Communications in Computer and Information Science   2119

Rationale

The CCIS series is devoted to the publication of proceedings of computer science conferences. Its aim is to efficiently disseminate original research results in informatics in printed and electronic form. While the focus is on publication of peer-reviewed full papers presenting mature work, inclusion of reviewed short papers reporting on work in progress is welcome, too. Besides globally relevant meetings with internationally representative program committees guaranteeing a strict peer-reviewing and paper selection process, conferences run by societies or of high regional or national relevance are also considered for publication.

Topics

The topical scope of CCIS spans the entire spectrum of informatics ranging from foundational topics in the theory of computing to information and communications science and technology and a broad variety of interdisciplinary application fields.

Information for Volume Editors and Authors

Publication in CCIS is free of charge. No royalties are paid, however, we offer registered conference participants temporary free access to the online version of the conference proceedings on SpringerLink (http://link.springer.com) by means of an http referrer from the conference website and/or a number of complimentary printed copies, as specified in the official acceptance email of the event.

CCIS proceedings can be published in time for distribution at conferences or as post-proceedings, and delivered in the form of printed books and/or electronically as USBs and/or e-content licenses for accessing proceedings at SpringerLink. Furthermore, CCIS proceedings are included in the CCIS electronic book series hosted in the SpringerLink digital library at http://link.springer.com/bookseries/7899. Conferences publishing in CCIS are allowed to use Online Conference Service (OCS) for managing the whole proceedings lifecycle (from submission and reviewing to preparing for publication) free of charge.

Publication process

The language of publication is exclusively English. Authors publishing in CCIS have to sign the Springer CCIS copyright transfer form, however, they are free to use their material published in CCIS for substantially changed, more elaborate subsequent publications elsewhere. For the preparation of the camera-ready papers/files, authors have to strictly adhere to the Springer CCIS Authors' Instructions and are strongly encouraged to use the CCIS LaTeX style files or templates.

Abstracting/Indexing

CCIS is abstracted/indexed in DBLP, Google Scholar, EI-Compendex, Mathematical Reviews, SCImago, Scopus. CCIS volumes are also submitted for the inclusion in ISI Proceedings.

How to start

To start the evaluation of your proposal for inclusion in the CCIS series, please send an e-mail to ccis@springer.com.

Constantine Stephanidis · Margherita Antona ·
Stavroula Ntoa · Gavriel Salvendy
Editors

HCI International 2024 Posters

26th International Conference
on Human-Computer Interaction, HCII 2024
Washington, DC, USA, June 29 – July 4, 2024
Proceedings, Part VI

 Springer

Editors
Constantine Stephanidis
University of Crete and Foundation for
Research and Technology - Hellas (FORTH)
Heraklion, Crete, Greece

Margherita Antona
Foundation for Research and Technology -
Hellas (FORTH)
Heraklion, Crete, Greece

Stavroula Ntoa
Foundation for Research and Technology -
Hellas (FORTH)
Heraklion, Crete, Greece

Gavriel Salvendy
University of Central Florida
Orlando, FL, USA

ISSN 1865-0929 ISSN 1865-0937 (electronic)
Communications in Computer and Information Science
ISBN 978-3-031-61965-6 ISBN 978-3-031-61966-3 (eBook)
https://doi.org/10.1007/978-3-031-61966-3

This Springer imprint is published by the registered company Springer Nature Switzerland AG
The registered company address is: Gewerbestrasse 11, 6330 Cham, Switzerland

If disposing of this product, please recycle the paper.

Foreword

This year we celebrate 40 years since the establishment of the HCI International (HCII) Conference, which has been a hub for presenting groundbreaking research and novel ideas and collaboration for people from all over the world.

The HCII conference was founded in 1984 by Prof. Gavriel Salvendy (Purdue University, USA, Tsinghua University, P.R. China, and University of Central Florida, USA) and the first event of the series, "1st USA-Japan Conference on Human-Computer Interaction", was held in Honolulu, Hawaii, USA, 18–20 August. Since then, HCI International is held jointly with several Thematic Areas and Affiliated Conferences, with each one under the auspices of a distinguished international Program Board and under one management and one registration. Twenty-six HCI International Conferences have been organized so far (every two years until 2013, and annually thereafter).

Over the years, this conference has served as a platform for scholars, researchers, industry experts and students to exchange ideas, connect, and address challenges in the ever-evolving HCI field. Throughout these 40 years, the conference has evolved itself, adapting to new technologies and emerging trends, while staying committed to its core mission of advancing knowledge and driving change.

As we celebrate this milestone anniversary, we reflect on the contributions of its founding members and appreciate the commitment of its current and past Affiliated Conference Program Board Chairs and members. We are also thankful to all past conference attendees who have shaped this community into what it is today.

The 26th International Conference on Human-Computer Interaction, HCI International 2024 (HCII 2024), was held as a 'hybrid' event at the Washington Hilton Hotel, Washington, DC, USA, during 29 June – 4 July 2024. It incorporated the 21 thematic areas and affiliated conferences listed below.

A total of 5108 individuals from academia, research institutes, industry, and government agencies from 85 countries submitted contributions, and 1271 papers and 309 posters were included in the volumes of the proceedings that were published just before the start of the conference, these are listed below. The contributions thoroughly cover the entire field of human-computer interaction, addressing major advances in knowledge and effective use of computers in a variety of application areas. These papers provide academics, researchers, engineers, scientists, practitioners and students with state-of-the-art information on the most recent advances in HCI.

The HCI International (HCII) conference also offers the option of presenting 'Late Breaking Work', and this applies both for papers and posters, with corresponding volumes of proceedings that will be published after the conference. Full papers will be included in the 'HCII 2024 - Late Breaking Papers' volumes of the proceedings to be published in the Springer LNCS series, while 'Poster Extended Abstracts' will be included as short research papers in the 'HCII 2024 - Late Breaking Posters' volumes to be published in the Springer CCIS series.

I would like to thank the Program Board Chairs and the members of the Program Boards of all thematic areas and affiliated conferences for their contribution towards the high scientific quality and overall success of the HCI International 2024 conference. Their manifold support in terms of paper reviewing (single-blind review process, with a minimum of two reviews per submission), session organization and their willingness to act as goodwill ambassadors for the conference is most highly appreciated.

This conference would not have been possible without the continuous and unwavering support and advice of Gavriel Salvendy, founder, General Chair Emeritus, and Scientific Advisor. For his outstanding efforts, I would like to express my sincere appreciation to Abbas Moallem, Communications Chair and Editor of HCI International News.

July 2024   Constantine Stephanidis

HCI International 2024 Thematic Areas
and Affiliated Conferences

- HCI: Human-Computer Interaction Thematic Area
- HIMI: Human Interface and the Management of Information Thematic Area
- EPCE: 21st International Conference on Engineering Psychology and Cognitive Ergonomics
- AC: 18th International Conference on Augmented Cognition
- UAHCI: 18th International Conference on Universal Access in Human-Computer Interaction
- CCD: 16th International Conference on Cross-Cultural Design
- SCSM: 16th International Conference on Social Computing and Social Media
- VAMR: 16th International Conference on Virtual, Augmented and Mixed Reality
- DHM: 15th International Conference on Digital Human Modeling & Applications in Health, Safety, Ergonomics & Risk Management
- DUXU: 13th International Conference on Design, User Experience and Usability
- C&C: 12th International Conference on Culture and Computing
- DAPI: 12th International Conference on Distributed, Ambient and Pervasive Interactions
- HCIBGO: 11th International Conference on HCI in Business, Government and Organizations
- LCT: 11th International Conference on Learning and Collaboration Technologies
- ITAP: 10th International Conference on Human Aspects of IT for the Aged Population
- AIS: 6th International Conference on Adaptive Instructional Systems
- HCI-CPT: 6th International Conference on HCI for Cybersecurity, Privacy and Trust
- HCI-Games: 6th International Conference on HCI in Games
- MobiTAS: 6th International Conference on HCI in Mobility, Transport and Automotive Systems
- AI-HCI: 5th International Conference on Artificial Intelligence in HCI
- MOBILE: 5th International Conference on Human-Centered Design, Operation and Evaluation of Mobile Communications

List of Conference Proceedings Volumes Appearing Before the Conference

1. LNCS 14684, Human-Computer Interaction: Part I, edited by Masaaki Kurosu and Ayako Hashizume
2. LNCS 14685, Human-Computer Interaction: Part II, edited by Masaaki Kurosu and Ayako Hashizume
3. LNCS 14686, Human-Computer Interaction: Part III, edited by Masaaki Kurosu and Ayako Hashizume
4. LNCS 14687, Human-Computer Interaction: Part IV, edited by Masaaki Kurosu and Ayako Hashizume
5. LNCS 14688, Human-Computer Interaction: Part V, edited by Masaaki Kurosu and Ayako Hashizume
6. LNCS 14689, Human Interface and the Management of Information: Part I, edited by Hirohiko Mori and Yumi Asahi
7. LNCS 14690, Human Interface and the Management of Information: Part II, edited by Hirohiko Mori and Yumi Asahi
8. LNCS 14691, Human Interface and the Management of Information: Part III, edited by Hirohiko Mori and Yumi Asahi
9. LNAI 14692, Engineering Psychology and Cognitive Ergonomics: Part I, edited by Don Harris and Wen-Chin Li
10. LNAI 14693, Engineering Psychology and Cognitive Ergonomics: Part II, edited by Don Harris and Wen-Chin Li
11. LNAI 14694, Augmented Cognition, Part I, edited by Dylan D. Schmorrow and Cali M. Fidopiastis
12. LNAI 14695, Augmented Cognition, Part II, edited by Dylan D. Schmorrow and Cali M. Fidopiastis
13. LNCS 14696, Universal Access in Human-Computer Interaction: Part I, edited by Margherita Antona and Constantine Stephanidis
14. LNCS 14697, Universal Access in Human-Computer Interaction: Part II, edited by Margherita Antona and Constantine Stephanidis
15. LNCS 14698, Universal Access in Human-Computer Interaction: Part III, edited by Margherita Antona and Constantine Stephanidis
16. LNCS 14699, Cross-Cultural Design: Part I, edited by Pei-Luen Patrick Rau
17. LNCS 14700, Cross-Cultural Design: Part II, edited by Pei-Luen Patrick Rau
18. LNCS 14701, Cross-Cultural Design: Part III, edited by Pei-Luen Patrick Rau
19. LNCS 14702, Cross-Cultural Design: Part IV, edited by Pei-Luen Patrick Rau
20. LNCS 14703, Social Computing and Social Media: Part I, edited by Adela Coman and Simona Vasilache
21. LNCS 14704, Social Computing and Social Media: Part II, edited by Adela Coman and Simona Vasilache
22. LNCS 14705, Social Computing and Social Media: Part III, edited by Adela Coman and Simona Vasilache

https://2024.hci.international/proceedings

Preface

Preliminary scientific results, professional news, or work in progress, described in the form of short research papers (4–11 pages long), constitute a popular submission type among the International Conference on Human-Computer Interaction (HCII) participants. Extended abstracts are particularly suited for reporting ongoing work, which can benefit from a visual presentation, and are presented during the conference in the form of posters. The latter allow a focus on novel ideas and are appropriate for presenting project results in a simple, concise, and visually appealing manner. At the same time, they are also suitable for attracting feedback from an international community of HCI academics, researchers, and practitioners. Poster submissions span the wide range of topics of all HCII thematic areas and affiliated conferences.

Seven volumes of the HCII 2024 proceedings are dedicated to this year's poster extended abstracts, in the form of short research papers, focusing on the following topics:

- Volume I: HCI Design Theories, Methods, Tools and Case Studies; User Experience Evaluation Methods and Case Studies; Emotions in HCI; Human Robot Interaction
- Volume II: Inclusive Designs and Applications; Aging and Technology
- Volume III: eXtended Reality and the Metaverse; Interacting with Cultural Heritage, Art and Creativity
- Volume IV: HCI in Learning and Education; HCI in Games
- Volume V: HCI in Business and Marketing; HCI in Mobility and Automated Driving; HCI in Psychotherapy and Mental Health
- Volume VI: Interacting with the Web, Social Media and Digital Services; Interaction in the Museum; HCI in Healthcare
- Volume VII: AI Algorithms and Tools in HCI; Interacting with Large Language Models and Generative AI; Interacting in Intelligent Environments; HCI in Complex Industrial Environments

Poster extended abstracts were accepted for publication in these volumes following a minimum of two single-blind reviews from the members of the HCII 2024 international Program Boards, i.e., the program committees of the constituent events. We would like to thank all of them for their invaluable contribution, support, and efforts.

July 2024

Constantine Stephanidis
Margherita Antona
Stavroula Ntoa
Gavriel Salvendy

Preface

26th International Conference on Human-Computer Interaction (HCII 2024)

The full list with the Program Board Chairs and the members of the Program Boards of all thematic areas and affiliated conferences of HCII 2024 is available online at:

http://www.hci.international/board-members-2024.php

HCI International 2025 Conference

The 27th International Conference on Human-Computer Interaction, HCI International 2025, will be held jointly with the affiliated conferences at the Swedish Exhibition & Congress Centre and Gothia Towers Hotel, Gothenburg, Sweden, June 22–27, 2025. It will cover a broad spectrum of themes related to Human-Computer Interaction, including theoretical issues, methods, tools, processes, and case studies in HCI design, as well as novel interaction techniques, interfaces, and applications. The proceedings will be published by Springer. More information will become available on the conference website: https://2025.hci.international/.

General Chair
Prof. Constantine Stephanidis
University of Crete and ICS-FORTH
Heraklion, Crete, Greece
Email: general_chair@2025.hci.international

https://2025.hci.international/

Contents – Part VI

Interaction in the Museum

HCI in Healthcare

Interacting with the Web, Social Media and Digital Services

Growing Up with Passwords

Sarah Abdi[✉][iD] and Elizabeth Stobert[iD]

Carleton University, Ottawa, Canada
sarahabdi@cmail.carleton.ca, elizabeth.stobert@carleton.ca

Abstract. Children's development progresses through developmental stages, but there is little understanding about how these stages impact children's understanding of passwords and security. In this work, we conducted a semi-structured interview with parents of children ranging in age from 3 to 18, and our thematic analysis showed that there did seem to be a relationship between Piagetian and Montessori models of cognitive development and how children interact with passwords. We suggest that interfaces may be able to be designed for specific developmental stages to appropriately support children in learning about security as they mature.

Keywords: Children · Passwords · Authentication · Cognitive Development

1 Introduction

As more interactions take place online, it becomes more important for children to understand how to secure themselves online. Children are interacting with passwords and devices at young ages, but it is not clear how their age and development impact their capacity to understand passwords and security.

Children's cognitive and psychosocial development progresses through developmental stages [5,7], and we hypothesize that children's security understanding may follow a similar pattern of development. Specifically, children's ability to behave securely may be limited by their cognitive development.

In this work, we conducted interviews with parents of children aged 3 to 18 to ask about how their children interact with technology, and understand security mechanisms such as passwords. We used thematic analysis to investigate how these children's understanding aligned with Piaget's developmental phases.

Our findings support the idea that there are loose developmental stages of security understanding and password use. Children's ability to manipulate and comprehend passwords grows as they mature, and this supports their increasing independence. We suggest that the design of passwords and security controls for children should acknowledge the developmental stage of the children using them.

C. Stephanidis et al. (Eds.): HCII 2024, CCIS 2119, pp. 3–9, 2024.
https://doi.org/10.1007/978-3-031-61966-3_1

2   Background

In this section we provide some background on children's development and current research on children and authentication.

2.1   Developmental Milestones

In developmental psychology, one popular idea is that children go through various developmental "stages" as they mature, and there are several prominent theories of development. One of the most well-known of these is Piaget's model of stages of intellectual development [7], which posits that children's cognitive abilities develop as they grow. Montessori proposed a similar theory, called the Planes of Development [5]. As children grow older, Piaget's theory centres the child's growth towards of abstract thinking, while Montessori's theory emphasizes the child's independence (intellectual, emotional, and financial [9]).

Piaget's theory of children's cognitive development is that the child will actively seek new information to incorporate into their knowledge base through assimilation and accommodation (called a *constructivist* view) [7,9]. Children go through four stages, each qualitatively different from the last (Table 1). At younger ages, children construct their knowledge of the world through physical activities and interaction with objects. As they grow older, they begin to move towards more understanding of complex concepts, and more ability to reason abstractly. In Piaget's model of development, stages must be completed in order and no stage may be skipped.

Montessori's Planes of Development [5] categorize early childhood (birth to 6 years) as having sensitive periods, childhood (6–12 years) as having imagination and intellectual independence, and adolescence (12–18 years) as having emotional independence. Though Montessori's model preceded Piaget's, Piaget's stages of intellectual development are more well-known. There is overlap between the two, as Piaget drew upon Montessori's ideas [6,9].

In developmental psychology, Piaget [6] and Montessori's [5] frameworks discuss the milestones of different age groups.

Although the notion of developmental stages is widely accepted, Piaget and Montessori's models are not uncontested models of development. Critics of Piaget's theory have shown that if the evaluation methodology is slightly altered, more children are successful at an earlier age. Other critics have demonstrated that the ages defined for each stage can be influenced by the environment and culture [3,9].

The relationship between developmental stages and security understanding has not been directly explored. In this work, we focus on Piaget's stages of development as an analytic framework because passwords are abstract concepts that will be harder to grasp at younger ages. Piaget's theory suggests that older, literate children should have the capacity to understand passwords as abstract entities, and the cognitive capacity to remember more than one password at a time. In this work, we are interested not only in what children are capable of understanding, but also how can we ask children to do appropriate security tasks and scaffold their learning.

Table 1. Piaget's Stages of Cognitive Development [6].

Age	Stages of development
Birth to 18 to 24 months	**Sensorimotor period** exploring objects, cause-and-effect, mental representation, object permanence
18 to 24 months to 7 years	**Pre-operational period** mental structures and symbols, especially in language; intuitive problem-solving, semi-logical; ego-centrism; reversibility
7 to 11 years	**Period of Concrete Operations** logical reasoning limited to real, physical, and present objects; solves problems intuitively without understanding how and why they work; more complex
11 to 18 years	**Period of Formal Operations** more logical and flexible, mental hypothesis testing entertain many possible solutions to a problem; reason about abstract ideas; philosophical ideas, real and ideal world; integrated and complex view

2.2   Children's Authentication

Children's online authentication practices have been shown to be overall inse-
cure; and it is possible that their behaviour is limited by their psychological
development. Maqsood, Biddle and Chiasson [4] conducted a lab study of how
children choose passwords and found that they overwhelmingly chose simple
passwords, and often included personal information in passwords. Children were
also likely to overestimate the security of the passwords they chose.

Children's confidence about their password practices is mismatched with
their actual practices [8]. Of the 22 children (5–11 years old) interviewed by
Ratakonda, French, and Fails [8], 68% indicated they would willingly share their
username and passwords to a parent, sibling, teacher, or peer. While 63% of the
children said they would never reuse a password, 63% of their parent or teachers
claimed that the children would.

Social influences over children's security knowledge and habits are also evident. Children's security practices are greatly impacted by those of their parents [1,4], and Maqsood et al. found that parents' poor understanding of security
or poor password choices often end up being taught to children [4]. Parents and
teachers have extensive influence over how children generate, maintain, and use
passwords [4,8].

3 Study

To map their children's ability to manage, maintain, and memorize passwords to their developmental stages, we conducted a semi-structured interview study with parents of children aged 3–18. We chose to interview parents (rather than children) for greater consistency in reporting, and to allow us to explore the parents' perspectives on development.

In the interview, we asked parents about their perceptions of their child's security understanding. We asked how their children understand secrets or passwords are to see if this matches to Piaget's abstraction of ideas for the concept of passwords. We asked if their child had any or multiple passwords memorized or if they reused passwords to match their cognitive development. We also asked how many devices and applications the child uses to check for cognitive or motor developmental effects. The interview took about 20 min, and participants were not compensated.

We recruited 6 parents of 14 children aged 3 to 18 years old. If a parent had more than one child within this age range, they completed the study once per child. We excluded children under the age of three because they are unlikely to have the verbal skills to comprehend passwords.

Our study was cleared by our university's research ethics board. Besides asking the age group (3–6; 7–9; 10–12; 13–15; 16–18) to which their child belonged, no identifying or demographic data was collected. The interviews were not audio- or video-recorded, and anonymous notes were taken during the interview.

3.1 Analysis

Using the notes taken during the interviews, we conducted a thematic analysis [2]. We took a deductive approach to coding, using Piaget's and Montessori's developmental stages as a basis for our codes. We traversed our notes line by line to assign open codes, and then reviewed our open codes to find patterns relating to the developmental stages.

4 Results

We categorized our interviews into groups based on the age of the participant's child that corresponded roughly to Piaget and Montessori's stages of development (Early childhood 3–6; Middle childhood 7–12; and Late Childhood 16–18 years old).

4.1 Early Childhood: Ages 3–6

Younger children had limited access to online activities, sometimes by using applications that do not require user profiles or authentication. Parents consistently mentioned parental controls on devices for younger children.

Young children were likely to understand passwords as a barrier to access, and generally did not interact independently with passwords or PINS. Parents were described helping young children input passwords and PINS (either entering them for the child, or directing the child in doing so), but some parents said that older children in this age range were beginning to have memorized simple PINS.

Accounts used by this age group were also not independently owned or created. Children were mainly using parents' accounts or accounts set up specifically for family use. Children were generally accessing family devices such as tablets or computers, and were likely to be accessing video games and video streaming services. Parents frequently described using parental controls to mediate access.

4.2 Middle Childhood: 7–12

As children mature (7 to 12 years old), they gain greater memory capacity and understanding of what passwords are used for. Now in school, they were beginning to access their own school-created accounts and devices. Parents were also starting to share access to personal accounts, while still monitoring device and application usage through parental controls and physical access controls.

Children in middle childhood were starting to be able to remember passwords and understand their purpose. Whereas younger children might understand secrets as a "surprise" or feel that they are "part of the club" by knowing passwords, parents said that their 7 to 12 year old children understood the importance of keeping passwords "secret and safe". However, this understanding may not be complete: one parent described their child's understanding of passwords as "flippant" and said that the child was over-confident in their understanding of passwords and security. Children's password identity still seemed to be integrated in their role as a family member, and one participant described how their child had offered a complex password they had memorized at school to add security to a family-shared account – essentially "lending" a secure password to the family.

Though children in this age group were accessing more accounts, they were not typically fully independent online. Parents frequently shared accounts with their children, including sharing access to social media accounts, gaming and streaming services. Parents described this shared access as a way of scaffolding or mediating internet access for their child, and helping them learn to be online. School-created accounts also started to be common in this age group, and multiple participants mentioned accounts regulated by the school, including email accounts as well as login information for Chromebooks or other websites.

4.3 Late Childhood: 13–18

Older children were moving toward complete independence online, and were likely to be in control of more accounts and devices. Many of these older children had their own smartphones with internet access, and parental controls were much less used. Physical access was less likely to be limited, and many parents described access to devices including smartphones, game consoles, and personal computers. Children in this age group were likely to be talking to friends and engaging socially online, especially on social media, and gaming platforms.

Parents described their teenagers as having a more sophisticated understanding of password composition and security. These children were able to create and remember more complex passwords, and were sometimes even moving beyond their parents' expertise. Teenagers were more aware of the implications of security to the extent that they "might not trust a [password] manager".

Children in this group were likely to be separating their online identity from that of the family. In a few cases, they were beginning to create personal and business accounts, separating their private life from their family life. Parents of children in this age range described not knowing their children's passwords and having less awareness of their online activities.

5   Discussion

Although exploratory, our work supports the idea that Piagetian stages of development may be related to how children understand and use passwords and security. As they grow older, children are more able to independently understand and manipulate passwords. Although age range is not the only determinant of password behaviour, it appears that children do go through similar stages of understanding of passwords and security.

Although we chose to focus our analytic lens in this work around Piaget's stages of development, we see some evidence of the increased independence emphasized in Maria Montessori's planes of development [5]. As children mature, they not only understand passwords and security better, but also handle more of it by themselves, and separate their identity from their parents'.

We suggest that it might be possible to design more accessible password and security protocols for children. Currently, there is little done towards this – most security controls for children's applications simply shunt access control to parents. This removes potentially useful opportunities for children to learn about password mechanics and understanding [1]. For example, even young children could understand the difference between an identifier (the username) vs a shared secret (the password). Although it simplifies children's interaction, hiding login pages from children obscures the opportunity for children to learn, and for parents to scaffold learning about passwords, security, and access.

Developmental stages are also widely applied in the design of childhood education (e.g. Montessori-based schools). A better understanding of the developmental stages of passwords could also be used to design appropriate educational programs on security and privacy for young children. Further investigation from these results could test the use of an adapted Montessori-style as a teaching mechanism of password privacy and online security of children.

As there is wide variability in how children move through developmental stages, we saw similar variability in these results. Parents prioritized and taught password practices differently, and mediated growth and independence differently for different children. Future work should concentrate on larger scale and longitudinal studies following the developmental growth of parents yielding control to their children.

6 Conclusion

The abstract nature of passwords and security practices makes it difficult for children to understand their purpose and secretiveness. In this work, we used Piaget's developmental stages as a framework to understand what limits might be imposed upon children when interacting with these topics. We interviewed parents and conducted a thematic analysis of their responses, and found evidence suggesting a relationship between developmental stages and security understanding and password use. We suggest that a better understanding of development and the relation to security understanding could be used to design more effective authentication interfaces for young children, and also better educational strategies.

References

1. Choong, Y.Y., Buchanan, K., Williams, O.: Parents, passwords, and parenting: how parents think about passwords and are involved in their children's password practices. In: Moallem, A. (ed.) HCI for Cybersecurity, Privacy and Trust. LNCS (including subseries Lecture Notes in Artificial Intelligence and Lecture Notes in Bioinformatics), vol. 14045, pp. 29–48. HCI International Conference. Springer, Cham (2023). https://doi.org/10.1007/978-3-031-35822-7_3
2. Clarke, V., Braun, V.: Thematic analysis. J. Posit. Psychol. **12**(3), 297–298 (2017). https://doi.org/10.1080/17439760.2016.1262613
3. Lourenço, O., Machado, A.: In defense of Piaget's theory: a reply to 10 common criticisms. Psychol. Rev. **103**(1), 143–164 (1996). https://doi.org/10.1037/0033-295X.103.1.143
4. Maqsood, S., Biddle, R., Maqsood, S., Chiasson, S.: An exploratory study of children's online password behaviours. In: Proceedings of the 17th ACM Conference on Interaction Design and Children, IDC 2018, pp. 539–544. Association for Computing Machinery, New York, NY, USA, June 2018. https://doi.org/10.1145/3202185.3210772
5. Montessori, M.: The Absorbent Mind (May 1949)
6. Piaget, J.: The Stages of the Intellectual Development of the Child (1965)
7. Piaget, J.: Part I: Cognitive development in children–Piaget development and learning. J. Res. Sci. Teach. **40**, 11 (2003). https://doi.org/10.1002/tea.3660020306
8. Ratakonda, D.K., French, T., Fails, J.A.: 'My name is my password:' understanding children's authentication practices. In: Proceedings of ACM Interaction Design and Children (IDC 2019), pp. 501–507 (2019). https://doi.org/10.1145/3311927.3325327
9. Parke, R.D., Gauvain, M., Schmuckler, M.A.: Child Psychology: A Contemporary Viewpoint, 3rd edn. McGraw-Hill Ryerson, New York (2010)

GovMark: A Local Government Benchmarking Webapp for the Philippine Department of the Interior and Local Government

Eugenio Emmanuel A. Araullo[✉], Marcus Louis G. Averia, Madeleine S. Lim, Francoise Therese G. Tuala, and Elcid A. Serrano

Mapúa University, Makati Philippines, 1191 Pablo Ocampo Sr. Ext, Makati, Metro Manila, Philippines

{eeaaraullo,mlgaveria,mslim,ftgtuala}@mymail.mapua.edu.ph,
easerrano@mapua.edu.ph

Abstract. This case study delves into the development and evaluation of "Gov-Mark," a prototype of a web portal designed to consolidate, and publicly present government performance scores derived from the Seal of Good Local Governance for Barangays (SGLGB) scores achieved by barangays in the Philippines. Gov-Mark aims to promote transparency and accountability by publishing SGLGB scores in an easy-to-understand manner for the public to better and more objectively understand their local governments. The study aims to understand in the context of Human-Computer Interaction on how useful and effective the Gov-Mark prototype is at showing and providing transparent and intelligible data on barangay performance in the Philippines.

Keywords: E-Government · Philippines · DILG · Usability · LGU · Barangay · Seal of Good Local Governance

1 Introduction

1.1 Background of the Study

Electronic Government, commonly known as e-Government, leverages information and communication technologies (ICT) to enhance governance effectiveness [1]. Governments can streamline administrative processes by strategically integrating ICT, improving intra-governmental communication, and facilitating decision-making. In the Philippines, the burgeoning adoption of internet usage and the digitization wave experienced during 2020–2021 underscores the critical importance of effective information dissemination using digital tools [2, 3]. However, despite the increased internet penetration and digitalization, significant gaps persist in the accessibility and quality of online government services. Many essential government services remain offline, while those available online often lack adherence to modern web design standards and suffer from performance issues, such as server crashes during peak demand periods. Consequently, the current state of digital government services in the Philippines raises concerns about

© The Author(s), under exclusive license to Springer Nature Switzerland AG 2024
C. Stephanidis et al. (Eds.): HCII 2024, CCIS 2119, pp. 10–22, 2024.
https://doi.org/10.1007/978-3-031-61966-3_2

transparency, trustworthiness, and accessibility [4]. At the local level, the websites of cities, municipalities, and barangays are still in nascent stages of development, primarily serving basic informational purposes without transactional or interactive features. Particularly concerning is the dearth of information available about barangay-level websites, a gap this study seeks to address. Despite these challenges, measures such as the Seal of Good Local Governance [5] and the Seal of Good Local Governance for Barangays [6] are designed to provide citizens with insights into the performance of local governments and foster transparency and trust between the government and the citizenry. Analyzing the website implementations across various government departments reveals a diverse landscape, with differing interpretations of standards and design norms.

While certain websites may exhibit shortcomings in adherence to design standards, they generally provide the necessary functions and information, from basic content display to transactional capabilities, characteristic of either Web 1.0 or 2.0 platforms.

1.2 Reference Studies

[7] E-Government in the Philippines: An Assessment
This study delved into the landscape of e-government services in the Philippines, focusing on 21 government websites chosen for their alignment with constitutional mandates. It analyzed their visibility on search engines, finding that eight of them ranked prominently within the first 1.3 search results, while one was notably less visible, ranking at the 2.7th position. Notably, Google.com was the most utilized search engine, whereas Yahoo.com had lower utilization rates. The study underscores the importance of search engine optimization (SEO) for directing users to the correct URLs, especially considering that a significant majority of users rely on first-page search results. Despite variations in design standards, all executive government agency websites examined provided fundamental information such as agency functions, mission, vision, and charter. Moreover, these websites typically offered transactional functions and features for accessibility, certain level of autonomy among government agencies in managing their e-government platforms. While there may be differences in implementation standards, the core functionalities and information necessary for classification as webs 1.0 or 2.0 are generally accessible to the public.

[8] Maturity Assessment of Local E-government Websites in the Philippines
The study examined the sophistication and technology implementation of local government websites, categorizing them into Emerging, Enhanced, Transactional, and Connected Information Services types. It aimed to assess the current state of e-government websites in Philippine cities and municipalities, revealing that many are still in early stages of development. While most municipal websites are available in English, there's a clear need to prioritize e-government projects for improvement. Some municipalities lack their own websites, relying on the province website for essential information, hindering progress toward e-government objectives. The study, limited to 150 municipal websites, focused on services rather than service delivery methods. Despite limitations,

it offers insights for future studies and suggests the need for better implementation strategies for local government websites. Overall, the study highlights the insufficient online presence of local governments, indicating a need for significant improvement.

[9] Factors Affecting Trust in E-Government

This study emphasizes the critical role of trust in e-government within a democratic framework, highlighting its importance for citizen participation. Transparency and credibility are essential for successful e-government implementation. Research findings show that perceived effectiveness, privacy, and security are more influential than source credibility in determining e-government trust. Greater privacy and security measures lead to higher confidence in e-government, fostering citizen engagement. Building trust fosters connections between users and e-government, enabling the delivery of quality services and innovation. Trust also facilitates effective governance and cooperation between local government officials and the public.

[10] E-Government Initiatives of Local Governments in the Philippines

This study aimed to explore e-Government activities in municipal governments in Sorsogon, Philippines. Through surveys, documentation analysis, and interviews, researchers found that these activities are primarily conducted in collaboration with National Government Agencies. Despite some technological advancements, such as Real Property Tax Assessment Software and Enhanced Tax Revenue and Collection System, there's limited focus on process automation. The findings suggest that while some municipalities have begun developing official websites, overall e-Government efforts remain in early stages, with significant potential for enhancing operational efficiency and frontline services.

1.3   Research Question

How does GovMark's user interface (UI) and user experience (UX) design affect the overall usability of the platform for residents and Department of the Interior and Local Government (DILG) officials within the National Capital Region (NCR)?

1.4   Research Objectives

- This research focuses on designing and evaluating a user-oriented prototype website named GovMark. This website aims to address the critical needs of barangays in the Philippines regarding online information dissemination and public transactions. The project adheres to three key objectives:
- Develop a clear and user-friendly version of GovMark that presents the Department of the Interior and Local Government's (DILG) Seal of Good Local Governance (SGLGB) scores in a way that is easily understood by the Filipino public.
- Incorporate modern human-computer interaction (HCI) design principles to ensure GovMark's usability and accessibility, catering to individuals with varying levels of technical expertise.
- Integrate a benchmarking tool powered by DILG data within GovMark. This tool will facilitate comparative analysis of Local Government Unit (LGU) services and their corresponding SGLGB scores.

1.5 Significance of the Study

This research explores the potential of creating an online platform to encourage competition between local government units (LGUs). This platform could ultimately benefit the public, government, and the entire city in several ways. It could provide the public with transparent access to data that allows them to objectively assess the performance of their LGUs. Additionally, the platform could simplify the online publication of information for both government employees and academic researchers.

1.6 Scope and Delimitation

This research pilot program in the National Capital Region (NCR) of the Philippines focuses on local governments and residents, employing the SGLG framework. Utilizing the Figma prototyping tool, the study develops a prototype showcasing city, local government, and regional performance indicators derived from SGLG criteria. The Seal of Good Local Governance for Barangays (SGLGB), established by the Department of the Interior and Local Government, serves as the basis for recognizing and rewarding barangays for their effective operations and moral character. The pilot integrates a content management system into the web prototype to facilitate easy profile management for DILG and Barangays without the need for coding.

2 Review of Related Literature

2.1 Related Terms

E-Government: E-Government encompasses the strategic use of information and communication technology (ICT) to enhance governance efficiency, promote public access to information, and facilitate citizen engagement in policy decision-making processes [11]. It aims to digitize governance processes, improve service delivery, and foster transparency to combat corruption.

Benchmarking: Benchmarking involves comparing organizational practices, goods, and services with those of industry leaders to identify areas for improvement and enhance overall performance [12]. It enables organizations to glean insights, streamline operations, and add value to products and services through informed decision-making.

Information Dissemination Portal: Information dissemination portals serve as digital platforms designed to store, organize, and provide access to a diverse array of information across various domains [14]. Leveraging service-oriented architecture (SOA) and web technologies, these portals aim to enhance accessibility and facilitate seamless information retrieval for users.

Content Management System (CMS): A Content Management System (CMS) empowers non-technical users to create, manage, and modify website content without coding expertise [15]. Offering user-friendly interfaces and a plethora of extensions, CMS platforms facilitate efficient website development and maintenance, enabling organizations to deliver compelling online experiences.

Seal of Good Local Governance: The Seal of Good Local Governance (SGLG) symbolizes the ethical conduct and effective operation of local government units (LGUs) [6]. Instituted under Republic Act No. 11292, the SGLG emphasizes results-based governance, with LGUs required to demonstrate excellence across ten evaluation areas to earn the prestigious seal.

2.2 Related Literature

Digital 2022: The Philippines: The Philippines has witnessed exponential growth in internet usage, with a significant portion of its population now connected online [2]. This surge in internet penetration presents opportunities for enhanced information dissemination and improved decision-making among Filipinos.

E-Government Initiatives of Local Governments in the Philippines: The province of Sorsogon exemplifies proactive e-Government initiatives aimed at enhancing citizen services and governance efficiency [10]. Through a range of technology-based programs and information dissemination portals, Sorsogon has endeavored to uplift the livelihoods of its citizens and promote digital literacy.

Web Content Management: Systems, Features, and Best Practices: Modern content management systems (CMS) play a pivotal role in managing online content and facilitating effective communication with target audiences [16]. With evolving features and functionalities, CMS platforms empower organizations to deliver engaging digital experiences and optimize content delivery.

2022 Seal of Good Local Governance: The SGLG represents a comprehensive assessment system recognizing outstanding local government performance across diverse governance areas [6]. Through rigorous evaluation criteria, the SGLG incentivizes LGUs to uphold integrity, accountability, and sustainable development.

Assessment of the Performance Challenge Fund and the Seal of Good Local Governance: The Performance Challenge Fund (PCF) complements the SGLG, providing financial incentives to top-performing LGUs for priority projects and initiatives [17]. While the SGLG has incentivized local governance excellence, there is room for refinement in incentivization strategies to foster greater competitiveness and inclusivity among LGUs.

3 Methodology

The researchers aim to develop a prototype platform suitable for both the DILG and the general population of the Philippines to access the Seal of Good Local Governance for Barangays performance metrics in an easy-to-understand and transparent manner. The methodology involves creating the prototype platform and conducting comprehensive testing with two types of end-users: the DILG central office and public users.

3.1   SGLG Metrics

The performance metrics for the benchmarking tool are sourced from Republic Act 11292, commonly referred to as RA 11292, and are supplemented by technical notes from the SGLGB program provided by the DILG. RA 11292 delineates the comprehensive assessment criteria for the Seal of Good Local Governance. These metrics will be integrated into the system, enabling users to compare performance across various barangays and local government units (LGUs) (Fig. 1).

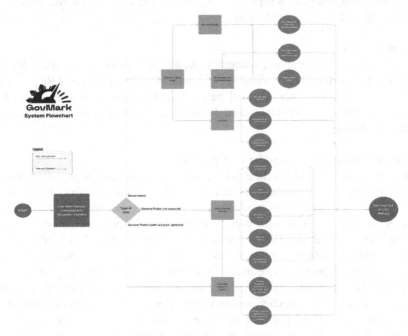

Fig. 1. GovMark System Flowchart

The user can choose between any of the following user types which have the following abilities:

DILG Central Office: This role manages user accounts, edits city and regional information, and has access to national-level scores.

DILG Assessor: Responsible for grading barangays, editing City-Municipality LGU information, and deciding on program participation.

City/Municipality: Can edit their personal city/municipality information and choose program participation options (opt-in/opt-out states). Also moderate comments on their personal SGLGB page and their constituent barangay page.

Barangay: Responsible for editing barangay information and deciding on program participation options (opt-in/opt-out states). Also moderate comments on their personal SGLGB page.

Citizen User: Accesses and views scores at the barangay and national levels. They are able to edit their profile and leave comments.

Public: Has access to view scores at the barangay, regional, and national levels.

Nonfunctional Requirements

Pages of the design web application must have matching themes and eye-pleasing designs for uniformity. Pages and clicks on the prototype web application must be responsive and respond in a manner that is expected of end-users. The design of the web pages must be convincing and must not mislead users.

Research Design

The study employs a quantitative research approach, specifically a descriptive type, to understand the situation on the ground in cities within the National Capital Region of the Philippines. Face-to-face interviews will be conducted with representatives from DILG regional and central offices to understand the SGLG system and gather requirements for the platform prototype.

Gathering of Data and Respondents of the Study

Initial discussions with DILG offices informed the GovMark prototype design, aiming to address the online information dissemination and transaction needs of barangays in the Philippines. The study targets adults aged 18 and above residing in the National Capital Region (NCR) for at least a year, ensuring relevant experiences. It involves eight public participants and four DILG representatives to assess GovMark's effectiveness from user and administrative perspectives. The prototype caters to two user groups: residents seeking transparent information and interaction with barangay government, and DILG officials monitoring SGLGB scores and barangay performance. GovMark aims to streamline data collection and reporting, benefiting both residents and DILG officials. Feedback will be gathered via a Google Forms survey-test questionnaire to enhance user experiences and preferences regarding government services and online platforms.

Research Instrument for Surveying

A user experience survey-based questionnaire will be used to collect data on participants' interactions with government services and their perceptions of the e-Government system in the Philippines. Additionally, a system usability scale will assess the overall usability of the platform according to user requirements.

Data Gathering

The data shall be collected by means of an anonymous online survey which will be sent via Google Forms. The survey will be carried out among residents above 18 years, who reside in the National Capital Region and have at least one experience of dealing with barangays. Participation is voluntary.

Sample and Sampling Technique

Purposive sampling, a strategic selection method, will be utilized to ensure participants possess relevant firsthand knowledge and experience. This method involves selecting individuals who meet specific criteria aligned with the research objectives. In this case, the target population will be:

Individuals aged 18 and above residing in the National Capital Region of the Philippines. Individuals with experience interacting with their barangay government.

4   Results and Discussion

Survey Results

The data collected through the survey provide insights into participants' perceptions and preferences regarding the GovMark platform. Figures 2, 3, 4, 5, 6, 7, 8, 9 and 10 present the key findings and trends observed among respondents.

A. **User Experience Questionnaire (UEQ) Results**

End-user experiences with the GovMark prototype revealed a generally positive

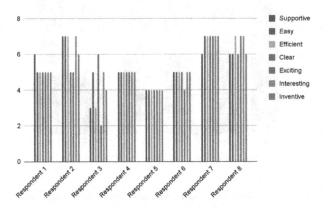

Fig. 2. User Experience Questionnaire

outlook based on the System Usability Scale (SUS), though individual responses varied. While aspects like ease of use and clarity received mostly high ratings, "Exciting" received lower scores, suggesting potential areas for improvement in user engagement and platform appeal.

B. **Individual Task Results**

Task 1: Choose/Search for an LGU: Half of the respondents stated that this task was hard.

Task 2: Look for LGU details: Half of these respondents regarded this task as difficult while others stated it was easy.

Task 3: Create an account/Login: 13.5% experienced it as hard while 37.5% said they had some difficulties doing this task. For 50%, they found it easy and successful.

Task 4: Create a comment: 50% of the respondents said it was difficult, whereas 50% mentioned easy.

Task 5: Edit profile: 37.50% considered that this task was hard, while 62.50% said that they had no difficulty performing this task.

Task 6: Find more details about how a score is graded: 37.5% of respondents indicated that this task was hard or unsuccessful while 62.5% said it was simple or successful.

C. Survey Results

The figure shows that 50% of the respondents are aware of SGLG and SGLGB, while 50% are not aware of it.

In this figure, it shows that the (87.5%) of the respondents are not aware of their city or municipality score and performance metrics while (12.5%) of the respondents are aware of their city or municipality scores and performance metrics.

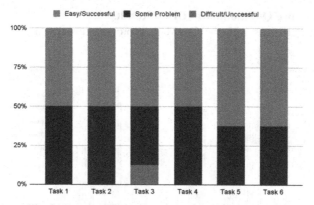

Fig. 3. Results of Task Questions for Citizen User type

Before taking this survey, were you aware of a government award called the Seal of Good Local Governance (SGLG) and/or the Seal of Good Local Governance for Barangays (SGLGB)?
8 responses

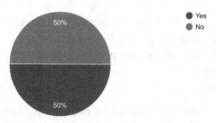

Fig. 4. Percentage of the Respondents' Awareness of Seal of Good Local Governance (SGLG) and/or the Seal of Good Local Governance for Barangays (SGLGB).

The figure shows that (12.5%) of the respondents are less interested and moderately interested, (50%) of the respondents are quite interested, and (25%) of the respondents

Are you aware of your city or municipality scores and performance metrics on SGLGB?
8 responses

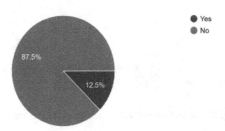

Fig. 5. Percentage of the Respondents Awareness to their City or Municipality Scores and Performance Metrics on SGLGB.

How interested are you in knowing more about your barangay's performance, transparency, and accountability.
8 responses

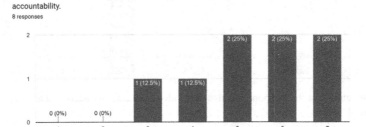

Fig. 6. Interest in Barangay Performance Metrics Bar Chart

How knowledgeable are you of the programs your barangay offers as well as how your barangay performance compares to other barangays?
8 responses

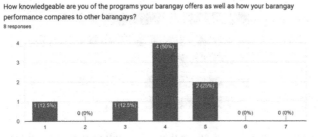

Fig. 7. Knowledge on Barangay Programs and Services

are extremely interested in recommending the GovMark platform to other government officials or agencies for benchmarking. This means that users are generally interested in promoting transparency of the government to their fellow.

This figure shows that 62.5% or 5 of the respondents are more interested in Barangay Scores, 50% or 4 respondents are interested in City/Municipality Scores and Comparative data between cities/barangay, 37.5% or 3 of the respondents are interested Performance metrics of government services and 25% or 2 of the respondents are interested in National Scores.

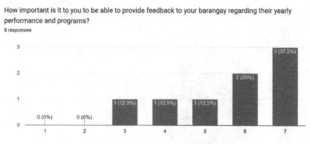

Fig. 8. Importance of yearly feedback to Barangays

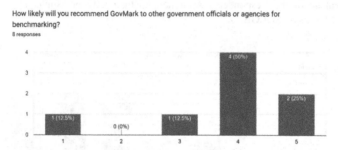

Fig. 9. Percentage of the Respondents that would Recommend GovMark to Other Government Officials or Agencies

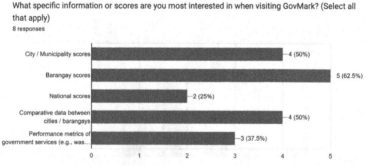

Fig. 10. Percentage of the Respondents on the specific information or scores most interested in visiting GovMark.

5 Conclusion and Recommendation

In conclusion, this study has explored the user experience and awareness relating to the GovMark benchmarking tool, with which the respondents were shown a prototype of a portal collating LGU "Seal of Good Local Governance for Barangay" scores. Based on the survey results, it is evident that the GovMark prototype platform has made significant strides in promoting awareness and understanding of LGU "Seal of Good Local Governance for Barangay" scores. However, there are several key findings and recommendations to consider: According to the quantitative survey results, the respondents have mixed experiences while using the prototype GovMark platform according to the research. Notably, half of the respondents found some problems when searching for an LGU, and the same percentage also found commenting as needing improvement. Despite this, most people found it simple to alter their profiles and comprehend score information which is for the intent of the study the most important and vital part of the prototype. Respondents were equally divided between those who were aware of SGLG and SGLGB and those who were not. Awareness of City/Municipality ratings and Performance Metrics: A vast majority (87.5%) of respondents did not know what their city or municipality's ratings and performance metrics were.

Recommendations for GovMark: The majority of respondents (75%) are at least somewhat interested in promoting GovMark to other government officials or agencies, demonstrating a favorable attitude towards the platform's goals. The majority of respondents (62.5%) expressed a strong interest in barangay scores, followed by city/municipality scores and comparison information.

The survey results indicate that there is a positive attitude towards the GovMark platform's goals, with the majority of respondents interested in promoting it to other government officials or agencies. To capitalize on this positive sentiment, it is recommended that GovMark focus on continuous user interface enhancements in order to address the issues raised by respondents, particularly those related to the search function and commenting features. This will enhance the overall user experience. Such as user experience testing, feedback loops, and interface redesigns or enhancements, are essential for activities done through the prototype online portal. The fact that many people are unfamiliar with the SGLG, SGLGB, and local scores further emphasizes the need for awareness initiatives that use a variety of media. This reinforces the need for further tools that provide transparency to local government performance metrics. Additionally, agreements with government officials provide a chance to increase GovMark's effectiveness and reach, particularly given their apparent propensity to endorse the platform. Another suggestion would be to add a tutorial or onboarding guide for first-time users of the platform in order for would-be users to get more easily acquainted with the platform, its features, and how it works, and not get overwhelmed or lost in how to make the platform function as some do experience now.

Given the results and the analysis provided, the research concludes that the GovMark platform is a viable and realistic approach to providing transparency of government metrics to the public in a user-friendly manner. The GovMark prototype, while needing improvements and further refinements from a user interface perspective, can be further enhanced overtime. The tool, while in its infancy, can be used as one of the many ways to further bridge the information gap between government and citizenry, providing users and local governments alike with metrics on gaps existing in LGU performance, as well as ways to improve these gaps. These also promote citizen feedback on local governments, as well as raising awareness and positive outlook on well-performing local governments.

References

1. Santiago, C.S., Jr., Ulanday, M.L.P., Centeno, Z.J.R., Bayla, M.C.D.: Access, skills and constraints of barangay officials towards the use of information and communications technology

(ICT). Int. J. Knowl. Content Dev. Technol. **11**(2), 37–54 (2021). https://doi.org/10.5865/IJKCT.2021.11.2.037

2. Simon Kemp. 2022. DIGITAL 2022: THE PHILIPPINES. (February 2022). Retrieved from https://datareportal.com/reports/digital-2022-philippines#:~:text=There%20were%2076.01%20million%20internet,percent)%20between%202021%20and%202022

3. Devy, N.P.I.R., Wibirama, S., Santosa, P.I.: Evaluating user experience of english learning interface using user experience questionnaire and system usability scale. In: 2017 1st International Conference on Informatics and Computational Sciences (ICICoS), pp. 101–106. (2017) DOI: https://doi.org/10.1109/ICICOS.2017.8276345

4. Rouibah, K., Qurban, H., Al-Qirim, N.: Impact of risk perceptions and user trust on intention to re-use e-government: a mixed method research. J. Global Inform. Manag. **30**(1), 1–29 (2022). https://doi.org/10.4018/JGIM.307117

5. Dilg. 2022 SEAL OF GOOD LOCAL GOVERNANCE: PAGKILALA SA KATAPATAN AT KAHUSAYAN NG PAMAHALAANG LOKAL (2022). https://www.dilg.gov.ph/PDF_File/issuances/memo_circulars/dilg-memocircular-2022128_ec42c8c0c0.pdf

6. DILG: Pilot for the Seal of Good Local Governance for Barangay (2021). https://www.dilg.gov.ph/PDF_File/issuances/memo_circulars/dilg-memocircular-202176_3eaca16fe2.pdf

7. Jayson Troy Ferro Bajar. 2020. E-Government in the Philippines: An assessment. 1,1 (2020). https://doi.org/10.13140/RG.2.2.27627.36643

8. Khalid, S.A., Lavilles, R.Q.: Maturity assessment of local e-government websites in the Philippines. Procedia Comput. Sci. J. **161**(2019), 99–106 (2019). https://doi.org/10.1016/j.procs.2019.11.104

9. Pribadi, U., Iqbal, M., Restiane, F.: Factors affecting trust in e-government. J. Gov. Civ. Soc. **5**(2), 263 (2021). https://doi.org/10.31000/jgcs.v5i2.4848

10. De Castro, C.A., De Castro, E.G.: E-government initiatives of local governments in the Philippines. J. Commun. Dev. Res. Humanit. Soc. Sci. **15**(3), 55–70 (2022). https://doi.org/10.14456/jcdr-hs.2022.25

11. Getrude, N., Otike, J.: E-Government: Its role, importance and challenges (2017). https://www.researchgate.net/file.PostFileLoader.html?id=564b965d6225ffe6e98b4595&assetKey=AS:296884838125570@1447794269180

12. The Balance. What is benchmarking in Business? https://www.thebalancemoney.com/overview-and-examples-of-benchmarking-in-business-2275114

13. Isixsigma. Understanding the purpose and the use of benchmarking. https://www.isixsigma.com/methodology/benchmarking/understanding-purpose-and-use-benchmarking/

14. Energy & Wetlands Research Group. CES. Center for Ecological Sciences. Information Dissemination Portal. http://wgbis.ces.iisc.ernet.in/biodiversity/sahyadri_enews/newsletter/Issue62/article/Bindu/index.html

15. Optimizely. Content Management System (CMS). What is Content Management System? (2022). https://www.optimizely.com/optimization-glossary/content-management-system/

16. Deane Barker: Web Content Management (First Edition). O'Reilly Media, Inc. (2016)

17. Cabot, J.: Wordpress: a content management system to democratize publishing. IEEE Softw. **35**(3), 89–92 (2018). https://doi.org/10.1109/MS.2018.2141016

18. Sicat-Diokno, C.J., Mariano, M.A.P., Castillo, A.F., Maddawin, R.B.: Assessment of the performance challenge fund and the seal of good local governance: Perceptions from municipalities. EconStor (2020). http://hdl.handle.net/10419/240994

19. Van Casteren, W.: The Waterfall Model and the Agile Methodologies: A comparison by project characteristics (2017). https://doi.org/10.13140/RG.2.2.36825.72805

Automatic Verbalizer for Extracting Fine-Grained Customer Opinions from Non-English Social Media Comments

Carlin C. F. Chu[1]($\boxtimes$) , Jonathan H. Y. Leung[2] , Raymond So[3] , and Andy Chan[4]

[1] Department of Computing, The Hang Seng University of Hong Kong, Hong Kong, China
carlinchu@hsu.edu.hk
[2] Cheriton School of Computer Science, University of Waterloo, Waterloo, Canada
j23leung@uwaterloo.ca
[3] Big Data Intelligence Centre, The Hang Seng University of Hong Kong, Hong Kong, China
[4] IDDY Ltd., Hong Kong, China

Abstract. Social media comments serve as useful references for reflecting customer preference and help to devise appropriate business strategies. Apart from knowing the overall preference of a product, obtaining fine-grained opinions in specific aspects can be more insightful. Masked language modeling (MLM) is one of effective approaches to extract aspect opinions. It extracts fine-grained information by utilizing a Large Language Model, such as BERT, to make opinion-bearing textual predictions. In practice, the predicted results are not always as expected due to the nature of training data and computational constraints for MLM fine-tuning. A verbalizer is needed to map unexpected predictions to desired outcomes. Existing literature mainly focuses on handling English comments with single-token MLM predictions. This study addresses concerns for non-English multiple-token predictions and proposes a practical methodology to develop an automatic verbalizer using variants of the k-nearest neighbors (KNN) classifier.

The proposed approach does not rely on a predefined dictionary. It predicts an aspect opinion using contextualized embedding vectors which encompass the information from the opinion-bearing textual prediction together with its underlying context. Concerns for handling multiple-token predictions are discussed and workable solutions are proposed. Variants of KNN classifier are employed to consolidate information obtained from multiple tokens. The performance of proposed verbalizers is examined on a large Chinese Meituan-Dianping dataset with over 40k genuine user reviews. Methods for MLM task decomposition, prompt construction and model finetuning are also addressed in this study.

Keywords: Aspect-Category Sentiment Analysis · Prompt-Based Learning · Pre-trained Language Models

© The Author(s), under exclusive license to Springer Nature Switzerland AG 2024
C. Stephanidis et al. (Eds.): HCII 2024, CCIS 2119, pp. 23–32, 2024.
https://doi.org/10.1007/978-3-031-61966-3_3

1 Introduction

Pre-trained language models (PLMs) have fundamentally changed how we design and build real-world natural language processing (NLP) applications. We can transfer the semantic knowledge of a PLM to different domains to perform NLP tasks (such as classification, named-entity recognition, question-answering, etc.) by finetuning the PLM's parameters with task-specific training data. A new paradigm called prompt-based learning (PBL) [6,11,12,14] has recently received much attention because it performs satisfactorily with minimal or no finetuning when using ultra-large PLMs such as the GPT-3 [1]. While ultra-large PLMs are ideal for PBL due to the massive amount of semantic knowledge they learned in the pretraining stage, they are often less accessible than smaller but publicly available models such as BERT [5]. This paper discusses using PBL with medium-sized PLMs for aspect category sentiment analysis (ACSA) [3,9,15].

In using PBL for ACSA, we design an aspect-specific prompt containing a masked word token that will hold an opinion-bearing textual prediction. We then supply an input text together with the prompt to a PLM to obtain a predicted masked word. We then *infer* the sentiment polarity using a *verbalizer*, which is a function that maps the predicted masked word to sentiment polarity labels such as "positive", "negative", and "neutral" [4,7,8,16]. Generally, a verbalizer is implemented as a dictionary that maps different opinion-bearing words to their corresponding sentiment labels. However, such an approach relies on expertise to generate a vocabulary list that covers jargon used in specific domains. Furthermore, traditional verbalizers cannot handle incoherent predictions that can arise from multiple-token predictions. We propose an automatic verbalizer implemented using variants of the k-nearest neighbors (KNN) classifier that does not require domain expertise and generalizes beyond single-token MLM predictions.

The main contributions of this paper are:

1. We present a practical methodology for creating automatic verbalizers using variants of the KNN classifier that supports non-English multiple-token predictions. The methodology is demonstrated on a large Chinese restaurant review dataset [2].
2. We discuss how to use PBL effectively with medium-sized PLMs such as BERT. We decompose ACSA into a collection of aspect-specific multi-label classification sub-tasks that can be solved using PBL.

The remaining of this paper is structured as follows. We present a methodology for using PBL with BERT and an automatic verbalizer to accomplish the ACSA task in Sect. 2. We describe our experiment settings and evaluate our work in Sect. 3. We conclude this paper with a summary of our experience and the lessons learned.

2   Methodology

2.1   Task Definition and Decomposition

Let $x = \{x_1, x_2, \ldots, x_z\}$ represent an opinion-bearing text. Aspect sentiments are *fine-grained* sentiments toward specific attributes (i.e., aspects) that we can identify in x. For $i \in \{1, 2, \ldots, N\}$, let a_i represent an aspect and $y_i \in \{\texttt{positive}, \texttt{neutral}, \texttt{negative}, \texttt{unknown}\}$ be the sentiment polarity of a_i.

We formally define an *aspect sentiment* to be a tuple (a_i, y_i). The goal of ACSA is to output a list of tuples for any opinion-bearing text x: $f(x) \rightarrow \{(a_i, y_i)\}_{i=1}^{N}$ (Fig. 1).

"*I was very disappointed with this restaurant. I've asked a cart attendant for a lotus leaf wrapped rice and she replied back rice and just walked away. I had to ask her three times before she finally came back with the dish I've requested. Food was okay, nothing great. Chow fun was dry; pork shu mai was more than usually greasy and had to share a table with loud and rude family. I/we will never go back to this place again.*"

```
(RESTAURANT#GENERAL,            negative)
(FOOD#QUALITY,                  negative)
(SERVICE#GENERAL,               negative)
(AMBIENCE#GENERAL,              negative)
(RESTAURANT#PRICES,             unknown)
(RESTAURANT#QUALITY,            unknown)
(RESTAURANT#STYLE_OPTIONS,      unknown)
(RESTAURANT#MISCELLANEOUS,      unknown)
(FOOD#PRICES,                   unknown)
(FOOD#STYLE_OPTIONS,            unknown)
...
```

Fig. 1. Samples of opinion aspect extracted from a restaurant review [13]

Considering we use different vocabulary and language semantics to express sentiments towards different aspects such as prices or food quality, we decompose the ACSA task by using *aspect-specific* classifiers $f_{a_i}(x)$ to *predict* the sentiment polarity of each aspect a_i:

$$f_{a_i}(x) \rightarrow \hat{y}_i, \ i \in \{1, 2, \ldots, N\} \tag{1}$$

Figure 2 provides an overview about the flow of decomposing the ACSA task into a collection of classification sub-tasks.

2.2   Prompting

The design of our classifiers is inspired by the concept of *prompt composition* [10], which is a technique of decomposing a complex task into several subtasks and use subtask-specific prompts to make predictions at inference time. We design unique prompts τ_{a_i} for each aspect a_i, following Seoh et al. to include wordings of the aspect [14]:

$$\tau_{a_i} = \{\text{The } a_i \text{ is } [\texttt{MASK}].\} \tag{2}$$

The above prompt is adaptable to handle languages that express sentiment states with multiple-word phrase (such as Chinese and Japanese). The number of [MASK] tokens are tweaked accordingly.

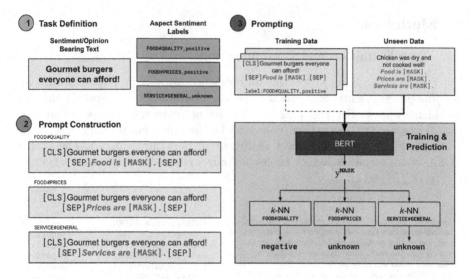

Fig. 2. An overview of methodology. We decompose ACSA into a collection of classification subtasks that can be solved using PBL. For each aspect, we create a distance-based KNN classifier. To predict the sentiment polarity of an aspect, we append an aspect-specific prompt to the unseen data and use BERT to predict the masked word in the prompt. We then predict the sentiment polarity with an automatic verbalizer, which uses KNN classifiers to find k closest matches of the predicted masked words y^{MASK} in the training data.

We append the aspect-specific prompt τ_{a_i} to input text x to obtain an *unanswered* prompt:

$$x_{a_i}^{\tau} = \{[\text{CLS}]\, x\, [\text{SEP}]\, \tau_{a_i}\, [\text{SEP}]\} \tag{3}$$

where [CLS] and [SEP] are special tokens that BERT uses to mark the beginning of its inputs and end of a sentence, respectively. We *prompt* BERT to predict the masked word(s) using MLM, and replace the [MASK] token(s) in $x_{a_i}^{\tau}$ with the predicted masked word(s) y^{MASK} to get an *answered* prompt:

$$\hat{x}_{a_i}^{\tau} = \text{MLM}(x_{a_i}^{\tau}) \tag{4}$$

Next, we extract the embedding of y^{MASK} in the answered prompt $\hat{x}_{a_i}^{\tau}$:

$$H_{\tau} = \text{BERT}(\hat{x}_{a_i}^{\tau}),\ H_{\tau} \in \mathbb{R}^{J*W*M} \tag{5}$$

where J and M are the number of hidden layers and hidden size of BERT respectively and W is the number of [MASK] in τ_{a_i}. If there are multiple [MASK] tokens, we take an average of H_{τ} along the W dimension:

$$H_{\tau} = \text{Avg}(H_{\tau}, \text{dim}=2),\ H_{\tau} \in \mathbb{R}^{N*M} \tag{6}$$

We use the output of the *last* hidden layer of BERT:

$$\hat{x}_{\text{encode}}^{\text{MASK}} = H_{\tau}[-1] \tag{7}$$

Algorithm 1. Aspect-Category Sentiment Polarity Classifier: $f_{a_i}(x)$

Input: x, Opinion-bearing text
Output: $\hat{y}$, Predicted sentiment polarity of a_i
 1: $\tau_{a_i} \leftarrow P(x, a_i)$ ▷ Equation (2)
 2: $x_{a_i}^\tau \leftarrow \{\,[\texttt{CLS}]\,x\,[\texttt{SEP}]\,\tau_{a_i}\,[\texttt{SEP}]\,\}$ ▷ Equation (3)
 3: $\hat{x}_{a_i}^\tau \leftarrow \text{MLM}(x_{a_i}^\tau)$ ▷ Equation (4)
 4: $H_\tau \leftarrow \text{BERT}(x_{a_i}^\tau)$ ▷ Equation (5)
 5: **if** number of [MASK] in $\tau_{a_i} > 1$ **then**
 6:     $H_\tau \leftarrow \text{Avg}(x_{a_i}^\tau, \dim = 2)$ ▷ Equation (6)
 7: **end if**
 8: $\hat{x}_{\text{encode}}^{\text{MASK}} \leftarrow H_\tau[-1]$ ▷ Equation (7)
 9: **for each** reference point $p \in \mathcal{D}_{a_i}^{\text{TRAIN}}$ **do**
10:     compute the Euclidean distance between $\hat{x}_{\text{encode}}^{\text{MASK}}$ and p;
11: **end for**
12: sort the computed distances;
13: select k-nearest reference points corresponding to k smallest distances;
14: $\hat{y} \leftarrow$ determine class label with equal or inverse weighted method;
15: **return** $\hat{y}$ (sentiment polarity of aspect a_i)

2.3 Automatic Verbalizer

The aspect-specific prompts that we append to the input texts provide additional semantic knowledge for BERT to create context-aware embeddings, which are used as input features for sentiment polarity classification. Inspired by the work of Hu et al. and You et al., we use automatic verbalizers that use KNN classifiers to infer the sentiment polarity class labels from $\hat{x}_{\text{encode}}^{\text{MASK}}$ (Fig. 3) [7,17]. We create a KNN classifier for each aspect. These classifiers find k examples of predicted masked words in the labeled training dataset that are most similar to $\hat{x}_{\text{encode}}^{\text{MASK}}$. The equally weighted and inverse distance weighted variants of the KNN classifer are used to determine the predicted sentiment polarity for the respective aspect.

The implementation of $f_{a_i}(x)$ (Eq. 1) is outlined in Algorithm 1. To predict the sentiment polarity of aspect a_i, we (a) obtain the embedding of the predicted masked word(s) $\hat{x}_{\text{encode}}^{\text{MASK}}$ (lines 1 to 8), (b) find k references in $\mathcal{D}_{a_i}^{\text{TRAIN}}$ that have the shortest Euclidean distances to $\hat{x}_{\text{encode}}^{\text{MASK}}$ (lines 9 to 13) and, (c) use the equal weighted and inverse distance weighted methods to determine the sentiment polarity label for aspect a_i (lines 14 to 15).

The inverse distance weighted method is implemented as:

$$\hat{y} = \underset{\text{class}}{\arg\max} \sum_{j=1}^{k} I(q_j = \text{class}) \cdot \frac{1}{\text{dist}(x_{\text{encode}}^{\text{MASK}}, q_j)} \tag{8}$$

where q_j are the k closest points to $x_{\text{encode}}^{\text{MASK}}$. The indicator function $I(\cdot)$ gives the value 1 when the closest point q_j belongs to a particular class label.

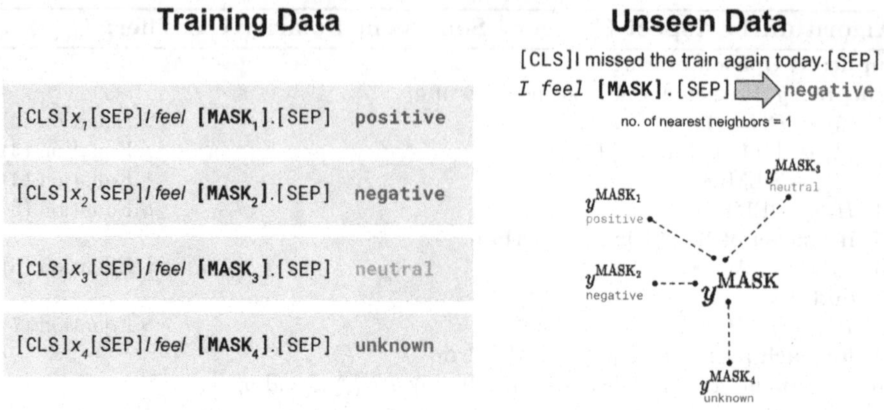

Training Data

$[CLS]x_1[SEP]$/ *feel* **[MASK$_1$]**.$[SEP]$ positive

$[CLS]x_2[SEP]$/ *feel* **[MASK$_2$]**.$[SEP]$ negative

$[CLS]x_3[SEP]$/ *feel* **[MASK$_3$]**.$[SEP]$ neutral

$[CLS]x_4[SEP]$/ *feel* **[MASK$_4$]**.$[SEP]$ unknown

Unseen Data

$[CLS]$I missed the train again today.$[SEP]$
I feel **[MASK]**.$[SEP]$ ⟹ negative

no. of nearest neighbors = 1

y^{MASK_3} neutral

y^{MASK_1} positive

y^{MASK_2} negative

y^{MASK} **MASK**

y^{MASK_4} unknown

Fig. 3. Automatic verbalizer using distance-based ACSA classifier with prompt-based learning. Our classifiers predict the sentiment polarity label of unseen data by (a) finding the closest matches of the predicted masked word y^{MASK} in the training data and (b) using the equally weighted/inverse distance weighted method for predicting the sentiment polarity class label. The number of closest matches in this example is one.

3   Experiments and Evaluation

3.1   Dataset

We tested our classifiers on a Chinese restaurant review dataset published by Meituan [2]. There are 36,851 and 4,941 examples in the training and testing datasets, respectively. Each example contains a review and sentiment polarity labels of eighteen aspects. Our objective is to predict the sentiment polarities of the five most rated aspects. These aspects are listed in Table 1.

Our aspect-specific prompts are designed for the Chinese language, which require using three [MASK] tokens for the expected aspect sentiments: 好满意 (positive sentiment), 还可以 (neutral sentiment), 很失望 (negative sentiment) and 没提及 (unknown sentiment). Table 1 shows the prompts we used in our experiments and the sentiment words for prompt-based finetuning.

Table 1. The five most rated aspects in the Chinese restaurant review dataset and correponding prompts.

Aspect	Prompt	Expected Masked Words
FOOD#TASTE	食物味道[MASK] [MASK] [MASK]。	好满意,还可以,很失望,没提及
SERVICE#HOSPITALITY	服务素质[MASK] [MASK] [MASK]。	好满意,还可以,很失望,没提及
PRICE#LEVEL	价格[MASK] [MASK] [MASK]。	好满意,还可以,很失望,没提及
AMBIENCE#DECORATION	用餐环境[MASK] [MASK] [MASK]。	好满意,还可以,很失望,没提及
FOOD#PORTION	食物份量[MASK] [MASK] [MASK]。	好满意,还可以,很失望,没提及

3.2   Experiment Results

We finetuned the Chinese version of BERT (`bert-base-chinese`[1]) with learning rate, epoch and batch size set at 0.001, 3 and 16, respectively. We observe that the performance of PBL improves substantially when the finetuned BERT (prompt-based finetuning) is used. We compared the inter and intra class distances of predicted masked words' embeddings produced by the vanilla and finetuned BERT using the values of the first two Principal Components as the axes. An example plot of the result of `FOOD#TASTE` aspect is depicted in Fig. 4 and the same finding are observed in other aspects. The finetuned BERT produces embeddings with shorter intra class distances (distances between predicted masked words of the same sentiment class) and larger inter class distances (distances between examples of different sentiment classes). Only the performance of finetuned BERT is reported in Table 2.

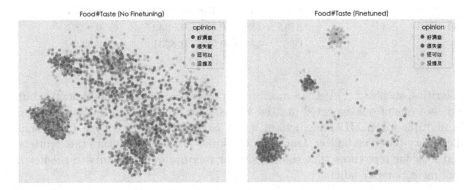

Fig. 4. Effects of prompt-based tuning on inter and intra class distances of predicted masked words.

Our classifiers are compared against two baselines: ZeroR and neural network classifier. The ZeroR classifier simply predicts the sentiment polarity of each aspect to be the majority class. We trained the neural network classifiers to output the correct sentiment polarity label for aspect a_i based on the embedding of the [CLS] tokens. The experiment results are shown in Table 2.

Overall, the inverse distance weighted BERT achieved a weighted F1 score of 0.83, which is 30% higher than achieved by the neural network classifier and 47% higher than achieved by the ZeroR classifer. The inverse distance weigted BERT attained an accuracy of 83%, outperforming the neural network classifier by 33% and the ZeroR classifer by 23%. We observe that BERT used with inverse distance weighted KNN performs marginally better than equally weighted KNN in each aspect in terms of accuracy and weighted F1 score.

We also observe that, in a minority of cases, the fine-tuned BERT predicts the masked tokens to be a combination of tokens representing different sentiment

---

[1] https://github.com/google-research/bert.

Table 2. Out-of-Sample Prediction Results.

Aspect	Metric	Model		PBL with KNN, k=15	
		ZeroR	NN	BERT (inverse weight)	BERT (equal weight)
FOOD#TASTE	ACC	0.5382	0.5912	**0.7946**	0.7935
	F1	0.3766	0.6321	**0.7931**	0.7920
SERVICE#HOSPITALITY	ACC	0.4412	0.5034	**0.8500**	0.8498
	F1	0.2701	0.5676	**0.8464**	0.8463
PRICE#LEVEL	ACC	0.5156	0.3178	**0.8215**	0.8208
	F1	0.3508	0.3793	**0.8228**	0.8221
AMBIENCE#DECORATION	ACC	0.5711	0.5881	**0.8831**	0.8826
	F1	0.4152	0.6054	**0.8805**	0.8800
FOOD#PORTION	ACC	0.5786	0.5399	**0.8167**	**0.8167**
	F1	0.4242	0.4709	**0.8134**	**0.8134**
Overall	ACC	0.5991	0.5081	**0.8332**	0.8327
	F1	0.3674	0.5311	**0.8331**	0.8326

polarities, such as "还满意" (a mixture of positive and neutral sentiments), but it is not one of our expected masked words. This is a problem uniquely arising in multiple-token MLM prediction, which cannot be handled by a traditional dictionary-based verbalizer. Our KNN classifiers are able to capture this subtlety and look for references that show a similar mixture of sentiments to predict a sentiment polarity label.

4   Conclusion

We presented a practical methodology for using PBL with BERT. We designed an automatic verbalizer using distance-based classifiers that require no training and minimal implementation efforts. The automatic verbalizer is able to handle non-English multiple-token MLM predictions. The automatic verbalizer also removes the dependency on domain expert knowledge in preparing the dictionary mapping. The proposed approach does not rely on a pre-defined dictionary. It predicts an aspect opinion using contextualized embedding vectors which encompass the information from the opinion-bearing textual prediction together with its underlying context. We also demonstrated a practical approach to using PBL with smaller PLMs such as BERT. Our automatic verbalizer is able to handle multiple-token predictions which are composed of a combination of tokens representing different sentiment polarities. This is a problem uniquely arising in multiple-token MLM prediction, which cannot be handled by a traditional dictionary-based verbalizer.

Acknowledgments. The work reported in this paper was supported by the Research Matching Grant Scheme (Project Reference No.: RMGS#700029) administrated by the University Grants Committee in Hong Kong.

Disclosure of Interests. The authors have no competing interests to declare that are relevant to the content of this article.

References

1. Brown, T.B., et al.: Language models are few-shot learners. In: Proceedings of the 34th International Conference on Neural Information Processing Systems. Curran Associates Inc., Red Hook (2020)
2. Bu, J., et al.: ASAP: a Chinese review dataset towards aspect category sentiment analysis and rating prediction. In: Proceedings of the 2021 Conference of the North American Chapter of the Association for Computational Linguistics: Human Language Technologies, pp. 2069–2079. Association for Computational Linguistics (2021). https://www.aclweb.org/anthology/2021.naacl-main.167
3. Cai, H., Tu, Y., Zhou, X., Yu, J., Xia, R.: Aspect-category based sentiment analysis with hierarchical graph convolutional network. In: Proceedings of the 28th International Conference on Computational Linguistics, pp. 833–843. International Committee on Computational Linguistics, Barcelona (2020). https://doi.org/10.18653/v1/2020.coling-main.72
4. Cui, G., Hu, S., Ding, N., Huang, L., Liu, Z.: Prototypical verbalizer for prompt-based few-shot tuning. In: Proceedings of the 60th Annual Meeting of the Association for Computational Linguistics, vol. 1: Long Papers, pp. 7014–7024. Association for Computational Linguistics, Dublin (2022). https://doi.org/10.18653/v1/2022.acl-long.483
5. Devlin, J., Chang, M.W., Lee, K., Toutanova, K.: BERT: pre-training of deep bidirectional transformers for language understanding. In: Proceedings of the 2019 Conference of the North American Chapter of the Association for Computational Linguistics: Human Language Technologies, vol. 1 (Long and Short Papers). pp. 4171–4186. Association for Computational Linguistics, Minneapolis (2019). https://doi.org/10.18653/v1/N19-1423
6. Gao, T., Fisch, A., Chen, D.: Making pre-trained language models better few-shot learners. In: Proceedings of the 59th Annual Meeting of the Association for Computational Linguistics and the 11th International Joint Conference on Natural Language Processing, vol. 1: Long Papers, pp. 3816–3830. Association for Computational Linguistics (2021). https://doi.org/10.18653/v1/2021.acl-long.295, https://aclanthology.org/2021.acl-long.295
7. Hu, S., et al.: Knowledgeable prompt-tuning: incorporating knowledge into prompt verbalizer for text classification. In: Proceedings of the 60th Annual Meeting of the Association for Computational Linguistics, vol. 1: Long Papers, pp. 2225–2240. Association for Computational Linguistics, Dublin (2022). https://doi.org/10.18653/v1/2022.acl-long.158
8. Hu, S., et al.: Knowledgeable prompt-tuning: incorporating knowledge into prompt verbalizer for text classification. In: Proceedings of 60th Annual Meeting of the Association for Computational Linguistics. pp. 6311–6322. Association for Computational Linguistics, Dublin (2022). https://aclanthology.org/2021.emnlp-main.509

9. Li, Y., et al.: A joint model for aspect-category sentiment analysis with shared sentiment prediction layer. In: Sun, M., Li, S., Zhang, Y., Liu, Y., He, S., Rao, G. (eds.) CCL 2020, pp. 388–400. Springer, Cham (2020). https://doi.org/10.1007/978-3-030-63031-7_28

10. Liu, P., Yuan, W., Fu, J., Jiang, Z., Hayashi, H., Neubig, G.: Pre-train, prompt, and predict: a systematic survey of prompting methods in natural language processing (2021). https://doi.org/10.48550/ARXIV.2107.13586

11. Liu, P., Yuan, W., Fu, J., Jiang, Z., Hayashi, H., Neubig, G.: Pre-train, prompt, and predict: a systematic survey of prompting methods in natural language processing. ACM Comput. Surv. **55**, 1–35 (2022). https://doi.org/10.1145/3560815

12. Ma, R., et al.: Template-free prompt tuning for few-shot NER. In: Proceedings of the 2022 Conference of the North American Chapter of the Association for Computational Linguistics: Human Language Technologies, pp. 5721–5732. Association for Computational Linguistics, Seattle (2022). https://doi.org/10.18653/v1/2022.naacl-main.420

13. SemEval-2016: International Workshop on Semantic Evaluation (2016). https://alt.qcri.org/semeval2016/task5

14. Seoh, R., Birle, I., Tak, M., Chang, H.S., Pinette, B., Hough, A.: Open aspect target sentiment classification with natural language prompts. In: Proceedings of the 2021 Conference on Empirical Methods in Natural Language Processing, pp. 6311–6322. Association for Computational Linguistics, Online and Punta Cana (2021). https://aclanthology.org/2021.emnlp-main.509

15. Sharma, T., Kaur, K.: Benchmarking deep learning methods for aspect level sentiment classification. Appl. Sci. **11**(22), 10542 (2021). https://doi.org/10.3390/app112210542

16. Wei, Y., Mo, T., Jiang, Y., Li, W., Zhao, W.: Eliciting knowledge from pretrained language models for prototypical prompt verbalizer. In: Pimenidis, E., Angelov, P., Jayne, C., Papaleonidas, A., Aydin, M. (eds.) ICANN 2022, vol. 13530, pp. 222–233. Springer, Cham (2022). https://doi.org/10.1007/978-3-031-15931-2_19

17. You, Y., et al.: Ti-prompt: towards a prompt tuning method for few-shot threat intelligence twitter classification. In: 2022 IEEE 46th Annual Computers, Software, and Applications Conference (COMPSAC), pp. 272–279 (2022). https://doi.org/10.1109/COMPSAC54236.2022.00046

Enhancing Usability in E-Voting Systems: Balancing Security and Human Factors with the HC3 Framework

Laura Cristiano[1]([⊠])[iD] and Chiara Spadafora[2][iD]

[1] Center for Cybersecurity, Fondazione Bruno Kessler, Trento, Italy
`l.cristiano@fbk.eu`
[2] Department of Mathematics, University of Trento, Povo, Trento, Italy
`chiara.spadafora@unitn.it`

Abstract. This short article proposes a new way to improve the security-usability tradeoff when developing an electronic voting (e-voting) system, through the usage of the Human-Centered Design methodology. Drawing from insights gained from a two-year study on e-voting, we propose a framework to bridge the gap between these diverse fields and demonstrate how it can be applied to design a coercion-resistant e-voting system.

Keywords: Human-Centered Design · Personas · User Journey · Service Blueprint · E-voting

1 Introduction

The right to vote is a fundamental pillar of a democratic society, ensuring that every individual has a voice in shaping the future of their nation. In order to uphold this right, it is essential that voting is made accessible and convenient for all citizens. With the advancement of technology, the introduction of e-voting[1] protocols has the potential to revolutionize the way we cast our ballots and increase the voter turnout [18], by allowing voters to vote wherever they are. This is particularly convenient for expatriates and citizens located in a city where they do not reside, but also for citizens who, for medical reasons or other circumstances, cannot leave their homes [16].

While security is undoubtedly crucial, neglecting user research can greatly impact the acceptance and adoption of such a system: voters must *believe* that the e-voting system is secure and they must *trust* it. By developing a user-friendly application that is also highly secure, we can maximize the adoption of e-voting technology and safeguard the integrity of the electoral process.

Context of Work. This article and the proposed *HC3* framework (see Sect. 2) originate as a form of reflection-on-action [24] on a completed research project,

---

[1] Throughout the paper, with *e-voting* we mean *remote e-voting*.

C. Stephanidis et al. (Eds.): HCII 2024, CCIS 2119, pp. 33–42, 2024.
https://doi.org/10.1007/978-3-031-61966-3_4

supported by Futuro & Conoscenza S.r.l., aiming to develop an e-voting proto-type [19] in which we took into account user needs from the early stages. To do this, we followed the Human-Centered Design methodology exploiting various methods. We identified possible user types through the definition of Personas [13], we outlined, for each of them, their User Journey [21]. The User Flow [15] and the Service Blueprint [14] helped us in delineating the voting process. To develop a prototype of the e-voting application, we designed an initial mockup with Balsamiq [2], followed by an interactive mockup created with Figma [6]. Once developed, the prototype was tested with real users.

Background on E-Voting Protocols. In order to be considered secure, an election must ensure voter privacy, vote verifiability and the correctness of the final results. There is one additional threat, however, that is equally crucial to address in a fair and democratic election process: coercion resistance. Informally, a coercion resistant protocol must defend voters from attackers that pressure them to vote in a specific way, either through threats or rewards.

When it comes to e-voting, the potential for coercion becomes even greater due to its remote nature. This significantly expands the range of possible attacks on coercion resistance compared to traditional in-person voting at polling sta-tions. Consequently, designing an e-voting protocol that successfully achieves coercion resistance is a challenging task. The JCJ voting scheme, introduced by Juels, Catalano, and Jakobsson in 2005 [12], was one of the earliest systems to rigorously define the property of coercion resistance.

Briefly, a voting protocol is coercion resistant if voters have the ability to create some kind of *fake credentials* [12], indistinguishable from a valid one, that can be given to a coercer in the event of an attack. This allows the voters to protect their valid credentials and maintain their voting rights. During the tally phase of the election process, any vote cast with fake credentials is discarded and only votes cast with valid credentials are counted.

Related Works. User acceptance of e-voting systems depends on both security and usability [32] and various studies highlight the importance of human factors in the design [17]. The study [1] evaluates three voting protocols and highlights how low success rates in completing the voting process were, primarily due to poor usability. This underlines the importance of a system not only being secure but also user-friendly to garner acceptance among voters. Few studies have pri-oritized user involvement from the early stages of solution design, despite the known tradeoff between security and usability. In the study conducted by [29], the authors developed an iterative design process to create a more usable system, involving a multi-level usability analysis and a survey on voters' past experiences. The factors promoting or hindering the adoption of internet voting are explored in [18], with political features, trust, and perception identified as critical. The paper [20] provides an overview of user study design challenges when investigat-ing end-to-end verifiable e-voting schemes and presents methods for assessing their usability metrics. The article [31] discusses the implications of introducing e-voting as an alternative to paper ballots, drawing on previous trials and suc-cessful e-enabled elections to issue technical recommendations for Internet voting in the European Union. While there are many insightful articles on the subject (e.g., [4,11,21,23]), this summary highlights only some of them for brevity.

2   The HC3 Framework

In this Section we present the *Human-Centered approach in Cryptography and Cybersecurity (HC3)* framework (see Table 1). The *HC3* framework is designed to prioritize the user in every step of the development of an e-voting system. It combines cryptographic and cybersecurity research with a focus on the end user, helping guide the project through its life cycle.

After an in-depth study of the state of the art (Step 1 of Table 1), it is necessary to identify the security, usability and accessibility requirements that the e-voting solution must meet (Step 2 of Table 1). Following this step, the operational phase of the design begins (Step 3 of Table 1), in which the cryptographic voting protocol is defined together with the User Flow to identify the main actions the user should perform during the protocol execution. Concurrently, to keep the user at the center of the development process and identify the possible critical points of the protocol, it is important to define the Personas and their respective User Journeys. The subsequent definition of the Service Blueprint (Step 4 of Table 1) integrates the aspects considered so far with the requirements related to cybersecurity. As the Back-End of the solution is being built, potential graphic designs for the prototype are explored and tested through an initial draft (Step 5 of Table 1). This should be followed by an interactive mockup, which marks the start of the Front-End development of the voting solution (Step 6 of Table 1). Lastly, to develop a solution that is usable and secure, it is mandatory to conduct a comprehensive evaluation of the e-voting system through both testing with potential users, that reflect the created Personas, and functional tests on the prototype (Step 7 of Table 1). After analyzing the data collected from the tests (Step 8 of Table 1), the *HC3* framework recommends starting again from Step 3:

- on the user research side, it is necessary to update the various methods employed, starting from the Personas, to ensure that they accurately represent the potential end users, up to improving the graphical interface;
- on the cryptography and cybersecurity research side, it is necessary to improve the protocol to make the steps, that have been found most critical, easier to follow and understand, without compromising security.

In Sect. 3 we will detail the Human-Centered Design methods we employed to develop a prototype of an e-voting system following the *HC3* framework.

Table 1. HC3 Framework Definition.

Steps	User Research	Research on Cryptography and Cybersecurity
1. *State of the art analysis*	State of the art on user experiences towards e-voting systems and gathering of socio-demographics data of possible users.	State of the art on e-voting protocols and techniques both from the mathematical and cybersecurity point of view.
2. *Identification of Requirements*	Identification of the usability and accessibility requirements.	Identification of requirements and properties that the e-voting protocol must satisfy.
3. *Design and Specification*	Definition of the User Flow. Definition of the Personas and their User Journeys.	Cryptographic protocol definition. Back-End Architecture.
4. *Refinement and Implementation*	Definition of the Service Blueprint for every possible voting flow allowed by the protocol.	Refinement of the cryptographic protocol. Back-End development.
5. *First graphical rendering and Implementation*	First draft of the Mockup.	Back-End and Front-End development.
6.*Prototype*	First interactive Mockup.	Front-End development.
7. *Tests*	Usability tests.	Functional tests.
8.*Continuous Evaluation and Iteration*	Based on the results, if necessary, start again from point 3.	Based on the results, if necessary, start again from point 3

3   Application of the HC3 Framework to an E-Voting System

This Section[2] demonstrates how we applied the *HC3* framework presented in Sect. 2 to the development of an e-voting system based on the *fake credentials* mechanism (see Sect. 1, [12]).

Research Users' Needs and Competitive Analysis. During the early stage of design, it is necessary to gain a deeper understanding of end user needs [28] via ethnographic field studies and contextual inquiry [30]. Following this principle, we began conducting in-depth research on potential users of the e-voting system. On one hand, we focused on understanding their needs, expectations, and concerns regarding e-voting systems in general. In the meantime, we sought to understand their digital skills and the factors that typically influence their participation in elections. In this initial stage, as defined by [22], a competitive analysis is crucial to have the chance to leverage successful strategies, avoid what does not work and identify areas for improvement. To conduct our competitive analysis, we examined the e-voting experiences already implemented in other countries, aiming to understand how voters perceived the online elections.

User Flow. Having understood, at a high level, the flow of an e-voting protocol based on the *fake credentials* mechanism (see Sect. 1, [12]), we defined the User Flow (see Fig. 1). As defined by [15] the User Flow represents a series of actions outlining the optimal sequence of steps required to complete the task using a product or a service. The User Flow was useful to have a first visual representation of the flow the end users should accomplish to vote.

---

[2] All the graphics have been created using Canva [3].

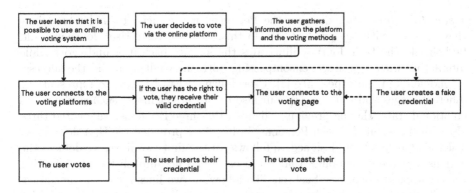

Fig. 1. User Flow of an e-voting system based on the *fake credentials* mechanism (see Sect. 1, [12]).

Personas. With the aim of consistently placing the user at the center of our design process, we have defined our user types through the creation of Personas (see Fig. 2). The Personas are a method that employs fictional characters to represent patterns of potential user types of a product or service [13]. They are designed based on the data collected during the early stage of the design process [30] and their definition helps the project team to gain a deeper understanding of the end users' by establishing a tangible representation that embodies consistent and reliable insights into the user groups [33]. We created three different Personas, defined based on the data collected while researching the user's needs and doing the competitive analysis. The Personas were defined in a narrative way. Each was assigned with a distinct name and biographical details, followed by a delineation of their interests and aspirations. Finally, we focused on their attitudes regarding political participation and their interaction with technology. In Fig. 2 we provided a shortened version of the three Personas.

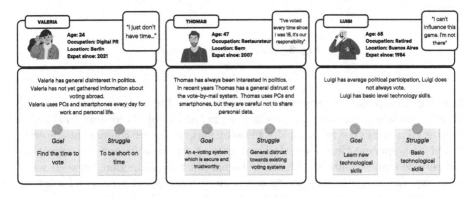

Fig. 2. Personas created to reflect potential users of the e-voting system.

User Journey. After defining the Personas, it is crucial to understand how they interact with the product. To do this, defining their User Journey could be helpful. The User Journey illustrates the journey each user undergoes while interacting with a product, encompassing both the challenges and the successful moments in the experience [5]. User Journeys can be used to represent the different stages and touchpoints, but also to capture elements such as the user's emotional state. Having previously defined the three Personas, we created three User Journeys, one for each Personas. In Fig. 3 we provided the User Journey of Valeria, that has been designed as follows. In the first two lines, we defined the actions and the touchpoints that the user should accomplish to vote following the e-voting protocol (see Sect. 1). The following two lines focus on the subjective perception of each Personas: in the *Thoughts* line, we defined the positive (indicated in green) and the negative (indicated in red) thinking, while in the *Feelings* line, we expressed the emotions they experience through the usage of emojis. Finally, we have the *Backstage opportunities* line, in which are defined the potential improvements we can make after reflecting as a team on the negative thoughts of each Personas.

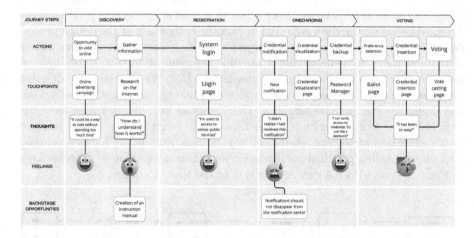

Fig. 3. Valeria's User Journey.

Service Blueprint. The Service Blueprint is a valuable method to map and visually explain a service or a product, as noted by [8]. According to [7], this diagram illustrates the relationships between various service components directly linked to a specific User Flow. It is structured on the different scenarios that the service can accommodate, and it highlights the distinction between what users experience *frontstage* and the operational and support processes *backstage*, during interactions with a product or service [10]. The Service Blueprint enables also the discovery of potential weaknesses and opportunities for improvement [7]. We defined the Service Blueprints based on the scenario arising from the usage of an e-voting protocol based on the fake credentials mechanism (see Sect. 1, [12]). We created two different Service Blueprints: one representing the scenario without the *fake credentials* request and one with (see Fig. 4). We designed the Service Blueprint following the key elements defined by [7]. In the first line, we defined the *User Actions*, i.e., the steps the end user performs to vote. In the second line, there are shown the *Frontstage Actions* that represent what occurs directly within the user's line of sight. Finally, we delineated the *Backstage Actions*, i.e., what happens behind the scenes to support Frontstage Actions.

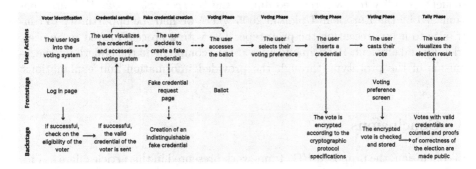

Fig. 4. Service Blueprint of an e-voting system based on the *fake credentials* mechanism (see Sect. 1, [12]). The Service Blueprint considers both the possible User Flows (see Sect. 3, Fig. 1).

Mockup and Prototype. Once the context is understood and user and process requirements are specified, it is appropriate to design a Mockup of the solution. A Mockup is a visual representation that allows to evaluate the design and the functional elements of a digital product from the user's point of view [25]. We designed two mockups. A first static Mockup, realized with Balsamiq [2], allowed us to reproduce low-fidelity interfaces focusing on structure and content, providing a first visual representation of the e-voting protocol. Subsequently, we updated the static Mockup to deliver a more interactive experience with animation and dynamic overlays, utilizing Figma [6].

After that, we designed the Prototype following the usability and accessibility requirements identified before. In addition, to put always the user at the center of the process, we decided to expand our design scope beyond the voting process itself, incorporating explanatory sections that guide users through different election procedures. These sections provide comprehensive information about how to vote in each different election.

Usability Test. Usability testing aims to find usability issues the project team had not thought about. Several studies underline the need to comprise usability testing with possible users [34] for validating new digital products, especially new e-voting systems [9]. Usability testing can be realized during various stages of the design: during the development to observe users' behaviour and make any changes under development, or when the product is already in use to understand user problems and redesign some components. Before conducting a usability test, it is necessary to organize at least one small pilot session, so the usability evaluation goes as smoothly as possible [26].

We organized respectively one pilot test session, followed by one main usability test. The pilot test was organized inside our company, and twelve colleagues tried to use our prototype. The pilot test allowed us to collect various feedback regarding how we designed the interfaces but also regarding the functionalities. It also allowed us to test how we organized the test and our scenarios. The subsequent usability test was realized during the *Sharper Night 2023* [27], an event launched by the European Union in 2005 where we had the opportunity to contribute to it by presenting the prototype. The voting process proved to be user-friendly and efficient. Participants were able to comprehend the underlying mechanisms of the prototype through the provided information and explanations.

4 Conclusions

In conclusion, the proposed *HC3* framework presented in this article offers a comprehensive approach to developing a user-friendly and secure e-voting system. By prioritizing user needs and integrating cryptography and cybersecurity research, the framework ensures that the system meets both security and usability requirements. Based on our experience, we learned that finding an effective approach to designing such systems can be challenging. This challenge is compounded by the diverse expertise within the project team and the intricate balance required between usability and security considerations.The application of the *HC3* framework enabled us to engage users from the early stages of the design process, and find the right balance between security and usability throughout the development of an e-voting prototype. Lessons learned from the application of the *HC3* framework include the importance of conducting thorough research on user needs and competitive analysis to gain a deep understanding of end users. Creating Personas, User Journeys, and Service Blueprints based on this research helps to design a system that meets the needs and expectations of users.

Drawing from our implementation of the *HC3* framework, we highly recommend its utilization not only in other e-voting system development scenarios but also in the development of diverse digital solutions. The framework's effectiveness in engaging users early in the design process and its ability to strike the right balance between security and usability make it a valuable asset across a spectrum of technological endeavors.

In future works, we aim to further expand the test base by incorporating a wider range of Personas and test scenarios to ensure comprehensive coverage of all possible outcomes. Our goal is to continually improve the accuracy and reliability of our framework by exploring new methods and methodologies.

Acknowledgements. This work has been partially supported by "Futuro & Conoscenza Srl", jointly created by the Fondazione Bruno Kessler and Poligrafico e Zecca dello Stato Italiano (IPZS, the Italian Government Printing Office and Mint).

References

1. Acemyan, C.Z., Kortum, P., Byrne, M.D., Wallach, D.S.: Usability of voter verifiable, end-to-end voting systems: baseline data for helios, prêt à voter, and scantegrity ii. USENIX J. Elect. Technol. Syst. (JETS) **2**(3), 26–56 (2014)
2. Balsamiq. https://balsamiq.com/
3. Canva. https://canva.com/
4. Eshet, E.: Human-centered design in mobile application development: emerging methods. Int. J. Mob. Hum. Comput. Interact. (IJMHCI) **4**(4), 1–21 (2012)
5. Fenn, T., Hobbs, J.: Applying user journey design to resolve complex design problems. In: University of Johannesburg Institutional Repository (2013). https://doi.org/10.13140/2.1.4704.6402
6. Figma. https://www.figma.com/
7. Gibbons, S.: Service blueprints: Definition (2017). https://www.nngroup.com/articles/service-blueprints-definition/
8. Haugen, M.: Service blueprints persistent qualities and future potential. In: Norwegian University of Science and Technology (2013). https://api.semanticscholar.org/CorpusID:195821409
9. Herrnson, P.S., Niemi, R.G., Hanmer, M.J., Bederson, B.B., Conrad, F.G., Traugott, M.: The importance of usability testing of voting systems. In: 2006 USENIX/ACCURATE Electronic Voting Technology Workshop (EVT 2006). USENIX Association, Vancouver, B.C. (2006). https://www.usenix.org/conference/evt-06/importance-usability-testing-voting-systems
10. Hossain, M.Z., Enam, F., Farhana, S.: Service blueprint a tool for enhancing service quality in restaurant business. Am. J. Ind. Bus. Manag. **07**, 919–926 (2017). https://doi.org/10.4236/ajibm.2017.77065
11. Hsu, J., Bronson, G.: E-voting technologies usability: a critical element for enabling successful elections. In: Tadj, L., Garg, A. (eds.) Emerging Challenges in Business, Optimization, Technology, and Industry: Proceedings of the Third International Conference on Business Management and Technology, Vancouver, BC, Canada 2017, pp. 61–78. Springer, Heidelberg (2018)
12. Juels, A., Catalano, D., Jakobsson, M.: Coercion-resistant electronic elections. In: Proceedings of the 2005 ACM Workshop on Privacy in the Electronic Society, pp. 61–70 (2005)
13. Junior, P.T.A., Filgueiras, L.V.L.: User modeling with personas. In: Proceedings of the 2005 Latin American Conference on Human-Computer Interaction, pp. 277–282 (2005)
14. Kalakota, R., Robinson, M.: Services Blueprint: Roadmap for Execution. Addison-Wesley Professional, Boston (2003)
15. Kaplan, K.: User journeys vs. user flows (2023). https://www.nngroup.com/articles/user-journeys-vs-user-flows/
16. Kulyk, O., Volkamer, M.: Usability is not enough: lessons learned from 'human factors in security' research for verifiability. In: E-Vote-ID 2018. TUT Press (2018)

17. Kulyk, O., Volkamer, M., Fuhrberg, N., Berens, B., Krimmer, R.: German voters' attitudes towards voting online with a verifiable system. In: Matsuo, S., et al. (eds.) FC 2022. LNCS, vol. 13412, pp. 335–350. Springer, Heidelberg (2022). https://doi.org/10.1007/978-3-031-32415-4_23

18. Licht, N., Duenas-Cid, D., Krivonosova, I., Krimmer, R.: To i-vote or not to i-vote: drivers and barriers to the implementation of internet voting. In: Krimmer, R., et al. (eds.) E-Vote-ID 2021. LNCS, vol. 12900, pp. 91–105. Springer, Heidelberg (2021). https://doi.org/10.1007/978-3-030-86942-7_7

19. Longo, R., Morelli, U., Spadafora, C., Tomasi, A.: Adaptation of an i-voting scheme to italian elections for citizens abroad. In: E-Vote-ID 2022. University of Tartu Press (2022)

20. Marky, K., Zollinger, M.L., Funk, M., Ryan, P.Y., Mühlhäuser, M.: How to assess the usability metrics of e-voting schemes. In: Bracciali, A., Clark, J., Pintore, F., Ronne, P., Sala, M. (eds.) FC 2019. LNCS, vol. 11599, pp. 257–271. Springer, Heidelberg (2020). https://doi.org/10.1007/978-3-030-43725-1_18

21. Moon, H., Han, S.H., Chun, J., Hong, S.W.: A design process for a customer journey map: a case study on mobile services. Hum. Fact. Ergon. Manuf. Serv. Ind. **26**(4), 501–514 (2016)

22. Neusesser, T.: Competitive usability evaluations (2024). https://www.nngroup.com/articles/competitive-usability-evaluations/

23. Olembo, M.M., Volkamer, M.: E-voting system usability: lessons for interface design, user studies, and usability criteria. In: Human-Centered System Design for Electronic Governance, pp. 172–201. IGI Global (2013)

24. Reymen, I.: Research on design reflection: overview and directions. In: Proceedings of ICED 2003. KTH Royal Institute of Technology (2003)

25. Rivero, J.M., Rossi, G., Grigera, J., Burella, J., Luna, E.R., Gordillo, S.: From mockups to user interface models: an extensible model driven approach. In: Daniel, F., Facca, F.M. (eds.) ICWE 2010. LNCS, vol. 6385, pp. 13–24. Springer, Heidelberg (2010). https://doi.org/10.1007/978-3-642-16985-4_2

26. Shade, A.: Pilot testing: Getting it right (before) the first time (2015). https://www.nngroup.com/articles/pilot-testing/

27. Sharper night 2023. https://www.sharper-night.it/

28. Siricharoen, W.V.: Human centered design and design thinking for entrepreneurship. EAI Endorsed Trans. Context-aware Syst. Appl. (2023). https://api.semanticscholar.org/CorpusID:260919001

29. Smith, M.A., Monfort, S.S., Blumberg, E.J.: Improving voter experience through user testing and iterative design. J. Usabil. Stud. **10**(4), 116–128 (2015)

30. Stefan, B.: Persona - an overview. In: Theoretical perspectives in Human-Computer Interaction (2002). https://api.semanticscholar.org/CorpusID:13518131

31. Trechsel, A.H., Kucherenko, V.V., Da Silva, F.F.: Potential and challenges of e-voting in the European union. Technical report, European University Institute (2016)

32. Volkamer, M., Spycher, O., Dubuis, E.: Measures to establish trust in internet voting. In: Proceedings of ICEGOV 2011. ACM Digital Library (2011)

33. Wang, X.: Personas in the user interface design. University of Calgary, Alberta, Canada (2014)

34. Zollinger, M.L., Distler, V., Rønne, P., Ryan, P., Lallemand, C., Koenig, V.: User experience design for e-voting: how mental models align with security mechanisms. In: E-Vote-ID 2019 TalTech Proceedings (2019). https://doi.org/10.13140/RG.2.2.27007.15527

Side Effect Reporting in Online Drug Reviews

Jie Mein Goh[1]([✉]) [iD] and Nathaniel Tok[2]

[1] Beedie School of Business, Simon Fraser University, Burnaby, BC V5A 1S6, Canada
jmgoh@sfu.ca

[2] Redmond High School, Redmond, WA 98052, USA

Abstract. Online drug reviews are an important resource for consumers and patients. However, potential misinformation from online drug reviews in the form of side effects reporting can bias consumer decisions about medications, potentially leading to detrimental health outcomes. The focus of this study is to understand the content discussed in online drug reviews and the potential risks in online drug reviews caused by patients' overreporting of certain kinds of side effects. For instance, patients may be more likely to report visible short term side effects compared to less visible side effects. Additionally, patients are more likely to report short term side effects compared to long term side effects. Patients relying on online drug reviews might select medications with less evident but potentially more severe side effects, misled by the over-representation of side effects in the reviews. Drawing on a sample of online drug reviews collected from a large popular online drug review platform, we employ state-of-the-art machine learning techniques to identify the themes being discussed and types of side effects reported in online drug reviews. Our preliminary findings detail the topics and side effects discussed in online drug reviews, as well as the different dimensions and the frequency with which topics appear. Results from this work can contribute to the overall literature on online reviews and provide useful insights to the public, policymakers and online platforms in their understanding of side effect reporting in online drug reviews.

Keywords: Side effect · review content · online reviews · drug reviews · GPT

1 Introduction

This study seeks to investigate the potential risks of online drug reviews, which are increasingly being utilized by patients seeking information on medications (Adusumalli et al., 2015; Hautala et al., 2021). While online drug review platforms such as, Drugs.com, WebMD.com, can offer valuable insights into various medications, misinformation poses a significant risk to users and can pose a significant threat to users and cause adverse health outcomes. In the absence of professional medical guidance, patients may rely on information from these online drug review sites to determine whether to initiate or continue with a drug treatment regimen. This reliance carries serious implications, as inaccurate information regarding medications can result in harmful decisions and significant negative health consequences on patients.

C. Stephanidis et al. (Eds.): HCII 2024, CCIS 2119, pp. 43–49, 2024.
https://doi.org/10.1007/978-3-031-61966-3_5

Online drug review sites frequently feature reports of side effects, which may be disproportionately represented. Such overrepresentation of side effects in online reviews can be problematic, as consumers might choose medications with lower efficacy and more severe though less visible side effects.

Although scholars in the Information Systems and Marketing fields have extensively researched the online word of mouth phenomena on e-commerce platforms (e.g., Amazon.com), surprisingly few studies have delved into online reviews in the realm of online drug reviews. The existing literature on online word of mouth predominantly focuses on online consumer reviews in non-healthcare context on consumer purchase behavior (Clemons et al., 2006; Duan et al., 2009; Luca & Vats, 2013). These studies highlight the pivotal role of online reviews as sources of information regarding product quality and fit, often serving as substitutes for traditional forms of word-of-mouth communication (Chevalier & Mayzlin, 2006). Prior research has also examined the effect of online review on sales (Chevalier & Mayzlin, 2006), firms' interactions on online review sites (Godes et al., 2005), seller strategies such as promotional reviews (Mayzlin et al., 2014) and user incentives like discounts (Mayzlin et al., 2014). Recent studies have investigated the effects of financial incentives on online review contribution (Khern-am-nuai et al., 2018; Qiao et al., 2020) as well as the spillover effects of online reviews in the e-commerce context (Kwark et al., 2014).

Surprisingly, contrary to the large body of literature on online reviews in e-commerce, studies focusing on online drug reviews are scarce. Research in e-commerce has explored how online reviews influence consumer perceptions, decisions and business outcomes for products and services categories (Ghose et al., 2014; Ghose & Ipeirotis, 2006). However, the distinct characteristics of online drug reviews suggest that these findings may not translate uniformly across different contexts. Given the growing reliance on online drug reviews for health-related decisions, understanding the impact of online drug reviews is of paramount importance, and this calls for more research in understanding how consumers make decisions based on online drug reviews. While there has been some exploration of online reviews in healthcare context such as online physician reviews and their impact (Gao et al., 2015; Saifee et al., 2019; Shukla et al., 2021, Wang et al. 2022), this study marks the first step in an attempt to investigate side effect reporting in online drug reviews.

Online drug reviews exhibit unique characteristics that set them apart from reviews of non-healthcare related products and services, potentially rendering findings from previous studies less relevant. The user base of online drug reviews primarily consists of individuals with unique needs seeking specialized information, often compounded by existing medical conditions or symptoms. Research indicates that drugs are considered experience goods due to the challenge consumers face in obtaining information prior to use (Zheng, 2021). Furthermore, the variability in drug characteristics, such as side effects, among individuals make online drug review sites a convenient means to search and compare across drugs.

Consumers may consult drug reviews to assess effectiveness (e.g., how fast symptoms are suppressed or disappear), hoping to alleviate their symptoms or find a cure for their condition, while others may seek insights into potential side effects of drugs reported by other users (Chew & Khoo, 2016). In the Computer Science field, studies have highlighted that online drug reviews tend to be emotionally charged and include personal anecdotes and attitudes, (Zheng, 2021). These differences raise the question of whether findings from other studies on online reviews focusing on non-healthcare related products and services can be extrapolated to online drug review sites.

Given the potential risks of online drug reviews on patients' health decisions, it is surprising that extant research do not focus on online drug reviews, and it is not clear what is reported in online drug review and whether the side effects reported in online drug reviews will influence consumers. Hence, to better understand what is reported in online drug reviews, this study aims to examine the research question: "What are the major themes reported in online drug reviews?" and as a precursor to understanding whether side effects reporting influence consumers, we ask the second research question: "What are the characteristics of side effects reported in online drug reviews?". Findings from this study will have important implications and be of high relevance to healthcare regulators and online review platforms in healthcare.

2 Method

2.1 Research Setting and Data Collection

Data was obtained from a large and popular online drug review platform hosted on IBM Cloud for consumers and healthcare professionals. Users can register on the web-based online community at no cost. Once registered, users have the ability to post online reviews about the drug or medication they have taken for their condition. Similar to other online review sites, this platform allows users to upvote reviews, effectively "likeing" them. A random sample of reviews was collected from this online drug review platform.

Our sample dataset contains 75,000 reviews, from which we gathered the review text, use duration of the drug, and the rating of the review. We focus our analysis on this sample of the data. Table 1 shows the summary statistics for this sample.

Table 1. Summary Statistics.

Duration	n	percent
Use duration (options provided by platform)		
-Short term use duration (< 1 month)	14,147	18.86
-Medium term (1–6 months)	12,293	16.39
- 6 months – 1 year	3644	4.86
-1–2 years	3158	4.21
-2–5 years	2740	3.65
-5–10 years	1359	1.81
- > 10 years	1050	1.42
Number of reviews without use duration	36,609	48.8
Average rating of reviews	6.69	

2.2   Data Processing for Thematic Analysis

User comments and reviews posted to the online community were analyzed to identify specific themes related to the reporting of side effects. For this thematic analysis, we utilized user specified prompts using ChatGPT. Developed by OpenAI, ChatGPT is a generative text-based AI model designed for various applications. ChatGPT employs the state-of-the-art Generative Pre-Trained Transformers (GPT) technology, and it has been recognized for its effectiveness and accuracy in natural language processing tasks. We employed the following prompt with ChatGPT: "Look through the review [text] column and identify common topics or themes across the reviews." The output generated from ChatGPT is shown in Table 2 and will be discussed in Sect. 3.1.

2.3   Data Analysis for Classification

For classification of side effects into categories of none, low, medium and high visibility, we made use of GPT-3.5 Turbo API. All 75,000 data points were processed using this API. The model, operated through a script hosted on an Azure cloud PC, analyzed each user reviews and classifies each review text according to the visibility of the side effects. The performance metrics for visibility classification were as follows: overall accuracy was 0.7267, precision was 0.7572, recall was 0.6229, and F1 score was 0.6795. We used the model to classify all reviews in the sample and obtained the distribution of reviews in each category across different use durations. These results will be discussed in Sect. 3.2.

3   Results

3.1   Themes Identified

Table 2 presents the four main topics identified using ChatGPT and their frequency within the data. As shown in the table, the most frequently mentioned themes in the online reviews are:

– Experience and pain management: This theme being most mentioned makes sense because patients primarily seek medications to alleviate symptoms or manage conditions. Their reviews often focus on the effectiveness of the drug in managing pain or other symptoms related to certain conditions. Patients may describe their overall experience, highlighting the positive and / or negative aspects of taking the drug.
– Cost and specific medications: The cost of medications emerges as a significant concern for many patients which is reflected in the online reviews. Discussions often involve comparisons between the costs of different medications.
– Medication and side effects: Many reviews delve into the side effects experienced by patients, a critical area of interest for most patients seeking information about drugs. Reviewers often describe the onset, nature and severity of the side effects experienced.
– Treatment outcomes and feelings: Information regarding the effectiveness of a drug in treating a medical condition is a common focus, with patients reporting on their feelings and the effects experienced after taking the medication.

Table 2. Themes extracted from GPT

Themes	Sample words	% of reviews
Medication and Side Effects	Days, day, period, just, started, pill, weight, effects, medication	75
Experience and Pain Management	taking, started, felt, work, doctor, effects	84
Treatment Outcomes and Feelings	Feel, medication, weeks, going, mg, effects, life, better	74
Cost and Specific Medications	Effects, taking, use, started, pain, price, days	76

3.2 Characteristics of Side Effects Reported in Online Reviews

To address the second research question "What are the characteristics of side effects reported in online drug reviews?", we analyzed the dataset using the classifications for low, medium and high visibility, along with the use duration information provided by the patients. From Table 3, it is evident that among patients who report use duration, typically discuss drugs taken within the first 6 months of use. Moreover, patients often report side effects of medium or high visibility across all durations of use. Few patients post reviews without mentioning visible side effects. In instances where visible side effects are mentioned, the majority of online drug reviews discuss side effects with medium to high visibility. However, we urge caution in interpreting these results, as they are influenced by the performance of our classification model, which has significant potential for improvement.

Table 3. Analysis of side effect reporting using visibility and use duration

Use Duration	Predicted Rating			
	None	Low	Medium	High
-Short term use duration (<1 month)	183	160	8478	5326
-Medium term (1–6 months)	95	228	8822	3148
−6 months – 1 year	33	57	2753	801
−1–2 years	33	50	2394	681
−2–5 years	47	76	2112	505
−5–10 years	8	40	1108	203
−>10 years	8	31	859	152

4 Discussion

Online drug reviews are an important source of information when consumers are considering various medications for treating a medical condition. In this study, we employed GPT technology, including both ChatGPT and its API, to analyze topics mentioned in online drug reviews, and to gain insights into side effect reporting on online drug reviews. Our initial findings suggest that side effects are a prominent theme being discussed in online reviews. Furthermore, patients are more inclined to report visible, short-term side effects compared to less visible, long-term side effects. These results can contribute to a better understanding of online drug reviews, and we aim to extend this work through further empirical studies to investigate whether side effect reporting has a negative impact on drug choice. The outcomes of our study are poised to provide important implications for both policymakers and pharmaceutical companies.

References

Adusumalli, S., Lee, H., Hoi, Q., Koo, S.-L., Tan, I.B., Ng, P.C.: Assessment of web-based consumer reviews as a resource for drug performance. J. Med. Internet Res. **17**(8), e4396 (2015)

Chevalier, J.A., Mayzlin, D.: The effect of word of mouth on sales: online book reviews. J. Mark. Res. **43**(3), 345–354 (2006)

Chew, S.W., Khoo, C.S.G.: Comparison of drug information on consumer drug review sites versus authoritative health information websites. J. Am. Soc. Inf. Sci. **67**(2), 333–349 (2016)

Clemons, E.K., Gao, G.G., Hitt, L.M.: When online reviews meet hyperdifferentiation: a study of the craft beer industry. J. Manag. Inf. Syst. **23**(2), 149–171 (2006)

Duan, W., Gu, B., Whinston, A.B.: Informational cascades and software adoption on the internet: an empirical investigation. MIS Q. **33**(1), 23–48 (2009)

Gao, G.G., Greenwood, B.N., Agarwal, R., McCullough, J.S.: Vocal minority and silent majority: how do online ratings reflect population perceptions of quality? MIS Q. **39**(3), 565–589 (2015). https://doi.org/10.25300/MISQ/2015/39.3.03

Ghose, A., Ipeirotis, P.G.: Designing ranking systems for consumer reviews: the impact of review subjectivity on product sales and review quality. In: Proceedings of the 16th Annual Workshop on Information Technology and Systems, pp. 303–310 (2006)

Ghose, A., Ipeirotis, P.G., Li, B.: Examining the impact of ranking on consumer behavior and search engine revenue. Manage. Sci. **60**(7), 1632–1654 (2014)

Hautala, G.S., et al.: Most orthopaedic trauma patients are using the internet, but do you know where they're going? Injury **52**(11), 3299–3303 (2021)

Khern-am-nuai, W., Kannan, K., Ghasemkhani, H.: Extrinsic versus intrinsic rewards for contributing reviews in an online platform. Inf. Syst. Res. **29**(4), 871–892 (2018)

Kwark, Y., Chen, J., Raghunathan, S.: Online product reviews: implications for retailers and competing manufacturers. Inf. Syst. Res. **25**(1), 93–110 (2014)

Luca, M., Vats, S.: Digitizing Doctor Demand: The Impact of Online Reviews On Doctor Choice. Harvard Business School, Cambridge, MA (2013)

Mayzlin, D., Dover, Y., Chevalier, J.: Promotional reviews: an empirical investigation of online review manipulation. Am. Econ. Rev. **104**(8), 2421–2455 (2014)

Qiao, D., Lee, S.-Y., Whinston, A.B., Wei, Q.: Financial incentives dampen altruism in online prosocial contributions: a study of online reviews. Inf. Syst. Res. **31**(4), 1361–1375 (2020)

Saifee, D.H., Bardhan, I.R., Lahiri, A., Zheng, Z.E.: Adherence to clinical guidelines, electronic health record use, and online reviews. J. Manag. Inform. Syst. **36**(4), 1071–1104 (2019)

Shukla, A.D., Gao, G.G., Agarwal, R.: How digital word-of-mouth affects consumer decision making: evidence from doctor appointment booking. Manag. Sci. **67**(3), 1546–1568 (2021)

Wang, W., Luo, J., Dugas, M., Gao, G.G., Agarwal, R., Werner, R.M.: Recency of online physician ratings. JAMA Intern. Med. **182**(8), 881–883 (2022)

Zheng, L.: The classification of online consumer reviews: a systematic literature review and integrative framework. J. Bus. Res. **135**, 226–251 (2021)

Influence Based Group Recommendation System in Personality and Dynamic Trust

Cheng-En Huang[1,2] and Yi-ling Lin[1,2(✉)]

[1] Department of Management Information Systems, National Chengchi University, Taipei, Taiwan
brianhuang881215@gmail.com
[2] 64, Section 2, Zhinan Road, Wenshan District, Taipei 11605, Taiwan

Abstract. Given the frequent engagement in group activities within daily life, recommending content to a group of users becomes an important task. In heterogeneous groups, a conflict situation may arise more easily if the preferences of group members are incompatible. The challenge with dynamic groups lies in reconciling the diverse preferences of its members to reach a collective decision that satisfies everyone. While social dynamics such as personality traits, and mutual influence play a pivotal role in shaping group decision-making, this study employs the TKI personality traits, which have demonstrated efficacy in mitigating conflicts during group decision processes. Besides, we have developed a novel dynamic trust mechanism that adeptly captures the evolving trust values within a group integrated into our refined group recommendation algorithms. In order to achieve our research objectives, we executed a four-week empirical study by deploying a responsive web application tailored for our group recommendation system. Users in the experiment interacted with two distinct algorithms: traditional influence-based aggregation and the influence matrix algorithm, each over the course of two consecutive weeks. Through the experiment, we are able to better capture the variability of social factors in group decision-making, achieving higher accuracy and satisfaction as well as laying the foundation for a milestone in group recommendation within the restaurant domain.

Keywords: Group Recommendation · Trust · Personality traits · Group decision-making · Social Influence

1 Introduction

Recommendation systems (RS) solve the problem of information overload and are increasingly used in various domains. Certain items, like restaurants and museum exhibits, are frequently experienced in groups rather than alone, so addressing recommendations to groups can actually be conventional [16]. In heterogeneous groups, a conflict situation may arise more easily if the preferences of group members are incompatible [19]. While several group recommendation algorithms [2, 13, 20] are effective for homogeneous groups, they often fall short for heterogeneous ones. The challenge with heterogeneous groups lies in reconciling the diverse preferences of its members to

© The Author(s), under exclusive license to Springer Nature Switzerland AG 2024
C. Stephanidis et al. (Eds.): HCII 2024, CCIS 2119, pp. 50–57, 2024.
https://doi.org/10.1007/978-3-031-61966-3_6

reach a collective decision that satisfies everyone. Factors like personality and mutual influence are key in group decisions [24].

Conflicts arising from differing individual preferences are common, and inaccurate recommendations can reduce the satisfaction of group recommendations. Many studies have confirmed that TKI personality traits can effectively resolve conflicts during group decision-making. Juan A. Recio-Garcia [19] improved accuracy by adding TKI personality to standard aggregation methods. Abolghasemi [1] devised an influence matrix method based on TKI personality to produce a ranked list of recommendations via Markov chain iterations. However, the factors influencing decision-making are not solely due to personality traits. The nature of relationship or expertise, can also impact the degree to which you allow them to make decisions.

After reviewing literature on social group recommendation systems [4, 9, 10, 15, 18, 21], we discovered that the factor of trust can encompass various social factors beyond personality traits. In the past, trust factors in group recommendation systems mostly derived their data from social network connections, utilizing indicators like the number of mutual friends, length of acquaintance, social status, and contact frequency to measure trust levels, as in Capuano [3]. However, this approach may not be well-suited to real-life group interactions, as trust is likely to be influenced by the context of each group gathering and the composition of individuals, which can vary over time. Therefore, the primary objective of this study is to design a dynamic trust mechanism that captures the current fluctuating trust values within a group.

In order to achieve our research goals, we conducted a four-week on-site experiment using a web app for group restaurant recommendations. Participants test our two refined algorithms (one is based on traditional influence aggregation method [24], and the other is the influence matrix method [1, 3]) over two separate two-week periods to assess effectiveness via accuracy and feedback. This paper makes several significant contributions to the group recommendation. Firstly, it is the pioneer study to ground personality traits and trust value in group recommendation systems to allow for their actual user interaction. Secondly, we design a novel mechanism that dynamically detects trust, offering a more precise computation of trust. Lastly, we refine and compare two proposed methods with TKI personality and dynamic trust, improving accuracy and satisfaction, and setting a new standard in restaurant recommendation algorithms.

2   Literature Review

2.1   Personality Test

Personality is commonly applied in recommendation systems, and it can be acquired in both implicit and explicit ways [7]. The former approach acquires user personality by observing users' behavioral patterns on online social network data. It requires less effort from users, but less accurate compared with the explicit one. The explicit personality measurements approaches are generally based on questionnaires and one of the most widely used personality theories is known as the Five Factors Model (FFM) [12]. Besides, there are another explicit measurement of personality called Thomas-Kilmann Conflict Mode Instrument (TKI) [26]. It directly describes a person behavior in conflict situations with five personality modes: competing, collaborating, avoiding, accommodating and compromising. In real life, people have different expectations that usually appear to be incompatible, leading to "conflict situations" [19]. Therefore, many studies are applying the TKI personality to address challenges of group decision-making.

2.2 Social Influence Based on Trust

Many studies have tried to incorporate social influence into group recommendation scenarios. A social-aware group recommendation framework which uses both social relationships and social behaviors can not only predict a group's preferences but also capture the tolerance and altruism traits of group members [25]. In order to gain a better understanding of how individuals within a group are affected by their respective social influences, trust has been recognized as a significant factor impacting the consensus-building process in group decision-making [5]. Besides, trust is inherently dependent on interpersonal relationships, and their perceived outcomes and risks. In addition, there is another term commonly used to indicate the strength of trust between groups called tie-strength which encompasses the time spent, emotional intensity, closeness, and reciprocal exchanges defining a relationship [14]. Regarding the source of relationships, Tyler [27] has proposed a well-known social relationship theory called Relational Model Theory. This theory classifies everyday group interactions into four primary relationship types. It helps in understanding the various dynamics that underlie different group interactions. While traditional group recommendation systems have relied on data from social networks to evaluate trust factors [3], to gain a better understanding of the meaning of trust beyond simply distinguishing it based on the strength of relationships, we have explored various definitions and measurement methods related to trust.

Trust, in previous research, is fundamentally subjective, varying based on individual perspectives. It is inherently asymmetric and may not be reciprocated equally within a dyad. Besides, trust in social settings is not always transitive; one's trust in a person does not automatically extend to their trusted contacts. Trust is also dynamic, liable to diminish over time without ongoing interaction. Lastly, trust is context-dependent, influenced by situational factors, and the level of trust adjusts as circumstances evolve. According to Jiang [17], explicit or direct trust stems from the connections between entities that interact directly; on the other hand, implicit or indirect trust can be inferred from the trust scores by intermediaries. As for indirect trust, Massa [23] introduces a method to calculate trust value called MoleTrust. There are two important components it. First is the trust propagation horizon, which specifies the maximum distance from the source to the end user. The second component is threshold, which evaluates all the incoming trust edges and considers only the ones coming from users with a predicted trust score exceeds a specified minimum value. Therefore, we can use this method to indirectly obtain the trust values between individuals without directly rating.

2.3 Group Recommendation Algorithm on Social Elements

Numerous studies have converged on the consensus that the social aspect plays a pivotal role in shaping group recommendations. Research is increasingly applying the TKI personality to mitigate group decision-making conflicts [1, 6, 19]. While TKI traits are useful, group decisions are also affected by other social factors like relationships.

Gartrell [9] designed a Heuristic Group Consensus Function that factors in social ties, expertise, and diversity to arrive at collective item ratings, suggesting that stronger relationships enhance satisfaction in decision outcomes. Guo [15] considered multiple social dimensions, including TKI personality, relationship strength, expertise, and preference similarity in group recommendation systems, finding that a combined approach yields better accuracy and satisfaction than adding factors separately. Additionally, Sun [25] proposed a social-based system that differentiates between one-way (celebrity/expert) and two-way (friend) relationships, proving its effectiveness through ad-score and hit rate. Notably, one-way relationships were found to reflect user preferences more than two-way connections.

Regarding the research on group recommender systems that integrate personality traits and trust, Quijano-Sanchez [24] proposed two novel aggregation methods:

1. Delegation-Based Rating Prediction: Inspired by Golbeck [11], this method suggests that people form their opinions based on trusted friends' recommendations, taking into account both the friends' personalities and their trust levels.

$$pred'(u, i) = dbr(u, i) = \frac{1}{\left|\sum_{v \in G} t_{u,v}\right|} \sum_{v \in G \cap^v \neq u} t_{u,v}(pred(v, i) + p_v) \quad (1)$$

2. Influence-Based Rating Prediction: This method accounts for how much friends' ratings influence an individual's rating. It posits that a person might adjust their rating based on others' ratings, whose trust and TKI personality are high.

$$pred'(u, i) = ibr(u, i) = pred(u, i) + (1 - p_u)\frac{\sum_{v \in G \cap^v \neq u} t_{u,v}(pred(v, i) - pred(u, i))}{|G| - 1}$$
$$(2)$$

Besides, Capuano [3] proposed an enhanced GDM-based model for group recommendations that incorporates social elements. They utilized both interpersonal trust and personality to create an influence matrix weight for group recommendations. The method for calculating trust continues to utilize the approach mentioned by Quijano-Sanchez [24], which is a combination of 10 factors measured on Facebook profiles. Although the proposed method differs from traditional aggregation-based approaches, the experimental results were analyzed using only simulated data generated by the authors themselves, leaving the effectiveness of real-life group recommendations unclear. Therefore, in Sect. 3, we will introduce two refined influence-based algorithms with TKI personality and trust. Both incorporate our dynamic trust mechanism to optimize and compare which method is better in real-life group recommendations.

3   Personality-Based Dynamic Trust Group Recommendation System

3.1   TKI Personality Value

In our study, we employ the Thomas-Kilmann Conflict Mode Instrument (TKI) [26] to assess individual behavioral responses in conflict situations, which convert five TKI modes into numerical values to calculate their Conflict Mode Weight (CMW). The CMW score ranges from 0 to 1, with higher values suggesting selfish personalities and lower values indicating easygoing personality.

3.2 Dynamic Trust Mechanism

Previously, group recommendation systems primarily gauged trust using social network data by mutual friends, acquaintance duration, social status, and contact frequency [3]. To better reflect real-life group decisions, we have developed a dynamic trust mechanism based on diverse trust definitions in our experiment. Firstly, the trust questions rated by the group members are summarized by Evans [8] in Likert seven-point scale:

- How close was your working relationship with each person?
- How often did you communicate with each person?
- To what extent did you typically communicate with each person?
- Source of a relationship?

Regarding the source of relationships, we employed the Relational Model Theory [27], which categorizes everyday group interactions into four primary relationship types(Equal Matching, Market Pricing, Authority Ranking, and Communal Sharing). We can automatically classify the group's purpose into one of these types. Besides, the expertise of each individual in selecting restaurants is also taken into consideration. If a person is trusted by the group but lacks the ability to choose good restaurants, their recommendations are less likely to be heavily weighted by others. Furthermore, our dynamic trust mechanism also integrates global and indirect trust metrics [18], along with the subjective and context-dependent of trust from Marsh [22]. For global trust, group members are asked to provide a collective rating instead of mutual peer ratings, to prevent trivial assessments. We then calculate average indirect trust using the MoleTrust method with threshold of 0.6 and a trust propagation horizon of 2. To sum up, the following is the final equation of our dynamic trust mechanism:

$$Trust_{AB} = \frac{\frac{1}{T}\sum_{i=1}^{T} trustItem_i + expertise(B) + moleTrust_{AB}}{3} \qquad (3)$$

The dynamic trust value of $Trust_{AB}$ is computed as the average of trustItems, expertise and MoleTrust. $trustItem_i$, where i ranges from 1 to 4, representing the individual trust factors [8]. $Expertise(B)$ is a value between 0 and 1. Last, $moleTrust_{AB}$ is derived from the past trust levels among group members. In summary, our dynamic trust mechanism effectively mitigates the cold start issue for newcomers and reduces the burden of mutual peer rating. Moreover, it enables dynamic updating of trust scores, reflecting the changes in trust that occurs in different group interaction contexts.

3.3 Integration of Personality and Social Trust

According to Quijano-Sanchez [24], the author proposed two methods to optimize traditional aggregated group recommendations. However, the application of TKI personality and trust in these models seems underutilized. The delegation-based approach (Eq. (1)) averages the ratings of group members, excluding the individual's rating, and adds the value of p into the prediction rating without fully capturing the nuances of TKI personality traits. The influence-based model (Eq. (2)) adjusts user u's rating of item i based on personality and trust strength but falls short in different group sizes, TKI personalities, and trust value, compared with Eq. (1). Therefore, we propose a revised influence-based model based as shown in Eq. (4).

$$pred'(u, i) = ribr(u, i) = p_u \times pred(u, i) + (1 - p_u) \sum_{v \in G \cap v \neq u} t_{u,v} \times pred(v, i)$$

(4)

The algorithm uses parameter p as a weighted average to reflect user assertiveness; a higher p indicates a user's preference reliance. The complement, $1 - p$, gauges other group members' influence on the user. Unlike previous research, we detect $t_{u,v}$ through our dynamic trust mechanism for more accurate trust assessment. The final prediction $pred'(u, i)$ is computed for each user using the traditional average satisfaction method to establish the group's collective rating for item i.

Recently, some papers have explored the influence matrix method for group dynamics and decision-making, but their accuracy compared to traditional methods remains uncertain. Therefore, we propose an influence matrix method based on TKI personality and trust according to [1, 3] and compare it with the revised influence method mentioned above. Firstly, in order to mitigate the effects of social influence, the authors adopt the TKI personality to measure the users' attitudes to remain faithful to their initial preferences. Given the assertiveness $a(u_i^G)$ and the cooperativeness $c(u_i^G)$ of user $u_i^G \in G$, the personality of u_i^G between 0 to 1 can be obtained as follows:

$$p(u_i^G) = \frac{1 + a(u_i^G) - c(u_i^G)}{2}$$

(5)

As for the acquisition of trust values, we will use the dynamic trust mechanism to detect. According to the normalization property of trust value, the influence of peers on each user should sum to one. $\forall i \in \{1, 2, ..., m\}$, $\sum_{j=1}^{m} W_{ij} = 1$ (m is the number of group). So, the influence weight of pears j on i (w_{ij}) as:

$$w_{ij} = \begin{cases} (1 - p(u_i^G)) \cdot \dfrac{trust\left(u_i^G, u_j^G\right)}{\sum_{k \in \{1,...,m\} \backslash i} trust\left(u_i^G, u_k^G\right)} & if\ i \neq j, \\ p(u_i^G) & if\ i = j. \end{cases}$$

(6)

Given that matrix W is a square stochastic matrix, it serves as the transition probability matrix for a Markov chain with m states and stationary transition probabilities [1]. If we consider $G = \{g_1, g_2, ..., g_m\}$, g as a group of m members, then $y_x^{(1)} = [r_{g_1x}, r_{g_2x}, ..., r_{g_mx}]$ will be a vector, representing the group members' rating for item x. After the group members interact, their opinions will change based on different social influence. Mathematically, $y_x^{(2)} = W \cdot y_x^{(1)}$ where $W = (w_{ij})$ is an $m \times m$ weight matrix. After iterating t times, the group members' opinions are as follows:

$$y_x^{(t)} = W \cdot y_x^{(t-1)} \text{ which equals to : } y_x^{(t)} = W^{t-1} \cdot y_x^{(1)}$$

(7)

For example, if there is a group G with three people g_1, g_2, g_3, and their respective TKI personality values are: $p_1 = 0.5, p_2 = 0.2, p_3 = 0.8$, and the trust values between them are: $t_{12} = 0.3$, $t_{13} = 0.9$, $t_{21} = 0.8$, $t_{23} = 0.8$, $t_{31} = 0$, $t_{32} = 0.8$. After applying the Eq. (6), we can obtain the following weight matrix.

$$W = \begin{pmatrix} 0.5 & 0.125 & 0.375 \\ 0.4 & 0.2 & 0.4 \\ 0 & 0.2 & 0.8 \end{pmatrix}. \tag{8}$$

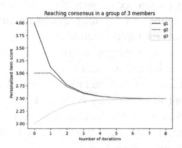

Fig. 1. Example of group preference in one restaurant

Assuming that group G's ratings for a particular restaurant are as follows: g1: 4, g2: 3, g3: 2. After eight iterations, as seen in Fig. 1, the final group rating stabilized at 2.5, aligning with g3's high-trust, high-TKI personality preference. This process helps identify the top 30 restaurants for recommendations to the group.

4   Methodology

To achieve our research goals, we conducted a four-week on-site experiment employing a responsive web application. This study focuses on group restaurant recommendations, as this scenario closely aligns with everyday life, where individuals frequently find themselves dining out with different people. Participants, primarily students from National Chengchi University, engaged with two distinct algorithms (one is based on delegation, and the other is a novel algorithm that we have developed) over two separate two-week periods to assess their effectiveness through accuracy and user feedback. Participants could easily join the study by scanning a QR code, registering, and creating a personal profile. Once users formed groups within the interface, group recommendation functions became available, with recommendations tailored based on the trust levels and personality traits of the group members.

References

1. Abolghasemi, R., et al.: A personality-aware group recommendation system based on pairwise preferences. Inf. Sci. (N Y). **595**, 1–17 (2022)
2. Boratto, L., Carta, S.: State-of-the-art in group recommendation and new approaches for automatic identification of groups. In: Soro, A., Vargiu, E., Armano, G., Paddeu, G. (eds.) Information Retrieval and Mining in Distributed Environments, pp. 1–20. Springer Berlin Heidelberg, Berlin, Heidelberg (2011). https://doi.org/10.1007/978-3-642-16089-9_1

3. Capuano, N., et al.: Fuzzy group decision making for influence-aware recommendations. Comput. Human. Behav. **101**, 371–379 (2019)
4. Cho, J.-H., et al.: A survey on trust modeling. ACM Comput. Surv. **48**(2), 1–40 (2015)
5. Chu, J., et al.: Social network analysis based approach to group decision making problem with fuzzy preference relations. JIFS **31**(3), 1271–1285 (2016)
6. DeGroot, M.H.: Reaching a consensus. J. Am. Stat. Assoc. **69**(345), 118–121 (1974)
7. Dunn, G., Wiersema, J., Ham, J., Aroyo, L.: Evaluating interface variants on personality acquisition for recommender systems. In: Houben, G.J., McCalla, G., Pianesi, F., Zancanaro, M. (eds.) UMAP 2009. LNCS, vol. 5535, pp. 259–270. Springer, Heidelberg (2009). https://doi.org/10.1007/978-3-642-02247-0_25
8. Evans, M.M., et al.: The strength of trust over ties: investigating the relationships between trustworthiness and tie-strength in effective knowledge sharing. Electron. J. Knowl. Manag. **17**(1), 19–33 (2019)
9. Gartrell, M., et al.: Enhancing group recommendation by incorporating social relationship interactions. In: GROUP'10, pp. 97–106 (2010)
10. Gilbert, E., Karahalios, K.: Predicting tie strength with social media. In: CHI'09, pp. 211–220 (2009)
11. Golbeck, J.: Combining provenance with trust in social networks for semantic web content filtering. In: Moreau, L., Foster, I. (eds.) IPAW 2006. LNCS, vol. 4145, pp. 101–108. Springer, Heidelberg (2006)
12. Goldberg, L.R.: The structure of phenotypic personality traits. Am. Psychol. **48**(1), 26–34 (1993)
13. Gorla, J., et al.: Probabilistic group recommendation via information matching. In: WWW'13, pp. 495–504 (2013)
14. Granovetter, M.S.: The strength of weak ties. Am. J. Sociol. **78**(6), 1360–1380 (1973)
15. Guo, J., et al.: A social influence approach for group user modeling in group recommendation systems. IEEE Intell. Syst. **31**(5), 40–48 (2016)
16. Jameson, A., Smyth, B.: Recommendation to groups. In: Brusilovsky, P., Kobsa, A., Nejdl, W. (eds.) The adaptive web. LNCS, vol. 4321, pp. 596–627. Springer, Heidelberg (2007). https://doi.org/10.1007/978-3-540-72079-9_20
17. Jiang, W., et al.: Understanding graph-based trust evaluation in online social networks: Methodologies and challenges. Acm Comput. Surv. (Csur). **49**(1), 1–35 (2016)
18. Jiang, W., et al.: Understanding graph-based trust evaluation in online social networks: methodologies and challenges. ACM CSUR **49**(1), 1–35 (2016)
19. Recio-Garcia, J.A., et al.: Personality aware recommendation to groups. In: RecSys'09, pp. 325–328. Association for Computing Machinery (2009)
20. Kim, J.K., et al.: A group recommendation system for online communities. Int. J. Inf. Manage. **30**(3), 212–219 (2010)
21. Marsden, P.V., Campbell, K.E.: Measuring tie strength. Soci. Forces **63**(2), 482–501 (1984)
22. Marsh, S.P.: Formalising trust as a computational concept (1994)
23. Massa, P., Avesani, P.: Trust-aware recommender systems. In: Proceedings of the 2007 ACM Conference on Recommender Systems, pp. 17–24 (2007)
24. Quijano-Sanchez, L., et al.: Social factors in group recommender systems. ACM Trans. Intell. Syst. Technol. **4**(1), 1–30 (2013)
25. Sun, L., et al.: Social-aware video recommendation for online social groups. IEEE Trans. Multimedia **19**(3), 609–618 (2016)
26. Thomas, K.W.: Thomas-kilmann conflict mode. TKI Profile and Interpretive Report. 1, 11 (2008)
27. Tyler, T.R., Lind, E.A.: A relational model of authority in groups. In: Advances in Experimental Social Psychology, vol. 25, pp. 115–191. Elsevier (1992). https://doi.org/10.1016/S0065-2601(08)60283-X

Did Japanese Students Change Their Social Media Usage Toward Learning After COVID-19?

Toshikazu Iitaka[✉]

Kumamoto Gakuen University, Oe 2-5-1, Kumamoto, Japan
iitaka2@yahoo.co.jp

Abstract. This article constitutes an investigation into the ramifications of the COVID-19 pandemic on educational technology. Notably, in May 2023, the Japanese government reclassified COVID-19 as a commonplace infection. Analyzing the juxtaposition between the pandemic era and the post-redefinition period is pivotal for comprehending the ultimate impact of COVID-19 on Japanese online learning. Consequently, this comparative assessment will furnish valuable insights for designing an optimal e-learning framework in the aftermath of the pandemic.

This article addresses the comparative analysis between the empirical findings of Iitaka's study in 2023 and the survey conducted in September of the same year. Iitaka's research specifically explored the utilization of social media platforms for educational purposes. Given that social media constitutes a substantial repository of voluminous data, and considering that contemporary artificial intelligence (AI) systems heavily rely on this extensive data, this investigation holds promise in illuminating optimal strategies for harnessing big data within diverse modern e-learning frameworks, all of which are underpinned by AI methodologies.

Literature [3] unearthed intricate associations between social isolation and the utilization of social media for educational purposes. Were this outcome replicable, signifying the persistence of these intricate connections, it would necessitate a reevaluation of system design. However, the survey conducted in 2023 failed to reveal such a correlation. Consequently, we may exploit voluminous data within AI-supported e-learning systems.

Keywords: Social-Media · COVID-19 · Big-Data · Social-Isolation

1 Introduction

This study investigates the influence of the COVID-19 pandemic on the utilization of social media platforms for educational and learning objectives.

The shift from traditional in-person work and study to online modalities due to the pandemic has been widely recognized, resulting in a conspicuous alteration in the dependence on social media for educational purposes. Literature [2, 3] discerned this transition through rigorous statistical analysis, and the outcomes corroborated the observed fluctuations. Should this transformation endure, it signifies a significant metamorphosis in the realm of e-learning.

However, certain journalistic articles have documented a restoration of normalcy, attributing it to the reclassification of COVID-19 as a commonplace infectious ailment. Consequently, it becomes imperative to ascertain whether analogous trends endure within the domain of e-learning.

To assess these trends, an online survey was administered, and its findings were subjected to meticulous statistical scrutiny. The outcomes corroborate the aforementioned transitions. This study expounds upon the survey methodologies and subsequent analytical procedures.

First, we outlined the background and significance of this research, followed by a detailed presentation of the online survey and the statistical techniques employed. Finally, we discussed the analysis results to understand the characteristics of the phenomenon. The discussion tries to suggest the proper design for e-learning systems using big data.

2 Background and Significance

This study is based on two primary contexts: first, it examines the social media usage for educational purposes, and second, it evaluates the influences of the COVID-19 pandemic on learning methodologies.

Firstly, we examine the background concerning the utilization of social media for educational purposes.

Literature [1] conducted an in-depth exploration into the intricate fabric of social media usage within academic milieus. These meticulous analyses unveiled that approximately 40% of Japanese students availed themselves of Twitter as a digital repository for their scholarly endeavors. Furthermore, a multifaceted tapestry of educational applications emerged across this demographic. Literature [1] underscored the pivotal role of social media as a rich reservoir of big data. E-learning systems, underpinned by robust data analytics, hold the promise of efficacious learning outcomes. Notably, recommender systems, which curate tailored information for individual learners, warrant rigorous investigation within e-learning frameworks.

The emergence of the COVID-19 pandemic is conjectured to have fundamentally reconfigured this milieu. My subsequent scholarly inquiry in 2022 corroborated this paradigm shift. While a substantial cohort of Japanese students persisted in utilizing social media as an educational conduit, a discernible diminution in engagement became apparent [3]. Simultaneously, salient metamorphoses within the Twitter ecosystem, notably encompassing a transition in executive stewardship and a subsequent corporate rebranding, may bear implications for its pedagogical assimilation.

Subsequently, we expound upon the secondary background, namely, the impact of the COVID-19 pandemic on the educational landscape. Literature [3] accentuated the burgeoning specter of social isolation during the pandemic. Considering that one of the cardinal functions of social media platforms lies in fostering interpersonal linkages, these platforms may be construed as ameliorative instruments in countering such isolation. This postulation forms the bedrock upon which the ensuing analyses are predicated.

Subsequent to the abatement of COVID-19 restrictions in Japan in April 2022, my survey in Literature [3] was undertaken in August of the same year. Moreover, the pandemic's dynamic landscape experienced yet another metamorphosis in May 2023.

Consequently, any analytical inferences drawn from data postdating May 2023 hold the potential to yield profound insights.

3 Method

This study implemented an online survey to investigate the subsequent research question.

3.1 Description of Survey

This study implemented an online survey to investigate the subsequent research question.

- RQ: Does the transformation identified by Iitaka (2023) exhibit temporal character-istics?

Then we describe the research design (Table 1).

Table 1. Research Design.

Type of Survey	Online Research	
Period	2023.9.15–2023.9.19	
Number	560	
Gender		
female	50%	
male	50%	
Age	%	Number of Samples
−19	25.2	141
20–29	31.8	178
30–39	10.4	58
40–49	10.2	57
50–59	10.0	56
60-	12.5	70

The research design closely mirrors that of Literature [3]. Literature [3] posited the necessity of offline surveys, and consequently, an offline survey was conducted. Although the analysis remained incomplete at the time of Literature [3]'s writing, the outcomes were akin to those reported by Literature [3]. However, the social media adoption rate observed in the offline research cohort was inferior to that documented by Literature [3]. The online survey conducted in 2022 revealed that 68% of respondents utilized X (specifically, Twitter). Conversely, the offline survey in the same year indicated that 59% of participants engaged with X (Twitter). Notably, the Generation Z demographic, as per the 2022 Offline survey, exhibited a mere 44.4% adoption rate for X (Twitter), despite a prominent Japanese research entity asserting that 66% of Generation Z users in Japan actively employ X (Twitter) [5]. Consequently, the fundamental dataset diverges significantly from the reliable data. The research firm responsible for the survey had preemptively acknowledged the challenges associated with obtaining reliable data due to the non-utilization of offline (postal) surveys for sample collection. Furthermore, the correlation coefficients between social media usage for educational purposes and social isolation scales tend to exhibit lower magnitudes (Table 2).

This paper uses the same variables as that of Literature [3]. So, important variables are frequencies of social media uses for learning and social isolation scales. Table 3 shows the distribution of variables.

Table 2. Questions of the Japanese version of the UCLA loneliness scale and the direct question.

	Text	Abbreviation
Q1	I am happy doing so many things with friends. (reverse)	With Friends
Q2	I have nobody to talk to	nobody to talk to
Q3	There is no one I can turn to.	no one I can turn to.
Q4	I am not alone. (reverse)	not alone
Q5	I am a necessary person for my friends. (reverse)	necessary person
Q6	My friends and I have many things in common. (reverse)	in common
Q7	I am no longer close to anyone	no longer close
Q8	My interests and ideas are not shared by those around me	not shared
Q9	I prefer going out.(reverse)	prefer going out
Q10	There are people who are close to me.(reverse)	people close to me
Q11	I am ignored.	Ignored
Q12	My social relationships are superficial.	Superficial
Q13	No one really knows me well	No one knows me
Q14	I feel isolated from others	feel isolated
Q15	I can make friends anytime if I want. (reverse)	can make friends
Q16	There are people who know me well. (reverse)	knows me well
Q17	I am unhappy being so withdrawn	Withdrawn
Q18	Though I have friends, their ideas are different from mine.	different idea
Q19	There are people to whom I can talk.(reverse)	people I can talk
Q20	There are people to whom I can turn.(reverse)	people I can turn
Q21	I am lonely (Original)	Direct isolation

Table 3. Distribution of the variables.

	Minimum	Maximum	Mean	Std. Deviation	Skewness	Kurtosis
Direct isolation after commonization	1	4	2.25	.970	.293	−.901
Direct isolation after restriction	1	4	2.49	.871	−.081	−.679
Direct isolation during restriction	1	4	2.25	.967	.285	−.898
Direct isolation before COVID-19	1	4	2.17	.957	.371	−.830
UCLA loneliness scale after commonization	21.00	80.00	47.90	10.16	.176	.856
UCLA loneliness scale after restriction	41.00	59.00	50.15	3.01	−.120	.267
UCLA loneliness scale during restriction	20.00	80.00	48.1	10.62	.141	1.109
UCLA loneliness scale before COVID-19	20.00	80.00	47.19	10.6	−.016	.907
Uses of Facebook for learning	11.00	44.00	15.57	7.38	1.474	1.079
Uses of Twitter (X) for learning	11.00	44.00	16.49	7.69	1.250	.498
Uses of Line for Learning	3.00	12.00	5.08	2.40	.946	−.016

3.2 Statistical Analysis

Initially, we focused on examining the frequency of social media adoption for educational purposes, followed by determining the correlation between such usage and established social isolation scales.

Analyzing the usage patterns across multiple social media platforms revealed that several Japanese students use social media for academic endeavors. Approximately 40% of these students use Platform X (Twitter) for digital note-taking. Notably, compared with the findings of Literature [3], the prevalence of using social media for learning has increased. Moreover, these frequencies exhibited signs of resurgence. An analysis of variance (ANOVA), comparing the outcomes of surveys from 2018, 2020, 2022, and 2023, reveals a statistically significant deviation among 2018, 2020, and 2022 surveys, as indicated by $F(3, 1116) = 3.585$, $p < 0.05$. Evidently, the utilization frequency of

Twitter (X) for educational purposes exhibited a precipitous decline in the year 2020. Subsequently, this frequency demonstrates a gradual recuperation. Notwithstanding, as of 2023, the frequency remains inferior to that observed in 2018; however, the discernible disparity does not attain statistical significance (Tables 4, 5, 6 and 7).

Table 4. Frequencies of social media use for learning in 2022.

	Use Facebook for note-taking (text data)			
	Never	Seldom	Sometimes	Often
Not Student	227	33	14	6
	81.1%	11.8%	5.0%	2.1%
Student	190	43	36	11
	67.9%	15.4%	12.9%	3.9%
Total	417	76	50	17
	74.5%	13.6%	8.9%	3.0%
	Use Twitter for note-taking (text data)			
	Never	Seldom	Sometimes	Often
Not Student	224	32	18	6
	80.0%	11.4%	6.4%	2.1%
Student	182	48	41	9
	65.0%	17.1%	14.6%	3.2%
Total	406	80	59	15
	72.5%	14.3%	10.5%	2.7%

This study examined the correlation between the frequency of social media utilization for educational purposes and various measures of social isolation. These measures were categorized into four distinct temporal periods: "pre-COVID-19" (up to March 2019), "during Restriction" (April 2019 to March 2022), "post-Restriction" (April 2022 to April 2023), and "post-Commonization" (from May 2023 onward). Notably, among Japanese students, as highlighted by Literature [3], a noteworthy pattern emerges specifically between social media engagement for learning and the social isolation scale corresponding to the "post-Restriction" phase.[*]1 This intricate relationship implies that the UCLA loneliness scale and responses to direct inquiries about social isolation exhibit different associations with social media use (particularly on platforms like Line) for educational purposes, despite the substantial similarity between the two independent variables. However, during other time periods, a consistent positive correlation persists between the frequency of social media adoption for learning and the respective social isolation scales. Consequently, the observed intricate trend is likely transient in nature.

If the transient nature of the intricate pattern were not the case, we might have been compelled to reconfigure our preexisting e-learning frameworks, leveraging big

Table 5. Frequencies of social media use for learning in 2023.

	Use Facebook for note-taking (text data)			
	Never	Seldom	Sometimes	Often
Not Student	231	26	21	2
	82.5%	9.3%	7.5%	0.7%
Student	183	51	37	9
	65.4%	18.2%	13.2%	3.2%
Total	414	77	58	11
	73.9%	13.8%	10.4%	2.0%
	Use Twitter for note-taking (text data)			
	Never	Seldom	Sometimes	Often
Not Student	227	31	19	3
	81.1%	11.1%	6.8%	1.1%
Student	171	53	41	15
	61.1%	18.9%	14.6%	5.4%
Total	398	84	60	18
	71.1%	15.0%	10.7%	3.2%

Table 6. Analysis of variance on the use of Platform X for learning among Japanese Students.

Dependent Variable			Mean Difference (I-J)	Sig
Use of Twitter for Learning	2018.00	2020.00	**1.85357***	**.044**
		2022.00	**2.05714***	**.020**
		2023.00	1.71071	.075
	2020.00	2018.00	**−1.85357***	**.044**
		2022.00	.20357	.992
		2023.00	−.14286	.997
	2022.00	2018.00	**−2.05714***	**.020**
		2020.00	−.20357	.992
		2023.00	−.34643	.961
	2023.00	2018.00	−1.71071	.075
		2020.00	.14286	.997
		2022.00	.34643	.961

Table 7. Correlations between Social Isolation and Social Media Uses for Learning among Japanese Students.

	Use of Facebook for Learning	Use of Twitter (X) for Learning	Use of Line for Learning
UCLA social isolation scale after Commonization	.268**	.212**	0.004
UCLA social isolation scale after Restriction	−.128*	−0.071	0.03
UCLA social isolation scale during COVID-19	.220**	.171**	0.004
UCLA social isolation scale before COVID-19	.335**	.277**	0.079
Direct Question after Commonization	.269**	.237**	0.076
Direct Question after Restriction	−0.043	−0.014	.160**
Direct Question during COVID-19	.338**	.305**	.188**
Direct Question after Commonization	.239**	.220**	0.034

**. Correlation is significant at the 0.01 level (2-tailed).
*. Correlation is significant at the 0.05 level (2-tailed).

data, given that social media serves as a pervasive source of such data. However, an immediate overhaul of the existing e-learning system is unnecessary, as the change appears enduring. Nevertheless, social isolation, in and of itself, holds considerable significance for the learning process. Consequently, exploring the underlying origins of this temporal intricacy becomes desirable. Such an investigation could facilitate the enhancement of our e-learning systems.

4 Discussion of Result

This section confirms what this paper has discussed and shows the limitations and future issues of this research.

The analytical outcomes of Literature [3] suggested a potential imperative to modify the approach to studying social media usage. Such an alteration could hold crucial implications for research concerning social media application. Because social media is a major source of big data, this must affect the design of e-learning systems using big data and AI. However, findings from this current study suggest that this proposed shift might be unnecessary, as the observed changes appear to be transient. So, the investigation into e-learning systems which make use of data from social media must be encouraged, because social media can provide good big data for AI.

Nevertheless, the current empirical evidence underscores the existence of nuanced phenomena associated with social isolation. The principal constraint of this research lies in the context of these intricately manifested phenomena. In a broader context, the social isolation experienced by adolescent learners poses a formidable challenge for educators. Consequently, strategies aimed at ameliorating this issue ought to be incorporated into the design specifications of e-learning systems. As such, this phenomenon warrants further scholarly inquiry.

Acknowledgement. This work was supported by JSPS KAKENHI Grant Number JP15K12175 and 20K03196.

References

1. Iitaka, T.: An analysis on digital note-taking using social media in Japan. In: Stephanidis, C., Antona, M. (eds.) HCI International 2020 – Posters: 22nd International Conference, HCII 2020, Copenhagen, Denmark, July 19–24, 2020, Proceedings, Part III, pp. 177–184. Springer International Publishing, Cham (2020). https://doi.org/10.1007/978-3-030-50732-9_24
2. Iitaka, T.: An analysis on social media use for learning under the COVID-19 condition in Japan. In: Zaphiris, P., Ioannou, A. (eds.) Learning and Collaboration Technologies. Designing the Learner and Teacher Experience: 9th International Conference, LCT 2022, Held as Part of the 24th HCI International Conference, HCII 2022, Virtual Event, June 26–July 1, 2022, Proceedings, Part I, pp. 253–264. Springer International Publishing, Cham (2022). https://doi.org/10.1007/978-3-031-05657-4_18
3. Iitaka, T.: Change in Social Media Use for Learning Among Japanese Internet Users During the COVID-19 Pandemic. In: Coman, A., Vasilache, S. (eds.) Social Computing and Social Media: 15th International Conference, SCSM 2023, Held as Part of the 25th HCI International Conference, HCII 2023, Copenhagen, Denmark, July 23–28, 2023, Proceedings, Part II, pp. 308–323. Springer Nature Switzerland, Cham (2023). https://doi.org/10.1007/978-3-031-35927-9_22
4. Kaplan-Rakowski, R.: Addressing students' emotional needs during the COVID-19 pandemic: a perspective on text versus video feedback in online environments. Educ. Tech. Research Dev. **69**(1), 133–136 (2020). https://doi.org/10.1007/s11423-020-09897-9
5. NHK: KoronaGorui RemoteWork · ZaitakuKinmuKara Shusshani KaikiSuru Ugokimo (2023). https://www.nhk.or.jp/shutoken/newsup/20230515c.html). Accessed 9 Oct 2023
6. Cyber Agent: Cyber Agent Zisedaiseikatsukenkyuuzyo ,"Z sedaino SNS riyouritsu wo happyou (2023). https://www.cyberagent.co.jp/news/detail/id=29609#:~:text=2022%E5%B9%B4%EF%BC%88%E8%AA%BF%E6%9F%BB%E6%9C%9F%E9%96%93%EF%BC%9A2022,%E3%81%AA%E3%81%A3%E3%81%9F%E3%81%93%E3%81%A8%E3%81%8C%E6%98%8E%E3%82%89%E3%81%8B. 19 Dec 2023

Unveiling Digital Literacy Dynamics in Social Media Usage Patterns: Comparison of Digital Skill and Critical Information Behavior

Eunbi Kang[1] (iD), Soyeong Choi[1] (iD), Xu Li[2] (iD), and Hyesun Hwang[1]([⊠]) (iD)

[1] Department of Consumer Science, Convergence Program for Social Innovation, Sungkyunkwan University, Seoul, South Korea
h.hwang@skku.edu
[2] Department of Consumer Science, Sungkyunkwan University, Seoul, South Korea

Abstract. Social media has profoundly transformed human-computer and interpersonal interactions, enabling communication acros temporal and spatial barriers and expanding access to information. Nevertheless, the widespread dissemination of unverified personal content underscores the critical importance of digital literacy in contemporary society. Unvetted content frequently lacks credibility, impeding consumers' critical thinking and exacerbating information overload. Given the indiscriminate sharing of content on platforms like social media, active engagement in critical information searching is paramount. Despite extensive discussions on the digital divide, previous research has primarily concentrated on material access, skills, and technology usage, overlooking consumers' social media usage patterns and digital literacy, especially concerning critical information behavior (CIB). To address this gap, this study draws on data from the Korea Media Panel Survey 2022 and utilizes Latent Profile Analysis (LPA) to classify individuals based on their social media behaviors. LPA's person-centered approach identifies five distinct user groups: light users, lurkers, casual users, likers, and network leaders. Subsequent ANOVA analysis reveals that light users demonstrate the lowest scores in digital device usage skills and CIB, while network leaders exhibit the highest overall scores. However, even among network leaders, there exists a significant deficiency in CIB scores, underscoring the necessity to not only address digital literacy related to usage but also emphasize comprehensive information evaluation skills. This study underscores the need for comprehensive digital literacy education that encompasses both technical skills and critical information evaluation, ensuring individuals can navigate the digital landscape responsibly and effectively.

Keywords: Digital Literacy · Social Media Usage Patterns · Information Behavior

1   Introduction

In contemporary digital societies, the prevalence of digitalization facilitates the easy expression and dissemination of opinions, often resulting in a proliferation of unverified personal content [1]. The abundance of user-generated media content underscores the

C. Stephanidis et al. (Eds.): HCII 2024, CCIS 2119, pp. 67–77, 2024.
https://doi.org/10.1007/978-3-031-61966-3_8

increasing significance of digital literacy in discerning and evaluating content critically [2–4]. This is particularly pertinent in the realm of social media platforms, where individuals freely generate, share, and rapidly disseminate content, necessitating consumers to adopt critical information-searching behaviors.

Digital literacy is delineated qualitatively distinct from digital accessibility or mere usage. South Korea, renowned as a digital powerhouse, boasts a smartphone penetration rate of approximately 97% as of 2023, indicating widespread digital accessibility and consequently, proficient overall digital device usage skills [5]. However, in terms of digital literacy—specifically, the ability to critically evaluate information and discern between facts and opinions—the country falls somewhat short, scoring only 26%, which is below the OECD average of 47% [3]. This dissonance accentuates novel challenges regarding the nature of the digital divide within digitally advanced societies.

While discussions abound regarding bridging the gap in digital access and device usage skills [6–8], there remains a dearth of research concerning consumers' social media usage patterns and their corresponding digital literacy levels. Consequently, the aim of this study is to delineate patterns based on consumers' social media usage behaviors, ascertain the number of latent profiles, and juxtapose them with critical information-searching behaviors and digital device usage skills. The study underscores the necessity for literacy and behaviors that enable individuals to objectively scrutinize content consumed through technology, transcending mere technical proficiency. This will furnish invaluable insights for future consumer digital literacy education initiatives.

2 Literature Review

2.1 Digital Device Usage Skills

The digital divide has been extensively deliberated upon and categorized into three principal dimensions: access, skill, and usage [9]. Digital access pertains to the physical availability of digital devices and internet connectivity, which has become pervasive in contemporary digital society. The digital divide, emblematic of variances in digital proficiency, is predominantly explored in terms of fundamental device usage skills and the adeptness to employ them at an advanced level to accomplish specific objectives [10]. These digital proficiencies may exhibit discrepancies contingent upon demographic attributes and even within identical consumer cohorts, diverging based on the type of device employed [11]. Consequently, this study also investigates rudimentary skills in utilizing digital devices, classified into mobile and computer usage categories.

2.2 Digital Literacy and Critical Information Behavior

Digital Literacy In light of the rapid digital transformation catalyzed by the COVID-19 pandemic, discourse surrounding the digital divide has transitioned from its conventional emphasis on usage skills to encompass additional dimensions [12–14]. Despite the widespread proficiency of individuals in employing digital technology in their everyday routines, it remains challenging to assert that they have attained complete digital competency. This is because the skills necessary for operating digital devices and the ability to critically comprehend and navigate content consumed through them represent distinct competencies necessitating discrete examination [15].

Digital literacy denotes the capacity to critically comprehend and effectively apply multimedia information encountered online [2, 16, 17]. The landscape of information dissemination has become increasingly fragmented in modern digital society owing to the proliferation of media content, including videos and images [4]. Notably, social media platforms have emerged as pervasive channels deeply integrated into consumers' daily routines, facilitating the active sharing of user-generated content. Consequently, this proliferation poses a significant challenge for the cultivation of critical reasoning skills [18]. The focal point of this study centers on scrutinizing consumers' social media usage behaviors, given the paramount importance of cultivating the ability to critically examine information in today's digital milieu.

Critical Information Behavior. To assess consumers' digital literacy, critical information behavior (CIB) serves as a valuable indicator. Defined within the Korean Media Panel Survey, CIB encapsulates how individuals scrutinize various information encountered in digital media using digital technology, and the frequency with which they engage in such practices [19–21]. This encompasses behaviors such as verifying information accuracy, scrutinizing sources, identifying biases or intentional manipulation, and discerning political or commercial motivations. These actions reflect the active exercise of critical thinking by consumers in navigating information consumption within the digital society, thus signaling their level of digital literacy.

While prior studies have classified groups based on social media usage behavior and motivations [22–24], this research hones in specifically on digital literacy, particularly crucial within the context of social media as a platform for individual-generated communication. In doing so, it employs CIB as a key indicator. By juxtaposing the ability to critically consume content with traditional digital skills, this study endeavors to draw comparisons. The classification of social media usage patterns serves as the foundation for this comparative analysis.

Hence, this study poses the following research question.

RQ1. What distinct patterns of social media usage types emerge from consumers' behaviors including catching up, uploading, sharing, reacting, and time spent on social media?

RQ2. How do consumers' critical information behavior (CIB) and digital device usage skills (mobile and PC) vary across the types of social media usage patterns?

3 Methods

3.1 Data

This study draws upon data from the Korea Media Panel Survey, conducted in 2022. Initiated in 2010, the Korea Media Panel Survey is primarily dedicated to investigating media usage behaviors across more than 5,000 households and individuals nationwide, thereby furnishing valuable insights into the evolving media landscape in tandem with technological advancements. By leveraging data from the most recent survey iteration, conducted in 2022, this study endeavors to explore consumers' social media usage patterns and digital competencies within the contemporary media milieu.

The analysis concentrated on individuals aged 20 to 59 who had actively engaged with social media platforms within the past 3 months. Specifically targeting adults not categorized as elderly, the study sought to examine individuals who might not conventionally be perceived as digitally vulnerable [25]. The demographic distribution of the respondents is delineated in Table 1.

Table 1. Descriptive statistics of respondents (N = 4206).

Variables		N	(%)
Gender	Male	1941	46.15%
	Female	2265	53.85%
Age	20–29	1145	27.22%
	30–39	743	17.67%
	40–49	1157	27.51%
	50–59	1161	27.60%
Education Level	High School or less	1078	25.63%
	College or higher	3128	74.37%
Household Income per month (million KRW)[a]	Less than 2.00	49	1.17%
	2.00–3.99	694	16.50%
	4.00–5.99	1232	29.29%
	6.00–7.99	1075	25.56%
	More than 8.00	1156	27.48%

Notes. a KRW 1.00 million = USD 758.34.

3.2 Variables

Social media usage behaviors were evaluated based on the frequency of engaging in various activities, including catching up, uploading content, sharing others' posts/images/videos, reacting to others' posts/images/videos through comments/likes, and the average daily time spent on social media for both weekdays and weekends. The frequency of catching up was assessed using an 8-point scale, ranging from 'less than once a month' to '5 or more times a day'. Similarly, the frequencies of uploading, sharing, and reacting were gauged on a 9-point scale, spanning from 'no experience' to '5 or more times a day'. The daily time spent on social media for weekdays and weekends was quantified in minutes. These variables were utilized to delineate social media usage profiles.

To assess digital competence, CIB, mobile device usage skills, and PC usage skills were evaluated. CIB was appraised using five items that gauge the frequency with which individuals critically scrutinize the accuracy and validity of information encountered during media usage. The assessment of mobile skills comprised five questions probing the ability to execute fundamental tasks, such as configuring settings and creating documents using smart devices. For PC skills, four questions were employed to ascertain proficiency in tasks such as installing programs and connecting external devices using a computer.

3.3 Latent Profile Analysis

In this study, we employed latent profile analysis (LPA) using STATA 17.0 to delineate distinct patterns of social media usage behavior. LPA constitutes a form of finite mixture model, representing a person-centered analytical approach [26]. Through iterative reclassifications, an optimal classification of individuals was iteratively refined based on their observed values across various items. Consequently, individuals were allocated to the group with the highest probability of membership, termed the posterior probability [27]. Compared to cluster analysis, LPA offers the advantage of determining the number of groups on a more statistically sophisticated basis [28].

4 Results

4.1 Estimating the Number of Latent Profiles

To determine the appropriate number of groups for classification using LPA, we evaluated the model fit by incrementally increasing the number of groups. The outcomes are presented in Table 2. Both the Bayesian Information Criterion (BIC) and Sample-size Adjusted Bayesian Information Criterion (SSABIC) values exhibited a decreasing trend as the model complexity increased. The Entropy value, a standardized coefficient ranging from 0 to 1, indicated the degree of distinctiveness in group classification, with higher values suggestive of clearer distinctions between groups [29]. While scholarly discourse may vary regarding the definition of a satisfactory cutoff, values exceeding 0.8 are generally deemed favorable [30]. The results of the Lo-Mendell-Rubin likelihood ratio test (LMR-LRT) scrutinized the goodness of fit by juxtaposing a model with a population of k profiles against a model with k-1 profiles. Significance in the p-value of the test indicates a well-fitting model [31]. The table delineates that with an increase in the number of groups, both BIC and SSABIC values declined. Additionally, the adjusted LMR-LRT results indicated that a greater number of groups significantly enhanced model fit. Notably, the entropy value peaked notably at 0.978 for the five-group model. Considering these metrics and their interpretability, the five-group model was selected for this study.

4.2 Results of Latent Profile Analysis

To address RQ1, LPA was conducted to delineate the types of consumers based on their social media usage behavior, as depicted in Table 3 and Fig. 1. The analysis yielded five distinct patterns of social media usage behavior: *Light Users, Lurkers, Casual Users, Likers,* and *Network Leaders.*

The first group identified was *Light Users* (Class 1), comprising individuals least inclined to utilize social media across various modes and time frames. Their engagement

Table 2. Fit statistics for latent profile analysis.

Fit statistics	2 Classes	3 Classes	4 Classes	5 Classes
Latent Profile Model				
BIC	154309.2	151864.9	149907.1	149023.0
SSABIC	154248.8	151713.9	149715.6	148790.8
Entropy	0.971	0.964	0.970	0.978
Adj.LMR-LRT (*p-value*)	-2502.75^{***}	-2016.15^{***}	-942.53^{***}	-887.57^{***}
Group size [n (%)]				
Class 1	2761 (65.64%)	2068 (49.17%)	1922 (45.70%)	1464 (34.81%)
Class 2	1445 (34.36%)	1583 (37.64%)	1231 (29.27%)	509 (12.10%)
Class 3		555 (13.20%)	477 (11.34%)	1148 (27.29%)
Class 4			576 (13.69%)	484 (11.51%)
Class 5				601 (14.29%)

Notes. *** $p < .001$; BIC = Bayesian Information Criteria; SSABIC = Sample size adjusted BIC; Adj. LMR-LRT = Sample size adjusted Lo-Mendell-Rubin likelihood ratio test; n = class sample size.

in browsing others' posts on social media was infrequent, and they seldom expressed their own opinions or uploaded media such as photos. On both weekdays and weekends, they allocated an average of 23 and 28 min per day to social media usage, respectively.

The second group, *Lurkers* (Class 2), exhibited a predilection for social media catch-up activities, primarily involving passive consumption of posts and content shared by others. Notably, they demonstrated a significantly higher catch-up score of 5.98 compared to other behavior types, whereas their scores for uploading (0.83), sharing (0.63), and reacting (1.21) were relatively lower. While they integrated social media into their daily routines frequently, their engagement leaned more towards passive consumption rather than active participation through content creation or interaction with others.

The third group, identified as *Casual Users* (Class 3), demonstrated a relatively even and less frequent representation across all behavior types, without a pronounced skew towards any specific type. Although they spent less time on social media compared to *Lurkers*, *Likers*, and *Network Leaders*, they engaged in uploading and sharing activities more frequently than *Light Users*, *Lurkers*, and *Likers*. Despite their comparatively reduced overall time spent, they exhibited a tendency to contribute opinions and media such as photos to the social media sphere.

Comparable to *Lurkers*, *Likers* (Class 4) prioritize the consumption of content generated by others over creating and posting their own. However, unlike *Lurkers*, whose focus primarily lies in passive viewing, *Likers* exhibit greater interactivity by engaging in activities such as commenting on and liking other users' content. Remarkably, among the five identified groups, *Likers* allocate the most extensive duration to social media usage, surpassing even *Network Leaders*, who are regarded as the most active users of social media platforms.

Lastly, *Network Leaders* (Class 5) exhibit the second-highest frequency in catching up, reacting, and overall time spent on social media, trailing *Likers*. However, they stand out as the most active group in terms of uploading and sharing activities. *Network Leaders* commonly express their opinions on social media platforms and actively disseminate self-created content such as photos and videos. Despite their propensity for frequent social media use, their behavior leans towards greater activity compared to receptive groups like *Lurkers* and *Likers*, who primarily focus on consuming content generated by others.

Table 3. Social media usage pattern by latent profile class.

	Class 1	Class 2	Class 3	Class 4	Class 5
	Light Users	*Lurkers*	*Casual Users*	*Likers*	*Network Leaders*
N (%)	1464 (34.81%)	509 (12.10%)	1148 (27.29%)	484 (11.51%)	601 (14.29%)
Catch up	2.29	5.98	4.07	6.71	6.39
Upload	0.91	0.83	3.02	2.36	5.43
Share	0.73	0.63	2.90	1.67	5.70
React	1.04	1.21	3.06	6.26	5.89
Weekday Time Spent (min./day)	23.29	41.06	32.49	59.28	53.40
Weekend Time Spent (min./day)	28.06	50.20	40.02	75.61	65.56

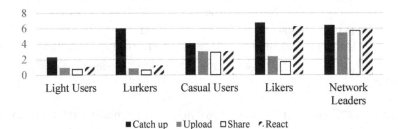

■ Catch up   ■ Upload   □ Share   ⌐ React

Fig. 1. Characteristics of the latent profiles on all four social media usage patterns.

4.3 Digital Literacy and Skills by Social Media Usage Patterns

To address RQ2, an analysis of variance (ANOVA) test followed by *Scheffé* post-hoc analysis was conducted to compare CIB, mobile usage skills, and PC usage skills across the latent profile groups. The outcomes of the analysis are summarized in Table 4.

Network Leaders, identified as the most active users of social media, emerged as the group exhibiting the highest level of engagement in CIB. It is posited that their frequent and extensive use of social media as creators and sharers fosters an active approach to assessing the accuracy of encountered information online. This may equip them with enhanced skills to critically evaluate information, particularly when it lacks objectivity. However, according to the *Scheffé* post-hoc test, the CIB score of *Network Leaders* did not exhibit a statistically significant difference from that of *Lurkers* and *Likers*. Furthermore, these two groups did not demonstrate a statistically significant difference from the lowest scores observed in *Light Users* and *Casual Users*. The average score, hovering around 3 on a 5-point scale, indicates a relatively modest level of engagement in CIB. While *Network Leaders*, as the most active social media consumers, are statistically more inclined to engage in critical information seeking compared to *Light Users* and *Casual Users*, this does not unequivocally imply absolute activity in this regard.

However, a statistically significant difference was not observed between *Casual Users* and *Likers* in terms of mobile skills, in contrast to *Network Leaders* and *Lurkers*. Conversely, PC skills were notably lower for *Casual Users* and *Likers* compared to *Network Leaders*, suggesting a trend of technology leapfrogging. This phenomenon implies that groups adept in mobile usage may exhibit relative inexperience in PC usage [11]. It is conceivable that consumers, propelled by rapid technological advancements, have become more adept in mobile device usage while lagging in PC skills. Notably, *Casual Users* and *Likers* also demonstrate relatively lower proficiency in PC usage compared to mobile usage, indicative of their predominant use of social media in mobile environments.

Table 4. Digital literacy by latent profile class.

	Class 1	Class 2	Class 3	Class 4	Class 5	F
	Light Users	*Lurkers*	*Casual Users*	*Likers*	*Network Leaders*	
N (%)	1464 (34.81%)	509 (12.10%)	1148 (27.29%)	484 (11.51%)	601 (14.29%)	
Critical Information Behavior	3.10^b (0.76)	3.20^{ab} (0.92)	3.12^b (0.77)	3.23^{ab} (0.88)	3.26^a (0.87)	5.77^{***}
Mobile Usage Skills	3.87^c (1.07)	4.16^b (1.05)	4.26^{ab} (0.81)	4.24^{ab} (0.94)	4.37^a (0.77)	43.61^{***}
PC Usage Skills	3.54^c (1.21)	3.89^b (1.17)	3.97^b (0.94)	3.91^b (1.05)	4.15^a (0.91)	45.40^{***}

Notes. *** $p < .001$; *Scheffé post hoc test* a > b > c

5 Discussion

This study identifies five distinct patterns in consumer social media usage behavior. *Light Users* engage with social media infrequently, spending the least amount of time. *Lurkers* dedicate considerable time but focus on consuming content rather than active participation. *Casual Users* spend moderate time and exhibit higher frequencies of content sharing compared to *Lurkers* and *Likers*. *Likers* spend the most time on social media, primarily consuming content and actively reacting. *Network Leaders* display the most proactive usage, engaging in content consumption, opinion expression, and media posting. These classifications provide valuable insights into consumer behavior on social media. Despite its potential for real-time, bidirectional interaction, only *Network Leaders* actively engage in such interactions, representing a mere 14.29% of the total sample. This study suggests that despite social media being a novel form of communication, its usage pattern mirrors that of traditional media, characterized by few active senders and numerous receivers. However, while traditional media channels disseminated verified information professionally [32], contemporary social media platforms propagate personalized and unverified content [33], necessitating users' vigilance in information consumption. Hence, the findings underscore the importance of consumers critically assessing information received on social media and the imperative of digital literacy for effective navigation.

Upon scrutinizing the levels of CIB, mobile usage skills, and PC usage skills across the types of social media usage behavior classified through LPA, it emerged that all three aspects were statistically significantly lowest in *Light Users*. While *Casual Users* and *Likers* exhibited mobile usage skills akin to those of *Network Leaders*, their PC usage skills were inferior in comparison. Notably, CIB displayed sporadic frequencies, predominantly falling within the 3-point range, signaling the imperative of enhancing literacy skills to comprehend digital content effectively. Despite being identified as *Network Leaders*, a group characterized by active expression of opinions and content creation, active engagement in CIB was notably lacking. This highlights the necessity of broadening digital literacy education beyond mere device usage and functionality [17, 34]. As digital technology becomes increasingly integrated into modern consumers' daily lives, it transforms how information is acquired and shared [35, 36]. While providing convenience, its rapid evolution has also led to the proliferation of biased media and misinformation [37, 38]. Consequently, individual consumers' critical judgment and comprehension—referred to as digital literacy—have become crucial. Even among those actively involved in social media, the lack of proactive engagement in CIB underscores educational deficiencies. Given the prevalence of low digital literacy among adults not deemed digitally vulnerable [39], tailored educational policies are urgently needed.

While this study using Korean data provides valuable insights into the domestic context, its applicability to the global landscape is limited. Additionally, the focus on individuals aged 20–59 indicates a need for further investigation into adolescents and the elderly. Future research could address these limitations by exploring variations in social media use and digital literacy patterns across different countries or age groups. Furthermore, the reliance on secondary data constrains the analysis to general social media usage patterns, overlooking nuances among various platforms. Given the diversity of social media platforms available today, future studies should examine how these usage patterns and interpretations of digital literacy vary across different platforms.

References

1. Viviani, M., Pasi, G.: Credibility in social media: opinions, news, and health information—a survey. WIREs Data Min. Knowl. Discovery **7**(5), 1–25 (2017)
2. Gilster, P.: Digital Literacy. Wiley Computer Pub, New York (1997)
3. OECD: https://www.oecd.org/publications/21st-century-readers-a83d84cb-en.htm. Last accessed 10 March 2024
4. Oh, E.: A study on information literacy in social media age: focusing on redefinition, contents, and media of information literacy. J. Korean Soc. Library Inform. Sci. **47**(4), 385–406 (2013)
5. Gallup Korea: https://www.gallup.co.kr/gallupdb/reportContent.asp?seqNo=1405. Last accessed 10 Mar 2024
6. Van Dijk, J.A.: Digital divide research, achievements and shortcomings. Poetics **34**(4–5), 221–235 (2006)
7. Soomro, K.A., Kale, U., Curtis, R., Akcaoglu, M., Bernstein, M.: Digital divide among higher education faculty. Int. J. Educ. Technol. High. Educ. **17**, 1–16 (2020)
8. Adam, I.O., Dzang Alhassan, M.: Bridging the global digital divide through digital inclusion: the role of ICT access and ICT use. Transform. Gov.: People, Process and Policy **15**(4), 580–596 (2021)
9. Van Dijk, J.A.: A framework for digital divide research. Electron. J. Commun. **12**(1), 1–7 (2002)
10. Kim, S., Choi, S.: The influence of digital literacy on privacy concern. Korean Soc. Public Adm. **30**(2), 257–284 (2019)
11. Hwang, H.: Consumers' smart media usage divides: focusing on technology leapfrogging. Consumer Policy Educ. Rev. **12**(2), 145–168 (2016)
12. Choi, Y.: A study on the effect of digital utilization capabilities on life satisfaction after COVID-19: focusing on the moderating effect of digital social capital. The Korean Assoc. Governance **28**(3), 25–58 (2021)
13. Aissaoui, N.: The digital divide: a literature review and some directions for future research in light of COVID-19. Global Knowl., Mem. Commun. **71**(8–9), 686–708 (2022)
14. Cheshmehzangi, A., Zou, T., Su, Z.: The digital divide impacts on mental health during the COVID-19 pandemic. Brain Behav. Immun. **101**, 211–213 (2022)
15. Jeong, H., Jang, E.: The implications of digital media literacy education on korean language curriculum. J. CheongRam Korean Lang. Educ. **88**, 7–39 (2022)
16. Lanham, R.A.: Digital literacy. Sci. Am. **273**(3), 198–199 (1995)
17. Bawden, D.: Origins and concepts of digital literacy. Digital Literacies: Concepts, Policies Pract. **30**, 17–32 (2008)
18. Nisar, T.M., Prabhakar, G., Strakova, L.: Social media information benefits, knowledge management and smart organizations. J. Bus. Res. **94**, 264–272 (2019)
19. Heinström, J.: Fast surfing, broad scanning and deep diving: the influence of personality and study approach on students' information-seeking behavior. J. Documentation **61**(2), 228–247 (2005)
20. Weiler, A.: Information-seeking behavior in generation Y students: motivation, critical thinking, and learning theory. J. Acad. Librariansh. **31**(1), 46–53 (2005)
21. Bates, M.J.: Information behavior. Encycl. Libr. Inform. Sci. **3**, 2381–2391 (2010)
22. Baek, Y., Cho, Y., Kim, H.: Attachment style and its influence on the activities, motives, and consequences of SNS use. J. Broadcast. Electron. Media **58**(4), 522–541 (2014)

23. Keum, B.T., Wang, Y.W., Callaway, J., Abebe, I., Cruz, T., O'Connor, S.: Benefits and harms of social media use: a latent profile analysis of emerging adults. Curr. Psychol. **42**(27), 23506–23518 (2023)
24. Zawacki-Richter, O., Müskens, W., Krause, U., Alturki, U., Aldraiweesh, A.: Student media usage patterns and non-traditional learning in higher education. Int. Rev. Rese. Open Distrib. Learn. **16**(2), 136–170 (2015)
25. Murthy, N., Gopalkrishnan, S.: Exploiting fear and vulnerabilities of senior citizens: are regulatory changes required to prevent digital frauds? Working Older People **28**(1), 84–95 (2024)
26. Bergman, L.R., Magnusson, D.: A person-oriented approach in research on developmental psychopathology. Dev. Psychopathol. **9**(2), 291–319 (1997)
27. Vermunt, J.K., Magidson, J.: Latent class cluster analysis. Appl. Latent Class Anal. **11**, 89–106 (2002)
28. No, U., Jung, S., Hong, S.: Classifying latent profiles in delinquency of children and adolescents and testing the effects of determinants. Studies on Korean Youth 25(4), 211–240 (2014)
29. McCutcheon, A.L.: Latent Class Analysis. Sage, Newbury. Park, CA (1987)
30. Tein, J.Y., Coxe, S., Cham, H.: Statistical power to detect the correct number of classes in latent profile analysis. Struct. Equ. Modeling **20**(4), 640–657 (2013)
31. Lo, Y., Mendell, N.R., Rubin, D.B.: Testing the number of components in a normal mixture. Biometrika **88**(3), 767–778 (2001)
32. Talarico, J.M., Kraha, A., Self, H., Boals, A.: How did you hear the news? The role of traditional media, social media, and personal communication in flashbulb memory. Mem. Stud. **12**(4), 359–376 (2019)
33. Hermida, A.: Tweets and truth: journalism as a discipline of collaborative verification. J. Pract. **6**(5–6), 659–668 (2012)
34. Lee, S.: Digital literacy education for the development of digital literacy. Int. J. Digit. Literacy Digit. Competence **5**(3), 29–43 (2014)
35. Eshet, Y.: Digital literacy: a conceptual framework for survival skills in the digital era. J. Educ. Multimedia Hypermedia **13**(1), 93–106 (2004)
36. Rainie, L., Wellman, B.: The internet in daily life: the turn to networked individualism. The turn to networked individualism. In: Rainie, L., Wellman, B. (eds.) Society and the Internet: How Networks of Information and Communication are Changing Our LivesHow Networks of Information and Communication are Changing Our Lives, pp. 27–42. Oxford University Press (2019). https://doi.org/10.1093/oso/9780198843498.003.0002
37. Özkan, E., Tolon, M.: The effects of information overload on consumer confusion: an examination on user generated content. Bogazici J.: Rev. Soc., Econ. Adm. Stud. **29**(1), 27–51 (2015)
38. Bawden, D., Robinson, L.: Information overload: an introduction. In: Bawden, D., Robinson, L. (eds.) Oxford Research Encyclopedia of Politics. Oxford University Press (2020). https://doi.org/10.1093/acrefore/9780190228637.013.1360
39. Choi, S., Li, X., Kang, E., Hwang, H.: Typology of digital information literacy among middle-aged and elderly consumers: using latent class analysis (LCA). J. Consum. Stud. **34**(4), 135–161 (2023)

Digital Democracy, Digital Dangers: Tracing Cybercrime Victimization in Finnish Online Political Discourse

Aki Koivula[1], Pekka Räsänen[1(✉)], and Teo Keipi[2]

[1] University of Turku, FIN-20014 Turku, Finland
{akjeko,pekka.rasanen}@utu.fi
[2] Aalto University, 00067 Espoo, Finland
teo.keipi@aalto.fi

Abstract. This study investigates the relationship between online political engagement, political preferences, and cyberhate victimization in a Nordic country. We utilize longitudinal, population-level data from over 3,750 Finnish respondents surveyed between 2017 and 2021. The data affords a nuanced understanding of cyberbullying victimization trends over time and how such victimization reflects the respondents' online behavior. The findings reveal a notable association between experiencing cyberhate and the respondents' political activity, highlighting the polarizing nature of the online political environment in Finland. The data indicates also that left-wing supporters are disproportionately targeted by online hate. The study raises concerns about the urgent need for effective measures to mitigate the impact of cyberhate, toward more respectful online discourse among individuals with differing political beliefs.

Keywords: Political Activity · Social Media · Cyberhate Victimization

1 Introduction

Social media has emerged as a potent catalyst for ideological formation and political struggles, effectively drawing together individuals with shared beliefs, facilitating the broad dissemination of ideas, and granting direct access to a spectrum of opposing viewpoints [1]. Ever-evolving social media platforms provide open spaces for political participation, social connectivity, and exchange of opinions. However, these dynamic and democratic spaces can also have the potential for negative consequences for individuals. Different media platforms can facilitate increased conflicts, dissemination of misinformation, and cyberbullying.

Prior research, conducted particularly in the United States and certain European countries, have explored the contours of online victimization as it intersects with political ideologies and activities [2, 3]. These studies are often framed within the polarized setting of a two-party system where ideological divisions are clearly identified. This raises intriguing questions about the nature of such interactions in a multiparty representative democracy, suggesting a different, multilayered, landscape of online political engagement and its attendant challenges.

In this paper, we examine how online political participation and political preferences associate with cyberhate victimization in Finland. We examine three different forms of cyberhate, which offer us a multi-dimensional overview of the exposure to the phenomenon. These include victimization to hate speech, false accusation, and sexual harassment. We are particularly interested in what kind of consequences political activity can have in digital environments. In addition, explore how different political ideologies connect the observed associations guided by the following research questions:

sRQ1: What is the relationship between participation in online political activities and the likelihood of becoming a victim of cybercrime?
RQ2: Does individuals' political preference influence the association between their online engagement and experiences of victimization?

The links between political activity and online hate victimization in Finland represent a significant research gap that this study aims to fill by using a proven theoretical framework, nationally representative data, and novel findings. By combining the theoretical frameworks of routine activity theory and affective polarization the study examines the ability of supporters from various groups to express their views safely in the online environment.

2 Theoretical Background

2.1 Routine Activity Theory and Political Participation

Routine activity theory (RAT) has played a significant role in criminological research in the past, originally developed in the 1970s [4]. This approach has been well established and extensively used to study various forms of aggressor behavior both online and offline. As such, it has been widely used for victimization research [5]. According to RAT, routines carried out in daily life place individuals at risk for victimization by exposing them to risky people, places, and situations. RAT puts forth that the convergence of a motivated offender, a suitable target and a lack of capable guardians will lead to victimization experiences [6].

Four components are central in RAT for the victimization process, namely: value, inertia, visibility, and accessibility. In terms of value, the offender makes a calculation in terms of the value of targeting someone in a destructive manner. Second, the offender makes an estimate of how much resistance to the threat a potential target can carry out in self-defense. Third, a target must be visible and therefore identifiable to some degree by the aggressor. Finally, offenders are concerned with how easily escaping from a victimization event might be, given the environment in which it takes place.

The online setting presents a highly dynamic environment in which to apply the RAT framework, as accessibility, visibility and inertia are all potentially significantly affected by how interaction takes place. On social media, for example, interaction is highly accessible, as is the route to exit an aggressive interaction, for example. Online, visibility can be managed, and interacting partners are more easily found compared to offline communities sharing antagonistic points of view, for example. Furthermore, in terms of inertia, potential victims are less able to avoid or defend against initial threats through content creation or text-based hate, for example. As such, RAT has

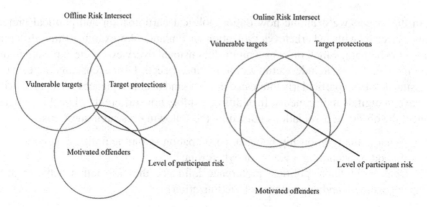

Fig. 1. Offline and online routine activity risks.

successfully been applied to various Internet-based phenomena including hate speech and harmful content [7], victimization experiences [8], cybercrime and cyberbullying [8], and cyberstalking.

Figure 1 above illustrates the dynamics of online vs. offline routine activity risk. As vulnerable targets become more available, potential number of motivated offenders grows and ability to defend against unwanted content online diminishes, the convergence area grows and so does the risk of user participation online. This sets the stage for key components that make online victimization more likely through participation in that environment.

Currently, social media plays a pivotal role in enabling unprecedented levels of engagement in discussions and the initiation of new social movements [10]. It allows individuals to openly share their political views and objectives by engaging in the public domain via social media platforms [11]. Compared to offline environments, online platforms enable messages to reach large audiences quickly. Opinions shared online can easily be disseminated beyond the original social circle, reaching individuals with opposing views who may respond with hate speech. Here, once a negative or hostile response is initiated, it can quickly escalate as more people join in. The absence of non-verbal cues present in face-to-face interaction can lead to depersonalization, where people view those with opposing views not as individuals but as faceless members of an outgroup, making it easier to justify directing hate speech towards them [7].

Also, the algorithms used by social media platforms significantly influence the information users are exposed to, with the platforms' algorithmic filtering further enhancing this effect. For example, individuals are inclined to engage with information that aligns with their existing beliefs and to form networks with others who share their views [12]. This results in social interactions that occur within echo chambers, limiting exposure to diverse viewpoints and exacerbating the polarization among different social groups [13]. Furthermore, these homogeneous groups become fertile grounds for spreading cyberhate, and studies have shown that active engagement in political discourse can lead individuals towards participating in online 'echo chambers' [14].

2.2 Affective Polarization and Cybercrime Victimization in Multiparty System

Affective polarization is an important concept for grasping the emotional and social rifts within modern political landscapes [15]. In contrast to ideological polarization, which is grounded in differing policy preferences and political ideologies, affective polarization is concerned with the emotional and affective reactions that people have towards those from rival political factions. It emphasizes the emergence of negative emotions, such as distrust, aversion, or animosity, which can be directed at individuals simply because of their political party membership, rather than their actual opinions or deeds [16]. This dynamic has been increasingly identified and explored across various democratic nations.

Social media discussions highlight topics that arouse strong emotions across the political spectrum, such as immigration and the environment [17]. Citizens form online networks with politically similar people, and these networks increasingly differentiate themselves from opposing clusters providing fertile base for partisan sorting. Online politics also seem to reinforce opinion barriers, creating an effect that reduces constructive social debate [18]. As social media platforms have made political controversies increasingly visible, many people now choose to refrain from political discussions in offline contexts due to the presence of non-like-minded others [19].

In Finland, for example, it has been demonstrated that differences between supporters of different parties are growing on social media [20]. The debate has been particularly intense between the Finns (FP), the Greens (GL) and the Left Alliance (LA). The FP is known as a far-right populist party that has made significant electoral gains in the 2010s and 2020s by promoting conservative and nationalist values, while at the same time stirring up debate, particularly against humanitarian immigration. At the same time, GL and LA have acted as counterparts to FP by emphasizing equality, tolerance, and minority rights, especially in relation to income, race and ethnicity, and sexual orientation.

3 Method

3.1 Participants

Our study draws from a comprehensive longitudinal survey conducted from 2017 to 2021. Initially, it targeted a random cohort of approximately 10,000 Finns aged 18–74, yielding a response from 3,724 individuals. Subsequently, the survey was administered three more times at 15-month intervals, exclusively to participants who opted to continue in the study. The development of this panel is detailed in a separate research report [21].

Participation activity decreased over time, with 1,137 respondents in the second survey, 735 in the third, and 543 in the fourth. Altogether, this research utilizes all 6,131 observations collected from these participants.

The survey included questions about the participants' basic demographics, such as gender, education, and age. The data represent both sexes well as 51 per cent of the participants were male and 49 per cent female. The final sample is also relatively representative in terms of education, as 51 per cent of the sample has secondary level education and 34 per cent holds master's or bachelor's degree. Respondents age ranged from 18 to 74 years, average age being 51 years, which makes the age distribution of the data slightly skewed towards the older age groups (the population average is 46 years).

3.2 Measures

We formed the dependent variable by considering different angles of cyberhate. We used three items of self-reported online victimization by examining whether participants have victimized by 1) hate speech, 2) sexual harassment, or 3) false accusation. According to the composite variable created, there were 901 victims in the data (indicating a victimization probability of 15%).

The independent variable was online political participation, measured through activities on social media such as sharing, creating, and discussing political content. Respondents assessed the frequency of engagement in these activities on a scale from never (1) to daily (4). We combined these responses into a 10-point index to measure the extent of participation, where 1 indicates no participation and 10 indicates daily participation in all activities. Descriptive analysis revealed that about 35 per cent of participants participated in some form of political activity online during the study period. However, active participation was limited, with only 15 per cent scoring 4 or higher on the index, indicating that most respondents participated infrequently and in limited forms.

Political party preference was utilized as a moderating variable, measured by reported voting intentions for the 2019 parliamentary elections. This was measured only during the second survey wave, restricting its utilization in longitudinal analyses to participants of this wave who provided their preference (n = 1,125). To have enough observations for the analysis, we focused on the six largest political parties in Finland, with 250–712 observations per party. The distribution was the following: the Centre Party 7.1 per cent, the Finns Party 9.1 per cent, the Coalition Party 15.9 per cent, the Social Democrats 15.8 per cent, the Greens 20.2 per cent, and the Left Alliance 10.6 per cent.

3.3 Analytic Strategy

We conducted multilevel linear probability models to predict the probability of victimization at the respondent level. In all models, we account for the clustering of responses at the respondent level, and the models include random intercepts. The analysis was performed using the Stata 18 software, using *meglm* and *xtreg* commands. The main results were plotted by using the *coefplot* command.

First, we examined the overall manifestation of victimization in terms of political participation and voting preferences. After this, we implemented an interaction model to find simple effects of online political participation across different political parties.

4 Results

First, we analyzed the general associations in the longitudinal data design. The findings are given in Fig. 2. The findings indicate a marked increase in the incidence of cybercrime correlating with the level and diversity of political participation on social media. Specifically, an increase by one unit in the participation activity associates with a six-percentage point increase in the probability of victimization, as substantiated by a statistically significant coefficient ($B = 0.06$, $p < 0.001$).

The data also revealed notable disparities in victimization rates according to the political preferences of the respondents. Individuals expressing a preference for the Left had a notably higher propensity for becoming targets of cybercrime in comparison to supporters of alternative political factions. The result showed that left-wing supporters were up to 30 per cent more likely to become a victim. This is also illustrated in Fig. 2.

Finally, we conducted an interaction analysis to find the simple effects of online political participation among different party preferences. Findings are shown in Fig. 3. This analysis indicated that online participation significantly elevates the risk of victimization for individuals aligned with left-wing and green political parties. Conversely, this trend does not manifest with equivalent clarity among affiliates of other political entities. Among supporters of the Coalition and the Finns cybercrime experiences are unlikely to increase as participation becomes more active or diverse.

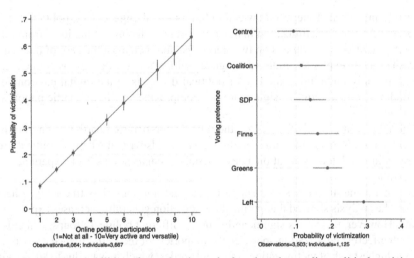

Fig. 2. Predicted probabilities of experiencing cyberhate based on online political participation and party preference. Estimated from the generalized linear mixed effects models.

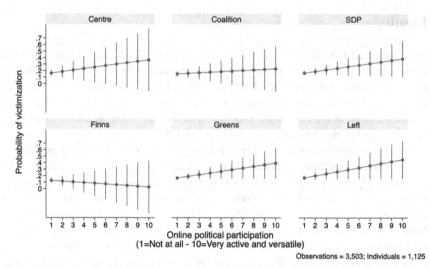

Fig. 3. Predicted probabilities of experiencing cyberhate based on heightened online political participation, differentiated by party preference. Estimated from the fixed-effect models.

5 Discussion

The study investigated the link between online political engagement, political preferences, and cyberhate victimization in a Nordic country, distinguishing itself from other research that often concentrates on two-party systems such as in the case of the United States. The study explored a multi-ideological political scene with various political conflicts, especially underlining the rise of political divisions in the digital environment. The findings provide novel insights into the complexities of digital participation and democracy.

Our empirical analysis focused on the relationship between participation in online political activities and cybercrime victimization. We also asked whether political preference influenced the association between online engagements and experiences of victimization.

In general, the study lent strong support for the assumptions of routine activity theory (RAT). The analysis showed that political participation generally increases experiences of hate. However, this varies significantly among different political groups, which is in line with affective polarization approaches. Supporters of the Left Alliance appeared to have the highest risk of victimization among all parties, which may be due to left-leaning individuals being more visible on social media and potentially more vulnerable due to the relative smallness of their party. In the Finnish political landscape, large parties, particularly those leaning more to the right, tend to dominate.

As individuals' political activity increases, victimization rises especially among the Green and the Left Alliance supporters. In contrast, supporters of the Finns Party and the National Coalition Party tend to experience relatively less harassment, even if their activity levels increase. These observations thus highlight that in Finnish social media, it seems easier to be "on the right" than "on the left".

The research raises several intriguing follow-up questions. For instance, to what extent has the polarization between the left and the right begun to manifest in voting behavior? In recent political elections, the right-wing parties have notably prevailed. If active left-leaning individuals face more harassment and hate speech on social media, how does this reflect on traditional forms of social participation? Conversely, if the activity of right-wing parties attracts less hate speech, does this facilitate political visibility in other channels of participation? Answers to these questions remain open for future investigations.

This study naturally has its limitations. The primary limitations stem from its original research design and data collection methodology. The data were gathered through general survey questionnaires. Therefore, a detailed analysis at the message level that might reveal variations in communication styles among supporters of different political parties, was not possible. Moreover, the data originated from a single, small European nation, underscoring the need for broader data collection across multiple countries to enable cross-national comparisons. The analysis conducted in this study was constrained by a limited number of instances suitable for individual-level longitudinal observation across various intervals. Consequently, it was not feasible to evaluate how shifts in political allegiance and style of discourse could affect personal experiences.

Despite these complexities, our study demonstrates that the interplay between political preferences and online activities offers an important subject that illuminates prevailing digital inequalities within today's society.

Acknowledgments. This research received funding from the European Union's Horizon 2020 research and innovation program under the Marie Skłodowska-Curie grant agreement No. 861047.

Disclosure of Interests. The authors have declared no competing interests.

References

1. Beaufort, M.: Digital media, political polarization and challenges to democracy. Inf. Commun. Soc. **21**(7), 915–920 (2018)
2. Butler, D.M.: Representing the Advantaged: How Politicians Reinforce Inequality. Cambridge University Press, New York (2014)
3. Caiani, M., Parenti, L.: European and American extreme right groups and the internet. Routledge (2016)
4. Felson, M., Cohen, L.E.: Human ecology and crime: a routine activity approach. Hum. Ecol. **8**, 389–406 (1980)
5. Akdemir, N., Lawless, C.J.: Exploring the human factor in cyber-enabled and cyber-dependent crime victimisation: a lifestyle routine activities approach. Internet Res. **30**(6), 1665–1687 (2020)
6. Hawdon, J., Oksanen, A., Räsänen, P.: Exposure to online hate in four nations: a cross-national consideration. Deviant Behav. **38**(3), 254–266 (2017)
7. Keipi, T., Näsi, M., Oksanen, A., & Räsänen, P. (2017). Online hate and harmful content: Cross-national perspectives (Vol. 200). Taylor & Francis
8. Räsänen, P., Hawdon, J., Holkeri, E., Keipi, T., Näsi, M., Oksanen, A.: Targets of online hate: examining determinants of victimization among young Finnish Facebook users. Violence Vict. **31**(4), 708–725 (2016)

9. Kaur, P., Dhir, A., Tandon, A., Alzeiby, E.A., Abohassan, A.A.: A systematic literature review on cyberstalking. An analysis of past achievements and future promises. Technol. Forecast. Soc. Change **163**, 120426 (2021)
10. Bennett, W.L., Toft, A.: Identity, technology, and narratives: Transnational activism and social networks. In: Routledge handbook of Internet politics, pp. 246–260. Routledge (2008)
11. Kidd, D., McIntosh, K.: Social media and social movements. Sociol. Compass **10**(9), 785–794 (2016)
12. Brunnermeier, M.K.: Asset Pricing Under Asymmetric Information: Bubbles, Crashes, Technical Analysis, and Herding. Oxford University Press, USA (2001)
13. Barberá, P., Jost, J.T., Nagler, J., Tucker, J.A., Bonneau, R.: Tweeting from left to right: Is online political communication more than an echo chamber? Psychol. Sci. **26**(10), 1531–1542 (2015)
14. Koivula, A., Kaakinen, M., Oksanen, A., Räsänen, P.: The role of political activity in the formation of online identity bubbles. Policy Internet **11**(4), 396–417 (2019)
15. Iyengar, S., Sood, G., Lelkes, Y.: Affect, not ideology: a social identity perspective on polarization. Public Opin. Q. **76**(3), 405–431 (2012)
16. Diniz Bernardo, P., Bains, A., Westwood, S., Mograbi, D.C.: Mood induction using virtual reality: a systematic review of recent findings. Journal of Technology in Behavioral Science **6**, 3–24 (2021)
17. Kubin, E., von Sikorski, C.: The role of (social) media in political polarization: a systematic review. Ann. Int. Commun. Assoc. **45**(3), 188–206 (2021)
18. Sunstein, C.: # Republic: Divided democracy in the age of social media. Princeton University Press (2018)
19. Hampton, K.N., Shin, I., Lu, W.: Social media and political discussion: when online presence silences offline conversation. Inf. Commun. Soc. **20**(7), 1090–1107 (2017)
20. Koiranen, I., Koivula, A., Saarinen, A., Keipi, T.: Ideological motives, digital divides, and political polarization: how do political party preference and values correspond with the political use of social media? Telematics Inform. **46**, 101322 (2020)
21. Koivula, A., Vainio, E., Sivonen, J., Uotinen, J.: Research Report on the Finland in the Digital Age Round 3 Panel-survey. Working Papers in Economic Sociology (XIV). University of Turku, Turku (2020)

An Analysis of the Dissemination Status of Makeup and Skincare Videos on the Bilibili

Weiqi Li[1], Shichao Zhang[2(✉)], Jiayi Zhang[1], Kunhe Li[3], and Tao Huo[1]

[1] School of Film Television and Communication,
Xiamen University of Technology, Xiamen, Fujian, China
[2] Department of Media and Communication, Kyungpook National University,
Daegu, South Korea
zhshch@knu.ac.kr
[3] Department of Journalism & Visual Communication College of Social Science,
Keimyung University, Daegu, South Korea

Abstract. This paper explores the dissemination characteristics of videos related to makeup and skincare on Bilibili, a prominent video community in China. Through analyzing the annual distribution, content creators' characteristics, and video view counts of 88 makeup and skincare videos, we observed a growing trend in video production from 2019 to 2022, followed by a decline in 2023. The study reveals that creators who have distinct personal styles, produce short-duration videos, and utilize suspenseful titles are more effective in spreading their content. Consequently, it suggests that novice creators can improve their videos' visibility by focusing on personalized content and crafting titles that ignite viewer curiosity. This research not only provides strategic insights for producing makeup and skincare content but also contributes to the broader understanding of beauty content dissemination on social media, particularly within the Chinese context.

Keywords: Beauty · Makeup and Skincare Video · BiliBili · Self-media

1 Introduction

Throughout history, China has maintained a tradition of using makeup to enhance personal appearance, with beauty and cosmetics becoming indispensable aspects of women's lives [1]. With the rapid rise of social media and video platforms, the ways in which beauty and skincare knowledge is acquired, as well as how products are purchased, have undergone significant changes [2]. In recent years, beauty and skincare videos have gained prominence on the video platform Bilibili. Content creators produce and upload videos that introduce makeup, skincare, and beauty products, sharing their expertise [3]. Makeup enthusiasts engage with these tutorials, exchange beauty tips and techniques, and interact with creators via comments. In the first quarter of 2022, the number of beauty content creators on Bilibili increased by 68% year over year, while searches related to beauty rose by 180% [4]. This paper explores the characteristics of successful makeup and skincare videos on Bilibili and provide insights for content creators to help them produce more attractive and popular content.

© The Author(s), under exclusive license to Springer Nature Switzerland AG 2024
C. Stephanidis et al. (Eds.): HCII 2024, CCIS 2119, pp. 87–93, 2024.
https://doi.org/10.1007/978-3-031-61966-3_10

To investigate the dissemination of makeup and skincare videos on Bilibili in China, this study targets videos listed on the Weekly Must-See catalog list as subjects for analysis. Initiated in March 2019, Weekly Must-See is a curated selection of weekly video highlights, meticulously chosen by Bilibili editors from a broad spectrum of content uploaded by creators. This feature aims to swiftly navigate new users to premium content [5]. Accordingly, the focus of this research is on makeup and skincare videos that have been featured on the Weekly Must-See catalog list.

2   Methods

2.1   Research Framework

This study is structured into main sections. Firstly, it explores the yearly distribution of 88 videos. Secondly, it examines the characteristics of content creators who have more than two videos featured in on the Weekly Must-See catalog list rankings. Thirdly, it performs descriptive statistical analyses and content analyses focusing on aspects such as view counts, video duration, and title strategies of the videos. Additionally, it examines the videos that have garnered over 5 million views to identify trends and interests of the audience in the realm of makeup and skincare videos.

2.2   Data Collection

During the data collection phase, a Python script was utilized to gather metadata from videos featured in the Weekly Must-See catalog list on Bilibili, covering the period from its inception in March 2019 through to the 250th edition in December 2023. This metadata included video titles, view counts, creator, durations, and category. Videos categorized under the makeup and skincare genre were subsequently selected for in-depth analysis. The criterion for selecting makeup and skincare videos was based on the platform's official genre label "tname" (see Fig. 1). Thus, videos tagged with the genre label "makeup and skincare (美妆护肤)" were the primary focus of this study.

'stat': {'aid': 50342560,
         'coin': 22807,
         'danmaku': 7960,
         'dislike': 0,
         'favorite': 22471,
         'his_rank': 15,
         'like': 52507,
         'now_rank': 0,
         'reply': 2730,
         'share': 10503,
         'view': 1499971,
         'vt': 0,
         'vv': 1499971},
'state': 0,
'tid': 157,
'title': ' [ONLee] 把男友化成抖森浩基去看《复联4》首映，路人的反应是...',
'tname': '美妆护肤',
'videos': 1},

Fig. 1. Example of JSON data returned by the Bilibili API

During the data cleansing phase, the 90 videos initially identified as belonging to the makeup and skincare genre were manually reviewed, culminating in the selection of 88 videos as the definitive subjects for analysis.

3   Result

3.1   Annual Distribution of Makeup and Skincare Video

From 2019 to 2023, the number of makeup and skincare videos exhibited a significant upward trend. In 2019, only three videos were featured on the list. This number increased to five in 2020, rose to fourteen in 2021, and surged to thirty-eight videos in 2022, marking the peak of this trend. However, a slight decline was observed in 2023, with twenty-nine videos making the list (see Fig. 2).

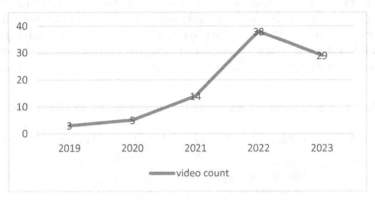

Fig. 2.   Trends in makeup and skincare video on Bilibili from 2019 to 2023. The line graph reflects the annual variation in the number of videos.

3.2   The Status of Makeup and Skincare Content Creators

Among a total of 88 videos, there are 54 creators, which 15 creators have more than 2 videos featured. After removing 3 creators not focused on beauty, we retain only those primarily focused on beauty content [6], we focus on 12 content creators primarily dedicated to beauty content, as analyzed in Table 1. These creators are classified into four types based on their content style: (1) hair styling, (2) outfits transition/celebrity-inspired makeup, (3) makeup tutorials, and (4) makeup plus other topics. Before 2019, the makeup and skincare sector were predominantly occupied by creators excelling in makeup tutorials, blending fashion with beauty, and showcasing daily makeup routines. However, in 2022, there was a noticeable increase in the variety of content, with more hair styling, outfits transition and celebrity-inspired makeup creators making their mark.

Among these, the most noteworthy is "Haircut Diaries by Mountain City's Xiao Lixun" (hereafter referred to as "Xiao Lixun") which made its debut on Bilibili in 2022. The series, crafted in dramatic style, quickly gained traction. Each episode begins with "Xiao Lixun" inviting clients to discuss their hairstyling preferences, followed by engaging conversations, and culminates in a showcase of transformative before-and-after hair styling results. Xiao Lixun's exceptional hair styling talent, coupled with his humorous and relatable video presentation, catapulted him to fame in 2022, earning the highest number of featured videos on the platform that year.

Outfits transition creators, such as "A Jingzi" and "Biri Boy", showcase a outfits transition content in their videos that begins with a simple setting and sloppy wearing, then dramatically transformation to a polished look following a costume, hair styling and makeup change [19]. This approach attracts viewer interest through the striking contrast between the initial and final appearances. Similarly, celebrity-inspired makeup content creators (e.g., "Tao A Gou" and "Bobo the Most Stylish") engage their audiences with exceptional makeup imitation skills, replicating celebrity looks with remarkable accuracy. Creators of this classification also garnered significant attention in 2022, with their videos occupying a substantial count of the Weekly Must-See catalog list.

Among the more stable genres of beauty and makeup tutorial creators, "King BBBB Famous Crosstalk Actor" began sharing videos in 2019 but only started to receive significant recognition in 2021. Her rise to popularity was due to her time studying abroad in South Korea that year, where she captivated audiences with the "Get Ready with Me" format, infused with humorous takes on South Korean culture and everyday life.

Table 1. Types of Content Creators and Their Representation in Featured Videos

Contents type	Creator	Years of Debut	Total Videos	Featured Videos	Percentage
Hair Styling	Haircut Diary by Mountain City's Xiao Lixun [7]	2022	147	10	6.8%
Outfits Transition / Celebrity-Inspired Makeup	A Jingzi- [8]	2021	130	5	3.85%
	Biri Boy [9]	2022	101	2	1.98%
	Tao A Gou [10]	2017	299	2	0.67%
	Bobo the Most Stylish [11]	2022	17	2	11.76%
Makeup Tutorials	Starlet Zhouzhou [12]	2021	72	2	2.78%
	Yiyi is a Black Cat [13]	2019	174	4	2.3%
	XiaoSang Cai Nai [14]	2019	120	2	1.67%
Makeup + Other Topics	Famous Crosstalk Actor King BBBBB [15]	2019	139	4	2.88%
	Plastic Fork FOKU [16]	2019	172	3	1.74%
	Sword Sister-in-Law [17]	2017	332	4	1.24%
	Nationally Famous Ice Cream [18]	2018	279	2	0.72%

3.3 Analysis of View Counts, Video Duration, and Title Strategies in Makeup and Skincare Videos

Analysis of View Counts for Makeup and Skincare Videos. An examination of the view counts for makeup and skincare videos indicates that 14 videos (16%) have accumulated over five million views. The category with the highest number of videos features those with view counts ranging from one million to five million, encompassing 67 videos (76%). This is followed by videos with fewer than one million views, comprising 7 videos (8%) (see Fig. 3). The highest viewed video is titled "Essential Tutorial for Beginners! Simply Stunning ~" achieving a total of 10,934,706 views. The video with the lowest view count is titled "Sourcing Ingredients through Scrounging, Recreating Helena Rubinstein Night Cream for My Assistant!" with 351,521 views.

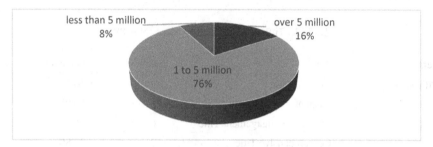

Fig. 3. Distribution of Video Views Count

Analysis of Video Duration for Makeup and Skincare Videos. In terms of video duration, shorter videos significantly dominate, with 40 videos (46%) being under 5 min in length, and 32 videos (36%) between 5 to 10 min, cumulatively making up over 80% of the videos not exceeding 10 min in duration. This trend is noteworthy even on video platforms like Bilibili, which is not primarily focused on short video content, indicating a clear consumer preference towards short video formats (Fig. 4).

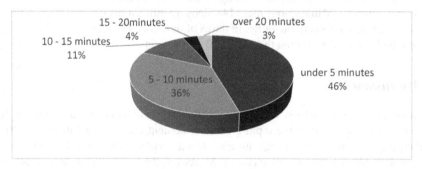

Fig. 4. Distribution of Video Duration

Analysis of Title Strategies Duration for Makeup and Skincare Videos. Based on existing research and classification standards for video title strategies, this study categorizes video title strategies into four main types: (1) General Title, (2) Suspenseful Title, (3) Interactive-Stimulating Title, and (4) Comprehensive Title [20]. General titles directly and concisely describe the video content, while Suspenseful titles create intrigue or pose questions to spark viewer curiosity. Interactive-Stimulating titles use strong language to encourage viewers to click, watch, save, or share the content. Comprehensive titles combine elements of the above strategies, delivering information directly while also incorporating aspects of suspense or interactive stimulation.

As shown in Table 2 in terms of the distribution of video title strategies, Suspenseful titles are the most common, accounting for 52 videos (59.09%), followed by Comprehensive titles at 23.8% with 21 videos. Additionally, there are 9 General titles (10.23%) and 6 Interactive-Stimulating titles (6.82%).

Table 2. Title Strategy for 88 Videos (N = 88)

Item	Type	Count	Percentage
Title strategy	General Title	9	10.23%
	Suspenseful Title	52	59.09%
	Interactive-engagement Title	6	6.82%
	Comprehensive Title	21	23.8%

Analysis of Makeup and Skincare Videos Garnering over Five Million Views. Among the 14 videos that surpassed five million views, one was published in 2019, three in 2021, seven in 2022, and three in 2023. These include "Bad Haircuts Aren't Illegal" by "Xiao Lixun" in January 2023, "Celebrity-Inspired Makeup Compilation (13th Edition)" by "Bobo the Most Stylish" in June 2023, and "The Ultimate Fringe for Every Face Shape!" by "Liu Qifu" in August 2023. Among these, two are hairstyling videos, and one is a celebrity-inspired makeup video. Notably, "Xiao Lixun" contributes seven of the 14 videos, making up over 50% of the total.

We also discovered that among these 14 videos, 13 utilized suspenseful titles, whereas only one featured a conventional title. In terms of duration, 13 videos were shorter than 10 min, with a single exception that lasted 10 min and 54 s.

4   Discussion

While the period from 2019 to 2022 saw a yearly increase in makeup and skincare video content, particularly due to the rapid growth of content creators on Bilibili [4], 2022 marked an explosive year for makeup and skincare videos. However, by 2023, there was a noticeable decrease in video counts. Moreover, the rise of hairstyle tutorials and fashion transition/celebrity-inspired makeup videos in 2022 injected new life into the makeup and skincare video scene, which had previously been dominated by makeup tutorials alone.

The practical significance of this study lies in its insights for content creators. First, influential creators often possess distinctive personal characteristics, underscoring the need for emerging creators to pinpoint their personal positioning and develop a unique creative style to better attract and retain audience attention. Second, adopting appropriate strategies in video titles and durations—keeping videos under 10 min and using suspenseful titles to pique audience curiosity—can enhance video dissemination.

Although this research provides fresh insights into the analysis of makeup and skincare videos on Bilibili, its analytical scope is somewhat limited, concentrating primarily on quantitative descriptions rather than engaging in more in-depth discussions. Future research could further explore case studies of content creators who have demonstrated exceptional performance in terms of dissemination and influence, such as "Xiao Lixun".

Acknowledgments. This study was funded by High-level Talents Research Initiation Project at Xiamen University of Technology (grant number YSK23011R).

References

1. Liu, N., Hu, R.: The self-construction of the female image in beauty short videos. Media **24**, 48–50 (2019). (in Chinese)
2. Smith, R.K., vanDellen, M.R., Ton, L.A.N.: Makeup who you are: Self-expression enhances the perceived authenticity and public promotion of beauty work. J. Consum. Res. **48**(1), 102–122 (2021)
3. Kedveš, A.: Beauty Is (Beyond) Make Up? Critical Discourse Analysis of UK Beauty Community. Conference Presentation, In: 6es Rencontres de Sémantique et Pragmatique, Orléans (2013)
4. Bilibili: https://www.bilibili.com/read/cv16736586/. Last accessed 15 Mar 2024
5. SocialBeta: https://socialbeta.com/t/reports-bilibili-marketing-planning-2021-02-22. Last accessed 15 Mar 2024
6. Liu, T.: Opinion leaders' perspectives on the communication strategies and optimization paths of TikTok beauty bloggers (in Chinese). Voice Screen World **9**, 113–115 (2023)
7. Homepage of "Haircut Diary by Moun-tain City's Xiao Lixun": https://space.bilibili.com/1869712375
8. Homepage of "A Jingzi-": https://space.bilibili.com/501687003
9. Homepage of "Biri Boy": https://space.bilibili.com/504630061
10. Homepage of "Tao A Gou": https://space.bilibili.com/17364274
11. Homepage of "Bobo the Most Stylish": https://space.bilibili.com/422292755
12. Homepage of "Starlet Zhouzhou": https://space.bilibili.com/1529865934
13. Homepage of "Yiyi is a Black Cat": https://space.bilibili.com/3725622
14. Homepage of "XiaoSang Cai Nai": https://space.bilibili.com/31438993
15. Homepage of "Famous Crosstalk Actor King BBBBB": https://space.bilibili.com/15892313
16. Homepage of "Plastic Fork FOKU": https://space.bilibili.com/130636947
17. Homepage of "Sword Sister-in-Law": https://space.bilibili.com/113362335
18. Homepage of "Nationally Famous Ice Cream": https://space.bilibili.com/77587039
19. Abidin, C.: Mapping internet celebrity on TikTok: exploring attention economies and visibility labours. Cult. Sci. J. **12**(1), 77–103 (2021)
20. Xu, J., Liu, Y.: Study on the factors affecting the communication effectiveness of science popularization videos: the case of the "Institute of Physics, CAS in the second dimension" Bilibili Account. Libr. J. **42**(11), 108–116 (2023). (in Chinese)

Electronic Government: Culture and Tax Collection

Jose Ricardo Mondragon Regalado[1]([✉]) [iD], Alexander Huaman Monteza[1] [iD],
Jaime Mundaca Araujo[2] [iD], Grimaldo Heredia Pérez[3] [iD],
Sonia Luz Leandro Inocencio[4] [iD], Sabina Acho Ramirez[5] [iD],
and Edith Marlene Gavidia Olivera[5] [iD]

[1] University National of Jaen, Cajamarca, Peru
jose.mondragon@unj.edu.pe
[2] University Cesar Vallejo, Lambayeque, Peru
[3] University Catholic of Trujillo Benedict XVI, La Libertad, Peru
[4] Institute of Higher Education Horacio Zeballos Games, Ucayali, Peru
[5] University National Intercultural of the Amazon, Ucayali, Peru

Abstract. The purpose of the study was to determine the influence of electronic government on tax collection in companies and microenterprises in the Cajamarca region. A basic methodology with a quantitative approach was used, adopting a non-experimental and cross-sectional design, the type of study was descriptive correlational. The sample was made up of 60 commercial establishments from the provinces of Jaén, Cutervo, San Marcos and San Ignacio; The technique applied in the study was the survey, using the questionnaire to collect information. Regarding the results, it was shown that the significance value obtained for both variables was 0.000, indicating values less than 0.05. In fact, the alternative hypothesis that the collected data does not follow a normal distribution is supported. In summary, it is concluded that electronic government has a direct influence on tax collection. Furthermore, the association between the variables showed a value of 0.999, indicating a very strong positive association. This implies a higher level of e-governance that improves the tax collection rate. The government must implement control strategies through intelligent systems with the aim of reducing levels of tax evasion. This measure will not only contribute to an increase in state revenue, but will also facilitate a more efficient allocation of resources for public investment projects.

Keywords: Electronic · government · culture · tax · collection

1 Introduction

Generally speaking, e-governance plays a fundamental role in the use of information and communication technologies (ICT) in government, especially with respect to tax collection. Although its importance is recognized, some countries are still in the implementation process. According to Akbar et al. (2022), Lima et al. (2022), Kamal and Ghani (2022), Urra et al. (2022) and Carbonaro (2022), e-governance focuses on aspects such as application interoperability, citizen-centric modernization, security and data quality management; These aspects are considered important in the context of e-governance and technology.

The generation of user satisfaction through information systems has a significant and favorable effect on net profit. In short, the implementation of the Electronic Invoice optimizes the management of tax invoices and Value Added Tax (VAT) returns, offering users convenience, effectiveness and efficiency (Wagiman et al., 2023).

In that sense the use of information systems through big data in the field of tax collection and management has the potential to reduce the costs associated with online tax filing and simplify the identification of preferential tax policies through an intelligent search system (Deng and Yang, 2022).

A study in Indonesia, presented by the Directorate General of Taxation, seeks to increase tax collection through technological modernization, including the Tax Information System, with a focus on electronic filing, considered a key component of tax reform (Millenia et al., 2022).

Likewise, tax collection by Income Tax Departments and staff is impacted by training and familiarity with technology, as it improves the efficiency and effectiveness of the information system, thus contributing to the reduction of tax evasion (Altarwneh et al., 2015).

In the Cajamarca region, the commercial sector is made up mainly of small and microenterprises, as well as informal businesses. The lack of innovative strategies, such as the insufficient use of information systems, may be contributing to low tax collection, which has a negative impact on the decrease of public revenues, making it difficult to provide services to citizens.

In accordance with the above, the research question posed is: How does e-governance influence the tax collection of companies and micro-enterprises in the Cajamarca Region, 2023?

The study is important from a practical point of view because the results will help the competent authorities to develop technological strategies to improve tax collection. From the social point of view, with more tax collection there will be more public investment, i.e., public resources will be allocated to improve basic sanitation works, build more schools, more hospitals, among others.

The general objective of the study was to determine the influence of electronic government on the tax collection of companies and microenterprises in the Cajamarca region.

Hypothesis H1: "Electronic government significantly influences the tax contribution in the Cajamarca Region, 2023." H0: "Electronic government does not influence the tax collection of companies and microenterprises in the Cajamarca Region, 2023".

2 Methodology

Office supplies: computer, printer, pens, A4 bond paper. Data processing: Spss software version 26 and Microsoft Word. The focus of the study is quantitative; Non-experimental and transversal design, according to its correlational descriptive level. Variables: electronic government, culture and tax collection. In the first variable, the dimensions were: information security, data processing and integration of functions. In the second variable, the tax was addressed.

The population was made up of natural persons with businesses and legal entities from the provinces of Jaén, Cutervo, San Marcos and San Ignacio. And the sample was composed of 60 companies and microenterprises from the four provinces selected through non-probabilistic sampling.

The technique was the survey and the questionnaire was used as an instrument, this was validated through expert opinion and its reliability was evaluated using Cronbach's Alpha coefficient.

Procedure: The study began with the observation of the problems that have to do with electronic Government and tax collection. Then, the participation of micro and small business managers was requested to collect information through the instrument. Subsequently, a background search was carried out and relevant theoretical doctrines were also reviewed. The information was then processed and through observation the results were analyzed allowing general conclusions to be drawn.

The data were processed using descriptive and inferential statistics; This method allowed us to test the hypothesis and the normality of the data.

Data analysis method: The collected data were tabulated in Excel, and processed with the SPSSv 26 program. The reliability of the instrument was evaluated and its level of confidence is considered. The relationship between variables was also verified through evaluation tests.

3 Results

It is established that electronic governance significantly influences tax collection, according to Table 1. The statistical significance (sig. < 0.05) supports what was stated above, accepting the alternative hypothesis that states that "Electronic governance has a significant influence on the tax collection of companies and microenterprises in the Cajamarca Region, 2023" and rejecting the null hypothesis, which assumed the opposite. Furthermore, a strong direct correlation of 0.999 is observed, indicating that a higher level of electronic governance also increases tax collection rates.

Table 1. Hypothesis contrast between electronic government and tax collection

			Electronic government	Tax collection
Rho de Spearman	Electronic government	Correlation coefficient	0,900	0,999
		Sig. (bilateral)	–	0,000
		N	60	60
	Tax collection	Correlation coefficient	0,999	0,900
		Sig. (bilateral)	0,000	–
		N	60	60

With respect to the dimensions of e-governance, Table 2 shows that the dimensions of Information Security, Data Processing and Integration of Functions have a direct influence on tax collection. In other words, the entities responsible for tax collection as well as taxpayers achieve greater efficiency in the processing of their accounting movements. Also, data have greater security, i.e. they can be stored through robust digital media or also in the cloud, allowing to improve control and avoid tax evasion and finally the integration of functions dimension allows to cross internal and external information to improve control for the collecting institutions as well as for the taxpayer himself.

Table 2. Influence of the dimensions of electronic government and Tax collection.

		Information Security	Data Processing	Function Integration
Tax collection	Correlation coefficient	1,000	0,980	0,890
	Sig. (bilateral)	0,000	0,000	0,000
	N	60	60	60

4 Conclusions

The study concluded that electronic government has a direct influence on tax collection in companies and microenterprises in the Cajamarca region, with a degree of statistical significance of $0.000 < 0.05$. This indicates that greater e-government policies also increase tax collection. In terms of Information Security, Data Processing, and Integration of Functions, they have a direct relationship of p:1,000; p: 0.980; p: 0.890 respectively, indicating that these dimensions generate greater confidence and improve tax collection.

The government must implement control strategies through intelligent systems with the aim of reducing levels of tax evasion among taxpayers; This measure will not only contribute to an increase in state revenue, but will also facilitate a more efficient allocation of resources for public investment projects.

References

Altarwneh, H., Altarawneh, M., Alobisat, F.: The impact of computer information systems in the reduction of the tax evasion/exploratory study in jordanians firms. J. Theoret. Appl. Info. Technol. **78**(1), 9–14 (2015). https://www.scopus.com/inward/record.uri?eid=2-s2.0-849389 44162&partnerID=40&md5=c8e92acadbe9452838dcee41ddf897e7

Akbar, P., Nurmandi, A., Irawan, B., Loilatu, M.J.: Research Trends in E-Government Interoperability: Mapping Themes and Concepts Based on The Sco-pus Database. EJournal of EDemocracy and Open Government **14**(2), 83–108 (2022). https://doi.org/10.29379/jedem. v14i2.707

Carbonaro, A.: Interpretability of AI Systems in Electronic Governance. In: F., O.-R., S., T., M., S., A., N. (eds.) Communications in Computer and Information Science: Vol. 1666 CCIS, pp. 109–116. Springer Science and Business Media Deutschland GmbH (2022). https://doi.org/10.1007/978-3-031-22950-3_9

Deng, J., Yang, J.: Application of big data technology in tax collection and management and tax business environment. In: ACM International Conference Proceeding Series [Internet], pp. 71–6. School of Economics, Sichuan University, Association for Computing Machinery, Sichuan Province, Chengdu, China (2022). Available from: https://www.scopus.com/inward/record.uri?eid=2-s2.0-85145572801&doi=10.1145%2F3564665.3564678&partnerID=40&md5=90c6dae9183e52260ca343aa62f3c179

Kamal, Z.A., Ghani, R.F.: E-government based on the blockchain technology, and the evaluation of its transaction through the number of transactions completed per second. Periodicals of Eng. Natu. Sci. 10(1), 620–631 (2022). https://www.scopus.com/inward/record.uri?eid=2-s2.0-85129419736&partnerID=40&md5=5cec75eb5339fd0e4cd39623d5dbd571

Lima, D., Zego, E.P., Rodrigues, J.: Digital transformation in public finance: a paradigm that has contributed to cabo verde's growth. In: A. L., S. D., Z., L. (eds.), ACM International Conference Proceeding Series, pp. 570–572. Association for Computing Machinery (2022). https://doi.org/10.1145/3560107.3560198

Millenia, S., Kristianti, T., Prawati, L.D.: The success factors of e-filing tax reporting in Indonesia: an empirical analysis using the DeLone & McLean IS Success Model. ACM International Conference Proceeding Series, pp. 90–97 (2022). https://doi.org/10.1145/3512676.3512691

Urra, C.V, Pastene, F.R., Castro, S.O.: Electronic governance and social inclusion of the elderly through digital and information literacy strategies in Placilla, Chile. Palabra Clave (La Plata) 12(1), (2022). https://doi.org/10.24215/18539912e168

Wagiman, A.N., Aspasya, G.S., Prawati, L.D.: Net Benefit on E-Invoice Implementation: Applying the Delone & McLean Information Systems Success Model. In: M, T.N., null, N., S. E., B, F.T., (eds.) E3S Web of Conferences [Internet]. Accounting Departement, Faculty of Economics and Communication, p. 11480. Bina Nusantara University, EDP Sciences, Jakarta, Indonesia (2023). Available from: https://www.scopus.com/inward/record.uri?eid=2-s2.0-85160761660&doi=10.1051%2Fe3sconf%2F202338804054&partnerID=40&md5=21f62449d4c3ff302711fe1b3b39a308

Deceptive Patterns in Japan's Digital Landscape: Insights from User Experience

Naomi Victoria Panjaitan[✉] and Katsumi Watanabe

Waseda University, Shinjuku 169-8050, Tokyo, Japan
naomivp@toki.waseda.jp

Abstract. This study delves into the recognition and impact of deceptive patterns in Japan's digital environment, exploring how these manipulative design tactics influence user behavior and trust. Focusing on a Japanese context, the study investigates the role of demographic and psychological factors in detecting deceptive patterns and assesses their emotional and behavioral consequences on users. Findings reveal that higher awareness of deceptive patterns paradoxically does not enhance users' ability to identify or resist them. Instead, it indicates that knowledge alone is insufficient against such manipulative designs, highlighting a critical need for actionable understanding and strategies to combat these practices.

Keywords: Deceptive Patterns · User Behavior · Digital Ethics

1 Introduction

In the evolving realm of digital technology and human-computer interaction, the emergence of deceptive patterns, or dark patterns, has garnered widespread scrutiny. Coined by UX designer and cognitive scientist Harry Brignull in 2010, these design tactics are cleverly crafted by companies to sway user actions [2]. One example is a pre-ticked consent box that nudges users into unintended subscriptions. Such strategies are widespread across digital platforms, with evidence from studies in the U.S. [15] and the U.K. [21] highlighting their significant influence on consumer decisions.

While considerable attention has been paid to deceptive digital practices globally, there remains a critical need to explore these patterns within the context of Japan's unique digital culture [14]. Hence, this study seeks to address these two research questions:

RQ1: How do demographic and psychological factors influence Japanese users' recognition of deceptive patterns?

RQ2: How do these manipulative designs affect users' emotional responses, trust in digital platforms, and subsequent behavior?

By addressing these queries, the research endeavors to deepen our understanding of the influence of deceptive patterns on the user experience within Japan's unique digital ecosystem, ultimately informing the principles of digital ethics and user-focused design.

C. Stephanidis et al. (Eds.): HCII 2024, CCIS 2119, pp. 99–108, 2024.
https://doi.org/10.1007/978-3-031-61966-3_12

2 Literature Review

The term "deceptive patterns," first coined by Harry Brignull in 2010, has sparked important conversations about the ethics of digital design. Gray et al. were among the first to categorize these questionable practices, identifying five main types [11]. Since then, further research, including Mathur et al.'s identification of 15 dark patterns on 53,000 product pages [16] and Gray et al.'s ontology of 65 dark patterns [10], has provided a deeper understanding of the classifications of such design tactics.

Governments and organizations worldwide are taking steps to protect consumers from these practices. The European Data Protection Board issued guidelines in 2022 [7], the U.S. Federal Trade Commission released policies in 2021 [8], and India set out consumer guidelines in 2023 [17]. While Japan lacks specific regulations for dark patterns, recent revisions to its Specified Commercial Transactions Law [3] and a ban on stealth marketing in 2023 [4], signal a move towards future regulation.

The conversation around deceptive patterns extends to their implications in the business sector and their impact on consumers. Narayanan et al. pointed out their widespread use in various business sectors, where they were employed to subtly influence user actions to boost sales and gather data [18]. This raises questions about where to draw the line between effective marketing and ethical practice.

From a consumer perspective, the initial concerns were raised by BJ Fogg regarding the exploitation of vulnerabilities through persuasive technologies [9]. Building on this, Di Geronimo et al. [6] and Bongard-Blanchy et al. [1] explored how demographic factors affect the detection of deceptive patterns and introduced the concept of "dark pattern blindness," suggesting that repeated exposure to these manipulative strategies has made them seem like a normal part of online interfaces, leading to a decreased ability to identify when one is being subtly coerced or misled by design.

The existing literature on deceptive patterns highlights a growing concern over the ethical implications of digital design practices. While international initiatives are underway to address deceptive patterns, Japan represents a distinct digital landscape still unexplored in this context. This study aims to uncover how such patterns affect Japanese users, shedding light on the cultural nuances that shape interactions and trust in digital platforms.

3 Method

Our study employed a mixed-method approach, combining experimental design with demographic and psychological analyses, structured as follows:

1. Demographic Data Collection: We began by gathering participants' demographic information, focusing on age, gender, and internet usage habits, to understand the diverse backgrounds of our sample.
2. Experimental Design: Utilizing a between-participants design, participants were exposed to eight different user interfaces—four featuring deceptive patterns (DPs) as identified by Brignull [2], such as Preselection, Confirmshaming, Hidden Cost, and Fake Urgency, and four serving as controls without DP. The task involved identifying

manipulative elements within those interfaces, with their accuracy scored. Additionally, participants rated the perceived manipulativeness of each interface on a 1–5 Likert scale.

3. Awareness and Experience with DPs: Initially, we assessed participants' awareness of DPs without providing a definition to ensure unbiased responses. After gauging their initial awareness, we introduced the concept of DPs. This was followed by inquiries into their experiences with DPs, including the frequency and contexts of encounters, and concluded with an examination of the emotional and behavioral impacts of DPs on participants, such as trust in companies using DPs and the likelihood of continued website engagement.

4. Psychological Assessment: The Ten Item Personality Inventory Japanese version (TIPI-J) by Oshio et al. [19], which is based on the original TIPI model by Gosling et al. [13], was employed to assess the Big Five personality traits. We also included questions on susceptibility to deception, adapted from materials by the Japanese Consumer Affairs Agency [5]—which would be classified as a gullibility tendency.

Data collection was facilitated through Qualtrics, which was chosen for its comprehensive survey administration features. Participant recruitment was conducted via Yahoo! Crowdsourcing to ensure a wide demographic reach within Japan. The survey was designed for completion within approximately 15 min to balance detailed data collection with participant convenience. Statistical analyses were be conducted using MATLAB (MathWorks) for its advanced numerical analysis capabilities.

4   Results

In our analysis of 353 valid responses, after excluding 24 due to duplication or incompleteness, we observed a diverse age distribution among participants, with the 45–54 age group being the most represented at 34.84% (n = 123). The majority of respondents were male (70.25%, n = 248), nearly half held a Bachelor's degree (49.29%, n = 174), and over half were employed full-time (54.39%, n = 192). A high level of technology proficiency was reported, with 61.47% (n = 217) considering themselves intermediate users, and the vast majority (98.02%, n = 346) using the internet daily, predominantly via smartphones (51.84%, n = 183).

The Big Five Personality Traits assessed through the TIPI-J score revealed mean values for Openness to Experience (3.79, SD = 1.33), Conscientiousness (3.79, SD = 1.33), Emotional Stability (3.94, SD = 1.31), Agreeableness (4.67, SD = 1.17), and Extraversion (3.48, SD = 1.26). Alongside, we measured gullibility tendencies adapted from the Japanese Consumer Affairs Agency, revealing varied susceptibility among participants to deceptive practices. Notably, a portion showed a predisposition towards influence by external endorsements: 13.60% were swayed by media-highlighted products, 13.03% by celebrity endorsements, and 19.83% by expert advice, underscoring the nuanced impact of these factors on vulnerability to deceptive patterns.

Influence of Demographic and Psychological Factors on Japanese Users' Recognition of Deceptive Patterns (RQ1). The dark pattern recognition scores, derived from participants' evaluations, quantified their ability to identify deceptive elements within user interfaces. Participants' score distributions is depicted in Fig. 1. In evaluating the detection of deceptive patterns, we also applied Signal Detection Theory [12], which provided measures for sensitivity and bias. Sensitivity refers to the accuracy with which participants could distinguish between deceptive and non-deceptive interfaces (Fig. 2), while bias denotes the tendency to either overestimate or underestimate the frequency of deceptive patterns (Fig. 3).

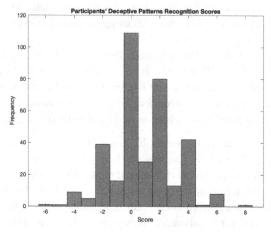

Fig. 1. Distribution of Deceptive Pattern Recognition Scores.

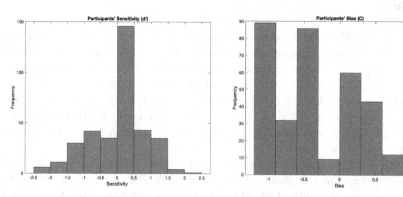

Fig. 2. Distribution of Sensitivity Scores.   **Fig. 3.** Distribution of Bias Scores.

As illustrated in Table 1, which encompasses the results with statistical significance ($p < 0.05$), our regression analysis unveiled key insights: Increased awareness of deceptive patterns negatively influenced recognition scores ($\beta = -0.34$, $p = 0.002$), suggesting that a higher consciousness of dark patterns does not necessarily enhance the ability to detect them. Moreover, participants who reported more frequent internet usage displayed a surprising increase in sensitivity ($\beta = 0.72$, $p = 0.019$), indicating that regular engagement with digital content could sharpen the ability to spot deceptive designs.

Conversely, the tendency to report deceptive patterns—bias—was found to vary with age, with older participants displaying greater bias ($\beta = 0.25$, p $= 0.003$). The inclination to trust celebrity endorsements (Tendency 2, $\beta = -0.74$, p $= 0.029$) and to be influenced by media-featured products (Tendency 1, $\beta = -0.24$, p $= 0.009$) were also significant factors, adversely affecting the accurate reporting of deceptive patterns. An interaction between age groups and extraversion further nuanced the understanding of bias ($\beta = -0.06$, p $= 0.010$), adding layers of complexity to how demographic and psychological factors interplay in the recognition of online deception.

Table 1. Significant Factors Influencing Recognition, Sensitivity, and Bias towards Deceptive Patterns

Metrics	Predictor	Coefficient	SE	t-Stat	p-value
Recognition Scores	Awareness	−0.34	0.11	−3.11	0.002
	Tendency 2	−0.74	0.34	−2.19	0.029
Sensitivity (d')	Awareness	−0.11	0.04	−2.79	0.006
	Internet Usage	0.72	0.31	2.36	0.019
Bias (C)	Age Groups	0.25	0.08	3.00	0.003
	Awareness	−0.09	0.03	−3.05	0.003
	Tendency 1	−0.24	0.09	−2.62	0.009
	Age Groups * Extraversion	−0.06	0.02	−2.60	0.010

Note: Tendency 2 is "I am tempted to buy products recommended by my favorite celebrities." Tendency 1 is "I am tempted to try a product that has been featured in the mass media."

Impact of Manipulative Designs on Emotional Responses, Trust, and Behavior in Digital Platform Users (RQ2). The participants reported encountering deceptive patterns with varying frequency, as depicted in Fig. 4: *7.93% 'Very Often', 30.31% 'Somewhat Frequent', 43.91% 'Rare', and 17.85% 'Never'.*

The locations of these encounters varied, with *'Subscription services' (20.80%), 'E-commerce sites' (13.82%), and 'Email marketing or promotional emails' (12.78%)* being the most common, as shown in Fig. 5.

The emotional responses to deceptive patterns (Fig. 6) were predominantly negative, with *'Annoyed' (15.09%), 'Anxious' (14.15%), and 'Angry' (10.58%)* being the top emotions reported, indicating a significant emotional toll on users.

This emotional impact translated into a considerable trust deficit towards digital platforms employing deceptive patterns, with *41.36% reporting a 'Decrease to some degree' in trust and 34.84% noting a 'Significantly lower' trust level*, as illustrated in Fig. 7.

Regarding the likelihood of discontinuing the use of digital services employing deceptive patterns (Fig. 8), a significant portion of participants indicated *a high possibility (41.08%) or were very likely (17.56%) to stop using such services.*

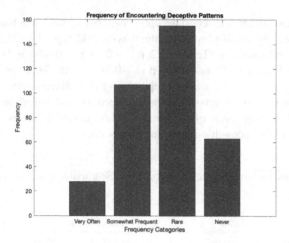

Fig. 4. Frequency of Deceptive Pattern Encounters.

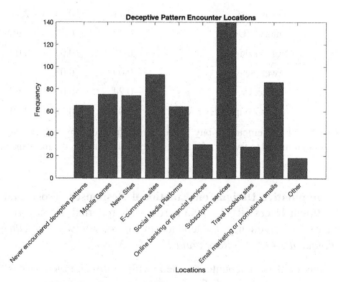

Fig. 5. Locations of Deceptive Pattern Encounters.

Despite these negative sentiments, the reasons for continuing to use websites with deceptive patterns included *the need for necessary services (39.01%), familiarity and convenience (28.91%), and the absence of known alternatives (20.99%)*, as summarized in Fig. 9.

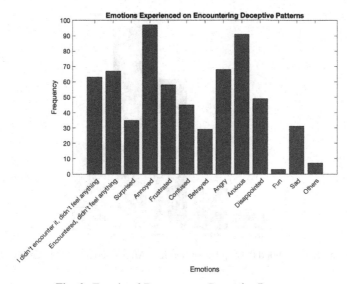

Fig. 6. Emotional Responses to Deceptive Patterns.

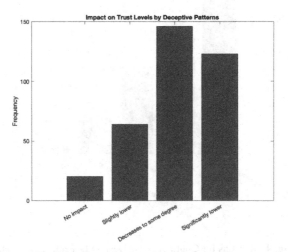

Fig. 7. Impact of Deceptive Patterns on Trust.

These findings highlight the pervasive nature of deceptive patterns across digital platforms, their detrimental effect on user emotions and trust, and the complex decision-making process users undergo when contemplating the discontinuation of services that employ such manipulative designs.

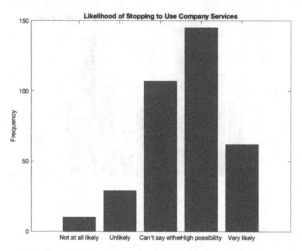

Fig. 8. Customer Likelihood to Stop Using Services After Encountering Deceptive Patterns.

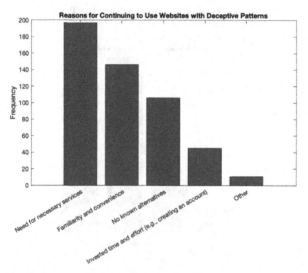

Fig. 9. Reasons for Continued Use Despite Deceptive Patterns.

5   Discussions

This research has unveiled that heightened awareness of dark patterns does not necessarily translate into better detection, a somewhat paradoxical discovery. The finding indicates that merely knowing about dark patterns is not sufficient to guard against them. Instead, it appears that increased familiarity with these tactics may lead to a form of complacency or overconfidence, thus reducing vigilance.

The results align with Bongard-Blanchy et al. [1], who posited that recognizing deceptive designs is not solely dependent on awareness. This suggests that current approaches to educate users about dark patterns might need to be revised to be more effective. Developing more interactive and engaging forms of education that simulate real-world scenarios could help individuals better identify and resist such patterns in practice.

In light of these findings, it becomes crucial to consider the specific context of the Japanese digital landscape. The strong emphasis Japanese consumers place on quality, sensitivity to social cues, and group dynamics [20], suggests that unethical digital practices could lead to a significant backlash, especially as understanding of deceptive patterns grows. This backdrop sets the stage for a broader discussion on the potential for regulatory measures to address deceptive patterns in Japan.

Building on these insights, future research should focus on creating transparent user engagement strategies that support user autonomy without compromising ethical standards. By integrating sustainable business practices with digital ethics, the goal is to foster a consumer-friendly digital environment that upholds ethical engagement and mutual respect.

6 Conclusion

The present study delved into the recognition and implications of deceptive patterns within Japan's digital landscape, revealing that heightened awareness does not necessarily translate into an increased ability to detect deceptive designs. This underscores a disconnect between theoretical understanding and practical recognition skills, highlighting the need for education that goes beyond awareness to develop real-world discernment capabilities.

In a culture that highly values ethical practices, like that of Japan, these findings suggest that deceptive online tactics could prompt significant consumer pushback. This presents an opportunity for regulatory action to safeguard consumer interests, aligning with Japan's societal values of trust and community. Moving forward, the challenge lies in crafting initiatives that educate and enable users to navigate digital spaces critically, enhancing transparency and reinforcing user autonomy. Our study contributes to a foundational understanding of the complex nature of dark patterns, setting the stage for the development of strategies that ensure digital environments are ethical and centered on user experience.

References

1. Bongard-Blanchy, K., et al.: I am definitely manipulated, even when I am aware of it. It's ridiculous! - Dark Patterns from the End-User Perspective. In: Designing Interactive Systems Conference 2021, pp. 1–13 (2021). https://doi.org/10.1145/3461778.3462086
2. Brignull, H.: Deceptive Patterns (2010). https://www.deceptive.design/
3. Consumer Affairs Agency, Government of Japan: 令和3年特定商取引法・預託法の改正について [Revision of the Act on Specified Commercial Transactions and Deposits in 2021] (2021). https://www.caa.go.jp/policies/policy/consumer_transaction/amendment/2021/

4. Consumer Affairs Agency, Government of Japan: 令和5年10月1日からステルスマーケ
   ティングは景品表示法違反となります [Stealth Marketing has been a Violation of the
   Act Against Unjustifiable Premiums and Misleading Representations Since October 1,
   2023] (2023). https://www.caa.go.jp/policies/policy/representation/fair_labeling/stealth_m
   arketing/
5. Consumer Affairs Agency, Government of Japan: だまされやすさを測る 心理傾向チェ
   ック![Measuring Gullibility. Psychological Tendency Check!] (n.d). https://www.caa.go.jp/
   future/project/project_001/material/pdf/project_001_190329_0001.pdf
6. Di Geronimo, L., Braz, L., Fregnan, E., Palomba, F., Bacchelli, A.: UI dark patterns and where
   to find them. In: Proceedings of the 2020 CHI Conference on Human Factors in Computing
   Systems (2020). https://doi.org/10.1145/3313831.3376600
7. European Data Protection Board: Dark Patterns in Social Media Platform Interfaces: How
   to Recognise and Avoid Them (2022). https://edpb.europa.eu/system/files/2022-03/edpb_03-
   2022_guidelines_on_dark_patterns_in_social_media_platform_interfaces_en.pdf
8. Federal Trade Commission: FTC to Ramp up Enforcement Against Illegal Dark Patterns
   That Trick or Trap Consumers into Subscriptions (2021). https://www.ftc.gov/news-events/
   news/press-releases/2021/10/ftc-ramp-enforcement-against-illegal-dark-patterns-trick-or-
   trap-consumers-subscriptions
9. Fogg, B.J.: Persuasive technology: using computers to change what we think and do. Morgan
   Kaufmann (2003)
10. Gray, C.M., Bielova, N., Santos, C., Mildner, T.: An Ontology of Dark Patterns: Foundations,
    Definitions, and a Structure for Transdisciplinary Action (2023). https://doi.org/10.48550/
    arXiv.2309.09640
11. Gray, C.M., Kou, Y., Battles, B., Hoggatt, J., Toombs, A. L.: The Dark (Patterns) Side of
    UX Design. In: Proceedings of the 2018 CHI Conference on Human Factors in Computing
    Systems (2018). https://doi.org/10.1145/3173574.3174108
12. Green, D.M., Swets, J.A.: Signal Detection Theory and Psychophysics. Wiley & Sons, Inc
    (1966)
13. Gosling, S.D., Rentfrow, P.J., Swann, W.B., Jr.: A very brief measure of the big five personality
    domains. J. Res. Pers. **37**, 504–528 (2003)
14. Hidaka, S., Kobuki, S., Watanabe, M., Seaborn, K.: Linguistic dead-ends and alphabet soup:
    finding dark patterns in Japanese Apps. In: Proceedings of the 2023 CHI Conference on
    Human Factors in Computing Systems (2023). https://doi.org/10.1145/3544548.3580942
15. Luguri, J., Strahilevitz, L.: Shining a light on dark patterns. SSRN Electron. J. (2019). https://
    doi.org/10.2139/ssrn.3431205
16. Mathur, A., et al.: Dark patterns at scale: findings from a crawl of 11K shopping websites.
    In: Proceedings of the ACM on Human-Computer Interaction, 3(CSCW), pp. 1–32 (2019).
    https://doi.org/10.1145/3359183
17. Ministry of Consumer Affairs, Food and Public Distribution Department of Consumer
    Affairs, Government of India: Draft Guidelines for Prevention and Regulation of Dark
    Patterns 2023 (2023). https://consumeraffairs.nic.in/sites/default/files/file-uploads/latest
    news/Draft%20Guidelines%20for%20Prevention%20and%20Regulation%20of%20Dark%
    20Patterns%202023.pdf
18. Narayanan, A., Mathur, A., Chetty, M., Kshirsagar, M.: Dark patterns: past, present, and
    future. Queue **18**(2), 67–92 (2020)
19. Oshio, A., Abe, S., Cutrone, P.: Development, Reliability, and Validity of the Japanese Version
    of the Ten Item Personality Inventory (TIPI-J). Jpn. J. Pers. **21**, 40–52 (2012)
20. Synodinos, N.E.: Understanding japanese consumers: some important underlying factors.
    Jpn. Psychol. Res. **43**(4), 235–248 (2001)
21. Zac, A., Huang, Y., Von Moltke, A., Decker, C., Ezrachi, A.: Dark Patterns and Online
    Consumer Vulnerability (2023). https://doi.org/10.2139/ssrn.4547964

Dissemination of Misinformation About COVID-19 on TikTok: A Multimodal Analysis

Kesha A. Patel[1] and Nirmalya Thakur[2](✉)

[1] Department of Mathematics, Emory University, Atlanta, GA 30322, USA
kesha.patel@emory.edu
[2] Department of Computer Science, Emory University, Atlanta, GA 30322, USA
nirmalya.thakur@emory.edu

Abstract. TikTok, a globally popular social media platform, that gained even more popularity amongst different age groups since the outbreak of COVID-19, has come under scrutiny in the recent past as the platform has significantly contributed to the dissemination of misinformation about COVID-19. Even though multiple works related to the analysis of misinformation about COVID-19 on social media have been published in the last few months, none of those works have focused on the analysis of misinformation by considering the user diversity and topics represented in TikTok videos. The work presented in this paper aims to address this research gap by presenting multiple novel findings from a comprehensive analysis of a dataset of TikTok videos containing different levels of misinformation (low, moderate, and high) about COVID-19. First, a diversity-based analysis showed that between male and female users of TikTok, males published a higher number of videos containing misinformation. Second, for videos containing low levels of misinformation, patients published a higher number of videos as compared to news sources or media outlets. Third, the analysis of the topics of these videos revealed multiple novel insights. For instance, for videos containing a moderate level of misinformation, the highest percentage of videos (18.889%) were videos that discussed the prevention of COVID-19. Finally, the average views, likes, and comments for videos with low levels of misinformation were found to be higher as compared to videos that contained moderate to high levels of misinformation.

Keywords: TikTok · COVID-19 · Misinformation · Big Data · Data Analysis · social media · Data Science

1 Introduction

The pandemic caused by COVID-19 presented a significant threat to public health worldwide. COVID-19 is caused by severe acute respiratory syndrome coronavirus 2 (SARS-CoV-2), initially detected in individuals at a seafood market in Wuhan City, Hubei Province, China, in December 2019 [1, 2]. While the mortality rate due to COVID-19 is lower compared to SARS and MERS, the resulting pandemic has been much more severe [3, 4]. As of February 25, 2024, there have been 774,771,942 confirmed cases

© The Author(s), under exclusive license to Springer Nature Switzerland AG 2024
C. Stephanidis et al. (Eds.): HCII 2024, CCIS 2119, pp. 109–120, 2024.
https://doi.org/10.1007/978-3-031-61966-3_13

due to COVID-19 [5]. Throughout history, humanity has faced numerous outbreaks of infectious diseases, each causing significant loss of life and economic impact [6–8]. In this context, social media platforms have emerged as crucial sources of information, providing valuable insights into the nature and status of such outbreaks [9, 10]. Text analysis of social media content has become a central focus in medical informatics research, particularly in conducting syndromic surveillance and monitoring public health-related discussions online [11, 12]. This approach is driven by the understanding that social media platforms serve as important channels for real-time public views, perspectives, and sentiment during outbreaks, offering valuable insights into the concerns and opinions of the general public through the analysis of user engagement, user behavior, and user interactions [13–16].

TikTok, a globally popular social media platform [17] with approximately 1.7 billion users [18], gained even more popularity amongst different age groups since the outbreak of COVID-19, as the global population started using social media platforms more than ever before, for seeking and sharing health-related information [19]. TikTok was considered to have the potential for *"disease prevention and health promotion"* in the context of COVID-19 during the first few months of the outbreak [20]. However, TikTok has come under scrutiny in the recent past as the platform has significantly contributed to the dissemination of misinformation about COVID-19 [21]. In general, misinformation can be defined as false or inaccurate information. It is crucial to differentiate between misinformation and misperceptions; misinformation pertains specifically to false information, often initially presented as true before being debunked. Misinformation can be spread deliberately, such as in anti-science campaigns, although this isn't always the case. Given the significant repercussions of misinformation, its origins and dissemination have garnered extensive attention from researchers across different disciplines [22–25].

Even though multiple works related to the analysis of misinformation about COVID-19 on social media platforms have been published in the last few months, none of those works have focused on the analysis of misinformation by taking into account the user diversity and topics represented in the videos, with a specific focus on TikTok. The work presented in this paper aims to address this research gap by presenting multiple novel findings from a comprehensive analysis of a dataset of TikTok videos containing different levels of misinformation about COVID-19 that received a total of 2333111000 views, 249970900 likes, and 2338867 comments. The rest of this paper is presented as follows. In Sect. 2, a review of recent works in this field is presented. Section 3 discusses the methodology that was followed for this research project which is followed by Sect. 4 where the results are presented. Section 5 concludes the paper which is followed by references.

2   Literature Review

Since the beginning of COVID-19, multiple social media platforms have served as prominent communication channels for the global population. An overview of recent studies in this area, with a particular emphasis on the mining and analysis of social media discussions regarding COVID-19 is presented in this section.

Silva et al. [26] analyzed Tweets containing misinformation about COVID-19. Their work showed that bots on Twitter were more likely to Tweet misinformation as compared to real users. Sharma et al. [27] gathered streaming data on Twitter related to COVID-19, starting March 1, 2020, and presented a public dashboard that tracked Tweets containing misinformation and presented the topics, sentiments, and related trends. Ahmed et al. [28] inspected the content and social network of Tweets during a 7-day period where #5GCoronavirus related to a conspiracy theory was trending on Twitter. Krittanawong et. al [29] studied 13,596 nonacademic Tweets and found that most of the tweets contained false or unverifiable information and that there were two categories of topics related to the 5G COVID-19 conspiracy theory on Twitter at that time. Singh et al. [30] studied COVID-19-related posts to understand themes of discussion, origins of the discussion, myths, and the connection with other information on the internet. Their work showed that there was a possible spatiotemporal relationship between information flow and new cases of the virus. Huang et al. [31] categorized users on Twitter based on home country, social identity, and political orientation from a dataset of 67 million Tweets. Their work showed that false information was most likely to spread, and the majority of influential Tweets were published by regular users rather than news media, government officials, or news reporters. Yang et al. [32] investigated the spread of misinformation between Twitter and Facebook and found that misinformation on both platforms tended to originate from low-credibility sources that were usually verified. Broniatowski et al. [33] collected 325 million posts on Twitter and Facebook where URLs were shared. Their work compared multiple characteristics of posts on both platforms before and after COVID-19. Using a partial least square-based structural equation modeling technique, Hossain et al. [34] developed a model to understand what affordances contributed to fake news on social media and how fake news affected supply chain disruption. Due to partial or complete lockdowns in different regions of the world, online learning was used as a primary mode of education in those regions for multiple months during COVID-19. As a result, researchers from different disciplines [35–38] also analyzed conversations on social media platforms related to online learning during COVID-19. Pranto et al. [39] developed a machine-learning model that detected fake news related to COVID-19 on social media, published in Bengali. Al-Zaman [40] performed a quantitative content analysis on 876 Facebook posts about COVID-19. The results of their work showed that 60.88% of users trusted the misinformation and 50.55% of users who had accepted the false information felt mostly happy. Ahmed et al. [41] tested Facebook's "fact-check policy". Their work used 454 posts related to COVID-19 and by utilizing SPSS, they found that in these posts, the tone was mostly serious, the most frequent topic was medical or public health, and 22.3% of these posts included misinformation. Similarly, multimodal components of posts on Facebook regarding COVID-19 have been investigated in prior works [42–45] in this field.

Li et al. [46] collected the top 75 videos associated with the keywords 'coronavirus' and the top 75 videos associated with 'COVID-19' on YouTube on March 21, 2020. Their analysis indicated that 27.5% of videos that passed screening had non-factual information and had gained over 62 million views in total. In another paper, Li et al. [47] found the top 150 videos associated with the keyword 'COVID-19 Vaccine' on July 21, 2021. The results of this work showed that about 11% of the data had information about COVID-19 that contradicted the information shared by reputable sources, such as WHO or the Centers for Disease Control and Prevention. Quinn et al. [48] performed a qualitative content analysis of 77 videos on YouTube that were related to the search terms "COVID", "coronavirus", and "vitamin D". Their results showed that over three-quarters of the videos contained misleading information about COVID-19 and vitamin D. Röchert et al. [49] collected data related to YouTube videos from January 2020 to March 2020. Using concepts of machine learning, they found that users or channels that spread false news were mostly in heterogeneous discussion networks that had content other than misinformation. Over 10 days, Quinn et al. [50] gathered the top 10 Instagram posts each day for the hashtags: #hoax, #governmentlies, and #plandemic, for a total of 300 posts. The results of the data analysis showed that the most common theme was mistrust, which was followed by conspiracy theories. In the last few months, multiple works related to the analysis of misinformation about COVID-19 on TikTok [51–59] have been published. However, none of those works have focused on the analysis of misinformation by taking into account the user diversity and topics represented in the videos. Addressing this research gap serves as the main motivation for this work. The methodology that was followed for the completion of this research work is described in Sect. 3.

3 Methodology

The dataset used for this research work was developed by Baghdadi et al. [60]. This dataset contains the data of 166 TikTok videos about COVID-19 which contain varying degrees of misinformation. These videos received a total of 2333111000 views, 249970900 likes, and 2338867 comments. To develop this dataset, the authors reviewed a random sample of user-created videos on TikTok associated with the hashtag #coronavirus published in English on or before the date of data collection (September 1, 2020). They excluded those videos that were not viewable due to privacy settings or were unrelated to COVID-19. The authors accessed video quality using two validated scales: the Patient Education Materials Assessment Tool (PEMAT) and DISCERN. Thereafter, they graded the presence of misinformation in each video as 0 (low or none), 1 (moderate), or 2 (high) based on the extent and degree of misinformation.

The flowchart shown in Fig. 1 presents an overview of the step-by-step methodology that was followed in this research work. As can be seen from Fig. 1, different types of analysis were performed in this research work. First, the computation of the average number of likes, views, and comments per misinformation level i.e. low, moderate, and high. Second, the investigation of the distribution of video sources per misinformation type. Here, source refers to the type of publisher such as a government agency, foundation, advocacy group, healthcare professional, news source, media outlet, or patient. For videos where the publisher did not belong to any of these sources, the source was considered as "other". Third, the investigation of the distribution of gender identity of TikTok users per misinformation type. Fourth, the analysis of the video descriptions per misinformation type. Here, the video description refers to the focus area of the videos such as risk factors, symptoms, modes of transmission, masks, demonstration of how to wear masks, eye protection, hand hygiene, social distancing, testing, prevention, quarantining, and commercial bias. The data regarding the video descriptions and gender identity of TikTok users who published these videos was available in the dataset. For performing all these data analysis tasks, Python 3.9.16 was downloaded and installed on a computer with the Apple macOS operating system (comprising of Apple M1 @ 3.2GHz, 3228 MHz, 8 Core(s), and 8 Logical Processors) and Visual Studio Code 2024.3.6 was used as the IDE for running the programs and compiling the results.

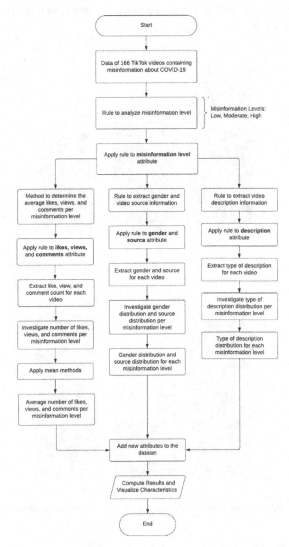

Fig. 1. Overview of the step-by-step methodology that was followed in this research work.

4　Results and Discussion

This section presents the results of this research work. Figures 2, 3 and 4 show the average number of views, likes, and comments in the videos per misinformation type. In these Figures, the X-axis stands for the level of misinformation, where 0 stands for low (or none), 1 stands for moderate, and 2 stands for high. From these Figures, it can be concluded that the average views, likes, and comments for videos with low levels of misinformation were higher as compared to videos that contained moderate to high levels of misinformation.

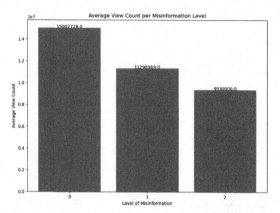

Fig. 2. Analysis of average views in the videos per misinformation level.

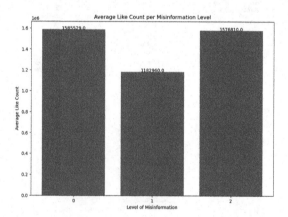

Fig. 3. Analysis of average likes in the videos per misinformation level.

The results of the investigation of the distribution of video sources per misinformation type are shown in Fig. 5. Multiple novel findings can be inferred from Fig. 5. For example, for videos containing low levels of misinformation, patients published a higher number of videos as compared to news sources or media outlets. Similarly, for videos containing low levels of misinformation, healthcare professionals published a higher number of videos

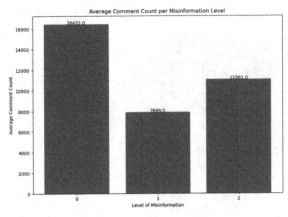

Fig. 4. Analysis of average comments in the videos per misinformation level.

as compared to official sources. The results of the investigation of the gender identity of TikTok users per misinformation type are shown in Fig. 6. Figure 6 also presents multiple novel findings. For instance, between male and female users of TikTok, males published a higher number of videos containing misinformation and this was observed for all types of videos i.e. videos with misinformation levels 0, 1, and 2. The results of the analysis of the video descriptions per misinformation type are presented in Figs. 7, 8 and 9.

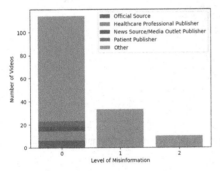

Fig. 5. Analysis of the distribution of video sources per misinformation level.

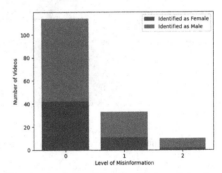

Fig. 6. Analysis of the distribution of gender identity of TikTok users per misinformation level.

Figures 7, 8 and 9 reveal multiple novel insights. For instance, for videos containing a moderate level of misinformation, the highest percentage of videos (18.889%) were videos that discussed the prevention of COVID-19. This was followed by videos that focused on masks, protection of eyes, modes of transmission of COVID-19, approaches for wearing masks, social distancing, quarantine, symptoms, hand hygiene, risk factors, and testing, respectively. Similarly, for videos containing a high level of misinformation, the highest percentage of videos (22.22%) were videos that discussed the prevention of COVID-19.

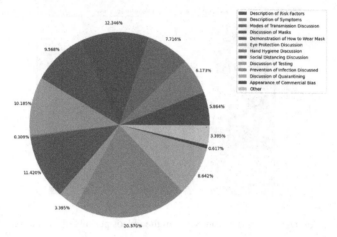

Fig. 7. Analysis of the distribution of video descriptions for misinformation level = 0.

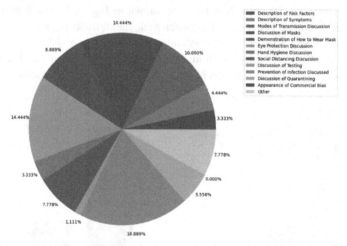

Fig. 8. Analysis of the distribution of video descriptions for misinformation level = 1.

This study has a limitation. The results presented in this paper indicate the findings of data analysis based on the data of the videos that are present in this dataset [60]. As TikTok is a globally popular social media platform where several videos related to COVID-19 have been uploaded since the publication of this dataset, it is possible that if a similar data collection (as presented in [60]) followed by a similar analysis (as presented in this paper) is performed, the results of data analysis could vary as compared to the results presented in this paper.

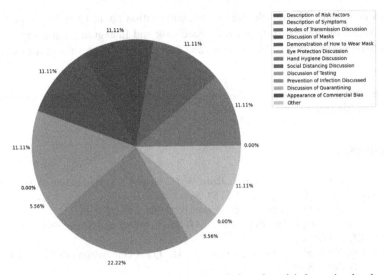

Fig. 9. Analysis of the distribution of video descriptions for misinformation level = 2.

5   Conclusion

Since the beginning of COVID-19 in December 2019, social media platforms have become pivotal for disseminating information about the pandemic. As a result, in the last couple of years or so, several studies from diverse fields have focused on analyzing information and misinformation about COVID-19 on social media platforms. TikTok, a widely used social media platform, has come under scrutiny in the last few months for being a source of misinformation about COVID-19. None of the studies that have been conducted in this field thus far have focused on the analysis of misinformation on TikTok by considering the diversity of users and topics presented in videos. The work presented in this paper aims to address this limitation and presents multiple novel results from a comprehensive analysis of a dataset containing 166 TikTok videos comprising varying degrees of misinformation about COVID-19. First, user diversity-based analysis revealed that TikTok users who identified as male uploaded a higher number of videos containing misinformation compared to TikTok users who identified as female. Second, videos with low misinformation were predominantly published by patients rather than news sources or media organizations. Third, in terms of video content analysis, for TikTok videos with moderate misinformation levels, videos discussing COVID-19 prevention constituted the highest proportion. This was followed by content addressing topics such as masks, eye protection, transmission modes, mask-wearing techniques, social distancing, quarantine, symptoms, hand hygiene, risk factors, and testing. Similarly, multiple novel results were obtained upon performing content analysis of the videos per misinformation type. Finally, the analysis of views, likes, and comments per video type showed that videos with low misinformation levels garnered higher average views, likes, and comments compared to those with moderate to high misinformation levels. As per the best knowledge of the authors, no similar work has been done in this field thus far. Future work in this area would involve performing similar data analysis of videos containing varying degrees of misinformation about COVID-19, published on other social media platforms, such as Facebook and Instagram, and comparing the findings to report the observed similarities and differences in the results of data analysis.

Disclosure of Interests. The authors have no competing interests to declare that are relevant to the content of this article.

References

1. Ciotti, M., Ciccozzi, M., Terrinoni, A., Jiang, W.-C., Wang, C.-B., Bernardini, S.: The COVID-19 pandemic. Crit. Rev. Clin. Lab. Sci. **57**, 365–388 (2020)
2. Watkins, J.: Preventing a covid-19 pandemic. BMJ **368**, m810 (2020)
3. Liu, J., et al.: A comparative overview of COVID-19, MERS and SARS: review article. Int. J. Surg. **81**, 1–8 (2020)
4. Hu, T., Liu, Y., Zhao, M., Zhuang, Q., Xu, L., He, Q.: A comparison of COVID-19. SARS and MERS. PeerJ. **8**, e9725 (2020)
5. COVID-19 cases: https://data.who.int/dashboards/covid19/cases. Last accessed 15 March 2024
6. Bhadoria, P., Gupta, G., Agarwal, A.: Viral pandemics in the past two decades: an overview. J. Family Med. Prim. Care. **10**, 2745 (2021)
7. Grubaugh, N.D., et al.: Tracking virus outbreaks in the twenty-first century. Nat. Microbiol. **4**, 10–19 (2018)
8. Nii-Trebi, N.I., et al.: Dynamics of viral disease outbreaks: A hundred years (1918/19–2019/20) in retrospect - Loses, lessons and emerging issues. Rev. Med. Virol. 33 (2023)
9. Thakur, N., Han, C.: An exploratory study of tweets about the SARS-CoV-2 Omicron variant: Insights from sentiment analysis, language interpretation, source tracking, type classification, and embedded URL detection. COVID. **2**, 1026–1049 (2022)
10. Gole, S., Tidke, B.: A survey of big data in social media using data mining techniques. In: 2015 International Conference on Advanced Computing and Communication Systems. pp. 1–6. IEEE
11. Haux, R.: Medical informatics: Past, present, future. Int. J. Med. Inform. **79**, 599–610 (2010)
12. Nawaz, M.S., Mustafa, R.U., Lali, M.I.U.: Role of online data from search engine and social media in healthcare informatics. In: Advances in Bioinformatics and Biomedical Engineering, pp. 272–293. IGI Global, Hershey, PA (2018)
13. Bello-Orgaz, G., Hernandez-Castro, J., Camacho, D.: A survey of social web mining applications for disease outbreak detection. In: Intelligent Distributed Computing VIII, pp. 345–356. Springer International Publishing, Cham (2015)
14. Thakur, N.: MonkeyPox2022Tweets: A large-scale Twitter dataset on the 2022 Monkeypox outbreak, findings from analysis of Tweets, and open research questions. Infect. Dis. Rep. **14**, 855–883 (2022)
15. Fernández-Luque, L., Bau, T.: Health and social media: perfect storm of information. Healthc. Inform. Res. **21**, 67 (2015)
16. Thakur, N.: Social media mining and analysis: a brief review of recent challenges. Information (Basel) **14**, 484 (2023)
17. Schellewald, A.: Understanding the popularity and affordances of TikTok through user experiences. Media Cult. Soc. **45**, 1568–1582 (2023)
18. TikTok users worldwide 2027, https://www.statista.com/forecasts/1142687/tiktok-users-worldwide. Last accessed 14 March 2024

19. Feldkamp, J.: The rise of TikTok: The evolution of a social media platform during COVID-19. In: Digital Responses to Covid-19, pp. 73–85. Springer International Publishing, Cham (2021)
20. Basch, C.H., Fera, J., Pellicane, A., Basch, C.E.: Handwashing videos on TikTok during the COVID-19 pandemic: potential for disease prevention and health promotion. Infect. Dis. Health. **27**, 31–37 (2022)
21. Lundy, M.: TikTok and COVID-19 vaccine misinformation: new avenues for misinformation spread, popular infodemic topics, and dangerous logical fallacies. Int. J. Commun. **17**, 24 (2023)
22. Vraga, E.K., Bode, L.: Defining misinformation and understanding its bounded nature: using expertise and evidence for describing misinformation. Polit. Commun. **37**, 136–144 (2020)
23. Van der Linden, S.: Misinformation: susceptibility, spread, and interventions to immunize the public. Nat. Med. **28**, 460–467 (2022)
24. Del Vicario, M., et al.: The spreading of misinformation online. Proc. Natl. Acad. Sci. U. S. A. **113**, 554–559 (2016)
25. Skafle, I., Nordahl-Hansen, A., Quintana, D.S., Wynn, R., Gabarron, E.: Misinformation about COVID-19 vaccines on social media: Rapid review. J. Med. Internet Res. **24**, e37367 (2022)
26. Silva, M., et al.: People still care about facts: twitter users engage more with factual discourse than misinformation--A comparison between COVID and general narratives on Twitter
27. Sharma, K., Seo, S., Meng, C., Rambhatla, S., Liu, Y.: COVID-19 on social media: Analyzing misinformation in Twitter conversations (2020). http://arxiv.org/abs/2003.12309
28. Ahmed, W., Vidal-Alaball, J., Downing, J., López Seguí, F.: COVID-19 and the 5G conspiracy theory: Social network analysis of Twitter data. J. Med. Internet Res. **22**, e19458 (2020)
29. Krittanawong, C., et al.: Misinformation dissemination in Twitter in the COVID-19 era. Am. J. Med. **133**, 1367–1369 (2020)
30. Singh, L., et al.: A first look at COVID-19 information and misinformation sharing on Twitter
31. Huang, B., Carley, K.M.: Disinformation and Misinformation on Twitter during the Novel Coronavirus Outbreak
32. Yang, K.-C., et al.: The COVID-19 Infodemic: Twitter versus Facebook. Big Data Soc. **8**, 205395172110138 (2021)
33. Broniatowski, D.A., et al.: Twitter and Facebook posts about COVID-19 are less likely to spread misinformation compared to other health topics. PLoS ONE **17**, e0261768 (2022)
34. Hossain, M.A., Chowdhury, M.M.H., Pappas, I.O., Metri, B., Hughes, L., Dwivedi, Y.K.: Fake news on Facebook and their impact on supply chain disruption during COVID-19. Ann. Oper. Res. **327**, 683–711 (2023)
35. Thakur, N., Pradhan, S., Han, C.Y.: Investigating the impact of COVID-19 on online learning-based web behavior (2022). http://arxiv.org/abs/2205.01060
36. Mukhtar, K., Javed, K., Arooj, M., Sethi, A.: Advantages, limitations and recommendations for online learning during COVID-19 pandemic era: online learning during COVID-19 pandemic era. Pak. J. Med. Sci. Q. **36**, S27 (2020)
37. Thakur, N.: A large-scale dataset of Twitter chatter about online learning during the current COVID-19 Omicron wave. Data (Basel) **7**, 109 (2022)
38. Lemay, D.J., Bazelais, P., Doleck, T.: Transition to online learning during the COVID-19 pandemic. Comput. Hum. Behav. Rep. **4**, 100130 (2021)
39. Pranto, P.B., Navid, S.Z.-U.-H., Dey, P., Uddin, G., Iqbal, A.: Are you misinformed? A study of COVID-related fake news in Bengali on Facebook (2022). http://arxiv.org/abs/2203.11669
40. Al-Zaman, M.S.: Social media and COVID-19 misinformation: how ignorant Facebook users are? Heliyon. **7**, e07144 (2021)
41. Ahmed, N., et al.: The COVID-19 infodemic: A quantitative analysis through Facebook. Cureus (2020)

42. Mejova, Y., Kalimeri, K.: COVID-19 on Facebook ads: Competing agendas around a public health crisis. In: Proceedings of the 3rd ACM SIGCAS Conference on Computing and Sustainable Societies. ACM, New York, NY, USA (2020)

43. Mori, E., Barabaschi, B., Cantoni, F., Virtuani, R.: Local governments' communication through Facebook. Evidences from COVID-19 pandemic in Italy. J. Public Aff. 21 (2021)

44. Guarino, S., Pierri, F., Di Giovanni, M., Celestini, A.: Information disorders during the COVID-19 infodemic: The case of Italian Facebook. Online Soc. Netw. Media. **22**, 100124 (2021)

45. Banker, S., Park, J.: Evaluating prosocial COVID-19 messaging frames: Evidence from a field study on Facebook. Judgm. Decis. Mak. **15**, 1037–1043 (2020)

46. Li, H.O.-Y., Bailey, A., Huynh, D., Chan, J.: YouTube as a source of information on COVID-19: a pandemic of misinformation? BMJ Glob. Health **5**, e002604 (2020)

47. Li, H.O.-Y., Pastukhova, E., Brandts-Longtin, O., Tan, M.G., Kirchhof, M.G.: YouTube as a source of misinformation on COVID-19 vaccination: a systematic analysis. BMJ Glob. Health. **7**, e008334

48. Quinn, E.K., et al.: COVID-19 and vitamin D misinformation on YouTube: Content analysis. JMIR Infodemiology. **2**, e32452 (2022)

49. Röchert, D., Shahi, G.K., Neubaum, G., Ross, B., Stieglitz, S.: The networked context of COVID-19 misinformation: Informational homogeneity on YouTube at the beginning of the pandemic. Online Soc. Netw. Media. **26**, 100164 (2021)

50. Quinn, E.K., Fazel, S.S., Peters, C.E.: The Instagram infodemic: cobranding of conspiracy theories, coronavirus disease 2019 and authority-questioning beliefs. Cyberpsychol. Behav. Soc. Netw. **24**, 573–577 (2021)

51. Shang, L., Kou, Z., Zhang, Y., Wang, D.: A multimodal misinformation detector for COVID-19 short videos on TikTok. In: 2021 IEEE International Conference on Big Data (Big Data), pp. 899–908. IEEE (2021)

52. van Kampen, K., Laski, J., Herman, G., Chan, T.M.: Investigating COVID-19 vaccine communication and misinformation on TikTok: Cross-sectional study. JMIR Infodemiology. **2**, e38316 (2022)

53. Baghdadi, J.D., et al.: #Coronavirus on TikTok: user engagement with misinformation as a potential threat to public health behavior. JAMIA Open **6** (2023)

54. Sidorenko Bautista, P., Alonso López, N., Giacomelli, F.: Espacios de verificación en TikTok. Comunicación y formas narrativas para combatir la desinformación. Rev. Lat. Comun. Soc. 87–113

55. O'Sullivan, N.J., Nason, G., Manecksha, R.P., O'Kelly, F.: The unintentional spread of misinformation on 'TikTok'; a pediatric urological perspective. J. Pediatr. Urol. **18**, 371–375 (2022)

56. Bhargava, P., MacDonald, K., Newton, C., Lin, H., Pennycook, G.: How effective are TikTok misinformation debunking videos? HKS Misinfo Review (2023)

57. Pandher, M., et al.: (324) TikTok's misinformation about COVID-19 infections and vaccinations on male fertility. J. Sex. Med. 20 (2023)

58. Pandher, M., et al.: Mp45–18 misinformation on TikTok about the effect of covid-19 infections and vaccinations on male fertility. J. Urol. 209, (2023)

59. Sidorenko-Bautista, P., Herranz de la Casa, J.M., Cantero de Julián, J.I.: Use of new narratives for COVID-19 reporting: From 360o videos to ephemeral TikTok videos in online media. Trípodos. **1**, 105–122 (2021)

60. Baghdadi, J., et al.: #Coronavirus on TikTok: User engagement with misinformation as a potential threat to public health behavior. https://doi.org/10.5061/DRYAD.BVQ83BKDP

Gamified Social Media Assistance for Children and Teens: Fostering Ethical Online Behavior

Anqi Qu[1] , Jiarui Liu[2(✉)] , Zilai Pan[3] , and Yiwa He[4]

[1] Wenzhou Business College, Wenzhou, People's Republic of China
[2] China Academy of Art, Hangzhou, People's Republic of China
lnfxljr@126.com
[3] Zhejiang University of Technology, Hangzhou, People's Republic of China
[4] New York University, New York, US

Abstract. This paper introduces the Gamification Social Media Assist App, an innovative solution designed to promote the ethical use of social media among children. With the growing concerns about the negative impacts of social media, there is an urgent need for effective interventions. The proposed App incorporates gamification strategies to engage children in a fun and interactive way, encouraging them to reflect on their online behaviors and understand the importance of ethical use. By integrating principles from behavioral psychology and leveraging the motivational power of game mechanics, the App aims to foster a healthier social media environment for young users. Initial findings suggest significant potential in using gamification to influence behavior positively, with users showing improved awareness and changes in usage patterns. This paper discusses the App's theoretical basis, and preliminary results from its deployment. It concludes with insights for future research and the potential scalability of gamification Approaches in educational and behavioral interventions.

Keywords: Gamification · Social Media Ethics · Youth Internet Behavior

1 Introduction

In the digital age, the Internet has eliminated geographical barriers, enabled sea less global communication and fostered a sense of global citizenship. However, this interconnectedness has also introduced significant challenges, particularly on social media platforms where misinformation and vested interests have led to misunderstandings, conflicts, and a chaotic online environment. These challenges are especially pronounced for children and adolescents, who, despite their curiosity, often lack the self-regulation necessary to navigate social media responsibly. Recognizing their vulnerability and crucial role as future digital citizens, there is a pressing need to cultivate ethical online behaviors and critical thinking skills among this demographic.

Addressing this need, our research introduces the Gamification Social Media Assist App, a novel solution designed to harness the educational and motivational aspects of gamification to guide young users towards ethical social media engagement. Unlike traditional digital literacy tools, this App uniquely combines the immersive Appeal of gaming with essential lessons in digital ethics and safety, aiming to embed moral standards and critical thinking in a manner that resonates with the young audience. By leveraging children's innate attraction to games, the App facilitates learning through interactive experiences, enabling users to discern reliable information, protect their privacy, and engage respectfully online.

This paper explores the transformative potential of the Gamification Social Media Assist App, delving into how gamification can innovatively address the complex issues children face on social media. Through a detailed examination of the App's design, implementation, and the broader implications for digital education, this research seeks to contribute valuable insights and practical solutions to enhance the digital well-being of children, paving the way for a healthier and more constructive social media landscape.

2 Literature Review

The digital transformation ushered by the Internet, particularly social media, has reshaped human interactions, offering unprecedented opportunities for global connectivity and information exchange. However, this transformation has not been without its challenges, especially for vulnerable demographics such as children and teenagers. The pervasive influence of social media on these young minds extends far beyond casual interaction, significantly affecting their auto-consciousness, shaping their worldviews, values, and personalities at a critical stage of their neurobiological development.

2.1 Previous Interventions and Their Effectiveness

The burgeoning concern regarding the negative impact of social media on children has prompted a range of interventions aimed at mitigating these effects.

One primary intervention approach has been digital literacy programs, which aim to equip children with the skills necessary to navigate the online world critically and safely. Studies have highlighted the potential of digital literacy to improve children's understanding of online risks and encourage more discerning engagement with social media [1]. However, the effectiveness of these programs often hinges on their ability to engage children actively and the extent to which they address the nuanced challenges children face online.

Parental mediation strategies represent another significant intervention, with parents monitoring and guiding their children's social media use. Active mediation can positively impact children's online experiences, reducing exposure to harmful content and cyberbullying [2]. Nonetheless, the effectiveness of parental mediation varies based on the communication quality between parents and children and parents' digital literacy levels.

Technological solutions, including content filters and usage monitoring tools, have also been deployed to protect children from the adverse effects of social media. While these tools can provide a layer of protection by restricting access to inappropriate content, their efficacy is limited by children's ability to circumvent controls and the potential for over-restriction, which may hinder the development of autonomous coping strategies [3].

2.2 The Role of Gamification in Educational and Behavioral Change

The role of gamification in educational and behavioral change has garnered significant attention in contemporary pedagogical research. Gamification, the Application of game-design elements and principles in non-game contexts, serves as a potent educational tool to enhance learning outcomes and influence behavior [4]. By integrating elements such as points, badges, and leaderboards into educational environments, gamification capitalizes on intrinsic motivation and engagement to foster deeper learning and behavioral modification [5]. In the realm of educational psychology, gamification is posited to enhance motivation and engagement through the provision of immediate feedback, clear goals, and a sense of achievement, thereby supporting the cognitive and affective processes involved in learning [6].

Despite its potential, the effectiveness of gamification in education and behavior change is contingent upon thoughtful implementation that aligns with pedagogical objectives and considers the diverse needs and preferences of learners [7]. Critical perspectives caution against over-reliance on extrinsic rewards, advocating for a balanced Approach that fosters intrinsic motivation and ensures the meaningful integration of game elements into the learning context [8].

2.3 Conclusion

In summarizing the exploration of gamification within educational and behavioral interventions, its potential as a significant tool for engagement and motivation emerges clearly, underscored by the necessity of grounding such strategies in robust pedagogical principles tailored to learners' needs. Addressing the negative impacts of social media on children reveals the complexity of crafting effective interventions, which depend on their design, implementation context, and individual child differences. Thus, a multi-faceted Approach, incorporating efforts from digital platforms, educational initiatives, and innovative gamification, is essential. This strategy aims not just to shield youth from misinformation's dangers but to empower them with critical thinking for ethical digital participation. Moving forward, prioritizing comprehensive strategies that promote children's digital well-being is crucial, setting the stage for nurturing informed, responsible digital citizens adept at navigating the digital world's ethical challenges.

3 User Research

3.1 Research Subject Positioning

The integration of social media into daily life has become a defining feature of contemporary society, significantly influencing the younger generation's interaction with the world. With the average age for initial social media use dropping to around 12 years, and instances of even younger engagements becoming increasingly common, the need to understand and guide children's social media use has never been more critical. This demographic's engagement with digital platforms, while marked by a robust curiosity, often lacks the necessary self-regulation and discernment skills to navigate the complex, and sometimes misleading, online landscape safely. The absence of comprehensive guidance from parents or educational institutions further exacerbates the risk, leaving young users vulnerable to Internet addiction and misinformation.

3.2 Semi-structured Interviews

To delve deeper into the challenges and perspectives surrounding children's interaction with social media, semi-structured interviews were conducted with parents and a primary school teacher, offering insights from both home and educational contexts.

Interviewee 1: The mother of an 11-year-old girl who actively uses social media daily. Despite efforts to engage with her daughter about online content, she struggles with limiting exposure to age-inappropriate videos and is concerned about the impact of harmful information on her family.

Interviewee 2: A father of two, whose demanding career in medicine limits his ability to monitor his children's social media usage. He notes a correlation between his eldest son's psychological distress and a lack of proper guidance on social media engagement.

Interviewee 3: An elementary school teacher observes widespread mobile phone and social media use among her students. She raises concerns about their vulnerability to fake news, aggressive opinions, and inappropriate content due to their strong curiosity but limited ability to discern truth from falsehood.

The interviews, encompassing two parental perspectives and that of a primary school educator, underscore a pressing requirement for tools and strategies that support children's safe and responsible social media use. The insights reveal a common theme of concern regarding exposure to inappropriate content, insufficient parental guidance, and the potential mental health implications of unsupervised social media interaction. These findings reinforce the importance of developing a comprehensive solution that addresses digital literacy, online safety, and the mental well-being of young social media users, suggesting a significant opportunity for educational interventions and parental support tools aimed at fostering a healthier digital environment for children.

4   Gamification Design for Social Media Assistance App

4.1 Concept and Objectives

Integrating insights from comprehensive interviews, the design focus of our application is to develop a holistic social media assistance App tailored for children, addressing three core needs: guiding children in the responsible use of social media, creating a virtual guardian for oversight, and facilitating mental health support. This initiative aims to balance the benefits of social media, such as broadening information access and facilitating communication, against the risks posed by misinformation and harmful content. By adopting a gamified Approach, which resonates well with children, the App intends to monitor social media usage, cultivate critical thinking and unbiased browsing, and establish effective communication channels between children and parents, thereby encouraging parental involvement in shaping their children's habits and values.

To safeguard young users and preempt potential harms, the design includes enhanced protective measures like age verification and educational interventions about the advantages and potential dangers of social media use. The envisioned gamified social media assistance App serves as a virtual guardian for children newly navigating social media, supervising their online activities to prevent negative impacts. Through engaging tasks and challenges, the App fosters the development of critical thinking skills among youth, offering them a comprehensive understanding of digital interactions. Meanwhile, it provides parents with tools to oversee and engage in their child's digital life, promoting a collaborative effort in guiding children towards becoming informed and conscientious digital citizens.

4.2 Core Gamification Elements

Minesweeper Game. The primary metaphor for our gamification design is the Minesweeper game, symbolizing the importance of viewing issues from multiple perspectives to uncover the truth. Similar to how Minesweeper requires revealing numbers that indicate the proximity of mines, our App encourages children to explore various viewpoints of news stories, thereby avoiding the dangers of one-sided information consumption.

Cultivating the Global Village. Reflecting on the idea that social media has created a global village, our app likens new users to villagers cultivating their land. By adopting multi-perspective Approaches to news and completing summary tasks, users can clear their land of mines, progressively earning their place in the Internet's global community [Fig. 1].

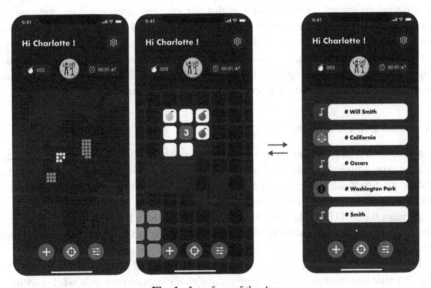

Fig. 1. Interface of the App

4.3 Engagement and Feedback Mechanisms

Topic Selection and Land Cultivation. Children choose topics of interest to start cultivating new land. The number at the center of each plot indicates how many different perspectives await exploration. Each mine represents a new content perspective for the user to discover.

Clearing Mines Through Reading. By reading content from different perspectives, users can clear mines related to a central topic. Successfully cultivated land marks an achievement for the user. If questions arise during reading, children can leave inquiries for their parents, who respond, enhancing understanding and parent-child communication.

Engagement with Tasks. Upon completing the cultivation of a topic's land, children encounter mini-tasks, such as crossword puzzles or timeline organization, rewarding them with extended social media usage or badges. These rewards motivate continued ethical social media practices.

Parental Involvement. The App provides parents with an avenue to monitor their children's progress and behavior within the App. Real-time reports allow parents to engage in meaningful discussions about social media use, ensuring a collaborative effort in guiding children's online habits.

5 Result

To validate the design and effectiveness, tailored for children aged 8–11 years and inclusive of parental involvement, a user test was meticulously orchestrated. We engaged ten elementary school students along with their parents, aiming to comprehensively assess the App's Appeal, usability, educational value, and to pinpoint any technical flaws or user experience issues. This evaluative phase was instrumental in testing the App's concept among our target demographic, uncovering aspects of the experience that may confuse users, evaluating its potential to instill positive habits, and identifying both the strengths and weaknesses inherent in the App's current iteration.

5.1 Findings for Children

Engagement and Recommendation: Children were queried on their willingness to engage with the App both in the short and long term and whether they would recommend it to their peers. Feedback indicated a general enthusiasm for the App, with its interactive and gamified elements capturing their interest.

Development of Good Habits: The App's effectiveness in fostering good social media habits was evaluated. Children expressed optimism about the App's role in guiding them toward healthier online behaviors, though the long-term impact remains to be seen.

Favorites and Challenges: Children shared their most and least favorite aspects of the App. Favorite features often included interactive challenges and rewards, while confusion arose from some of the navigation pathways and task instructions, indicating areas for simplification and clarification.

5.2 Findings for Parents

Parental Recommendation: Parents considered the App's potential as a supplementary educational tool for their children. There was a consensus that, with further refinement, the App could be a valuable resource for guiding children in responsible social media use.

Educational Value: Parents assessed the App's utility in contributing to their child's digital education. Many Appreciated the App's Approach to teaching digital literacy and safety, emphasizing the importance of active parental involvement in this learning process.

Favorites and Challenges: Similar to the children, parents identified their preferred features, often highlighting the App's informative content and the ability to monitor their child's progress. The main critiques centered around user interface issues and a desire for more in-depth content tailored to varying levels of prior knowledge.

5.3 Effectiveness Evaluation

The user test revealed several critical insights into the App's current design and functionality. Children's engagement and the App's educational potential were validated, while areas needing improvement, particularly in user experience and content depth, were identified. For an effective roll-out, the following steps are recommended.

Iterative Design Enhancements: Based on user feedback, refine the App's interface and navigation to ensure it is intuitive for both children and parents. Simplify task instructions and enhance interactive elements to maintain user engagement.

Content Expansion and Customization: Develop a wider range of content to cater to different knowledge levels and interests, ensuring the App remains relevant and informative for a diverse user base.

Continuous User Feedback Loop: Implement a mechanism for ongoing feedback collection and monitoring App usage patterns. This will facilitate timely updates and ensure the App evolves in alignment with user needs and technological advancements.

6 Conclusion

The gamification of social media assistance Applications represents a groundbreaking solution with significant advantages and potential. By integrating game elements with social media, this Approach not only captivates children's interest and participation but also plays a crucial role in developing their digital literacy and ethical awareness. The Application profoundly impacts fostering children's ability to use social media responsibly, discern true from false information, and cultivate critical thinking and values. This foundation equips children for future social media engagement, guiding them to become positive, responsible users.

This study emphasizes the importance of shaping positive habits and values from an early age. Despite making strides in conceptual design, limitations are acknowledged. Further refinement, particularly of the game mechanics' logic and the depth of parental supervision and communication features, is essential. Additionally, the Application's potential ethical concerns, such as privacy rights and manipulative behaviors, should be explored.

Looking ahead, the future brims with exciting possibilities. Developing the Application into a comprehensive "Children's Social Media School" offering diverse training modules to enhance children's social media skills represents a forward direction. Delving deeper into child psychology and game design theory will be paramount. By providing personalized services and mobile-friendly designs, the aim is to meet the needs of children, parents, and stakeholders, thereby enhancing the entire service ecosystem.

However, it's clear that an App alone cannot solve all issues related to children's use of social media. A collective effort from all sectors of society is called for to create a safer and more beneficial social media experience for children. Educational institutions, families, and social media platforms must collaborate closely, developing stricter standards and guidelines to ensure children grow up in a healthy online environment. This multi-faceted Approach promises not only to address the immediate concerns associated with social media use among children but also to pave the way for a future where digital citizenship is rooted in responsibility, respect, and an informed understanding of the digital world.

References

1. Livingstone, S., Mascheroni, G., Staksrud, E.: European research on children's internet use: Assessing the past and anticipating the future. New Media Soc. **20**(3), 1103–1122 (2018). https://doi.org/10.1177/1461444816685930
2. Wisniewski, P., Jia, H., Xu, H., Rosson, M.B., Carroll, J.M.: Preventative vs. reactive: How parental mediation influences teens' social media privacy behaviors. Proceedings of the ACM Conference on Computer Supported Cooperative Work & Social Computing (2015). https://doi.org/10.1145/2675133.2675293
3. Livingstone, S., Smith, P.K.: Annual research review: harms experienced by child users of online and mobile technologies: the nature, prevalence and management of sexual and aggressive risks in the digital age. J. Child Psychol. Psychiatry **55**(6), 635–654 (2014). https://doi.org/10.1111/jcpp.12197
4. Deterding, S., Dixon, D., Khaled, R., Nacke, L.: From game design elements to gamefulness: defining "gamification". Proceedings of the 15th International Academic MindTrek Conference: Envisioning Future Media Environments (2011). https://doi.org/10.1145/2181037.2181040
5. Hamari, J., Koivisto, J., Sarsa, H.: Does gamification work? -- A literature review of empirical studies on gamification. In: 47th Hawaii International Conference on System Sciences, pp. 1–10. IEEE (2014). https://doi.org/10.1109/HICSS.2014.377
6. Ryan, R.M., Deci, E.L.: Self-determination theory and the facilitation of intrinsic motivation, social development, and well-being. Am. Psychol. **55**(1), 68–78 (2000). https://doi.org/10.1037/0003-066X.55.1.68
7. Kapp, K.M.: The gamification of learning and instruction: Game-based methods and strategies for training and education. Pfeiffer, San Francisco (2012)
8. Nicholson, S.: A RECIPE for meaningful gamification. In: Gamification in Education and Business, pp. 1–20. Springer, Cham (2015). https://doi.org/10.1007/978-3-319-10208-5_1

Investigating the Accessibility and Usability of Multi-factor Authentication for Young People

Lukas Smith, Suzanne Prior$^{(\boxtimes)}$ ⓘ, and Jacques Ophoff ⓘ

Abertay University, Dundee DD1 1HG, UK
s.prior@abertay.ac.uk
http://www.abertay.ac.uk

Abstract. The rapid growth of young online users requires greater attention to balancing security needs with age-appropriate user experiences. Despite the well-publicised benefits of multi-factor authentication (MFA), uptake amongst this group remains low. This study examines young people's interaction with MFA methods to inform inclusive design for online security.

We present an evaluation involving 19 participants aged 10–14, assessing the accessibility and usability of six MFA methods within an Android mobile application. While traditional methods such as numerical MFA and push authenticators demonstrated high accuracy and faster completion times, the participants favoured the more novel MFA of copying a drawing. This highlights the need to balance speed with a positive user experience, mainly when promoting the uptake of good practices amongst young people.

The findings emphasise the potential for incorporating secure practices like MFA into platforms targeting children, contributing to building secure online habits from a young age.

Keywords: Inclusive Design · Children · Multifactor Authentication · Usability

1 Introduction

Young people represent a rapidly growing segment of online users [8]. An investigation into online scams found a 156% increase over three years of under 20-year-olds being scammed [6]. A well-known tactic is to convince the young person that the hacker is their friend and that if the young person gives them their password, the hacker will do something in return. Hackers typically promise something a child cannot do independently, like buying in-game currency or membership with real-world money.

One of the most common phishing scams on Roblox occurs when a malicious user creates a game that prompts the user to enter their username and password. The attacker normally promises a paid membership or Robux (an in-game currency which costs real money), which is appealing to naïve young people as they do not have their own money. This scam could easily be avoided if MFA was enforced on the site. Roblox is among the worst offenders for scams as many younger children play it. At the time of writing, there were 31 well-known phishing scams happening on the site [7].

While the security of young people's online data is important, developers may be concerned that additional measures, specifically multi-factor authentication (MFA), would impact their experience. The accessibility and usability of MFA needs careful consideration to ensure an inclusive design for all people [5]. However, there is limited knowledge about young peoples' interaction and experience with MFA to inform inclusive design.

While MFA is advocated to enhance online security, it is surprising that uptake remains problematic [3]. Accessibility requirements are proposed as a solution but only focuses on adult users [2,4]. Several authentication options may be suitable for young people [1] But, there is a need for more empirical data to guide inclusive design. Given this background, this study aims to compare the accessibility and usability of several MFA methods for young people. We designed and developed an MFA experience within an Android mobile application, which was evaluated by 19 participants. Data collection comprised of system interactions and a post-use survey.

2   Methodology

2.1   MFA Approaches

An Android mobile application was developed, including six MFA methods and an inbuilt survey regarding MFA experiences and opinions on the different methods. The platform was chosen due to its widespread adoption and the comfort young people have with mobile devices.

Four methods incorporated traditional text-based entry (Alphabetical, Alphanumerical, Alphanumerical + Generic Symbols, and Numerical). The other two methods were Push Authenticators and Drawing.

Drawing Authentication. Seventeen images were stored in the app and randomly selected for the Drawing authentication stage. Participants were shown the image and then asked to draw a copy on a blank canvas on the screen. The drawings had to be manually analysed to check whether the participants were correct. The template was split into a three-by-three grid to determine if the drawing was accurate. The line had to enter all the correct grid spaces and start and end in the same grid spaces (see Fig. 1). This example is listed as accurate as it starts and finishes in the same boxes as the template and enters all the correct grid slots.

By contrast, Fig. 2 would be labelled inaccurate as the drawing's endpoint is in the middle grid slot rather than the top middle slot.

Young people could attempt each method, with data collected about their performance and preferences. Performance was measured using accuracy (i.e., correctly authenticating) and time taken for each method.

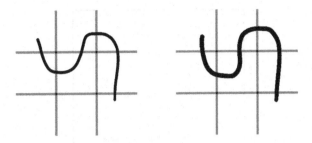

Fig. 1. Example of Correct Drawing Authentication

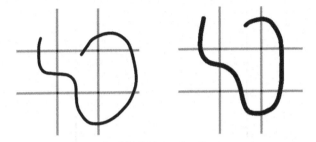

Fig. 2. Example of Incorrect Drawing Authentication

Push Authentication. The Push Authentication randomly selected one of two locations, 'Scotland, United Kingdom' or 'Melbourne, Australia'. The method randomly chose whether the login was genuine or malicious. The appropriate location (Scotland, United Kingdom being the genuine login location) is displayed, and the user is asked to press Yes or No (Fig. 3).

2.2   Evaluation

Nineteen participants between the ages of 10 and 14 took part in the evaluation with permission from their parents and guardians. The participants were split into groups of 4–5 and, before the evaluation, were given a brief explanation of MFA and why it is essential.

Participants were asked to use the Android mobile application to authenticate using each of the six MFA technologies. These were presented on the screen individually, and the participants were asked to authenticate using the information given.

Due to the age range, some younger participants initially struggled to understand words such as 'Alphanumerical' and 'Authentication' but understood after a verbal explanation.

Fig. 3. Example of Push Authentication

3   Results

Interaction data was stored in a database and extracted to determine each participant's accuracy over the six MFA methods. The overall accuracy results are summarised in Table 1. Two authentication methods stand out from the whole results set. The Push authenticator was the only method to have every participant answer correctly and had the third fastest time taken. In addition, the Numerical method only had one incorrect attempt and had the quickest time taken.

Table 1. Overall Accuracy of Results

Method	Time Taken (seconds)	Correct
Alpha	21.71	79%
AlphaNum	16.31	84%
AlphaNumSymbol	21.68	79%
Numerical	9.79	95%
Drawing	11.37	79%
Push	11.43	100%

However, these results varied according to the ages of the participants in the case study. For participants aged 10 the most accurate method was drawing while for 11 and 12 year olds it was numerical. The older participants aged 13 and 14 years old were most accurate with the Push notification. Participants were also asked to select their most/least favourite method, which was compared to the accuracy (Fig. 4). Overall, the authentication method the participants decided was their favourite was the Drawing authentication method, and the second favourite was Numerical. The least favourite authentication method was Alphanumerical and Symbols. No participants put Push authenticator as their least favourite method.

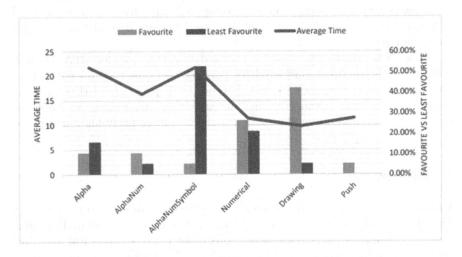

Fig. 4. Favourite & Least Favourites Vs Time Taken

Several key themes were discovered when the participants were asked for more details about their favourite authentication method. The Alphabetical, Alphanumerical, Numerical, and Drawing methods were all picked due to being 'fun', mainly the Drawing method. The Alphabetical, Numerical and Drawing methods had comments mentioning them as the easiest or simplest to use. The Drawing method was also described as 'cool'. One participant noted they liked the Push authentication method as it returns the location of the login attempt, so they know where the (potentially malicious) actor is.

4   Discussion

An important finding from this evaluation is that, generally, young people aged 10-14 can understand and use MFA. The authentication methods were also completed relatively quickly, with the longest average time being less than 30 s. As such, platform developers of games and tools aimed at children should consider this study and contemplate adding MFA to their platform. Many applications already use the Numerical authentication method, such as Google Authenticator and Microsoft Authenticator, making it easier for developers to implement such tools within their platforms.

The Drawing method was by far the most popular but was also one of the least accurate. The second most significantly popular method was the numerical method, which is the second most accurate. Push, the most accurate method was only the favourite method of one of the participants, and the Alphabetical method was the least accurate method. There does appear to be some connection between incorrect answers and least favourite methods. This can be seen most specifically with the Alphanumerical and Symbol method, with 21% of the participants getting it wrong and 52% stating it is their least favourite method. As such, it can be said that young people are least preferential to methods in which they struggle.

Whilst Numerical authentication is already a proven tool for MFA, Drawing authentication could be considered for younger users, as they do not have to copy text they may struggle to read. Several participants noted they preferred the Drawing method because it was 'fun' and 'easy'. By making an MFA tool that is enjoyable and usable for young people, it is more likely for young people to use it.

5   Conclusion

Young people are likely to be targeted by malicious actors due to their naivety. This study suggests pursuing MFA uptake for young people. Our findings illustrate two promising MFA options in terms of accuracy - Numerical and Push methods. Despite lower accuracy, participants also expressed a preference for Drawing methods. By using and understanding the importance of MFA at a younger age, young people will be more likely to carry this secure practice into their adult lives.

Acknowledgments. The authors express their thanks to the participants and their parents for taking part in this study.

Disclosure of Interests. The authors have no competing interests to declare that are relevant to the content of this article.

References

1. AL-Badi, F.A.: Child-friendly authentication (CFA) (2022). https://doi.org/10. 54938/ijemdcsai.2022.01.1.70
2. Andrew, S., Watson, S., Oh, T., Tigwell, G.W.: A review of literature on accessibility and authentication techniques. In: Proceedings of the 22nd International ACM SIGACCESS Conference on Computers and Accessibility, ASSETS 2020. Association for Computing Machinery, New York (2020). https://doi.org/10.1145/3373625. 3418005

3. Childers, D.: State of the auth 2021: Experiences and perceptions of multi-factor authentication. Duo Labs. Accessed 9 Jan 2023
4. Furnell, S., Helkala, K., Woods, N.: Disadvantaged by disability: examining the accessibility of cyber security. In: Antona, M., Stephanidis, C. (eds.) HCII 2021. LNCS, vol. 12768, pp. 197–212. Springer, Cham (2021). https://doi.org/10.1007/978-3-030-78092-0_13
5. Ophoff, J., Johnson, G., Renaud, K.: Cognitive function vs. accessible authentication: insights from dyslexia research. In: Proceedings of the 18th International Web for All Conference, W4A 2021. Association for Computing Machinery, New York (2021). https://doi.org/10.1145/3430263.3452427
6. Orcutt, A.M.: State of Internet Scams 2021—socialcatfish.com. https://socialcatfish.com/scamfish/state-of-internet-scams-2021/. Accessed 24 Jan 2024
7. RobloxWiki: Scam (2024). https://roblox.fandom.com/wiki/Scam. Accessed 24 Jan 2024
8. Smahel, D., et al.: Eu kids online 2020: survey results from 19 countries (2020). https://doi.org/10.21953/lse.47fdeqj01ofo

Expert Perspectives on UX Design Challenges for Solid-Enabled Personal Data Store Applications

Tim Theys[1]([envelope])[iD], August Bourgeus[2][iD], Peter Mechant[3][iD], Lieven De Marez[3][iD], and Jelle Saldien[1][iD]

[1] imec-mict-UGent, Department of Industrial Systems Engineering and Product Design, Ghent University, Ghent, Belgium
`tim.theys@ugent.be`
[2] imec-SMIT-VUB, Vrije Universiteit Brussel, Brussels, Belgium
[3] imec-mict-UGent, Department of Communication Sciences, Ghent University, Ghent, Belgium

Abstract. The growing complexity of managing personal data online has increased the need for enhanced transparency, control, and usability in data handling. Solid, a web specification being developed by a W3C Working Group, aims to offer a potential solution by providing users with a personal online data store or data vault. This enables users to transparently manage and control access to their data across various platforms. As Solid radically changes the way users interact with their personal data, it introduces new UX challenges for designers. This study uncovers the specific design challenges through twelve expert interviews with practitioners who have hands-on experience in designing Solid-enabled applications. By analyzing results from open-ended questions and a forced-choice ranking exercise and linking them with the Human-Data Interaction framework, we aim to assist practitioners in overcoming these challenges. We conclude by proposing a research agenda focusing on three key areas: 1) enhancing explainability, 2) investigating the balance between data control and usability, and 3) developing standardized design patterns.

Keywords: Solid · UX challenges · Human-Data Interaction

1 Introduction

In today's data-driven age, where personal information is scattered across various online platforms, there is a growing demand from individuals for more transparency, control, and user-friendly tools to manage their data [11]. Responding to these needs, Solid (SOcial LInked Data) has emerged as a promising solution, in line with Tim Berners-Lee's original vision of the web [2]. Solid differs from current data management models, such as those employed by major corporations like Alphabet, Apple, and Facebook, which keep data siloed. Instead, it presents

C. Stephanidis et al. (Eds.): HCII 2024, CCIS 2119, pp. 136–145, 2024.
https://doi.org/10.1007/978-3-031-61966-3_16

a decentralized web framework [5], separating data storage and user identity from the services users engage with [4]. Solid achieves this by providing users with a personal online data store, commonly referred to as a data vault, where data can be stored securely. Each data vault is associated with a unique identifier called a WebID, resembling a web address (e.g., use.id/username), granting users secure access and control over their data across platforms. The data stored in these vaults can be used across various services, with users retaining control over who can access their data and how it's utilized [6].

Despite the significant potential benefits of Solid-enabled data vaults for end-users, their adoption is still in its early stages. While some organizations like the BBC [1] and the Flemish government [7] have recognized Solid's potential and begun exploring its applications, widespread adoption among companies is hindered partly due to concerns about the potential burden of personal data management on users [10]. These concerns emerge from the fact that Solid significantly transforms how users manage their personal data online, introducing new and unique UX design challenges for designers.

To gain more insights into the specific UX challenges practitioners face during the design of Solid-enabled applications, we conducted twelve expert interviews with professionals experienced in designing Solid-enabled applications. This involved exploring their past experiences and employing a forced-choice ranking of predetermined UX challenges. By gaining an understanding of the challenges faced by practitioners and aligning these with relevant theoretical frameworks, we've set forth a research agenda dedicated to addressing the most pressing issues obstructing the design process.

2   Methodology

2.1   Study Design and Procedure

To examine the challenges faced by practitioners during the design and development of Solid-enabled applications, we conducted a series of twelve semi-structured expert interviews in June and August 2022. Each interview was divided into two segments. The first segment encompassed general questions concerning the interviewees' engagement and past experiences in the design of Solid-enabled applications. This included discussions on the challenges encountered in their role, as well as the methods and tools they currently employ to assist them in the design process. The second part of the interview featured a forced-choice ranking exercise in which participants were tasked with ranking challenges associated with designing Solid-enabled applications in terms of importance, ranging from 'most critical to address' to 'least critical to address'. Additionally, interviewees were encouraged to motivate their ranking choices. To facilitate expert participation and to address geographical constraints, all interviews were conducted online, using Microsoft Teams.

2.2   Sample Characteristics

To qualify as an expert, all interviewees needed to have practical experience designing Solid-enabled applications. We initially reached out to potential participants whom we knew met the criteria and expanded our sample using a snowball sampling method [9], resulting in a sample size of twelve experts. Among the interviewees, eight had engaged in the design of a Solid-enabled application professionally, with the majority affiliated with start-up companies (n=5), two employed by large enterprises, and one working within a government context. The remaining four interviewees acquired their experience through non-professional activities. The interviewees represented a spectrum of roles, encompassing UX designers (n = 4) and more technically oriented profiles (n = 8), such as developers, software engineers, and a CTO. These experts were actively operating in Europe (n = 9), North America (n = 2), and Australia (n = 1). An overview of the participants can be found in Table 1.

Table 1. Descriptive characteristics of the participants

Interviewee	Job title	Experience with Solid	Company type
1	UX designer	Professional	Start-up
2	UX designer	Professional	Large enterprise
3	UX designer	Professional	Large enterprise
4	UX designer	Professional	Government
5	Developer	Non-professional	N/A
6	Developer	Non-professional	N/A
7	Software engineer	Professional	Start-up
8	Software engineer	Non-professional	N/A
9	Software engineer	Non-professional	N/A
10	Head of engineering	Professional	Start-up
11	CTO	Professional	Start-up
12	CEO	Professional	Start-up

2.3   Data Analysis

The interviews were initially transcribed using Microsoft Teams' built-in tool and were subsequently cross-validated against the original recordings. Our data analysis adhered to an inductive thematic analysis methodology, chosen for its suitability to the exploratory nature of our research. While some of the interviews were originally conducted and analysed in Dutch, only specific excerpts featured in this paper have been translated into English to mitigate the potential loss of meaning during the translation process.

3 Results

3.1 Interview Part 1: Past Experiences

The analysis of the first part of the interviews, during which the experts answered open-ended questions regarding their past experiences and the hurdles they encountered in designing Solid-enabled applications, uncovered three predominant design challenges faced by the interviewees: 1) balancing user empowerment with usability, 2) simplifying WebID usability, and 3) lacking design examples.

Balancing User Empowerment with Usability. In the context of Solid's core affordance to enhance data transparency and user control, interviewees articulated the difficulty of striking a balance between empowering users over their personal data and ensuring that the task of managing this data does not become an overwhelming responsibility for users. Interviewee 1 insightfully noted: *"I think the most challenging part is that we are going to ask users to take more responsibility for their data. And that is a big ask for the people. How are we going to make it, so it is not overwhelming?"*. Moreover, concerns were voiced by the interviewees that while the data management feature enhances user empowerment and privacy, it might introduce friction in the user experience and overshadow the core functionalities that attract users to their platform.

This leads to a practical dilemma of deciding upon the level of granularity of control afforded to users, ensuring it meets their specific needs, while still being comprehensible. The optimal level of control desired by end-users is however challenging to anticipate due to its heavy reliance on context. Interviewee 3 illustrated this notion with insights from user testing, which revealed that people generally prefer more detailed management for sensitive data, like financial information, while opting for simpler management approaches for data that is perceived as less sensitive. Addressing this challenge will thus involve thoughtful consideration of data categorization, which according to interviewee 4 could be thematic, company-based, or sector-specific.

Simplifying WebID Usability. Given that Solid is still unknown to the general public, interviewees expressed concerns about the challenges in its wider adoption, particularly in familiarizing users with the concept of WebIDs. A WebID serves as a unique identifier linked to a user's data vault, facilitating authentication across different applications within the Solid ecosystem. Consequently, users have to log in with their WebID to access and utilize their data vault.

A recurring concern by the interviewees was that the URI structure of webIDs (e.g., user.id/username) may pose a challenge for users, especially in remembering their WebID for login purposes. This raised fears that users might repeatedly create new WebIDs upon login, thereby losing track of their various accounts. Interviewee 12 drew a parallel with the early days of email: *"Like how initially people had 10 email addresses, this seems like the same danger for WebIDs, that everybody will keep creating new WebIDs.*" Moreover, the resemblance of the WebID to a web address prompted worries regarding users potentially misinterpreting their WebID as a pathway to a personal website.

To address these complexities, several interviewees stated that they are exploring various solutions to simplify WebIDs. One approach, as proposed by Interviewee 11, involves incorporating a distinctive, easily recognizable symbol into WebIDs, such as the @ in an email address, enhancing their memorability. Another approach to improve memorability, as suggested by Interviewee 12, is to automatically generate a WebID based on the user's email address. For example, if a user's email is 'xxx@gmail.com', the system would automatically propose 'user.id/xxx' as the WebID.

Lacking Design Examples. A frequently employed practice by interviewees during the design process is examining existing Solid applications to find examples of frequently recurring design patterns such as consent or onboarding flows. However, this approach is hindered, as many interviewees pointed out, by the scarcity of high-quality examples that align with their needs. Given this lack of design examples, six interviewees expressed a strong desire for case studies showcasing best practices, which they believed could inform and enhance their design processes. The primary fear among these practitioners revolved around the potential for inferior application design due to a lack of exemplary applications, as concisely expressed by interviewee 6: *"If people do not have so many examples or the examples do not use the best UX, that is how applications will end up bad."*

Furthermore, the scarcity of high-quality examples of recurring design patterns is feared to lead to a lack of uniformity in user experience (UX) across Solid-enabled applications. Uniformity is considered crucial since Solid allows users to utilize their data vault across different applications, and inconsistencies in user flows across platforms could cause confusion. Consequently, a call was made for standardized UX guidelines addressing frequently recurring UX patterns in Solid-enabled applications, such as the creation of a WebID and the consent flow for data sharing. In the absence of standardized UX patterns, designers may resort to creating ad hoc solutions, leading to a fragmented landscape of user interfaces and hindering recognisability across platforms. *"I could just make stuff up here in terms of UX, but then every single solid app is going to look different."* remarked Interviewee 8, highlighting the challenge of maintaining a unified user experience in the absence of universal design guidelines.

3.2   Interview Part 2: Prioritizing UX Challenges

Following the first part of the interview, the second part entailed a forced choice ranking exercise. In this part, participants were presented with a predefined list of UX challenges specifically related to designing Solid applications. They were then asked to prioritize the challenges from 'most critical to address' to 'least critical to address' and were invited to motivate their choices.

The list of UX design challenges presented to the interviewees (see Fig. 1) was compiled by drawing upon our insights gained from prior consultations with UX practitioners, enriched by contributions from discussions within the Solid community forum[1] regarding UX design. This approach ensured that the challenges were reflective of real-world issues encountered when designing Solid applications. Additionally, the interviewees were also invited to identify any shortcomings of this list, however, no limitations were highlighted.

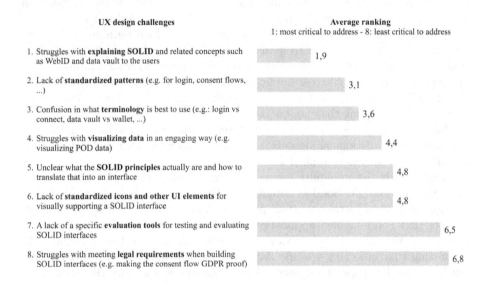

Fig. 1. Outcomes of the forced choice ranking task, where 1 indicates the most critical challenge to address and 8 the least.

Figure 1 presents these UX design challenges in order of their prioritized importance. The results reveal that the most pressing challenge to address is the difficulty of explaining and communicating the complex concepts of Solid, such as WebIDs and data vaults, in a concise and clear way to end-users. Interviewees highlighted the challenge of determining the optimal amount of information to share with end users, a complexity emphasized by Interviewee 7: *"It's a lot of information to communicate. How much do you communicate; how much do people care?"*. This closely matches insights from the initial open-ended segment of the interviews, where interviewees reported difficulties in finding a balance between user empowerment and usability. In response to this challenge, a shift in focus away from the technical details of Solid towards its practical advantages in user explanations was suggested. This approach was illustrated by interviewee 7 using the example of encrypted messaging: *"Most people don't know what encryption is. However, they use encrypted messages to text people. Just because*

---

[1] https://forum.solidproject.org/.

they have heard the concept and they kind of know that it is good and understand it protects their privacy. They don't even know how it works."

Consistent with the shortage of design examples, highlighted during the open-ended part of the interviews, the absence of standardized design patterns, especially for login and consent processes, emerged as the second most critical issue. Standardizing these flows is seen as crucial for building trust and enhancing the user experience. Interviewee 12 encapsulates this perspective, noting the value of a standard approach: *"I believe a standard flow adds a lot of trust. If you have to give consent everywhere in the same way, the user will feel like this is managed on a deeper level than just the application level. Repetition builds trust."*

The challenge ranked third is the confusion over which terminology to use. For instance, should we refer to 'pods' using terms like 'data vaults', and 'data wallets', or consider other alternatives? Many interviewees favour a uniform, recommended terminology across applications to simplify user understanding. On the other hand, some argue for context-specific terminology, allowing companies to choose terms fitting their unique audience and use cases.

Additionally, issues related to data representation and visualization, such as the challenge of distinguishing between verified and user-generated data within a user's data vault, were ranked forth.

Ranked fifth, the ambiguity surrounding certain Solid principles has provoked opposing opinions. As Solid is founded on the idea of granting users increased transparency and control over their personal data, it was argued by some interviewees that Solid-enabled applications should commit to specific data privacy principles. Alternatively, some view Solid primarily as a technical framework, suggesting that enforcing specific data privacy principles on companies might not be within its scope. They argue that companies should have the freedom to apply and align it with their own values. This division underscores a significant difference in viewpoints regarding the role and implementation of Solid.

The final three UX challenges for Solid-standardizing icons and UI elements, developing specific tools for evaluating Solid interfaces, and navigating legal requirements (like GDPR compliance)-were deemed less critical.

4   Discussion

By merging the outcomes of both the open-ended segment of the interviews and the forced choice ranking exercise, we identified the most prominent UX challenges and translated these into a list of research themes, forming the basis of a proposed future research agenda to address these issues.

The first key theme that emerged is the prevalent challenge among practitioners in efficiently explaining and conveying the complex concepts of Solid to users in a way that avoids overwhelming them with too much information. Practitioners especially struggle with conveying the concept of a WebID to users in a comprehensible matter and are exploring various ways to simplify and explain this concept. Achieving this proves to be a complex explainability challenge requiring a fine balance between ensuring interface transparency regarding data processes and holding users' interest in these processes. This leads to the first area of focus on the research agenda:

1. Explainability research involving co-creation with end users, leading to the development of strategies to simplify the presentation of complex Solid concepts like WebIDs and data vaults. The goal is to create a user-comprehensible terminology and a communication approach, ensuring these concepts are accessible to a non-technical audience.

The second theme emerging from our findings highlights the struggle practitioners face in striking a balance between user control and usability. This leads to the practical challenge of deciding upon the granularity of control users should be afforded over the data in their data vault. It involves tailoring the level of control to meet user-specific needs in a manner that remains understandable, ensuring that the complexity of what is presented and what engages users is thoughtfully managed. To address this challenge the Human-Data Interaction framework [8] could provide a roadmap for practitioners, as it suggests a practical approach toward improving legibility and agency over data processes. It underscores the critical need to go beyond mere transparency of data processes, advocating for a shift towards representations that are genuinely comprehensible to those impacted by them. Additionally, it put forward a personalized approach to data agency, ensuring interested users have the means to take control without imposing it on everyone, thus allowing for individual choice and flexibility [3]. In response to this second challenge, we propose the following topic for future research:

2. Research into the optimal balance between giving users control over their data and maintaining the usability of the application. This entails starting from the Human-Data Interaction framework to explore how much control is appropriate or required and how it can be integrated into the user experience without compromising ease of use.

The final prominent theme emerged from discussions about the shortage of design examples, resulting in a call for standardized design patterns and the establishment of a common terminology. While leading entities like the BBC [1] and the Flemish government [7] recognize Solid's promise and are pioneering its use, widespread adoption and the development of standardized design patterns and terminology are still emerging. This nascent stage of Solid adoption leads to uncertainty among designers when creating Solid-enabled interfaces as the general belief is that standardization will foster users' trust and application usability. Additionally, such standardization would also contribute to overcoming the aforementioned challenges regarding explainability. This introduces our final proposed subject for future research:

3. Identifying recurring design patterns in Solid applications for crafting universal guidelines in order to standardize these patterns. This effort is directed at lifting Solid's cross-platform recognizability, with the ultimate goal of enhancing user trust through familiarity and consistency in user experience.

Given that these themes emerged from the needs of practitioners, future studies in these areas will substantially benefit practitioners in their design efforts, ultimately leading to an improved user experience in Solid-enabled applications. This, in turn, is expected to promote broader adoption by refining interactions and usability.

5 Conclusion

Through a series of twelve expert interviews, we have shed light on the main UX challenges practitioners face during the design of Solid-enabled applications. By merging the results from both the open-ended questions and the forced choice ranking exercise and linking these with the Human-Data Interaction framework, we aim to aid practitioners in addressing these challenges. In conclusion, we therefore propose a future research agenda that concentrates on three key areas: 1) research into explainability, 2) exploring the balance between control and usability, and 3) the creation of standardized design patterns. These focus areas aim to tackle the most pressing issues currently obstructing practitioners in their design process. The insights garnered from these efforts have the potential to significantly enrich the field of Human-Data Interaction by translating theoretical knowledge into practical applications.

Acknowledgments. Supported by SolidLab Vlaanderen (Flemish Government, EWI and RRF project V023/10)

References

1. BBC: Together+data pod (2022). https://www.bbc.co.uk/taster/pilots/together-pod
2. Berners-Lee, T., Hendler, J., Lassila, O.: The semantic web: a new form of web content that is meaningful to computers will unleash a revolution of new possibilities (2001). https://scientificamerican.com/
3. Crabtree, A., Mortier, R.: Human data interaction: historical lessons from social studies and cscw. In: Boulus-Rodje, N., Ellingsen, G., Bratteteig, T., Aanestad, M., Bjorn, P. (eds.) ECSCW 2015, pp. 3–21. Springer, Cham (2015). https://doi.org/10.1007/978-3-319-20499-4_1
4. Dedecker, R., Slabbinck, W., Wright, J., Hochstenbach, P., Colpaert, P., Verborgh, R.: What's in a pod? - a knowledge graph interpretation for the solid ecosystem, vol. 3279, pp. 81–96 (2022). https://solidlabresearch.github.io/WhatsInAPod/
5. Mansour, E., et al.: A demonstration of the solid platform for social web applications, pp. 223–226. International World Wide Web Conferences Steering Committee (2016). https://doi.org/10.1145/2872518.2890529
6. Mechant, P., Wolf, R.D., Compernolle, M.V., Joris, G., Evens, T., Marez, L.D.: Saving the web by decentralizing data networks? a socio-technical reflection on the promise of decentralization and personal data stores. In: 2021 14th CMI International Conference - Critical ICT Infrastructures and Platforms (CMI), pp. 1–6 (2021). https://doi.org/10.1109/CMI53512.2021.9663788. https://ieeexplore.ieee.org/document/9663788/
7. Michiels, C.: Vlaanderen lanceert athumi: bepalen we binnenkort zelf wat er met onze online data gebeurt? (2023). https://www.vrt.be/vrtnws/nl/2023/05/04/vlaanderen-lanceert-athumi-bepalen-we-binnenkort-zelf-wat-er-me/

8. Mortier, R., Haddadi, H., Henderson, T., McAuley, D., Crowcroft, J.: Human-data interaction: the human face of the data-driven society (2014). https://doi.org/10.48550/arXiv.1412.6159

9. Parker, C., Scott, S., Geddes, A.: SAGE Publications Ltd. Snowball Sampling (2020). https://doi.org/10.4135/9781526421036831710

10. Stefanija, A.P.: Solid, mastodon, and the risk of overburdening the user. Internet Policy Review (2023). https://policyreview.info/articles/news/solid-mastodon-risk-of-overburdening-the-user/1688

11. Wang, C., Zhang, N., Wang, C.: Managing privacy in the digital economy. Fund. Res. 1, 543–551 (2021). https://doi.org/10.1016/j.fmre.2021.08.009. https://www.sciencedirect.com/science/article/pii/S2667325821001552

Could Chinese Users Recognize Social Bots? Exploratory Research Based on Twitter Data

Xinhe Tian[(✉)] 🆔 and Susan R. Fussell 🆔

Cornell University, Ithaca, NY 14850, USA
{xt246,sfussell}@cornell.edu

Abstract. Social bots have proliferated across global social media platforms such as Twitter, where they engage in sophisticated interactions with human users. We explored Chinese users' recognition of social bots through a survey-embedded experiment and in-depth interviews. Specifically, we conducted a 2 (frequent Twitter users vs. non-users) × 2 (informational tweets vs. emotional tweets) × 2 (human tweets vs. bot tweets) factorial design and selected participants for in-depth interviews based on the experimental results. Our results showed that Chinese users generally possess weak abilities in recognizing social bots, but more Twitter experience significantly improves their recognition abilities. However, we found no significant effect of tweet content on recognition abilities of Chinese users. Further analysis indicates that Chinese users' recognition abilities of Twitter social bots also involve factors such as language structure, basic account information, text content, and interaction. The findings of this study not only extend the theoretical framework but also offer valuable insights for both social media users and platform operators.

Keywords: Social bots · Human-machine communication · Computers are social actors · Affordances

1 Introduction

Advancements in machine learning have enabled social bots to produce tweets increasingly resembling human speech [1]. Social bots are automated or semi-automated accounts on digital social platforms, operated by computer software and displaying human-like actions [2]. Social bots can serve harmless objectives, such as aiding users with reading long content [3], but they can also be used for malicious intentions, such as manipulating public opinion [4]. Although the growth of social bots coincided with the evolution of social media, the year 2016 marked a turning point as they were implicated in influencing public opinion and voter behavior in the U.S. elections. According to a research report published by the project on computational propaganda at Oxford University [5], there has been a significant increase in the number of countries employing computational propaganda techniques. This study, set against this evolving landscape, aims to investigate the relationship between social bots and human users.

© The Author(s), under exclusive license to Springer Nature Switzerland AG 2024
C. Stephanidis et al. (Eds.): HCII 2024, CCIS 2119, pp. 146–156, 2024.
https://doi.org/10.1007/978-3-031-61966-3_17

Specifically, our research endeavors to explore users' ability to recognize social bots on Twitter, focusing particularly on Chinese users, from the perspective of communication studies, thereby contributing to the ongoing discussion in this area. Notably, in this article, the term "Chinese users" specifically refers to users who are native speakers of Chinese and live in the People's Republic of China. We emphasize this demographic for two reasons: First, despite Twitter's limited accessibility in mainland China, a significant number of Chinese users actively engage with the platform through virtual private network (VPN) or overseas connections [6], indicating their unique cross-cultural information behaviors. Second, these users have bilingual and multicultural backgrounds, making them adept at navigating both Chinese social media landscapes and international platforms like Twitter [7]. This distinction offers a valuable lens to study how cultural differences affect the recognition and interaction with social bots. In summary, we propose the following research questions:

RQ1: How effectively can Chinese users recognize social bots on social media?
RQ2: What factors significantly influence the ability of Chinese users to accurately recognize social bots?

We first review literature on human-social bot interactions, covering topics like misinformation spread, media operations, and computational propaganda. We then present our study design, including a survey-embedded experiment and in-depth interviews. Our findings indicate that Chinese users have a limited ability to recognize social bots, with Twitter experience significantly improving their recognition. Although tweet content had no significant effect, factors such as interactions and language cues also influence their abilities. The results have implications for more detailed studies into the interactions between humans and social bots and offer valuable insights for policymakers and industry professionals on the factors impacting users' detection capabilities.

2 Literature Review

In this section, we first review literature on the interactions between humans and social bots from the dimensions of misinformation spread, media operations, and computational propaganda. We then highlight the necessity of studying human abilities to recognize social bots from the perspective of social cognition.

2.1 Interacting with Social Bots

The social bot is a user account outfitted with features that automate interactions with other accounts [8], whether humans or otherwise. The term "bot" is a reduction of "robot", and these "bots" can essentially be considered as robots without physical form. The related research from the perspective of communication explores the interactions between humans and social bots, concentrating primarily on their impact on social, political, and informational dynamics.

From the perspective of misinformation spread, "fake news" is considered a specific form of misinformation [9]. Although its content is not based on facts, it is presented by content creators in a seemingly truthful manner. In certain cases, bots significantly facilitate the spread of misinformation (e.g., [10]). For instance, research has shown that bot accounts have significantly contributed to the spread of misinformation about anti-refugee sentiment on social media.

In terms of media operations, social bots, which are often conceptualized as news bots, serve as valuable tools for news outlets or journalists. These bots are designed to produce convenient social media data and amplify the relevance of the content on social platforms (e.g., [11]). It is interesting that articles generated by news bots can even attract more comments than those created by humans [12].

As a specialized form of political communication, computational propaganda employs algorithms and automation to intentionally manage and disseminate misleading content across social media platforms (e.g., [2]). This form of political manipulation has been widely applied in various political campaigns across multiple countries.

The complexity of the situation is further compounded by the fact that contemporary social bots are designed with increasingly human-like attributes, leading to a diverse array of nuanced cognitive, behavioral, and emotional responses from human users (e.g., [13]). As such, the ability of humans to recognize these ever-evolving, sophisticated social bots emerge as a focal concern.

2.2 Human Recognition of Social Bots

Research on interactions between humans and social bots not only explores the broad implications they hold for social, political, and informational landscapes, but also focuses on nuanced cognitive responses, achieving significant breakthroughs in the process (e.g., [14]). Among these compelling findings, the human ability to recognize social bots emerges as fundamentally important, setting the stage for an in-depth exploration of its wide-ranging applicability and ethical considerations. To be specific, social bots are increasingly being utilized in a wide range of online discussions on topics such as health [15], counter-terrorism [16], and education [17]. In these applications, the user's ability to accurately recognize a social bot could have a direct bearing on the effectiveness or even potential destructiveness of their interactions.

However, research on humans' ability to recognize social bots from a social cognition perspective is still quite limited, with only a few studies providing some insights. For instance, Calvo and colleagues found that journalism students improved their ability to recognize social bots after receiving specific educational interventions [18]; Yan and colleagues found that the characteristics of the participants and the stimuli used can influence the accuracy of bot identification [19]. Therefore, this study not only contributes to understanding how cross-cultural factors affect the recognition of social bots, but also offers a more holistic perspective, assisting social media platforms in adjusting their strategies to combat misinformation and malicious bot activities.

3   Theoretical Framework and Hypothesis Development

In this section, we discuss the concept of Computers are Social Actors (CASA) [20] and affordances. Building on them, we then propose hypotheses regarding the ability of Chinese users to recognize social bots.

3.1   Computers Are Social Actors (CASA)

Nass and colleagues' CASA model posits that human interactions with computers are fundamentally social and natural, suggesting that individuals infer that the machine has human-like social attributes, thereby applying the same social mechanisms to computers as they do in human-to-human interactions.

In the same way, when interacting with social bots, people may employ the same social mechanism and psychological expectations they use for human-to-human interactions. This inclination might further blur the lines in people's ability to discern social bots from human users, because individuals are more likely to interpret the behavior of these bots based on their previous social experiences and expectations, rather than critically analyzing whether they are interacting with a program or a human. Moreover, technological advancements, coupled with designers' efforts to make bots appear more human-like (e.g., [21]), have made it increasingly challenging to distinguish between human-generated and bot-generated tweets. To empirically investigate the recognition ability of Chinese users, this study proposes the following:

H1a: Chinese users demonstrate high accuracy in recognizing human tweets as human generated.
H1b: Chinese users demonstrate low accuracy in recognizing bot tweets as computer-generated.
H1c: The accuracy of Chinese users in recognizing bot tweets is significantly lower than their accuracy in recognizing human tweets.

3.2   Affordances

The concept of affordances originally refers to the possibility of action within a specific environment [22]. With the penetration of Internet technology in the field of journalism and communication, the concept of affordances has been adopted to explain the application of digital technology in media practice and human daily communication. For example, Hutchby defined affordances as "functional and relational aspects, which frame, while not determining, the possibilities for agentic action in relation to an object" [23]. Besides, Wellman and colleagues regarded the concept of affordances as the possibility that technology or objects influence daily life [24]. Moreover, Nagy and Neff proposed the concept of imagined affordances [25], which connected affordances with mediation, materiality, and affect, aiming to stimulate new vitality for it.

Many scholars place great emphasis on the value of mediation experiences, especially given that users tend to perceive communication media as an invisible entity mediated by human sensory, cognitive, and affective processes [26]. The perceptions of affordances are as much socially constructed for users as they are technologically configured [25]. For instance, Woolley and Howard noted the surprising lack of academic research demonstrating the use of robots and algorithms for computational propaganda in China [27], despite the increasing global prevalence of social bots. Consequently, we posit that Chinese social media users, when switching to Twitter, may struggle to recognize social bots due to differences in mediated experiences, such as lacking experience interacting with social bots. Familiarity with one platform's nuances might not translate well to another, complicating bot recognition. Therefore, we hypothesize the following:

H2: When exposed to bot tweets, frequent users demonstrate higher accuracy in recognizing social bots compared to users who have never used Twitter.

Nagy and Neff also underscore the significance of users' imagination and perception in their understanding and interaction with technology [25], which is particularly crucial for the analysis of the impact that affect in tweets has on social media users. On social platforms, users form emotional bonds with technology, viewing it as "relational entities" and exchanging emotional content to build connections. Consequently, we hypothesize that emotional content from social bots could impair users' recognition abilities, as emotions in tweets might confuse them. Besides, previous research found that strong information (data and research) is more persuasive than weak information (opinions and personal views) [28, 29], so we hypothesize that users can better recognize informational social bots due to the rich information provided. In conclusion, this study proposed the following:

H3: Chinese users demonstrate higher accuracy in recognizing informational social bots than emotional social bots.

4 Method

This study used mixed methods to investigate the recognition ability of Chinese social media users in regards to social bots. This investigation is comprised of two components: (1) A survey-embedded experiment that employed a 2 (frequent Twitter users vs. nonusers) × 2 (informational tweets vs. emotional tweets) × 2 (human tweets vs. bot tweets) factorial design. (2) After completing the survey, semi-structured in-depth interviews were conducted with a selected subset of participants to gain a deeper understanding of their experiences and perceptions.

4.1 Participants

This study recruited a total of 240 Chinese participants, half of whom were defined as frequent Twitter users, while the other half were non-Twitter users. To qualify, frequent users must own a Twitter account, which should be over one year old, and report using Twitter at least 4 days weekly. Each participant read 20 tweets and was given a 20

CNY incentive for successful completion of the survey, which was assigned through the Survey Star platform.

Following a manipulation check, 211 valid responses (128 females, 83 males) were collected and analyzed, and they were primarily from journalism and communication (N = 46), English (N = 87), and various other fields (N = 78), including computer science, economics, education, and geography. All participants in this study were fluent in reading English, given that the tweets used as materials were written in that language.

4.2 Survey-Embedded Experiment

The materials of this study involved 40 tweets, which were equally split between human and bot tweets. Specifically, it involved 20 informational tweets, comprising 10 human tweets and 10 bot tweets, as well as 20 emotional tweets, also including 10 human tweets and 10 bot tweets.

In order to distinguish between bot tweets and human tweets, all tweets were scored using BotoMeter [30], a social robot recognition program[1]. The program assigns a score of 0.3 or higher to bot tweets and a score of less than 0.3 to human tweets. To ensure maximum accuracy, all selected bot tweets in the study were scored 0.7 or higher and all human tweets were scored 0.3 or lower.

To minimize the impact of subjective perception on the participants' judgments, we selected a topic for the tweets that had less relevance to the Chinese participants: the "Taliban take over Afghanistan", a political event that took place outside of China in 2021.

All participants were randomly assigned to conditions, only told to identify tweet sources, unaware the study aimed to explore social bot recognition in advance. Upon completing the survey, they were tasked with identifying the source type of each tweet they read. They were given three possible answers to choose from: (1) media, (2) individual, and (3) bot. In reality, however, option (1) and (2) represented the same type of account – human accounts, while option (3) represented social bots.

4.3 In-Depth Interview

This study proceeds with in-depth interviews as a supplementary research method. We designed a semi-structured interview outline in alignment with the research questions, consisting of three primary sections: interviewees' social media usage, their basic perceptions of social bots, and their judgments about tweets. Participants were encouraged to express their views freely within the context of the established themes and frameworks.

Specifically, the interview participants were chosen based on their backgrounds (Table 1) and their performance during the experimental phase, with a focus on those who demonstrated either particularly strong or particularly weak abilities in recognizing social bots. Throughout this phase, a total of 13 participants were engaged in the in-depth interviews, with an average duration of 32 min per interview.

---

[1] Although the platform announced a temporary cessation of services on 30 June, 2023, and is currently in archival mode, the data for this study was collected in 2022 and was therefore not affected.

Table 1. Information about interviewees for in-depth interviews.

Rank	Code	Gender	Twitter experience	Type of tweets
01	NH	Female	Frequent	Information
02	YD	Male	Frequent	Information
03	DN	Female	Never	Emotion
04	JX	Male	Frequent	Information
05	HD	Male	Frequent	Emotion
06	SE	Male	Frequent	Emotion
07	WX	Female	Never	Emotion
08	LG	Male	Frequent	Emotion
09	ST	Female	Frequent	Information
10	FG	Male	Frequent	Emotion
11	NU	Female	Frequent	Information
12	FH	Male	Frequent	Information
13	OW	Female	Never	Emotion

5 Results

We conducted a series of chi-square tests to investigate Chinese users' recognition ability, as well as to examine the impact of Twitter experience and content type. Subsequently, we shared insights gained from our interviews.

5.1 Ability of Chinese Users to Recognize Social Bots

In this study, we calculated the recognition accuracy of 211 participants for social bots after they reviewed a series of tweets. General analysis revealed a recognition accuracy of 52.04%, with minor variation among participants (Table 2). However, deeper analysis revealed that 27.96% of participants consistently identified tweets as originating from human users, never selecting the bot option, and inherently achieved a half correct recognition rate by defaulting to human selections alone. Therefore, we calculated the accuracy rates of Chinese users in correctly identifying human and bot tweets respectively.

For human tweets, Chinese users had an accuracy rate of 88.44% to recognize them. In contrast, their ability to identify bot tweets was significantly weaker, with an average accuracy of just 15.64%. Furthermore, frequent Twitter users demonstrated a bot tweet recognition accuracy between 0 and 70%, averaging 17.80%, while non-users ranged from 0 to 60%, averaging 13.58%. In addition, Chinese users show low recognition accuracy for both informational and emotional bot tweets, with averages of 16.04% and 15.24% respectively.

The Kolmogorov-Smirnov test indicates that the data from both bot tweets and human tweets significantly deviate from a normal distribution. Therefore, this study

Table 2. Percentage of correct responses per condition.

Subcategory	Mean (Overall)	SD (Overall)	Mean (Frequent Users)	SD (Frequent Users)	Mean (Nonusers)	SD (Nonusers)	Number of Tweets
Human Tweets	88.44	1.89	87.65	1.46	89.17	1.28	10
Informational	88.68	1.68	88.82	1.21	88.55	1.38	10
Emotional	88.19	2.11	86.47	1.68	89.81	1.19	10
Bot Tweets	15.64	2.34	17.80	1.65	13.58	1.38	10
Informational	16.04	2.70	19.02	1.79	13.27	1.45	10
Emotional	15.24	2.00	16.67	1.51	13.89	1.32	10
Overall	52.04	1.61	52.75	1.43	51.38	1.08	20
Informational	52.36	1.70	53.92	1.43	50.91	1.11	20
Emotional	51.71	1.52	51.57	1.41	51.85	1.05	20

selected the chi-square test as the statistical method. First, a chi-square goodness of fit test indicated a significant difference between correct and incorrect identifications (CHI Sq (1) = 1246.86, p < .05), suggesting that Chinese users demonstrate high accuracy in recognizing human tweets. This finding supports H1a.

Following this, another chi-square goodness of fit test revealed that the number of bot tweets misidentified by Chinese users significantly exceeded the number of correct identifications (CHI Sq (1) = 996.45, p < .05), indicating that Chinese users demonstrate low accuracy in recognizing bot tweets. This supports H1b.

Finally, the chi-square test revealed a significant difference in the correct recognition of human and bot tweets by Chinese users (CHI Sq (1) = 2240.02, p < .05), indicating that the accuracy of Chinese users in recognizing bot tweets is significantly lower than their accuracy in recognizing human tweets. This finding supports H1c.

5.2 Influencing Factors of Chinese Users' Recognition Ability

Twitter Experience. Data analysis revealed a significant difference (CHI Sq (1) = 7.265, p = .007 < .05) between the group with Twitter experience and the group without it in terms of the number of correct identifications. This indicates that Twitter experience can enhance the ability to recognize social bots, thereby supporting H2.

Content Type. Despite a slightly higher accuracy for informational tweets than emotional tweets, we found no significant difference in Chinese users' ability to recognize bot tweets with different content types (CHI Sq (1) = 0.256, p = .613 > .05), which means H3 is not supported.

Additional Insights from Interviews. The effectiveness of Chinese users in distinguishing social bots from humans is increasingly challenged by bots' evolving "humanization". Advanced social bots now mimic human tweet characteristics, blurring traditional recognition cues.

In actual situations, "formal or overly detailed language might indicate a bot" (Participant JX), a perspective further supported by the observation that "excessive punctuation can also serve as a potential marker" (Participant PW), given that human users often overlook such details in their tweets. Overall, users still struggle with these subtleties, especially when bots mimic the writing style of human tweets.

The account's nickname and ID have a personalized impact on recognition, as robots' names are often regarded as "phone numbers or gibberish" (Participant DN), while "adding numbers to avoid name duplication on Twitter"(Participant LG) indicates that having a few numbers in the name does not necessarily mean it is a robot.

Hashtag usage further complicates bot recognition. Although social bots are known to "use hashtags to increase tweet visibility" (Participant, SE), this strategy is not exclusive to bots, as "human accounts sometimes do the same" (Participant, NH). Thus, hashtag frequency is unreliable for distinguishing bots.

Interactions such as likes, retweets, quotation, and comments, once reliable "indicators of human activity" (Participant, WX), are now exploited by bots to simulate engagement. This fake interaction, aimed at gaining trust, undermines the authenticity of engagement.

In summary, the advanced imitation capabilities of bots render traditional metrics based on account features, text content, and interaction patterns unreliable, as even seemingly human-like accounts can be social bots.

6 Limitations and Future Research

This study has some limitations that need to be addressed in future work. First, our study primarily focuses on investigating the ability of Chinese users to distinguish between tweets generated by humans and social bots. While the data from this specific demographic provides a valuable reference for users from other linguistic and cultural backgrounds, it obviously cannot serve as a comprehensive representation of the global user population. Therefore, future academic exploration could consider expanding the scope of research to include different linguistic and cultural contexts, aiming for a more holistic and nuanced understanding. Second, it is crucial to highlight that the usage and prevalence of social media and social bots exhibit temporal variations. Particularly, as the technology about social bots continues to evolve and improve, human capabilities in recognizing these bots are also likely to undergo corresponding changes. Consequently, the findings of this study may be subject to temporal limitations, and ongoing updates and adjustments are needed in future research to ensure both relevance and universality.

7 Conclusions

This study investigated the abilities of Chinese users in recognizing social bots and human beings. Based on the CASA model and affordances, we compared the abilities of Chinese users who frequently use Twitter with those who do not use Twitter at all in recognizing social bots, and also examined the impact of informational tweets and emotional tweets on the ability of Chinese users to recognize social bots. Through the survey-embedded experiment, we found that Chinese users generally have a weaker ability to recognize social bots, while users who frequently use Twitter demonstrate significantly stronger recognition capabilities. Furthermore, through in-depth interviews, we identified other factors that influence Chinese users' ability to discern social bots, offering valuable implications for future research in human-computer interaction. Our findings not only strengthen the explanatory power of affordances but also extend its applicability, enriching the theoretical landscape of human-computer interaction.

References

1. Orabi, M., Mouheb, D., Al Aghbari, Z., Kamel, I.: Detection of bots in social media: a systematic review. Inf. Process. Manage. **57**(4), 102250 (2020)
2. Kats, D., Sharif, M.: "I have no idea what a social bot is": on users' perceptions of social bots and ability to detect them. In: Proceedings of the 10th International Conference on Human-Agent Interaction, pp. 32–40. ACM, NY, USA (2022)
3. This bot unrolls Twitter threads and turns them into readable blog posts, https://tcrn.ch/31p TsRY. Last accessed 21 Mar 2024
4. Woolley, S.C., Howard, P.N.: Automation, algorithms, and politics| political communication, computational propaganda, and autonomous agents—Introduction. Int. J. Commun. **10**, 9 (2016)
5. Bradshaw, S., Howard, P.N.: The global disinformation order: 2019 global inventory of organised social media manipulation. https://digitalcommons.unl.edu/scholcom/207
6. Mou, Y., Wu, K., Atkin, D.: Understanding the use of circumvention tools to bypass online censorship. New Media Soc. **18**(5), 837–856 (2016)
7. Wu, S., Mai, B.: Talking about and beyond censorship: mapping topic clusters in the Chinese Twitter sphere. Int. J. Commun. **13**, 23 (2019)
8. Howard, P.N., Woolley, S., Calo, R.: Algorithms, bots, and political communication in the US 2016 election: the challenge of automated political communication for election law and administration. J. Inform. Tech. Polit. **15**(2), 81–93 (2018)
9. LWang, L., Fussell, S.R.: More than a click: exploring college students' decision-making processes in online news sharing. In: Proceedings of the ACM on Human-Computer Interaction, pp. 1–20. ACM, NY, USA (2020)
10. Zhen, L., Yan, B., Tang, J.L., Nan, Y., Yang, A.: Social network dynamics, bots, and community-based online misinformation spread: lessons from anti-refugee and COVID-19 misinformation cases. Inf. Soc. **39**(1), 17–18 (2023)
11. Santini, R.M., Salles, D., Tucci, G., Ferreira, F., Grael, F.: Making up audience: media bots and the falsification of the public sphere. Commun. Stud. **71**(3), 466–487 (2020)
12. Molina, M.D., Wang, J., Sundar, S.S., Le, T., DiRusso, C.: Reading, commenting and sharing of fake news: how online bandwagons and bots dictate user engagement. Commun. Res. **50**(6), 667–694 (2023)
13. Wischnewski, M., Ngo, T., Bernemann, R., Jansen, M., Krämer, N.: "I agree with you, bot!" How users (dis)engage with social bots on Twitter. New Media Soc. **26**(3), 1505–1526 (2024)
14. Laitinen, K., Laaksonen, S.M., Koivula, M.: Slacking with the bot: programmable social bot in virtual team interaction. J. Comput.-Mediat. Commun. **26**(6), 343–361 (2021)
15. Zhang, M., Qi, X., Chen, Z., Liu, J.: Social bots' involvement in the COVID-19 vaccine discussions on Twitter. Int. J. Environ. Res. Public Health **19**(3), 1651 (2022)

16. Alrhmoun, A., Winter, C., Kertész, J.: Automating terror: the role and impact of telegram bots in the Islamic state's online ecosystem. Terrorism Polit. Violence **36**(4), 409–424 (2023)
17. Chocarro, R., Cortinas, M., Marcos-Matás, G.: Teachers' attitudes towards chatbots in education: a technology acceptance model approach considering the effect of social language, bot proactiveness, and users' characteristics. Educ. Stud. **49**(2), 295–313 (2023)
18. Calvo, D., Cano-Orón, L., Esteban, A.: Materiales y evaluación del nivel de alfabetización para el reconocimiento de bots sociales en contextos de desinformación política. Revista ICONO14 Revista científica de Comunicación y Tecnologías emergentes **18**(2), 111–137 (2020). https://doi.org/10.7195/ri14.v18i2.1515
19. Yan, H.Y., Yang, K.-C., Menczer, F., Shanahan, J.: Asymmetrical perceptions of partisan political bots. New Media Soc. **23**(10), 3016–3037 (2021)
20. Nass, C., Steuer, J., Tauber, E.R.: Computers are social actors. In: Proceedings of the SIGCHI conference on Human factors in computing systems, pp. 72–78. ACM, NY. USA (1994)
21. Go, E., Sundar, S.S.: Humanizing chatbots: the effects of visual, identity and conversational cues on humanness perceptions. Comput. Hum. Behav. **97**, 304–316 (2019)
22. Gibson, J.J.: The Ecological Approach to Visual Perception. Houghton Mifflin, Boston (1979)
23. Hutchby, I.: Technologies, texts and affordances. Sociology **35**(2), 441–456 (2001)
24. Wellman, B., Quan-Haase, A., Boase, J., Chen, W., Hampton, K., Díaz, I., Miyata, K.: The social affordances of the Internet for networked individualism. J. Comput.-Mediated Commun. (2006). https://doi.org/10.1111/j.1083-6101.2003.tb00216.x
25. Nagy, P., Neff, G.: Imagined affordance: Reconstructing a keyword for communication theory. Soc. Media + Soc. **1**(2), 205630511560338 (2015). https://doi.org/10.1177/205630511560 3385
26. Renò, L.: Presence and mediated spaces: a review. Psychnol. J. **3**(2), 181–199 (2005)
27. Woolley, S.C., Howard, P.N.: Computational Propaganda: Political Parties, Politicians, and Political Manipulation on Social Media. Oxford University Press, Oxford, UK (2018)
28. Petty, R.E., Harkins, S.G., Williams, K.D.: The effects of group diffusion of cognitive effort on attitudes: an information-processing view. J. Pers. Soc. Psychol. **38**(1), 81–92 (1980)
29. Petty, R.E., Cacioppo, J.T., Schumann, D.: Central and peripheral routes to advertising effectiveness: the moderating role of involvement. J. Consum. Res. **10**(2), 135–146 (1983)
30. Botometer Homepage: https://botometer.osome.iu.edu/. Last accessed 21 Mar 2024

Emoji Interpretation and Usage in Bilingual Communication

Yadi Wang[1(✉)] ⓘ, Yu-Chen Chang[1], Linlin Li[1], Yunwei Sheng[1], Sheba Sow[2],
and Susan R. Fussell[1] ⓘ

[1] Department of Information Science, Cornell University, Ithaca, NY 14850, USA
{yw2547,yc2738,ll966,ys726,sfussell}@cornell.edu
[2] Department of Computer Science, Cornell University, Ithaca, NY 14850, USA
ss2956@cornell.edu

Abstract. Emojis help people to express their emotions in place of textual language, but the emotions they convey are often not consistent. Prior research has shown that the usage and interpretation of emojis vary across different languages and cultures, but little is known about those immersed in multiple cultural and linguistic environments at the same time. To address this gap in research, we surveyed 31 US university students who are bilingual in English and Mandarin to understand how they perceive emojis in different linguistic contexts. Our findings revealed their different emoji preferences across languages, alongside varying sentiment and semantic connotations attributed to the same emoji when used in different languages. Overall, our study provides valuable perspectives on the nuanced ways bilingual individuals navigate and imbue meaning into their emoji usage, shedding light on the multifaceted nature of this form of expression within diverse linguistic environments.

Keywords: Emoji · Language

1 Introduction

In the realm of computer-mediate communication (CMC), emojis have emerged as a mode of communication that transcends linguistic boundaries, facilitating the expression of emotions, nuances, and even cultural references in a way that text cannot [9]. However, this new form of communication is not universal. Our understanding of emojis can vary based on multiple factors, such as the subtleties in their visual representations [10, 16], as well as the identity of emoji senders and readers [5, 16]. While many prior studies have compared the use of emojis by people from various cultural backgrounds [7, 17, 19], little is known about bilingual or multilingual individuals who navigate multiple linguistic and cultural contexts daily. This presents an intriguing area of study for researchers.

Therefore, our research project aims to explore the nuances of emoji usage among bilingual individuals. In particular, we focus on English and Mandarin bilinguals in our study, as both languages are widely spoken around the globe, but represent very different cultural contexts [6]. As such, bilingual individuals proficient in both English

C. Stephanidis et al. (Eds.): HCII 2024, CCIS 2119, pp. 157–167, 2024.
https://doi.org/10.1007/978-3-031-61966-3_18

and Mandarin may need to constantly navigate linguistic and cultural challenges when they switch between languages. Thus, we ask the following research question:

RQ: Do English and Mandarin bilingual individuals use and interpret emojis differently when texting in different languages?

To explore this question, we recruited 31 undergraduate students proficient in both English and Mandarin. Each of them filled out an online survey, where they were asked to respond to five text messages accompanied by emojis they often use. Inspired by Miller et al. [10], we collected and analyzed the sentiment scores as well as text interpretations of the emojis from participants.

Our data lead to two main discoveries. First, when texting in different languages, participants exhibit partially similar but partially different emoji preferences. Second, the same emoji can convey different sentiments and semantics when used in different languages. For instance, when texting in Mandarin, participants tend to interpret emojis in a sarcastic and ambiguous manner, whereas in English, they associate emojis with clearer emotions. Overall, our study provides valuable perspectives on the nuanced ways bilingual individuals navigate and imbue meaning into their emoji usage, shedding light on the multifaceted nature of this form of expression within diverse linguistic environments.

2   Related Work

Previous research has provided valuable insights into factors associated with the usage and interpretation of emojis. A lot of these factors have to do with external elements, such as the appearance of the emojis and the context they are used. For example, both Cha et al. [1] and Cho et al. [3] found that the high specificity and complexity of graphics can cause divergent interpretations of stickers and pictorial images in texts. It has also been found that skin tones of emoji can affect text readers' perceptions of identity, even in cases where the accompanying text is linguistically neutral [16]. Moreover, Miller et al. [10] revealed that differences in the renderings of emojis on different platforms can significantly affect people's interpretation of them.

Another stream of work seeks to understand how the identities of emoji senders and readers affect their usage and interpretation of emojis. While some researchers focus on factors such as race [16], age and gender [5], we are particularly interested in the studies on language and culture. While some work found that linguistic and cultural background had little to no impact on people's interpretation of emojis [11], the majority observed a significant correlation between the two. For example, Togans et al. [19] found positive correlations between emoji use and scores on collectivism and interdependent self-construal. Having explored intensity gradations of face emojis across cultures, Krekhov et al. [7] concluded that people from linear-active cultures and multi-active and reactive cultures perceived emojis in very different ways. Additionally, Takahashi et al. [17] specifically studied how people from different cultural backgrounds recognize emotions in smiling emojis. They found that Japanese participants were more sensitive to emotions expressed by emojis than Cameroonian and Tanzanian participants.

There has been an abundance of work showing that bilingual and multilingual individuals exhibit different personalities, values, and behaviors [2, 13–15] when speaking different languages. However, to the best of our knowledge, there has been no work that explores such code-switching behavior [4] in the context of emoji use. Therefore, our research aims to address this gap in prior work by exploring the nuances of emoji usage among bilingual individuals, as we believe that understanding how bilinguals use emojis differently when texting in different languages can shed light on the intricate interplay between language, culture, and digital communication.

3 Methods

Our study is designed as a survey questionnaire that participants can complete on their own electronic devices. The survey implements a mixed design, in which participants are asked to interpret and respond to a series of texts accompanied by emojis in each of the two languages they are proficient in (i.e., English and Mandarin). In our study, the main variables are 1) the 2 languages each participant speaks (within-subjects), as well as 2) the 5 emojis they choose (between-subjects) from a list of 20 emojis we compiled. In total, each participant provided 10 responses.

3.1 Participants

We received 31 complete responses from participants who are bilinguals proficient in both English and Mandarin. All participants were Cornell students who received extra credit for participating in our study. They had an average age of 21.03 (SD = 1.89, min = 19, max = 28). Most of the participants (N = 26) used devices with an IOS system to answer the survey, and the rest used their laptops (N = 3) or Android (N = 2) devices. They all reported themselves using emojis in personal communication much more frequently than in professional contexts.

Among the 31 participants, 9 indicated English as their primary language, while 22 identified Mandarin as their primary language. When we asked them their frequency of using emojis when texting, 6 participants said they use emojis in nearly every message, 21 reported using one emoji in several messages, 3 stated they type emojis only when they feel strong emotions, and 1 participant indicated that they rarely emojis in their texts.

3.2 Study Design

In our survey, we compiled a list of 20 emojis (see Table 1), from which participants chose 5 that they used the most often in their daily lives in English and Mandarin respectively. This is due to our concern about our sample size, that we may not have enough data on each emoji to analyze if we give participants complete freedom to pick any emojis they want. We selected the emojis from *Emoji Sentiment Ranking* [12] based on the following criteria:

- the emoji's negativity and positivity scores are at least 0.3 (out of 1). In other words, we chose emojis that are loaded with both positive and negative emotions [12].
- the emoji has an occurrence of at least 300 in Novak et al.'s dataset of about 70,000 tweets [12].

- the emoji represents a facial expression instead of an object.

Those criteria allow us to identify emojis that are often interpreted differently by different users in different contexts (i.e., "controversial" enough), and commonly used in our daily life. The above criteria give us an initial list of 10 emojis, which are listed on the left of Table 1. Then, noticing the absence of seemingly positive emojis, and realizing that some non-facial expression emojis have also been misinterpreted fairly often in our daily lives, we manually added 10 other emojis listed on the right of Table 1.

Table 1. Emojis that are included in our survey. The descriptions are retrieved from Zeng's emoji package [20].

Emoji	Codepoint	Description	Emoji	Codepoint	Description
😭	0x1f62d	Loudly crying face	😀	0x1f600	Grinning face
😔	0x1f614	Pensive face	😁	0x1f601	Beaming face with smiling eyes
😳	0x1f633	Flushed face	😆	0x1f606	Grinning squinting face
😡	0x1f621	Pouting face	😅	0x1f605	Grinning face with sweat
😢	0x1f622	Crying face	😂	0x1f602	Face with tears of joy
😴	0x1f634	Sleeping face	😉	0x1f609	Winking face
😞	0x1f61e	Disappointed face	😇	0x1f607	Smiling face with halo
😪	0x1f62a	Sleepy face	🙄	0x1f644	Face with rolling eyes
😫	0x1f62b	Tired face	💀	0x1f480	Skull
😰	0x1f630	Anxious face with sweat	🙏	0x1f64f	Folded hands

Each emoji was then randomly paired with one of 5 neutral Q&A texts to form a scenario. We decided to ask participants to respond to emojis embodied in texts, instead of emojis only, for two reasons. First, the presence of texts helps to better simulate situations when participants text in English and Mandarin respectively. Second, based on prior research, when a text itself is neutral, readers' perceptions of the text will be affected by their perception of emojis: the presence of positive emojis makes them interpret the text more positively, and vice versa [11]. Therefore, we believe that participants' responses to the text and the emoji combined can serve as a reliable proxy for how they perceive the emojis. To make sure that the texts we use are neutral, we directly adapted the 5 neutral texts used in the study conducted by Neel et al. [11] and translated them into Mandarin (see Table 2). The resultant translation was proofread by an additional native Mandarin speaker besides the translator.

Table 2. The 5 neutral text scenarios in English and Mandarin. The [e] indicates where the emoji is inserted.

English	Mandarin
"How will you get there?" "By train [e]"	"你怎么过去？" "坐火车 [e]"
"When is it?" "It's on Wednesday [e]"	"是什么时候？" "星期三 [e]"
"When did you receive it?" "Yesterday [e]"	"你什么时候收到的？" "昨天 [e]"
"Did you get my email?" "I haven't checked it yet [e]"	"你收到我的邮件了吗？" "我还没有看邮箱 [e]"
"Did they respond?" "Not yet [e]"	"他们回复了吗？" "还没有 [e]"

Our survey has the following structure: after the informed consent form, we asked participants some basic demographic questions, such as their age, the languages they speak, and the device they use to fill in the survey. The first two questions are used to confirm that they are at least 18 years old and bilingual. The device requirement is to create consistency within the study by ensuring everyone has access to the same graphics of emojis [10]. However, we did end up including 5 non-IOS users' responses due to our limited sample size. We then asked some questions about their texting behavior, with an emphasis on how they use emojis in texts.

Then, for both English and Mandarin Chinese, we asked participants to choose the 5 emojis they most commonly use from the list of emojis we provided. We randomly paired each emoji with one of the 5 neutral texts to form a scenario. For each scenario, we then asked them to rate the sentiment score of the emoji that appears in the scenario and to provide text responses for their interpretations and potential reactions they would text back. The purpose of these questions is to see if we can understand the participant's perception of the emoji through their response to the text. In total, each participant responded to 10 such scenarios.

3.3 Data Collection and Analysis

Besides the demographic information and general emoji usage questions, the key data we collected are participants' responses to texts accompanied by emojis. Each of the 31 participants provided 10 responses (5 in English, 5 in Mandarin), so we collected 155 responses to emojis in the English texting context, and 155 in the Mandarin context. Because we asked participants to respond to emojis they use often, the data we collected skewed toward the relatively popular emojis. Therefore, in the following sections of the report, we will present the resultant analysis for the top emojis in each of the two languages because others do not have adequate data for us to run statistical analyses on.

Our data analysis proceeds as follows: we first separated responses by language. Then for each popular emoji in each of the languages, we extracted all participants for that particular emoji, regardless of which text scenario they saw the emoji paired with. Again, this is because we know that all texts are neutral and therefore should have minimum interference with the emotions participants reported feeling - the sentiment should mainly depend on the emoji. For the sentiment of each emoji, participants gave an integer from −5 to 5, from the most negative to the most positive [10]. In the analysis, we calculated the average sentiment score for each emoji, as well as the difference between two sentiment scores if an emoji is popular across two languages.

4   Results

We present our results derived primarily from two parts of our survey. First, we present the most popular emojis participants used when they texted in English and Mandarin respectively. Second, we compare their sentiment interpretation of those popular emojis in both linguistic contexts. In addition, we also provide some example text interpretations of emojis to complement our sentiment analysis results. Through a comparative analysis, we find both similarities and differences between how participants use and interpret those emojis when texting in different languages.

4.1   General Preferences

We first introduce the emojis that at least 10 participants reported themselves frequently using when texting in English or Mandarin. As shown in Fig. 1, in English responses, the top emojis, in decreasing order of frequency, were 😂, 😊, 🙏, 😅, 💀, 😄. In Chinese responses, the top emojis were 😂, 😊, 😅, 😄, 😄, 😊, 🙏, also following a decreasing order. It is noteworthy that 😂, 😊, 😅, 😄, and 🙏 emerged as common emojis frequently used in both English and Mandarin contexts. However, 💀 was observed predominantly in English texting, whereas 😄 and 😊 found popularity only in Mandarin texting.

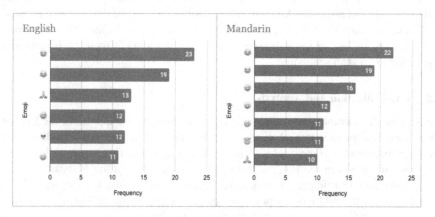

Fig. 1. The top six most frequently used emojis.

4.2 Sentiment Interpretation

We first analyze the sentiment scores of the emojis participants identified in previous questions. To make the comparison more straightforward, we focus on the frequently used emojis across both languages: 😀, 😩, 😆, 🙀 and 😁 (See Table 3).

Table 3. Means and standard deviations for sentiment scores of the selected emojis on a scale of −5 to +5, and results of t-tests comparing English vs. Mandarin sentiment. Note: **$p \leq .01$, + $p \leq .10$.

Emoji	English Mean (SD)	Mandarin Mean (SD)	T-Test DF	t
😀	1.91 (2.07)	-0.50 (2.20)	21	-2.76**
😩	-2.26 (1.05)	-0.89 (2.26)	40	-2.59**
😆	-0.05 (1.61)	-1.14 (2.34)	39	-1.70+
🙀	0.15 (1.72)	-0.60 (2.01)	21	-0.97
😁	-1.58 (1.51)	-1.31 (2.33)	26	0.35

Among the five emojis we analyzed, 😀 has the highest difference in mean sentiment scores (2.41) when being used in English compared to Mandarin. In English texts, the majority of participants (82%) perceive it as positive. However, in Mandarin texts, it elicited a mixed set of interpretations with 50% negative, and 25% neutral, 25% positive. Consequently, while it has a quite positive mean sentiment score of 1.91 in English, it leans neutral to slightly negative (−0.50) in Mandarin contexts. This shows a clear distinction in how participants attribute meanings to it in different linguistic contexts, which is also supported by our two-sample T-test result ($p \leq .01$).

On the other hand, 😁 has the lowest difference in mean sentiment scores (0.27) among the five emojis we investigated further. It was perceived as negative by most participants in both English (92%) and Mandarin (75%) contexts. The T-test result shows that the difference between its interpretations across the two languages is not statistically significant ($p > .10$).

Out of the five emojis we compare, 😀, 😩, and 😆 elicit notably divergent interpretations across the two languages. While being perceived as positive, negative, and neutral respectively in English contexts, they all tend towards neutrality to slight negativity in Mandarin contexts. On the other hand, participants did not report much sentiment differences between emotions conveyed by 🙀 and 😁 across languages: they are viewed as neutral and negative respectively in both languages.

An intriguing distinction arises when we compare the overall pattern of emoji interpretation in English v.s. Mandarin. When in English responses, clear categories emerge between positive (😀), negative (😩, 😆), and neutral (😆, 🙀) emojis based on their mean sentiment scores. Furthermore, the smaller overall standard deviations imply a higher level of agreement among participants regarding their sentiments. On the other hand, in Mandarin texts, all five emojis yield average sentiment scores ranging from neutral to slightly negative, accompanied by larger standard deviations above 2. This suggests that participants offered diverse sentimental interpretations for all those emojis.

4.3 Semantic Interpretation

To further illustrate the observation from the section above, in this section, we present some quotes from participants' text interpretations of 😁 and 😭, two emojis with opposite facial expressions (i.e., smiling v.s. crying) that were interpreted very differently in English vs. Mandarin contexts.

The "grinning face" emoji (😁) received a positive mean sentiment score in English, but a neutral to negative one in Mandarin. This is consistent with the text interpretations provided by participants. For example, when we asked how they interpret the English text scenario *"When is it?" "It's on Wednesday 😁"*, most participants perceived it quite positively. Some example interpretations are *"it is just a friendly emoji"*, *"she is looking forward to it"* and *"she's happy it's on Wednesday"*. On the other hand, when asked to interpret the Mandarin version of this text, all participants viewed it with a negative and sarcastic lens by saying *"she is nervous about the thing on Wednesday"* and *"he does not want to face this reality"*.

On the other hand, the "loudly crying face" emoji (😭) was rated as relatively negative in both English and Mandarin by our participants, and the text responses resonate with this overall negative connotation. However, they also reveal some additional nuances in how it is perceived differently in different languages. For example, when presented with the English text scenario *"When is it?" "It's on Wednesday 😭"*, many participants interpreted the message as the respondent having something bad coming up. For example, one participant wrote *"either the 'it' is something bad, or Wednesday is not a good time"*, while another speculated that *"there would be a prelim coming up and he did not study yet"*. When responding to the same message in Mandarin, however, participants gave a mix of positive (e.g., *"It's on Wednesday, expressed with gratitude or hope."*) and negative interpretations (e.g., *"I think my friend wants to express sadness and sorry about the event will be on Wednesday."*).

While we are not presenting a comprehensive analysis of the semantic interpretations of emojis, the examples above offer a glimpse into the potential reasons why participants attribute different sentiment scores to the same emojis in different linguistic contexts. In English texts, participants are likely to interpret emojis in alignment with their facial expressions. In Mandarin contexts, however, participants' interpretations are less contingent on emojis' facial expressions, leading to instances where the smiling 😁 is perceived as sarcastic, and the crying 😭 is understood as expressing gratitude sometimes.

From our analysis of participants' emoji preferences, as well as their sentiment and semantic interpretation of the emojis, we can now answer our *RQ*: although sharing some similarities, we have found clear evidence suggesting that English and Mandarin bilinguals' usage and interpretation of emojis differs across languages.

5 Discussion

In this study, we examined how bilinguals interpret emojis when texting in English and Mandarin respectively. By asking participants to pick the emojis they commonly use in English and Mandarin respectively, we found that they exhibit similar emoji preferences when texting in different languages. However, there are also some emojis that they only prefer using in one language than the other. Drawing upon this finding, we then specifically investigate their interpretation of five popular emojis across both languages: 😄, 😆, 😊, 😫 and 😁.

Examining each emoji's sentiment interpretations across languages, we found that 😄, 😆, and 😁 carry different emotional meanings depending on the language participants were using, while 😫 and 😊 do not exhibit statistically significant differences in their sentiment scores across languages. Thus our result suggests that English and Mandarin bilingual speakers do perceive some emojis differently in different linguistic contexts, although this is not true for every single emoji.

An interesting pattern emerges upon a closer look at participants' emoji interpretation within each of the two languages. In English contexts, participants attribute clearer emotional connotations to emojis, such as 😄 being positive, 😆 and 😁 being negative, while 😊 and 😫 being neutral, with a consensus. However, those emojis are interpreted in a more nuanced manner in Mandarin contexts. The overall negative sentiment scores for all five emojis, together with the divergence in individual interpretations, suggest that those emojis often carry layers of sarcasm and ambiguity. Consequently, individuals need to be more careful to "read between the lines", and interpret the emotions conveyed by emojis on a case-by-case basis in Mandarin contexts.

Overall, our findings are in line with the majority of studies on emoji usage in cross-cultural communication, which suggests that emojis carry different meanings in different cultural and linguistic contexts [3, 7, 17, 19]. More importantly, we found evidence that this difference exists not only for individuals coming from one single culture and speaking one language but also for those from a cross-cultural, multilingual background. Specifically, we have demonstrated that English and Mandarin bilingual speakers exhibit different emoji perception patterns when they are immersed in different linguistic contexts. Our findings also echo prior research on multilingual speakers, which suggests that people's psychological tendencies and behaviors change when they speak in different languages [2, 4, 13]. Our work extends this line of research by showing that this also holds for the context of emoji usage.

6 Limitations and Future Work

The biggest limitations of this work come from our participants' demographics and sample size. We only recruited Cornell students in our study, but this sample cannot represent the entire population due to their convergent age and educational background. In addition, we examined only English-Mandarin bilinguals, and we focused on a small subset of emojis in our analysis. Future research should involve a larger and more diverse participant pool, encompassing different age groups, and bilingual speakers of = a greater variety of languages. This will allow us to examine the emoji usage and interpretation for multilingual speakers more rigorously, potentially revealing more generalizable knowledge in the field.

Another limitation lies in the study design and data analysis. When we designed the text response questions, we wanted participants to respond in the same language the text scenario is written in (e.g., if they see a text exchange in Mandarin, they should type their potential response in Mandarin too). However, we did not make this requirement very clear in our survey. As a result, we got some English responses from Mandarin text scenarios, which is not what we desired, hence did not conduct a thorough analysis of the text response. Therefore, in the future, we aim to refine the survey design to elicit more precise responses from participants and to gather enough data on a larger scale to more accurately analyze the text responses using means such as the term frequency-inverse document frequency [8] or linguistic inquiry and word count [18].

7 Conclusion

This work presents an exploratory study of how bilingual individuals use emojis in different linguistic contexts. By asking 31 English and Mandarin bilingual undergraduate students at Cornell University to respond to text scenarios involving emojis in the two languages, we find that they use and interpret emojis differently when texting in different languages. Our findings are two-fold. First, we observe some divergent emoji preferences when participants text in different languages. Second, participants have different interpretations in terms of emotions conveyed by the same emoji in English v.s. in Mandarin. Specifically, when texting in English, participants are able to attribute clearer emotions to emojis. On the other hand, they seem to perceive emojis in a sarcastic and ambiguous way when seeing them in Mandarin texts. This emphasizes the need to consider cultural and language differences in understanding the emotional meanings conveyed by emojis in communication.

Disclosure of Interests. The authors have no competing interests to declare that are relevant to the content of this article.

References

1. Cha, Y., et al.: Complex and ambiguous: understanding sticker misinterpretations in instant messaging. Proc. ACM Hum.-Comput. Interact. **2**(CSCW), 30:1–30:22 (2018). https://doi.org/10.1145/3274299
2. Chen, S.X., et al.: Does language affect personality perception? A functional approach to testing the Whorfian hypothesis: language effects on personality perception. J. Pers. **82**(2), 130–143 (2014). https://doi.org/10.1111/jopy.12040
3. Cho, H., et al.: Human detection of cultural differences in pictogram interpretations. In: Proceedings of the 2009 International Workshop on Intercultural Collaboration, Palo Alto, California, USA, pp. 165–174. ACM (2009). https://doi.org/10.1145/1499224.1499250
4. Consani, C.: Code-Switching (2013). https://referenceworks.brillonline.com/entries/encyclopedia-of-ancient-greek-language-and-linguistics/*-SIM_00000427

 5. Herring, S.C., Dainas, A.R.: Gender and age influences on interpretation of emoji functions. Trans. Soc. Comput. **3**(2), 10:1–10:26 (2020). https://doi.org/10.1145/3375629
 6. Jiang, W.: The relationship between culture and language. ELT J. **54**(4), 328–334 (2000). https://doi.org/10.1093/elt/54.4.328
 7. Krekhov, A., et al.: Interpolating happiness: understanding the intensity gradations of face emojis across cultures. In: Proceedings of the 2022 CHI Conference on Human Factors in Computing Systems, pp. 1–17. Association for Computing Machinery, New York (2022). https://doi.org/10.1145/3491102.3517661
 8. Jing, L.-P., et al.: Improved feature selection approach TFIDF in text mining. In: Proceedings of the International Conference on Machine Learning and Cybernetics, Beijing, China, pp. 944–946. IEEE (2002). https://doi.org/10.1109/ICMLC.2002.1174522
 9. Logi, L., Zappavigna, M.: A social semiotic perspective on emoji: How emoji and language interact to make meaning in digital messages. New Media Soc. **25**(12), 3222–3246 (2023). https://doi.org/10.1177/14614448211032965
10. Miller, H., et al.: "Blissfully Happy" or "Ready toFight": varying interpretations of emoji. In: Proceedings of the International AAAI Conference on Web and Social Media, vol. 10, no. 1, pp. 259–268 (2016). https://doi.org/10.1609/icwsm.v10i1.14757
11. Neel, L.A.G., et al.: Emoji alter the perception of emotion in affectively neutral text messages. J. Nonverbal Behav. **47**(1), 83–97 (2023). https://doi.org/10.1007/s10919-022-00421-6
12. Novak, P.K., et al.: Sentiment of emojis. PLoS ONE **10**(12), e0144296 (2015). https://doi.org/10.1371/journal.pone.0144296
13. Paz, C., et al.: What happens when individuals answer questionnaires in two different languages. Front. Psychol. **12**, 688397 (2021). https://doi.org/10.3389/fpsyg.2021.688397
14. Ralston, D.A., et al.: Cultural accommodation: the effect of language on the responses of bilingual Hong Kong Chinese managers. J. Cross Cult. Psychol. **26**(6), 714–727 (1995). https://doi.org/10.1177/002202219502600612
15. Ramírez-Esparza, N., et al.: Do bilinguals have two personalities? A special case of cultural frame switching. J. Res. Pers. **40**(2), 99–120 (2006). https://doi.org/10.1016/j.jrp.2004.09.001
16. Robertson, A., et al.: Black or white but never neutral: how readers perceive identity from yellow or skin-toned emoji. Proc. ACM Hum.-Comput. Interact. **5**(CSCW2), 350:1–350:23 (2021). https://doi.org/10.1145/3476091
17. Takahashi, K., et al.: Is ☺ smiling? Cross-cultural study on recognition of emoticon's emotion. J. Cross-Cult. Psychol. **48**(10), 1578–1586 (2017). https://doi.org/10.1177/0022022117734372
18. Tausczik, Y.R., Pennebaker, J.W.: The psychological meaning of words: LIWC and computerized text analysis methods. J. Lang. Soc. Psychol. **29**(1), 24–54 (2010). https://doi.org/10.1177/0261927X09351676
19. Togans, L.J., et al.: Digitally saving face: an experimental investigation of cross-cultural differences in the use of emoticons and emoji. J. Pragmat. **186**, 277–288 (2021). https://doi.org/10.1016/j.pragma.2021.09.016
20. Zeng, X.: The emoji package Emoji support in (Lua)LaTeX

A User Review Analysis Tool Empowering Iterative Product Design

Qi Wu[✉]

Industrial Department, School of Mechanical Science and Engineering, Huazhong University of
Science and Technology, Wuhan 430074, China
qiwu5799@gmail.com

Abstract. Understanding user feedback and improving accordingly is an essential
phase in iterative product design. User reviews provide sufficient and various user
feedback about general experience, specific features, and bug reports. While the
traditional manual analysis may yield some insights, it is often constrained by limited sample sizes and potential biases. This paper introduces a user review analysis
tool equipped with a graphical user interface, based on multiple machine learning
and natural language processing techniques. This tool is designed to aid developers in rapidly acquiring a qualitative understanding of user experiences regarding
product features and topics, by illustrating user attitude evolution and summarizing diverse user opinions. The tool's performance is evaluated with datasets
from three different applications, each containing 50000 reviews. It was able to
identify major features and topics and illustrated the evolution of user attitudes.
Its effectiveness in summarizing diverse user opinions was also highlighted. The
user review analysis tool can enable developers to efficiently process and interpret large volumes of user feedback, thereby significantly enhancing the iterative
design process with data-driven insights.

Keywords: Iterative product design · User review analysis · Data-driven design

1 Introduction

App reviews are textual feedback associated with a star rating that app users can provide
to other users and app developers about their experience of an app [1]. App reviews
convey information on a variety of topics such as usability issues, feature requests, bug
reports or their attitudes towards the whole app or specific feature [2, 3]. Responding to
reviews not only keeps a better customer relationship [4] but also helps product iteration.
By analyzing app reviews, developers can learn how to maintain existing features to refine
user experience [5, 6], collect user test feedback for new-updated features [7], and even
gain insights for new features [8, 9].

Manual analysis is a direct method to understand user feedback. It provides a qualitative, in-depth understanding of user experiences from contextual expression, allowing
for the identification and prioritization of specific issues raised by users. However, manual analysis of user reviews is susceptible to various forms of human bias. Analysts may

C. Stephanidis et al. (Eds.): HCII 2024, CCIS 2119, pp. 168–177, 2024.
https://doi.org/10.1007/978-3-031-61966-3_19

unconsciously prioritize feedback that aligns with their preexisting personal experience, and cultural or linguistic background. Meanwhile, manual analysis is time-consuming and requires a vast human effort [10], which makes it only suitable for datasets with limited sample sizes.

Natural language processing (NLP) is the method that transforms user review's linguistic structure into data that can be processed by computers [11]. Pre-processing text data includes text normalization, cleaning and augmenting, where text is converted into a more consistent and standard form, unnecessary and irrelevant information is removed, and text data can be enriched with additional linguistic information to enhance its utility for further analysis [12]. After this, four key NLP techniques stand out, each serving a distinct purpose. Sentiment analysis interprets user emotions and presents with sentiment polarity, which gauges user satisfaction and attitude [13]. Text similarity identifies and groups reviews with similar viewpoints, enabling aggregating feedback about certain aspects of a product [14]. Pattern matching detects specific linguistic patterns or keywords, aiding in locating specific topics within the feedback [15]. Finally, collocation finding is utilized to uncover frequently co-occurring words or phrases, which can illuminate 'hot topics' or emerging trends in user feedback [16].

Machine learning (ML) techniques can be applied after the text data is vectorized, therefore advanced tasks such as information extraction, classification, and clustering become feasible [12]. These tasks enable product teams to gain a quantitative understanding of user feedback to inform future iteration. For instance, feature prioritization suggests considering features that matter [17], the impact of updates can be assessed by comparing feedback [18], and connecting user demographics and behaviour patterns may lead to new opportunities [19]. Integrating NLP and ML techniques offers a framework for product teams to make use of user feedback. When combined with qualitative insights, it can enable product teams to make data-driven decisions that align closely with user needs and market demands.

This study develops and introduces a tool that's feasible for non-tech developers in product teams to quickly gain an understanding of user experience from textual feedback. In this paper, how the tool was designed to make use of several NLP and ML algorithms to provide developers insights will be introduced, after introducing what constitutes the user review dataset and what can we expect from it. Then, the evaluation of this tool and the result will be presented to confirm its effectiveness in summarizing diverse user opinions.

2   User Review Dataset

A user review typically consists of 5 attributes: review text, 5-level rating, username, time, and app version. In this study, the user review datasets are collected from one mainstream app distribution platform, Google Play Store, with a node.js scraper, google-play-scraper module [20]. Gathering reviews from one platform eliminates the bias caused by app store [21] and frameworks [22]. The user reviews from the mentioned platform have additional attributes: review ID, thumbsUpCount (count of thumbs up one review receives from other users), and reply from the app holder with time (see Fig. 1). In this paper, the Twitter dataset is used for exemplification.

reviewId	userName	content	score	thumbsUpCount	at	replyContent	repliedAt	appVersion
cbe9f8f4-	Will Jones	THE VIDEOS ARE STILL GOING BLANK OR BLACK WHEN YOU CLICK ON THEN	1	1754	23/06/2023 00:14			9.94.0-release.0
e787429e	Frog	Cryptobots get priority over real humans. I can't post anything without seein	1	1050	22/06/2023 04:47			9.89.0-release.1
b719535c	Silver Jacka	Garbage app. Ads every other post. It's a very toxic place now.	1	987	21/06/2023 22:28			9.94.0-release.0
0a19bc0a	USERgame	Lately I haven't been able to watch a full video because either it suddenly st	4	1411	20/06/2023 07:34			9.93.0-release.1
24bd5554	Steve DeBe	Ad after ad after ad. So many ads. The ads aren't even good, it's all trash Ch	2	320	20/06/2023 02:54			9.93.0-release.1

Fig. 1. Part of the Twitter user review dataset

Additionally, some findings are extracted from inspecting the user review datasets: 1) One review may refer to a specific feature, a module, or the entire app. 2) Some features may have various names within reviews, especially when they are not labelled with text names. For instance, "algorithm", and "For you" may both refer to the mechanism that feeds users content based on a recommendation algorithm. 3) Multiple features may be mentioned in one review. 4) For usability issues, users tend to describe their goal, operation, and app's feedback, as well as how they fail to overcome the issue. 5) For new features, users tend to use adjectives to express their feelings about them.

3   User Review Analysis Tool

Inspired by the findings in the dataset section, I intend to make use of the reviews that mention specific product features and topics. A collection of user feedback on one feature or topic can be gathered from selecting concerned reviews. The collection can be analyzed by algorithms to illustrate users' attitude evolution. Furthermore, the collection can be clustered into groups, each of which stands for one major type of users' opinion on this feature or topic. Besides, the tool is expected to suggest popular features and topics for analysis, and a self-evaluation module for understanding and optimizing analysis performance will also be provided.

There are three major steps in using the tool to gain insights from user reviews:

3.1   Define Targets

In the first step, developers define the product features or topics for the tool to analyze, collectively called "targets". The process involves determining what are the valuable targets, identifying how users call them in reviews, and inputting target patterns for algorithm tracking. Two main sections, Reference and Input, are included to support this process.

Reference section (Fig. 2a) suggests developers about frequently discussed features and topics. Raw data table module, with reviews sorted in descending order of thumbUp-Count, enables developers to check reviews with more recognition first. In the exemplification, the developer could learn that users are experiencing issues with "Video", "Message", and "Notification" features, as well as they feel upset about the event "Elon Musk acquired Twitter". Meanwhile, Phrase detection module, making use of collocation to identify multi-word expressions, can automatically collect top-discussed topics from the reviews for developers, which is powered by gensim's models.phrases [16]. In the exemplification, topics like "Elon Musk", "video player", and "two factor authentication" are detected, indicating they should be inspected later.

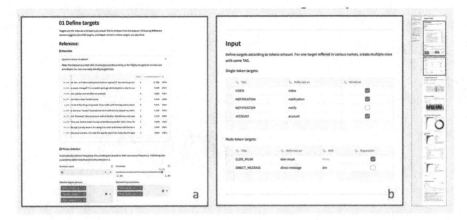

Fig. 2. Reference section proposes suggestions while Input section specifies patterns

Input section (Fig. 2b) is where developers specify the target patterns so that the algorithm, spacy's rule-based matching [15], can identify the targets from the reviews and extract concerning sentences. Two tables are provided in the tool, as identifying single-token targets and multi-token targets requires applying different linguistic features. "TAG" is a vital attribute across the tables, unifying all the names of one target, especially when the target is referred to more than one way. After specification, reviews mentioning multiple targets will be divided into parts by targets, and labelled with TAGs, preparing for upcoming process.

3.2 Visualize Users' Attitude

In the second step, developers can gain insights about users' attitudes towards each target. The algorithm will first perform sentiment analysis, powered by NLTK SentimentIntensityAnalyzer [23], on all targets' reviews. With the sentiment polarity assigned, a scatter plot and a boxplot are created to illustrate users' attitudes.

The scatter plot (Fig. 3a) provides developers with an overview of all targets' sentiment polarity trends. The tool allows checking each target individually by clicking the legend tag. In the exemplification, it can be interpreted that more than half of reviews on feature target "Video" are negative, and most of them are created during the week around 23rd April. This may indicate a common issue is frequently reported.

A boxplot (Fig. 3b) specifying users' sentiment distribution over time, i.e. the central tendency and variability, is built, especially when developers notice an abnormal pattern of one target in the previous step. The tool allows developers to adjust the time span with a slider. The boxplot not only makes users' attitude trend clearer but also highlights peak rises in review amount. In the exemplification, the number of reviews on "Video" reached about 60 to 80 per day in mid-to-late April, while no more than 20 in normal times. Meanwhile, the overall distribution of users' attitudes is negative. It is almost certain that this is caused by some updates during this period led to significant user experience issues.

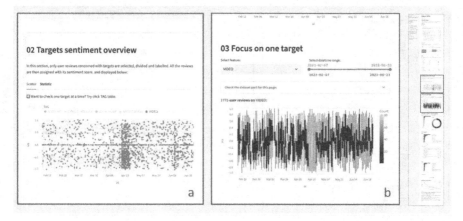

Fig. 3. Two graphs are provided to illustrate users' attitudes

3.3 Cluster User Opinions

In the final step, developers can gain qualitative insights from users' perspectives to learn why user experience is affected. The tool applied topic modelling algorithm, which is a NLP clustering technique powered by Gensim's model.ldamodel module [9]. For one target, semantically similar reviews are grouped into clusters. Each cluster is a collection of user reviews of similar opinions.

The tool provides a "Word count" histogram that list the words most relevant to the target as well as the number of occurrences (Fig. 4a). The default number of clusters to generate is set to 5, as the optimal number often lies into the range from 4 to 6 in practices, which can be adjusted accordingly by developers. Besides, a pie chart counts the number of reviews corresponding to each cluster, indicating the significance of each user opinions collection.

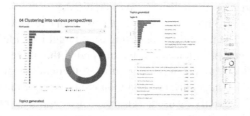

Fig. 4. Developers can check the ratio of clustered reviews before interpreting them

"Topics generated" (Fig. 4b) is where all the clusters are presented. The tool presents each cluster not only with the word-probability histogram, which lists the words constituting the cluster, but also with user reviews to make user opinions collection more interpretable. The reviews are scored with the word-probabilities and listed with a data frame. Reviews with higher scores are selected for interpretation as they manage more words of this cluster. By reading the reviews retrieved for each cluster, developers can quickly learn the major categories of user opinions. In the exemplification (Fig. 5), there are 5 (default number) clusters of user opinions on "Video":

- Topic 0, a collection of 355 reviews, is users expressing dissatisfaction towards the update around 20th – 30th April.
- Topic 1, a collection of 667 reviews, is users complaining video loading time too long, which is a long-term problem.
- Topic 2, a collection of 246 reviews, is users feeling upset about the new video module and asking it to be repaired or adjusted functions.
- Topic 3, a collection of 124 reviews, also concentrate around 20th – 30th April. Users reported that fast forwarding and rewinding function abnormally, wishing the app to restore the original version.
- Topic 4, a collection of 383 reviews, also concentrate around 20th – 30th April. Users describe various experience issues caused by the update.

Fig. 5. Exemplification of users' major opinions towards Twitter "Video" feature

The number of clusters is the essential parameter in the algorithm that affects the interpretability and the quality of the results. This tool provides a metric graph in the end, containing 3 metrics: Coherence, Perplexity, and topic average Jaccard Distance (JD), as well as the explanation. The graph indicates three aspects of the algorithm's performance, so developers can learn why when the result is hard to interpret and how to adjust to improve. To have an optimal clustering performance, developers may adjust the number of clusters at the beginning of this step.

4   Evaluation

4.1 Method

The tool's performance is assessed with user review datasets from three different apps: Twitter, Outlook, and Amazon, representing different categories: social media, professional productivity, and e-shopping. Each dataset contains 50,000 reviews, providing a comprehensive evaluation across these categories.

For each app mentioned, five targets including app features and non-feature topics discussed in reviews, single-token and multi-token, are defined. These targets were handpicked based on the reviews that received the most upvotes (thumbsUpCount). Every target's number of concerned reviews, scatter plot, boxplot, and metric graph are recorded. Initially, each target was set to generate five clusters, which was later adjusted according to inspect and metric graph. Cluster number, number of reviews gathered in each cluster, and each cluster's top 5 retrieved reviews are also recorded. To evaluate the performance, two major questions are proposed to measure: 1) For every target, do all the clusters talk about highly diverse content? 2) For the top 5 retrieved reviews in every cluster, are they all semantically related?

4.2 Result

Table 1. Evaluation records

App	Target	Class	Concerned reviews	Cluster number	Unique aspects	Retrieved reviews	Discrete reviews
Twitter	VIDEO	Feature	1775	6	3	30	4
	ACCOUNT	Topic	2068	6	5	30	6
	ELON_MUSK	Topic	4345	3	3	15	3
	DIRECT_MESSAGE	Feature	207	5	5	25	4
	NOTIFICATION	Feature	342	4	4	20	2
Amazon	SEARCH_BAR	Feature	852	5	5	25	1
	PRIME	Topic	395	6	5	30	3
	CART	Feature	372	5	4	25	3
	CRASH	Feature	562	5	3	25	3
	SEARCH_FILTER	Feature	195	4	3	20	3
Outlook	BROWSER	Feature	166	4	3	20	2
	JUNK_MAIL	Feature	681	4	4	20	1
	NOTIFICATION	Feature	1063	3	3	15	0
	INBOX	Feature	598	8	7	40	6
	DELETE	Feature	576	4	4	20	3

Table 1 is the overview of the evaluation records on the level of target. For all 15 targets formed from 3 apps: 72 topic clusters are generated, 61 of which can be considered as unique aspects; Among 360 retrieved reviews, only 45 of them discuss discrete opinions against others in the same topic clusters. All of them are distributed in different topic clusters, which makes it easy to identify to cause little confusion in interpretation.

As shown in Fig. 6, having a large number of reviews for one target does not necessarily yield a diverse range of meaningful topics. The figure illustrates a weak negative correlation between the volume of reviews and the number of meaningful topics generated for each target. This situation can be explained with: 1) The target topic is too simple to elicit diverse discussions. For example, although the Twitter topic "ELON_MUSK"

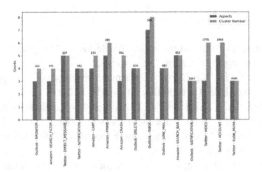

Fig. 6. Targets' proportion of clusters and unique aspects

had a high number of reviews, the reviews basically focused on two main subjects: his acquisition of the app, and the updates ever since. 2) The topic modelling algorithm may consolidate broader clusters if there are more unique aspects than the determined cluster numbers, therefor it treats smaller aspects as outliers.

By comparison, the Outlook "INBOX" feature produced seven unique aspects from just 598 reviews. This is likely because the inbox serves as the homepage and is multifunctional, dealing with email management and other activities. Reviews even mentioned aspects like junk mail filtering, which is another target feature.

In summary, the tool's performance can be comprehensively evaluated across different app categories, with specific metrics and adjustable parameters providing a nuanced understanding of user reviews.

5 Conclusion

The tool's target extraction function works well particularly when dealing with verbal or nominal targets, as well as multi-token topics that have up to two different names. The scatter plot effectively illustrates trends in user review volume, while the boxplot offers a coherent sentiment trend graph, aiding developers in comprehending user attitudes. By adjusting and iterating the number of clusters, the topic modelling algorithm categorizes semantically related reviews into thematic clusters, offering developers nuanced insights into user opinions.

On the other hand, the Phrase Detection module generates irrelevant target topics among the relevant ones, thereby necessitating manual verification. The target identification module has shortcomings when dealing with unnamed or unlabeled features. Moreover, although the tool offers quick insights, some manual intervention is still needed for cluster number adjustment to optimize its performance.

Overall, the tool provides a comprehensive understanding of user perspectives in most scenarios.

References

1. App Store: Ratings, reviews, and responses. Apple Inc. (2023) [Online]. Available: https://developer.apple.com/app-store/ratings-and-reviews/
2. Martin, W., Sarro, F., Jia, Y., Zhang, Y., Harman, M.: A survey of app store analysis for software engineering. IEEE Trans. Softw. Eng. **43**(9), 817–847 (2017)
3. Al-Hawari, A., Najadat, H., Shatnawi, R.: Classification of application reviews into software maintenance tasks using data mining techniques. Softw. Qual. J. **29**, 667–703 (2021)
4. G. P. S. Official: Reviews|Google Play Console Google (2023) [Online]. Available: https://play.google.com/console/about/reviews/
5. Maalej, W., Nabil, H.: Bug report, feature request, or simply praise? On automatically classifying app reviews. In: 23rd International Requirements Engineering Conference (2015)
6. Shams, R.A., Hussain, W., Oliver, G., Nurwidyantoro, A., Perera, H., Whittle, J.: Society-oriented applications development: investigating users' values from Bangladeshi agriculture mobile applications. In: Software Engineering in Society (SEIS) track of the 42nd International Conference on Software Engineering (ICSE), New York (2020)
7. Gao, C., et al.: Emerging app issue identification from user feedback: experience on wechat. In: Proceedings of the 41st International Conference on Software Engineering: Software Engineering in Practice, ICSE-SEIP '19. IEEE Press (2019)
8. Ceci, L.: Number of apps available in leading app stores as of 3rd quarter 2022. Statista, 8 Nov 2022 [Online]. Available: https://www.statista.com/statistics/276623/number-of-apps-available-in-leading-app-stores/
9. Blei, D.M., Ng, A.Y., Jordan, M.I.: Latent Dirichlet allocation. J. Machine Learn. Res. **3**, 993–1022 (2003)
10. van Vliet, M., Groen, E.C., Dalpiaz, F., Brinkkemper, S.: Identifying and classifying user requirements in online feedback via crowdsourcing. In: Madhavji, N.H., Pasquale, L., Ferrari, A., Gnesi, S. (eds.) Requirements engineering: foundation for software quality – 26th International Working Conference, REFSQ 2020, Pisa, Italy (2020)
11. Manning, C.D., Schutze, H.: Foundations of Statistical Natural Language Processing MIT Press (1999)
12. Dabrowski, J., Letier, E., Perini, A., Susi, A.: Analysing app reviews for software engineering: a systematic literature review. Empiri. Softw. Eng. **27**(2) (2022)
13. Buckley, K., Thelwall, M.: Sentiment strength detection in short informal text. J. Am. Soc. Inform. Sci. Technol. **62**(2), 419 (2010)
14. Wang, C., Zhang, F., Peng, L., Daneva, M., Sinderen, M.v.: Can app changelogs improve requirements classification from app reviews? An exploratory study. In: Proceedings of the 12th ACM/IEEE International Symposium on Empirical Software Engineering and Measurement, ESEM '18. ACM, New York (2018)
15. Spacy: Rule-based matching. Explosion AI (2023) [Online]. Available: https://spacy.io/usage/rule-based-matching#matcher
16. Řehůřek, R.: Phrase (collocation) detection. Gensim (2022) [Online]. Available: https://radimrehurek.com/gensim/models/phrases.html
17. Noei, E., Zhang, F., Wang, S., Zou, Y.: Towards prioritizing user-related issue reports of mobile applications. Empir. Softw. Eng. **24**(4), 1964–1996 (2019)
18. Wang, S., Wang, Z., Xu, X., Sheng, Q.Z.: App update patterns: how developers act on user reviews in mobile app stores in: service-oriented computing. In: 15th International Conference, ICSOC, Malaga, Spain (2017)
19. Tizard, J., Rietz, T., Blincoe, K.: Voice of the users: a demographic study of software feedback behavior. In: 28th IEEE International Requirements Engineering Conference, Zurich (2020)

20. Olano, F.: Google-play-scraper (2019) [Online]. Available: https://github.com/facundoolano/google-play-scraper
21. Ali, M.,Joorabchi, M.E.,Mesbah, A.: Same app, different app stores: a comparative study. In: Proceedings of the 4th International Conference on Mobile Software Engineering and Systems (2017)
22. Malavolta, I., Ruberto, S., Soru, T., Terragni, V.: End users' perception of hybrid mobile apps in the google play store. In: Proceedings of the 4th International Conference on Mobile Services (2015)
23. Bird, S., Klein, E., Loper, E.: Natural Language Processing with Python., O'Reilly Media Inc. (2009)

Interaction in the Museum

Augmented Reality and Interactive Experience Design of the Emperor Qianlong's San Xi Hall in the Palace Museum

Ying Chen and Dehua Yu[✉]

Beijing Institute of Technology, Beijing 100081, China
yudehuabit@163.com

Abstract. Augmented reality technology has been widely used in museums. Visitors can combine virtual images and real scenes through AR glasses, which can enhance the sense of experience, and achieve immersive viewing and interaction. The research was mainly applied to the Palace Museum's official study, San Xi Hall, a small window room with a heated brick bed surrounded by various cultural relics. The virtual emperor is set in there and combined with the real scene to restore the scene of the entire study. Visitors can put their hands into the view of AR glasses and use gestures to interact with the virtual emperor and relics, and the vivid virtual emperor will be presented in a variety of interesting poses. One finger click on the relic can enter a new page to see more information. Rotate wrist at any angle, or pinch it between thumb and forefinger to zoom in, to see the details more clearly. Click the hat on his head, he will put the hat on the hat rack; Click his hand and he will start to pick up the brush of Chinese calligraphy and say "Let me show you Chinese calligraphy!". It allows visitors to have a clearer understanding of relics in San Xi Hall, feel the daily study of Emperor Qianlong. It is a positive exploration and practice for the digital dissemination of traditional Chinese culture. And this interactive mode of immersive visits can be extended to all museums and galleries, which is a beneficial attempt.

Keywords: Augmented Reality · Scene Interaction Design · San Xi Hall · The Palace Museum

1 Introduction

San Xi Hall in the Palace Museum Beijing China was the study room where Emperor Qianlong of Qing Dynasty read and wrote. It is a small room near the window, which is equipped with a heatable brick bed, set up the hat rack, the four treasures of the study and other cultural relics [1].

In the traditional museum exhibition, there are problems such as boring display form or single interaction mode, so that visitors cannot deeply experience Chinese traditional culture and exquisite cultural relics. The common mobile AR display screen is too limited to achieve the effect of immersive viewing.

The research will explore the use of AR glasses and gesture interactive exhibition technology, try to break the deadlock of the traditional visiting mode and let the static cultural relics and scenes "move". It allows visitors to have a lot of interaction and communication with cultural relics and their former owners. So that visitors have an intuitive and interesting cognition of the scene and cultural relics, and explore the unknown culture with curiosity. Immersive knowledge experience can be more easily understood and remembered [2]. The new type of immersive experience is not yet widespread for most museums, and still needs to be deeply designed and explored. Therefore, the small and simple scene of San Xi Hall is selected as a case for interaction design practice. So that visitors can feel the use of cultural relics and the leisure of ancient Chinese literati in scene.

Before the visit, visitors can rent AR glasses at the rental equipment department at the entrance of the Palace Museum. The glasses form a system with the positioning device in the museum, and the corresponding AR effect will be displayed when visitors arrive at the corresponding palace. The whole system will be maintained by the Palace Museum staff. San Xi Hall immersive experience process consists of real scenes, cultural relics and virtual demonstrations of the Emperor Qianlong and his movements.

2 Interactive Display Effect of Relics

Simple gesture interaction can make the virtual cultural relics move in the hand. Visitors can not only carefully appreciate cultural relics, but also understand the knowledge of cultural relics in a more interesting way and explore the cultural connotation of cultural relics.

2.1 AR Glasses Recognize Relics

First, visitors need to wear AR glasses and approach the scene before visiting. Secondly, the AR glasses will automatically capture the cultural relics placed in the scene, and the edges of them are accentuated by bright solid lines (see Fig. 1). The sound of the glasses' legs and the text on the screen will give some instruction, guiding visitors to start interactive exploration in a certain order of gestures. The virtual emperor will say to visitors, "Hello, welcome to San Xi Hall, I am Emperor Qianlong, please start your journey of discovery!".

With instruction, visitors put their hands into the field of view of AR glasses to trigger interactive commands. Throughout the process, each time visitors enter a new step of interaction, AR glasses will be guided by sound and text. Placing index finger on the relic and clicking will trigger the selected command, and it will be highlighted. For example, when a visitor points to a Ruyi on a table, the glasses recognize it and say, "This is a decorative Ruyi, click again to see it in detail." Click again will trigger the display information command to enter the page for viewing the details of cultural relics (see Fig. 2).

Fig. 1. The state that visitors see through AR glasses before interaction.

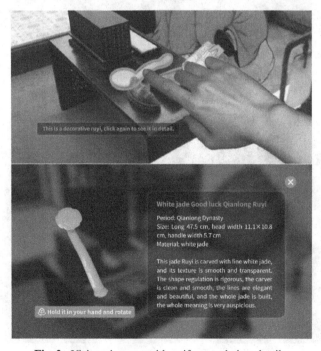

Fig. 2. Visitors interact with artifacts and view details.

2.2 A Gesture Interactive All-Round Display of Virtual Relics

After entering the cultural relic details page, visitors can see more information of the cultural relic, year of manufacture, storage location, material used and other information. And the page will prompt "Hold it in hand and rotate", and when the glasses catch the gesture of grip, it will "embed" the cultural relic in the hand (see Fig. 3). Visitors can rotate wrist at any angle, or pinch it between thumb and forefinger to zoom in, to see the details more clearly. When the glasses capture the finger scaling gesture, the cultural relics will be scaled with the finger pinching, to achieve the effect of magnifying the details. The page prompts "Release hand and return to the previous page.", open five fingers and return to the details page. Click the "cross" in the upper right corner to close the details page and return to the scene (see Fig. 4).

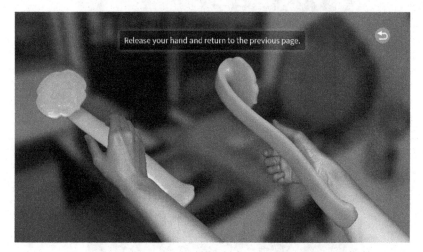

Fig. 3. Rotate wrist at any angle to see the details more clearly.

Fig. 4. Pinch it between thumb and forefinger to zoom in Ruyi.

3   Interactive Display Effect of Virtual Emperor

If only interacting with cultural relics and words, it is not enough to make tourists feel interesting and attractive. Adding the former protagonist of the scene to the scene can make the whole atmosphere more dynamic and vivid. In this way, visitors can have a direct conversation with the virtual emperor, which adds even more possibilities to the visiting experience. This section will be the essence of the immersive tour.

3.1   Set the Form of the Virtual Emperor in the Scene

Clicking on the image of the virtual emperor will bring visitors to a page where they can select the forms of the emperor. There are three forms of the virtual emperor that can be set: Write, Read and Rest (see Fig. 5). When the finger falls on the emperor in the "Write" state, he will say, "I can show you many excellent works of calligraphy." Visitors will enjoy the calligraphy of famous Chinese calligraphers in the scene. When the finger falls on the emperor in the "Read" state, he will say "I can talk to you." Visitors will see the virtual emperor demonstrate the use of various cultural relics in the scene. When the finger falls on the emperor in a "Rest" state, he will say "I am very sleepy." Visitors will trigger some unexpected interactions.

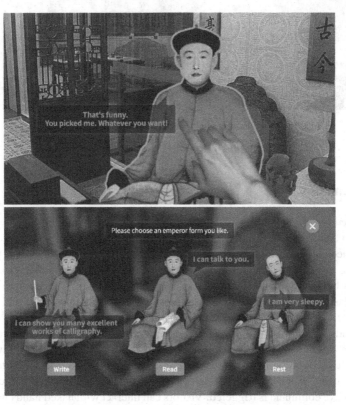

Fig. 5. The process of setting forms of Emperor Qianlong in scene.

3.2 Gesture Interact with the Virtual Emperor

After setting the form in the scene, visitors can click any part of the virtual emperor to trigger interesting interaction. Click the hat on his head, he will put it on the hat rack and scratch his head (see Fig. 6); Click his hand and he will start to pick up the brush of Chinese calligraphy and say "Let me show you Chinese calligraphy!" (see Fig. 7).

Fig. 6. Click the hat on emperor's head and trigger taking off hat interaction.

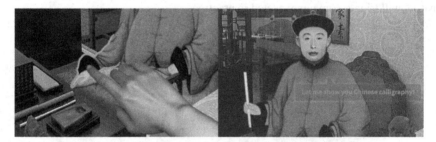

Fig. 7. Click the emperor's hand and trigger writing interaction.

4 Technology

Augmented reality technology is the perception of the real world, through some digital devices to add visual, text and sound information to the physical world [3]. It widely used in medical, education, entertainment and other fields, and it can also be used in interactive visits. This research can be realized by directly using AR glasses in the market as hardware and developing a system for maintenance by museums. Most of the AR glasses on the market already support simple gesture interaction and can easily manipulate the interface, such as Apple Vision Pro, Microsoft HoloLens, MIJIA and other brands. In addition, the MS COCO dataset released by the Microsoft can be used as training, combined with powerful real-time feedback algorithm of YOLOv4 [4].

Gesture recognition in this research adopts the naked hand interaction technology based on vision. When the camera on the glasses frame recognizes the four gestures set, the interactive command is triggered. Visitors can interact with naked hands without any sensors, which is more in line with users' interaction habits [5]. The whole process does not involve complex interaction, visitors only need to perform four semantic gestures of "click", "view", "zoom" and "release", and other demonstration parts are completed by the animation autonomously, with high usability and fault tolerance.

5 Conclusions

This research focuses on the digital display of Emperor Qianlong's daily studying, and the interaction between visitors and stationery in San Xi Hall in the Palace Museum Beijing China. With the help of AR technology and gesture interaction, visitors will have the opportunity to immerse themselves in the augmented reality display environment, interact with the real relics and virtual emperor.

Augmented reality technology is a good way to combine the real San Xi Hall scene of the Palace Museum with the virtual image of Emperor Qianlong in a humorous and understandable way, which is an interesting cultural design practice.

The whole process not only allows visitors to experience Chinese traditional culture, but also increases peoples' confidence in national culture, so that more visitors are interested in learning about it, which is conducive to the spread and innovation of traditional Chinese culture. This interactive and experiential design approach can be extended to the entire Palace Museum, where visitors can see virtual emperor, his concubines and ministers in the Palace Museum, and even break through the limitations of time and space to interact with virtual historical figures. This immersive visiting and interactive model can be promoted to all museums and art galleries, which is a beneficial and positive attempt.

Acknowledgments. Thank my tutor for providing me with valuable guidance and advice, and the school for giving me such a good platform and opportunity to do my research.

Disclosure of Interests. The authors have no competing interests to declare that are relevant to the content of this article.

References

1. Yan, G.: Appreciate the origin of "San Xi Hall." Art Panorama **6**, 110 (2011)
2. Crossley, T., Goepel, G., Guida, G: Augmenting beyond the physical: DMU constellation, a mixed reality exhibition experience that promotes participatory engagement and distributed access. In: Arai, K. (ed.) Proceedings of the Future Technologies Conference (FTC) 2023, Volume 3. FTC 2023. Lecture Notes in Networks and Systems, vol. 815, pp. 419–429. Springer, Cham (2023). https://doi.org/10.1007/978-3-031-47457-6_27
3. H. Lypak, N. Kunanets, N. Veretennikova, H. Matsiuk, T. Kramar and O. Duda: An information system project using augmented reality for a small local history museum. In: 2023 IEEE 18th International Conference on Computer Science and Information Technologies (CSIT), pp. 1–4. IEEE, Lviv (2023)
4. Li, W., Zhang, H., Zhang, Z., Li, C.: Human-computer interaction system based on gesture recognition. In: Proceedings of SPIE 12328, Second International Conference on Optics and Image Processing (ICOIP 2022), vol. 123281B (2022)
5. Zhang, W., Lin, Z.Y., Cheng, J., Ke, M.Y., Deng, X.M., Wang, H.A.: Survey of dynamic hand gesture understanding and interaction. J. Softw. **32**(10), 3051–3067 (2021)

Research on the Design of Science Museum Service System Based on User Experience

Xinran Huang(✉) ⓘ and Yuhong Shen ⓘ

Tsinghua University, Beijing 100000, China
hxr22@mails.tsinghua.edu.cn

Abstract. In the era of digitalization and the emergence of experience economy, science museums are facing a lot of difficulties and challenges: 1. The social function of museums is moving from "popularity enhancement" to "deepening of the degree of use" as a service challenge. 2. The popularization of science and education in commercial institutions is in full swing. More and more science popularization institutions are doing the same type of educational activities as museums. 3. The boundaries of the function of science museums are beginning to blur, not only the display of "objects", but also the diversified development of a single exhibition function can no longer meet the needs of the people. The main contradiction of domestic science museums is that the government-led construction of science museums has realized the importance of audience experience, but there is no way to provide users with immersive service experience.

In this paper, the pain points of the user needs of science museums are summarized as user experience oriented, and the interview method and user journey and service blueprint are utilized to construct a service design system of science museums, with a view to providing users of science museums with more complete services. It is complementary to science museums that already have a spatial base to provide visitors with a more complete service experience.

Keywords: science museum · service design · user experience

1 Challenges for Science Museums to Serve the Public

1.1 Transformation of the Social Function of Science Museums

At present, museums have become an important choice of life and leisure for urban citizens and an important window for domestic and foreign tourists to experience Chinese culture. With the free opening of museums and the convenience of traveling, the huge number of visitors has caused a sharp increase in the pressure on museum service facilities, service personnel and exhibition space, which in turn affects the quality of public visits and experience evaluation. As of 2016, China's various types of registered museums amounted to more than 4,690, receiving 850 million visitors annually. Among them, the top three visitors in 2016 were 16 million from the Palace Museum, 7.55 million from the National Museum, and 6.3 million from the Shanghai Science and Technology Museum. According to the national science and technology statistics released by the

Ministry of Science and Technology in 2021, there were 1,677 science and technology museums and science and technology museums in the country in 2021 [1]. Science and technology museums are large in number and fast in development, and they are the most dynamic type of museums, as well as the main force and vanguard in carrying out public science education [2].

At the same time, the problem of differentiated service needs of visitors is prominent, the China Youth Daily survey in 2015 showed that only 17.3% of respondents often go to the museum, 61.1% of respondents occasionally visit, the reasons for which include insufficient accessibility of the museum, inconvenient access to information, weak interaction and other service pain points. The above seemingly contradictory data reflects the challenge of the social function of science museums from "increasing popularity" to "deepening the degree of use", which is essentially a contradiction between the demand for social public services and the shape of museums.

1.2 Outstanding Contradiction Between Supply and Demand

Some scholars have identified six factors that influence visitors to museums: "socializing or interacting with others, tendency to do meaningful activities, desire to stay in a comfortable and carefree environment, accepting new challenges and experiences, learning and researching, and actively participating in leisure." Under these demands, contemporary museums have become a diversified venue for education, leisure, entertainment, and even public spirituality, and most of these non-exhibition behaviors take place in public spaces.

Science museums have long been limited by technology, space, operational thinking and exhibition capacity, and a series of contradictions between public demand and supply are prominent (weak visitor experience, little participation, a single tour line, low degree of openness, etc.). As museums have been positioned as an important part of the social public service experience, science museums, in addition to perfecting the traditional role of "keeping things" (collection, research, education), how to take root in the community and fulfill the responsibility of social services is the challenge of its new role. This challenge comes mainly from technological changes in the way public services are provided and from the consumer characteristics of visitors, such as open sharing and interactive experiences.

2 Current Situation and Service Design of Science Museums

2.1 Public Services in Science Museums

Museums belong to the public cultural service organizations, providing high quality public services to the audience. Since the advocacy of user-centered, so when they come to visit, at least they should be allowed to enjoy a home away from home service. But the interesting thing is that this consensus value judgment, not in the real world to get enough response, the museum does not have a restaurant, storage inconvenience, lack of seats and other phenomena are common. Epistemology is unable to bridge the gap between the "past" and the "reality" in a short period of time, and this gap is shaped by specific historical and social scenarios and their value positions. Because "the museum is in the society", the museum as a part of the society, is the product of the society. [3] Although how to provide services for the public has been the focus of museums since the advent of the public museum era, in fact, the awareness and enthusiasm of museums to serve the public have been perfected over the centuries in the process of socialization, and have not been achieved overnight.

The situation of museums in our country is different from that of foreign countries. China was influenced by the Soviet Union and had a serious object worship complex, while attaching importance to social propaganda. After the establishment of the People's Republic of China, China's museums basically adopted the macro and micro management mode of the former Soviet Union [4]. Macro, the former Ministry of Culture under the Administration of Cultural Relics, responsible for the management of the national cultural relics museums. At the beginning of its construction, it advocated the concept of "focusing on the protection of cultural relics", and the value judgment derived from it has been influential to this day. The issue of the public is not on the agenda, because only in the utilization of cultural relics, the service recipients will be discussed. Slightly different is that, at the micro level, China's museums, modeled on the Soviet Union's "Three Departments and One Room" model, created the Department of Publicity and Education or the Department of Mass Work, [5] objectively still partially allocated attention to the audience. However, at that time, the "Ministry of Mass Work", "Ministry of Propaganda and Education" is similar to the preaching institutions, with a condescending, passive indoctrination of the characteristics of the times, usually focusing on social propaganda, rather than public education.

In conclusion, since museums in China mainly adopt the curator responsibility system or the curator responsibility system under the leadership of the Party Committee, and both personnel and financial powers are vested in the higher authorities, museums in fact lack the motivation mechanism to really pay attention to the audience. Although the provision of quality services is the basic requirement of the museum as a public institution, but if not from the system, planning, funding, institutions, personnel, evaluation, incentives and other management and operational reforms, the internal motivation of the institution will not be activated, and intended to provide in-depth services, relying only on the goodwill of practitioners is not sustainable.

2.2 Service Design Thinking and Methods

Service design thinking was first proposed to solve the problem of total quality management, and after the research of service design by multiple scholars, service design is now commonly defined as a design thinking and methodology that integrates multiple disciplines, such as service science, design, management, and software engineering [6], which starts from the user's point of view, adheres to the principle of human-centeredness [7], and applies the method of user participation to globally analyze the service system, discover innovation points to create a perfect service experience journey for users [8]. The service design process is roughly divided into four stages: analysis and planning, innovation and design, design and evaluation, and organization and implementation [9], and the methods corresponding to each stage can help designers cultivate service design thinking and visualize complex problems.

From a theoretical point of view, service design is to improve the sustainability and adaptability of the service system by meeting the main needs of users throughout the service life cycle, thereby realizing value co-creation and benefit sharing. From a practical point of view, service design is to transform intangible services into tangible interactions through service touchpoints, creating a unified and coherent user experience journey for users. Therefore, the user is the core element of service design, and user-centered design can better focus on the users themselves, tap their needs, and design the best service experience journey. Therefore, cutting into the research of museum experience design from the perspective of service design brings more possibilities for the personalization and differentiation of museum experience services, and its focus on process and touchpoint visualization can help museums achieve emotional interaction and sustainability, which can better realize the public service nature of museums and enhance the audience's experience satisfaction.

3   Shanghai Planetarium Service System Design

3.1   Status of Service Design Issues in the Shanghai Planetarium

The above phenomenon triggered the planetarium to start thinking about how to give users a better experience. Shanghai Planetarium is located in Lingang New City, 70 km away from downtown. Although Metro Line 16 can be directly connected, the word journey still takes 1.5–2 h. The current status of service design problems of Shanghai Planetarium: 1. Let users give up the colorful commercial activities in the city center, choose to visit the planetarium, the public weekend entertainment time is only two days, the planetarium is far away from the city, need to give users a reason to stay in the planetarium for a day. 2. How to give young people to provide appropriate services, to win the sense of identity of young people. 3. How can exhibitions and educational activities be made more "dynamic" so that the public is willing to visit them regularly? Exhibitions and education are the two pillars of museums. The permanent exhibitions of museums are limited to a long renewal cycle, while educational activities are competing with commercial organizations, so how can museums always win and always be new [10].

3.2   Shanghai Planetarium User Journey Map

Based on the above background, the experience strategy design methodology is utilized to carry out research work on the future audience's visiting needs of the Shanghai Planetarium, and accordingly to carry out the top-level strategy design planning, to attract the audience who have not come to visit, and to attract the audience who have come to come again and again. This study introduces the service design research method into the museum field, and its purpose is to propose design strategies to enhance the adhesion between the target audience and the museum, and to improve the influence and reputation of the museum through the front-end research of audience experience.

Before visiting, visitors make preparations for the visit, such as checking the museum exhibitions, preparing travel supplies and taking transportation to the museum. Enter the museum to brush ID card to enter the museum security check and store items. Learn about the exhibitions in advance, understand the distribution of the museum and find the exhibition halls.

During the tour, visitors queue up to enter, scan the code to listen to the QR code explanation, and read the basic information of the pavilion. Interact with the interactive devices in the pavilion, leave the pavilion, take a short break, go to the next pavilion, and experience the science trivia game in the middle of the tour. At the end of the tour, look for restrooms to rest in the cafe, chat, drink water, browse the cultural and creative spots, and buy souvenirs.

After your visit, remove your stored items, take transportation, and leave the Science Museum. Share your visit with your friends and look up information to learn about places of interest.

3.3 Shanghai Planetarium Service System Construction

Through the analysis of the physical environment of the Shanghai Planetarium and user needs, the Shanghai Planetarium experience service system is constructed, and the service system contains the following features: **Introducing member services**: In addition to using data to enhance the visitor's experience in the offline planetariums, the planetariums need to actively utilize the power of data to provide better member services in other aspects, such as the establishment of a detailed membership system so that the customer service staff can quickly identify the user's membership level and relevant information when there is a telephone inquiry. For example, a detailed membership system should be established so that when a caller inquires, the customer service staff can quickly recognize the user's membership level and related information. At the same time, the use of these data is used to enhance the affinity with the members, the staff will further deepen the understanding of the state of members' needs, such as the number and content of the small activities they booked for science popularization, because mastering these data can help the planetarium to understand the members and provide them with more personalized exchanges. Through these membership services, not only can the planetarium keep in touch with its loyal members, but also attract more new members.

Offline Experience Optimization: For the Shanghai Planetarium, a huge museum space, is an important channel for the Planetarium to communicate with users and increase stickiness for cash. First of all, interest-based museum guidelines can maximize the user's preferences. App will analyze the user's relevant information to determine which exhibition hall the user likes to go to the most, when the user enters the museum is about to open the visit, app will be predicted exhibition halls of the highest priority recommended routes to the user, to remind the user of the guest target exhibition halls of the traffic flow, to help the user to stagger play to avoid crowds and so on. Secondly the app links the user's payment function, where food and souvenir cards can be easily purchased in the app. Users can also check the show time, bus waiting time and food ordering waiting time in the park on the app. The quantitative management helps users to avoid the embarrassment of waiting and also improves the user experience.

Constructing Social Circles and Stimulating Astronomical Topics: For young people, only by penetrating into their familiar social circles can they enter their world.

The planetarium hopes to appear repeatedly in the audience's social network, just like the Netflix tea, to stimulate the sense of "topic" in the circle of friends of young people. Combined with the trend that visitors are more and more inclined to show off, the museum will be able to bring its own attributes that are suitable for showing off. For example, in the NifreL Museum in Japan, due to the introduction of a large number of art installations in the museum, a large number of young people are attracted to come here to take pictures and post articles as a souvenir and a symbol of their lifestyle, in the hope that through the communication and dissemination of interpersonal communication, it will stimulate the audience's curiosity about the planetarium, and make the visit to the planetarium become a symbol of their identity (see Fig. 1).

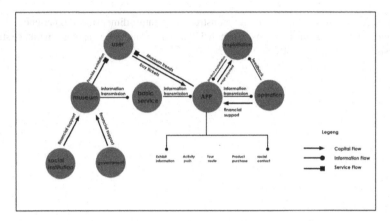

Fig. 1. Shanghai Science Museum Service System

4 Conclusion

The diversification of leisure and entertainment makes experience become the key to museum public service, and the thinking and methods of service design provide an effective way to improve museum user experience. Based on the environmental research of Shanghai Planetarium, the needs of user experience before, during and after the exhibition and the service design strategy of the museum are clarified, so as to construct a new museum service system. In the new service system through the combination of online applet and offline personalized experience, to improve the service quality and optimize the user experience. Therefore, the service design contributes to the maximization of the science education value of science museum exhibits, and also provides new ideas for science museum experience research.

References

1. Liu, J., Liu, X.: Research on "Internet+" museum public service design based on role cognition--taking the forbidden city museum as an example. Decoration (11), 118–119 (2017)

2. Ministry of Science and Technology. Ministry of Science and Technology releases national science and technology statistics for the year 2021 (2022). Accessed 10 June 2023
3. Yang, L., Pan, S. (eds.): Study on the Development Situation of Contemporary Western Museums, p. 19. Xueyuan Publishing House, Beijing (2005)
4. Yan, J.: Theory and Practice of Museums, p. 335. Zhejiang Education Press, Hangzhou (1998)
5. Duan, Y.: Contemporary Chinese Museums, p. 107. Yilin Press, Nanjing (2017)
6. Chen, J.: Service Design-Definition, Language, Tools. Jiangsu Phoenix Art Publishing House, Nanjing (2016)
7. Luo, S., Zou, W.: Status and progress of service design. Pack. Eng. **39**(24), 43–53 (2018)
8. Stickdorn, M., Schneider, J.: This is Service De-sign Thinking: Basics-Tools-Cases. AMS: BIS Publishers (2011)
9. Ning, F., Zhu, X., Zhang, Y.: Product Service Design. China Ocean Law Press, Qingdao (2017)
10. Chen, Y., Wang, C., Shi, C., et al.: Constructing a multi-dimensional experience of future science popularization museums--Shanghai Planetarium audience visiting experience strategy design. Ind. Des. Res. (00), 307–315 (2018)

Research on the Design of Art Healing Applications in Museums Under the Theory of Embodied Cognition

Xinran Huang(✉) 🆔

Tsinghua University, Beijing 100000, China
`hxr22@mails.tsinghua.edu.cn`

Abstract. Against the backdrop of global demographic and modern lifestyle changes, the public health crisis has become more acute and has led to many societal problems. Artistic healing in museums has presented itself as a place of healing in the wake of the new Crown Pneumonia. The historic shift in the educational focus of museums from promoting the information and value of collections to engaging in experiences filled with personal meaning has also changed the mindset of practitioners, policymakers, and the general public to be more convinced that the power of museums lies in creating a better world through healing and improving lives. The challenge, however, is how to make museums have a positive impact on people's health through artistic healing.

Art therapy in museums utilizes non-verbal media, including but not limited to artwork, weaving, interactive media, and robotics, to stimulate the senses of the visitor's body, assisting the visitor in transforming the world of direct experience into a cognitive or psychological world and projecting that cognition onto the objects in the collection. Thus, the essence of art healing in museums is the embodied interaction of the visitor's body with the medium and the environment. This paper explores the design method framework of art healing application of museums from the perspective of embodied cognition and proposes that the art healing function of museums can be systematically designed from the body perception layer, the behavior control layer, and the spirit construction layer. In the body perception layer, there are three ways in museum art healing: 1. Museum exhibits 2. Ways to collect exhibits 3. Museum environment. These three elements attract visitors and encourage them to participate in the experience. Five elements in the Behavioral Control layer: connecting, noticing, giving, continually learning, and being proactive. The five elements build a positive state of mind and body. In the Spirit Building Layer, visitors realize the creation of abstract concepts such as meaning and are soothed by the artwork during the embodied interaction of healing through multiple senses.

Keywords: Art Healing · Museum · Embodied Cognition

C. Stephanidis et al. (Eds.): HCII 2024, CCIS 2119, pp. 195–203, 2024.
https://doi.org/10.1007/978-3-031-61966-3_22

1 Introduction

The rapid pace of development in modern society has increased the pressure on people's mental world, and psychological symptoms such as anxiety and depression have become major problems for contemporary people. Compared with traditional physical medication and professional psychotherapy, art healing provides a solution with a lower threshold. Many scholars have gradually paid attention to the natural healing function of art in recent years. Among the many art forms, the visual medium of painting is the most widely used in art therapy. Art therapy cooperates with public institutions in non-medical environments, such as museums and art galleries, where the places surrounded by works of art provide a relaxing and pleasant atmosphere for the crowds that come to visit [1]. The development of museum functions has been diversifying in recent years, with museums not only providing new venues for patients in need of art healing, but also bringing a turning point in the development of museums. Focusing art healing on developing the emotional potential of museum collections highlights the healing function of art and helps museums advance change and development [2].

1.1 Art Healing in Museums

The concept of art healing is derived from the field of psychology and is a psychotherapeutic intervention in which ideas and emotions are materialized through the medium of art forms. There are many art forms of art therapy, mainly through the visual, music, dance and other art as the medium of intervention for patients [3]. Modern art psychotherapy developed with the psychiatry movement in the first half of the 20th century, relying on basic theories such as psychoanalysis and psychodynamics [4]. With the openness of the boundaries of modern psychology, art has gained new attempts to be integrated with psychological therapy because of its characteristics of stylistic expression, pattern generalization, symbolic symbolism, and application of color, as well as the emotional narrativity behind it [5].

Art is an important nourishment for human beings. The human brain is divided into left and right brains, with the left brain being responsible for logic and the right brain being in charge of image differentiation, etc. If too much logic is used, the left brain will become stressed. If too much logical thinking is utilized, the left brain will be under pressure, and the brain needs to be properly soothed by the right brain, and if it is not relaxed in time, the nervous system will continue to be tense. If not relaxed in time, the nervous system will continue to be tense. At this point, art therapy can provide good emotional relief. Compared with art therapy, art healing has a wider range of applicability, and its focus is on "healing" rather than treatment [6].

Art healing in museums refers to the creation of a peaceful and relaxing space for people through the appreciation of cultural and artistic works, helping them to reduce anxiety and pressure and alleviate the symptoms of mental illness. However, at present, art healing in museums still focuses on viewing visual images such as paintings and sculptures, and the evaluation and feedback mechanism for the healing effect of the viewers is not perfect. Research on other forms of art healing in museums is still relatively scarce.

1.2 Museums as Healing Environments for Mental Health, Personal and Social Development

Today, museums are engaged in a great deal of innovation and practice around health and well-being. Museums play a positive role in at least three ways. Museums can aid relaxation, which is an immediate intervention that promotes beneficial changes in physiology and mood; they also encourage people to socialize, as the process of viewing exhibitions is a process of understanding the feelings and thoughts of others, and will enhance interactive socialization with others; and they enhance health education, using public health campaigns to provide a wider range of healthy environments that actively contribute to the achievement of public health.

Reduce Anxiety and Stress and Improve Cognition. Studies have shown that physical, psychological and social aspects of a patient's condition can be improved when they are in a museum environment. Indeed, levels of stress hormones are reduced after a museum visit. Museums and their programs promote dynamic relationships by providing "safe space, pleasure, and time to think and connect" [7]. Art therapists have claimed that individual subjects or target populations can benefit greatly when museum visits are combined with art therapy [8]. In addition, when art history and critical analysis are introduced to art therapy, exhibition-goers experience greater self-esteem, self-awareness, sublimation, socialization skills, introspection, and creativity [9]. Consequently, it has been suggested that museum art therapy research should "seek new insights through our past experiences and share our thoughts and feelings with others" [10]. Thus, museums play a pivotal role in the emotional health and growth of their audiences.

Satisfy Emotional Needs and Enhance Social Interaction. Museums have long promoted social inclusion at the individual, community and societal levels [11]. On an individual level, visiting museums can boost self-esteem, self-confidence and creativity, and develop intelligence. In addition, it has been discussed how important it is to escape from daily activities and responsibilities to potter around in a museum. At the community level, museums can act as "catalysts for social rebirth", thus enabling communities to "increase their autonomy, improve their self-confidence, and develop the skills to take greater control of their lives and the development of the communities in which they live" [12] By reproducing these participating communities in their collections and exhibits, museums can help them to "develop a sense of ownership" of their lives. By recreating these engaged communities in their collections and exhibits, museums "have the potential power to increase inclusiveness, mutual respect between communities, and challenge stereotypes" [12]. Today, museums around the world are broadening their social roles, functions, and goals, aligning themselves with "health, welfare, social service, and other institutions" in an "effort to reverse disadvantage and achieve social outcomes" [12].

Providing Health Education and Promoting Public Health. 2014 RCMG, Research Centre for Museums and Galleries launched a year-long behavioral research project funded by Arts Council England and based at the School of Museum Studies, University of Leicester. This was followed by the publication of a book entitled Body and Mind: How Museums Impact on Health and Wellbeing [13]. The intention of this project was to show how museums can respond to changes in public health, using collections to improve people's health in order to combat health inequalities and actively contribute to the achievement of public health.

2 The Embodiment of Art Healing in Museums

2.1 Art Healing in Museums

Embodied cognition can be translated as cognition originating from the body; the sensory perceptions of a person's body and the way in which the body interacts with the world all affect the person's perception of the world [14]. Ye Haosheng believes that embodied cognition originated at the very beginning from the reflection on Plato's two worlds theory, a philosophically debated thesis, which is the beginning of mind-body dualism [15]; Heidegger believes that there should be existence before cognition, and that the world is connected; accordingly, he constructed the embryo of the theory of embodied cognition, which believes that the world is a whole, and that everything is connected to each other, and that it is an important source of integration of the body and the mind [16]. The publication of Merleau-Ponty's phenomenology of perception marked the formal birth of embodied cognition, which asserts that the subject of perception is the body, and that perception, the body, and the world are a unity [17].

Embodied cognition theory opens the door for art healing in museums beyond the visual. Embodied cognition theory believes that the body plays a crucial role in human cognitive processes, emphasizes that cognition is shaped by the body and its mode of activity, and focuses on the coupling process between the cognitive subject and his/her bodily actions and the specific context [18]. In other words, the content of healing should not be presented directly but explored independently by the person being healed, i.e., acquiring knowledge through the body and understanding the relationship between objects, scenes and subjects through actions [19].

2.2 Embodied Interaction and Art Healing Relevance

At present, the consensus formed by researchers on the understanding of embodiment theory can be summarized into three main points: first, perceptual experience directly affects cognitive processes; second, the motor system is an important connection between the brain and the body to cognition; third, cognition relies on the embodied context, and the brain nervous system, the body, and the environment are nested together to form a dynamic cognitive system of a person [20]. There are two advantages of art healing under embodied interaction, one is the directness of embodied interaction in art healing on people. The second is the expressive nature of embodied cognition in art healing, which accomplishes its self-representation through body movements or behaviors. From the perspective of embodied cognition, in order to construct the human-object-field relationship in art healing in museums.

3   How Embodied Interaction Affects Art Healing

The Five Ways to Happiness provides a useful framework for museums on how to enhance health and happiness. The concept of well-being includes two elements-feeling good and functioning well. Feeling good means we experience feelings of happiness, fulfillment, enjoyment, curiosity, and engagement. Living well means we have positive relationships, a sense of control over our lives and a sense of purpose, five ways that build on the inherent premise that mental health is happiness-a positive state of mind and body, being able to communicate, feeling safe, and feeling connected to people, communities, and the wider world. Each of these actions (connecting, noticing, giving, continually learning, being proactive) contributes to well-being in a positive way, making people feel good and improving their psychological capital (resilience, self-esteem, cognitive ability and emotional intelligence). Another important aspect of the Five Ways to Happiness is social engagement. Evidence suggests that for people of all ages, relationships are critical to promoting well-being and acting as a buffer against mental illness (see Fig. 1).

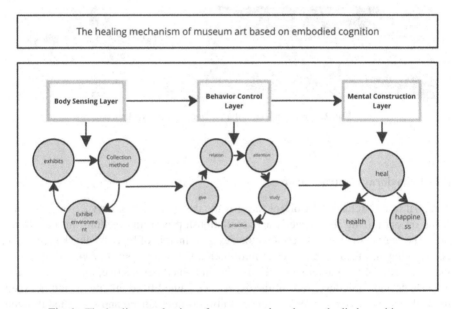

Fig. 1. The healing mechanism of museum art based on embodied cognition

3.1   Body Perception Layer

The goal of the perception layer of the body perception scene is the design of phenomenal experiences, focusing on the perceptual experience of the audience; the perception layer is based on the design principle of the body perception scene, i.e., to participate in cognition driven by instincts through different body perception modalities and perception degrees; embodied cognition emphasizes that an individual's perception of the world is not a reflex or an impression, but rather is the result of the body's participation in shaping it. The body's mode of perception and degree of perception play an important role in human healing, and viewers can obtain learning experiences through the joint participation of single or multi-sensory channels such as sight, hearing, smell, and touch. According to the theory of embodied cognition, the more sensory channels involved in interaction with the environment, the more complete the embodied experience will be.

At the "Emotion Map: Shared Healing Art Workshop" at the Liu Haisu Art Museum in Shanghai, participants will get to know each other and awaken their bodies through some simple team activities. After that, each participant will be given a piece of paper and choose five colors to represent his/her five emotions on the body of the little person on the paper, completing the first experience of personal creation; then, two by two, they will use their own bodies as the outline and use brushes, sponges, and other tools for the creation of the collective shared work, which is the one on display in the exhibition hall today. Finally, each person's self-statement of the work is the colorful statement that appears on the showroom (see Fig. 2).

Fig. 2. Emotion Map: Shared Healing Art Workshop

3.2 Behavioral Control Layer

The goal of the Behavioral Control Layer is the design of exploratory experiences that focus on optimizing the viewer's active relationship with the medium in the exhibition. The interaction layer is based on the design principle of body feedback scene, that is, receiving and feeding back scene information through physical or virtual, direct or indirect forms of body interaction. Under the embodied perspective, the subject's cognition is formed and developed in the experience gained from the interaction between the body and the environment, and the cognition is internalized and generated through the interaction. Studies related to the audience's learning process in museums have shown that interactivity promotes the audience's participation, understanding and recall of exhibits, and that people, both children and adults, remember their own body movements significantly more than they do those observed only by the naked eye. As new technologies continue to advance, technological tools such as body sensors and touch-screens act as mediators of audience interaction with the exhibition scene, integrating into the audience's perceptual experience and engaging with them in embodied learning.

Japanese design team "TeamLab" initiated an interactive art project "Flowers Bombing Home", which plays well with interactivity and the healing nature of natural graphics, the team planned a design to see the exhibition at home again! The team planned a design for the exhibition to be viewed at home. Participants were able to draw within the framework of flowers on paper, immersing themselves in the fun of self-creativity, and the completed drawings were scanned by their cell phones and transformed into a digital flower simulation of the dynamics of the bloom, opening up in the display screen. This simulated nature digital experience allows for a more diverse presentation of nature, in which the healing properties of nature for people are utilized to generate visualizations, and allows people living alone in their homes to feel a special connection to the outside world through a variety of flowers, creating a wide range of interactive communication (see Fig. 3).

Fig. 3. Flowers Bombing Home

3.3 Spiritual Construction Layer

The goal of the mental construction layer is the design of a relevance experience that focuses on the audience's active reflection on their own behaviors, feelings, thoughts, and experiences in a given situation; the meaning construction layer is based on the design principle of the body reflection scene, in which the audience consciously relates the exhibits to their personal meaning. For example, the Hongqiao Airport New Village Community Participatory Museum corresponds to the major historical phases of the airport new village, and with the change of the times, the new village has seen the emergence of three families, four families, single-parent families, singles, dormitory sisters, and temporary families of career tenants, and increasingly diversified family structures. The family structure is becoming more and more diversified, as well as the same kindergarten and elementary school class, the same airport team, the same volunteer team and the same square dance group. Family photos, videos and short videos are collected online and offline, and presented and interacted with through photo walls, electronic screens and interactive installations.

4 Museum Art Healing Strategies Under the Theory of Embodied Cognition

4.1 Content of Exhibits of a Phenomenal Nature

Exhibits are at the heart of the museum's role in art healing. Formally these collections give museums a unique role. A growing body of research suggests that objects enable us to make physical, cognitive, and emotional connections that are associated with a positive sense of well-being. Exhibits should be phenomenal in their selection, giving others a multi-sensory experience. Physical connections through touch and other senses stimulate cognition and emotion, setting off thoughts, ideas, feelings and memories. We learn through our bodies, and one of the ways through positive health is to keep learning.

4.2 Methods of Collection of Participatory Exhibits

Museums need to collect exhibits with more interactive and open-ended artworks that can engage the audience, thus better mobilizing their participation and reflection. Without the audience's participation, the role of public art and art healing will be impossible to talk about. For example, the Hope Flower Project 'Blooming at the right time' invited three artists to recreate the Hope Flower in an open manner. The audience can participate in the project by building a 'Hope Flower Sea' (DIY wall interaction), digital linkage between cell phones and the installation's LED screen (electronic screen interaction), and new media interactive flower blossoms (body sensing interaction), among many other forms. Through the power of art and the public to complete the Hope Flower program series of presentations, borrowing the power of art to heal the soul and awaken the vitality of the city.

4.3 Forms of Presentation of Exhibits that Allow People to Connect with People

Co-created exhibits are put on display through workshops. In an open workshop at the Hongqiao Airport New Village Community Participatory Museum, the artist invited all the residents of the new village and the social workers to join together to collaborate on a community work using tufted carpet craftsmanship. The participatory workshop transformed the production process into a platform for community exchange and co-creation. Residents of different ages and interests participated in the process. In the process, each participant's imagination, design, texture, brushstrokes and manual labor are accommodated into a community picture woven from diverse materials. The workshop interaction also increases the contact between different communities or families, promotes exchanges between different fields of work and age groups, strengthens the emotional integration and connection between neighbors, and creates a platform and atmosphere of exchange and integration for a better humanistic environment in the community.

5 Conclusion

Since the 1950s, art healing has gradually been recognized and used by the public. The scope and impact of art in healthcare proves that art can play a role in promoting health. Especially in the face of experiences during the New Crown Epidemic, art healing can serve as an expressive form of therapy that improves the physical, mental, and emotional state of participants through the creative process of art. Salom notes that "museums can provide healing experiences, which can have a significant impact on our sense of well-being and happiness if we focus on exploring ourselves and discovering ourselves through museum exhibitions and exhibits. " At the same time, "the diversity of museum collections can also reflect, in part, the value of unique personal expression. " Therefore, in this scenario, museums, because of their uniqueness, also encourage us to maintain an understanding of differences in our approach to self and others.

References

1. Meng, P.: Painting Art Assessment and Painting Art Therapy Intervention for Schizophrenic Patients. Beijing Normal University, Beijing (2004)
2. Camic, P.M., Chatterjee, H.J.: Museums and art galleries as partners for public health interventions. Perspect. Public Health **133**(1), 66–71 (2013)
3. Peng, J.: Research on art therapy in museums. Herit. Identificat. Appreciat. (17), 144–146 (2021)
4. Cai, C.H., Yang, L.H.: A developmental study of intentional inhibition in working memory. Psychol. Explorat. **29**(05), 32–36 (2009)
5. Lin, Y.-W., Zhu, R., Wu, J.-Y., Lu, W.-N., Liu, J.-J., Zhu, Y.-W.: The effect of drawing therapy in the rehabilitation of schizophrenia. Med. Food Therapy Health **18**(15), 209–210 (2020)
6. Cui, W., Wang, J.: Hot spots and dynamics of art healing research at home and abroad [J]. Media Criticism **01**, 1–28 (2023)
7. Silverman, L.: The Social Work of Museums. Routledge, New York (2010)
8. Fears, A.: The Museum as a Healing Space. Addressing Museum Visitors' Emotional Responses through Viewing and Creating Artwork. [MA in Art Education, Boston University, Boston] (2009)
9. Robertson, D.N.: Free time in an art museum: pausing, gazing and interacting. Leis. Sci. **33**(1), 70–80 (2011)
10. Williams, R.: Honoring the personal response: a strategy for serving the public hunger for connection. J. Museum Educ. **35**(1), 93–102 (2010)
11. Leonard, M.: Exhibiting popular music: museum audiences, inclusion and social history. J. New Music Res. **39**(2), 171–181 (2010)
12. Sandell, R.: Social inclusion, the museum and the dynamics of sectoral change. Museum Soc. **1**(1), 45–62 (2003)
13. Dodd, J., Jones, C.: Mind, Body, Spirit: How Museums Impact Health and Wellbeing (2014)
14. Liu, W.: Effective teaching in college English classroom based on embodied cognition. Exam. Eval. (Coll. Engl. Teach. Res. Ed.) **1**, 78–81 (2018)
15. Ye, H.: The meaning of the body: the epistemological value of physical education and sports from the perspective of phenomenology. Sports Sci. **41**(1), 83–88 (2021)
16. Fan, Y.: Research on the Generation and Criticism of Embodied Cognition and Development Trend. Shanxi University, Taiyuan (2019)
17. Song, J.H.: A few thoughts on the digital protection of intangible cultural heritage. Cult. Herit. (2), 1–8, 157 (2015)
18. Ye, H.: Embodied cognition: a new orientation of cognitive psychology. Adv. Psychol. Sci. **18**(05), 705–710 (2010)
19. Tang, L.T.: Body-consciousness in design. Pack. Eng. **40**(20), 1–8 (2019)
20. Zheng, H., Ye, H., Su, D.: Three theoretical models about embodied cognition. Psychol. Explor. **37**(03), 195–199 (2017)

Research on the Design of Multisensory Interactive Experiences in Museums Based on Embodied Cognition

Lin Lin and Lang Lu(✉)

School of Arts, Soochow University, Suzhou, Jiangsu, China
lulang@suda.edu.com

Abstract. With the arrival of the experienced economy and the intervention of virtual technology, museums pay more and more attention to people's sensory experiences in the space. The theory of embodied cognition emphasizes that human cognition and emotion come from the interaction between the body and the environment, which can provide theoretical references for the research of interaction design in museum environments.

The research content of this paper is as follows: 1. Explain the development of embodied cognition and analysis of the current situation of the museum interaction; 2. Combine with specific case studies to analyze the application of multisensory (vision, touch, hearing, smell) interaction design in the museum field, analyze the combinations and interactions between the human body and sensory experiences, and explore the potential impact and significance of multisensory experience interaction design on the audience's cognition, memory, and emotion, etc. 3. To propose a methodology for constructing multisensory experience interaction design at the theoretical and practical levels. At the theoretical level, the body is the crucial variable of cognitive and experiential activities in museums. Under the perspective of embodied cognition, multisensory experiences in the museum field can create infinite possibilities for simultaneously influencing the viewer's perception of his or her own body and, through the body, of the surrounding environment. At the same time, at the practical level, we can create a multifaceted experience mode in museums through the innovation of interactive forms of user experience, the application of embodied cognition in conjunction with multisensory experiences, and the combination of emerging technologies. At the practical level, through innovative interactive forms of user experience, the combination of embodied cognition and multisensory application, and the combination of emerging technologies to provide multiple experience modes, we can create vivid and compelling body and sensory experiences in the museum.

Keywords: Embodied Cognition · Multisensory Interactive Experiences · Museum Exhibitions · Interaction Design

C. Stephanidis et al. (Eds.): HCII 2024, CCIS 2119, pp. 204–211, 2024.
https://doi.org/10.1007/978-3-031-61966-3_23

1   Introduction

In the information age of rapid development of the economy, science and technology, and society, the cross-border integration of knowledge fields and the use of new technologies have become the driving force for the continuous development of museums and also prompted a shift in the center of attention of museums from "objects" to "people". The conception of multisensory experience and interaction design for museum exhibitions can help the audience effectively obtain diversified information through an immersive experience, which has also become an essential goal for the innovative development of museum exhibitions. Embodied cognition emphasizes the physical and spatial experience of the "human" body, providing an adequate basis for the design of information hierarchy and interactive actions [1]. Its application to designing multisensory interactive museum experiences can provide a theoretical basis and practical guidance for the innovative development of contemporary museum interaction design [2].

2   Embodied Cognition and Museum Interaction

The theory of embodied cognition can be traced back to the thinking of Heidegger, Merleau-Ponty, and others on the issue of body and mind at the beginning of the 20th century, which mainly refers to the strong correlation between physiological experience and psychological state [3]. The body is the basis of human perception of the environment and cognition, and the audience's experience and informal learning process in the museum space cannot be separated from the multisensory channels provided by the body [4]. In 2001, Paul Dourish proposed that embodied interaction is a participatory interaction between human beings and the environment and products and the creation and dissemination of meanings in the interaction process [5]. In 2007, the establishment of the TEI (Tangible Embedded and Embodied Interaction) conference is a sign that embodied interaction has become a hot research topic in the field of human-computer interaction. The body has a particular influence on the interaction process, and the theory of embodied cognition, which emphasizes the trinity of body, brain, and environment, provides us with a new perspective and path to explore the design of multisensory interactive experiences in museums.

The concept of interaction design emerged in the 1980s, focusing on the interaction and communication between people and machines to achieve the purpose of the user through the control of the interface in order to use the machine equipment and products through the "people" and "things" at the same time, the action and feedback, to realize the Closed-loop of interaction behavior [6]. In designing contemporary museum exhibition space to more effectively display and convey the information of exhibits to the audience, an important strategy is to change the visitors from "viewers" to "participants". The interaction mode in the museum exhibition space mainly includes three kinds of interaction modes: one is the multimedia interaction form mainly based on touch screen interaction, which mainly provides users with exhibition information, graphic descriptions, personalized visit routes, etc. [7]; the second is the interactive application of virtual devices mainly based on head-mounted displays [8]; and the third is the participatory interaction form, in which the users can obtain exhibition information and connotation through practical activities, as well as meet the immersive experience of the users in the scene space by the use of sound, light, electricity, images, video, and other elements.

3 Embodied Research on Interaction Design for Multisensory Experiences in Museums

3.1 Design Based on Visual Perception Development

The information obtained visually is more direct and objective than other senses, including visual organization, color, space, and object recognition. With the rapid development of science and technology, people have augmented reality technology, virtual reality technology, and other means to extend the concept of "viewing", the museum provides a new mode of experience. The "Teamlab Borderless" digital art museum uses many computers and projectors to capture the user's movements, behaviors, and reactions and manipulate the visual images to interact with the user, allowing him or her to explore the intersection of art, science, technology, and nature [9]. Among them, immersive interactive works such as Universe of Water Particles on a Rock where People Gather (see Fig. 1) present natural elements such as rocks, rivers, and flowers in the indoor space by digital means. Through the multi-sensory application of vision, hearing, and touch, they provide the experiencers with the possibility of immersive viewing of the exhibition, connecting the perception, cognition, and meaning generated by the users and effectively creating ways for users to control the virtual space. These simulated nature exploration experiences make the experiencers correspond the information about the fundamental nature in their mind with the symbols in the field and generate the intention of thought and emotion, completing the closed loop of "cognition-perception-experience" [10].

Fig. 1. Universe *of Water Particles on a Rock where People Gather*, teamLab, 2018, Interactive Digital Installation. Source: https://art.team-lab.cn/ew/waterparticles-rock-azabudai/

3.2 Design Based on Tactile Perception

The use of tactile perception in museums can meet the needs of the visually impaired in accessing information about exhibitions and collections. In recent years, many museums worldwide have been developing and expanding their accessibility resources and activities and updating their accessibility tools, including using Braille, audio devices, touching objects, and other initiatives to assist visually impaired groups in effectively accessing exhibition information. The Andy Warhol Museum in the United States has set up a particular area for touchable replicas of exhibits, including placing them on a rotating countertop so that users can rotate the perceptual objects. By coincidence, the Nanjing Museum has set up thematic digital experience areas to provide personalized services for visually impaired audiences with different degrees of blindness, amblyopia, photophobia, etc., such as setting up special fully automated disability carts to guide the users to the display points, replicating the exhibits in equal proportions for them to touch, and setting up a darker, independent display space for amblyopic and photophobic people (see Fig. 2). The display mode based on voice interpretation and tactile touch mobilizes multisensory experiences of the visually impaired, enabling them to identify and combine important information in the exhibition through their body's perception of the surrounding environment and enhancing their self-confidence and independence in exploring the visual arts exhibits [11].

Fig. 2. Thematic Digital Experience Area for the Visually Impaired at Nanjing Museum. Source: https://www.njmuseum.com/en/reviewDetails?id=529

3.3 Design Based on Auditory Perception Development

Sound is a tool for expressing their thoughts and a medium and material for artistic creation. It can not only expand the breadth and depth of space but also has a vital function of creating atmosphere, and its information-carrying capacity far exceeds that of words and images. In addition, compared with vision, sound can connect people's emotions and imagination, generating new meanings beyond its original expression. Sound communication has the function of attracting users' attention and triggering users' memories and associations. The Zhejiang Nature Museum has launched the "Bird Song Behavior Exhibition", which displays 238 bird songs of 106 species of birds through systematic multimedia equipment, guiding the users' attention with an orderly spatial and temporal cue (see Fig. 3). In the Nanjing Museum, the Republic of China Pavilion not only restores the scenes of the streets and houses of that time but also places a gramophone in the space to play the classic songs of the 1940s, such as Night Shanghai, which were popular in Shanghai, China, to trigger the users' memories of the past events. Sound is interactive, and when a certain kind of music is played, it triggers an auditory stimulus that produces behaviors such as swaying or singing along with the music. Compared with words, sounds in exhibitions have strong attraction and feedback, reflecting the spirit and cultural connotations of the venue, helping users to recognize information and feel spatial relationships in the transmission of sounds, and establishing emotional connections between exhibits and users, thus achieving ideal educational effects and viewing experiences.

Fig. 3. Exhibition scene of *Bird Song Behavior Exhibition* in Zhejiang Nature Museum. Source: https://weibo.com/2834193004/FxByBqHRC

3.4   Design Based on Olfactory Sensory Development

As an indispensable part of multisensory experience, smell is superior to the senses of "eyes, ears, tongue, and body" due to its ability to refer to the rich correlation between objects and reveal its complex characteristics. Due to the physiological characteristics of olfaction, which is naturally linked to emotion and memory, olfactory experience creates a unique place atmosphere, focuses on the experience mode across time and space, and retains a long-lasting and profound sensory memory, etc. In museums, there are two main design strategies for the olfactory experience; one is to stimulate the sense of smell by releasing odors, triggering bodily perception, and triggering the user's curiosity and desire to explore the exhibition space [12], such as the Paris Museum of Perfume and the International Museum of Perfumery of Grasse in the exhibitions displaying the ingredients of fragrances and the famous perfumes of the past and the present, which attracts the user's attention by stimulating the olfactory perception (see Fig. 4). The other is to use odors as part of a broader multi-sensory exhibition, researching and analyzing the characteristics of the type of odors that match the theme of the exhibition and the audience group as a way of awakening the user's memories, perceiving the surrounding environment with the sense of smell, and adjusting the body state, to better access to the information of the field.

Fig. 4. Scenes from the display of perfumes and raw materials in the Paris Perfume Museum. Source: https://musee-parfum-paris.fragonard.com/le-musee/

4 Multisensory Experience Interaction Design Application Strategies

4.1 Innovative Forms of User Experience Interaction

When designing experiential interactions in museums, the form of the interaction needs to be predetermined to guide the user's actions. Combined with new technologies and media, it instructs or guides the experiencer to produce interactive behaviors, leading to perceptual behaviors. For example, the interactive process can be completed through image prompts, voice commands, etc. Before the formal experience, warm-up training is provided to the users, and the association of front senses and interactive actions is used so that the experiencers can complete the learning of images, sounds, and smells in the spatial place. The interactive behaviors are guided through various types of media. The use of audio-visual, pictures, text, lighting, color, material, fragrance, indoor temperature changes, and other stimulation of human eyes, ears, nose, tongue, skin, and other multi-sensory, tapping the potential of human associative, flux, etc., stimulate human interest, enhance the depth of experience, visually create a diversified audio-visual experience, the use of smell triggers the conversion of the scene, enhance the depth of experience, tactile interaction to increase the sense of participation and the value of the experience, to form the user of the overall understanding of things, to achieve the effective dissemination of exhibits [13]. Designers can select the reference elements of interactive behaviors according to the main idea of multisensory experience design so that the multisensory experience design is more in line with the overall concept of the interactive field, and users can get multi-dimensional experience perception [14].

4.2 Combined Application of Embodied Cognition and Multisensory

Phenomenal space is a concrete, practical space closely linked to the perceptual and practical activities of the phenomenal body and the specific content of spatial experience [15]. Museum space needs to balance and coordinate the psychological and perceptual conditions between the audience and the exhibits, create a sense of intimacy and realism, and attract and strengthen the user's perceptual mode so that it not only relies on the visual appreciation of the exhibits, but also feels and understands the texture of the exhibits, the sense of touch and the symbolic system, and develops an active dialogue between the audience and the exhibits. Various display designs that activate the five senses make the audience think that they are in the "scene", the style, taste, atmosphere, and tone of being in the scene are constructed through the interaction of various senses. For the physical environment, reasonable flow lines and interactive areas can be set up, and fences, steps, lights, and color-contrasting signs can be used to guide the user so that the user's body and senses are controlled and attracted by the museum, experiencing the sensory stimulation brought by the museum and its exhibits. Dynamic elements will grab the audience's attention the first time. They can be set as the key elements of interactive operation, as well as through interactive objects and gesture prompt icons, etc., so that users can obtain a multi-dimensional personal experience.

4.3 Incorporate Emerging Technologies to Provide Multiple Modes of Experience

Embodied Cognition Theory emphasizes body perception and presence, suitable for new technologies such as Virtual Reality (VR) and Augmented Reality (AR). Designs combining AR and new materials can enhance the immersive experience of bodily participation and create emotional interactions among users; the combination of VR and new technologies, such as brainwaves, can place learning behaviors in intelligent environments constructed by the exhibition space, which can be applied to the research of education and teaching [16]. Exploring the movement of the body in interaction design, adding digital information and tangible interaction to the museum experience so that the user views the object while presenting relevant descriptive information, thus stimulating user participation. Combined with film art, graphic design, exhibition design, and many other directions, interaction design research under the perspective of embodied cognition still has broad development potential. In addition, we have strengthened our attention to the multi-sensory experience of specific groups, such as designing blind guide tools to help visually impaired people view the exhibition by combining tactile perception and physical behavior; designing exhibition supporting products for visually impaired people with the guidance of inclusive design and supplemented by embodied cognition; and continuously exploring new ways to provide users with more immersive exhibition viewing experience.

5   Conclusion

From the perspective of embodied cognition, this paper explores the multisensory experience of the audience by integrating digital technology and interaction technology to expand the multisensory joint interactive design method further. Under the comprehensive use of digital technology, sensing technology, and interaction design technology, not limited to two-dimensional expression, the multisensory experience is integrated into a spatial form, guiding the audience to explore the museum space, interact in the exhibition space, and create a sense of immersive spatial experience. Integrating digital art, science, and technology, the scenario is presented in three dimensions in the form of technological interaction, allowing participants to integrate into the narrative space in a multisensory form. In the future, designing a multisensory experience will be more widely used in interactive cultural experience places.

References

1. Bakker, S., Antle, A.N., Van Den Hoven, E.: Embodied metaphors in tangible interaction design. Pers. Ubiquit. Comput. **16**, 433–449 (2012)
2. Shaby, N., Vedder-Weiss, D.: Embodied interactions in a science museum. Sci. Educ. **105**(5), 938–960 (2021)
3. Lewis, A.L., Dietrich, E.: Merleau-Ponty, embodied cognition, and the problem of intentionality. Cybern. Syst. **28**(5), 345–358 (1997)
4. Shapiro, L.A.: Flesh matters: the body in cognition. Mind Lang. **34**(1), 3–20 (2019)
5. Dourish, P.: Where the Action is: The Foundations of Embodied Interaction. MIT Press, Cambridge (2001)
6. Weir, G.R.: Meaningful interaction in complex man-machine systems. Reliab. Eng. Syst. Saf. **38**(1–2), 151–156 (1992)
7. Zhuang, Q., Xu, W., Yang, D., Wei, N.: Multimedia analysis of digital museum user interface based on goal-oriented theory and information fusion and intelligent sensing. J. Sens. **2022** (2022)
8. Kim, K., Kwon, O., Yu, J.: Evaluation of an HMD-based multisensory virtual museum experience for enhancing sense of presence. IEEE Access (2023)
9. Varnava, C.: MORI Building DIGITAL ART MUSEUM: teamLab Borderless (2019)
10. Chen, S.X., Wu, H.C., Huang, X.: Immersive experiences in digital exhibitions: the application and extension of the service theater model. J. Hosp. Tour. Manag. **54**, 128–138 (2023)
11. Pawluk, D.T., Adams, R.J., Kitada, R.: Designing haptic assistive technology for individuals who are blind or visually impaired. IEEE Trans. Haptics **8**(3), 258–278 (2015)
12. Spence, C.: Scenting the anosmic cube: on the use of ambient scent in the context of the art gallery or museum. i-Perception **11**(6), 2041669520966628 (2020)
13. Vi, C.T., Ablart, D., Gatti, E., Velasco, C., Obrist, M.: Not just seeing, but also feeling art: mid-air haptic experiences integrated in a multisensory art exhibition. Int. J. Hum. Comput. Stud. **108**, 1–14 (2017)
14. Wang, S.: Museum as a sensory space: a discussion of communication effect of multi-senses in Taizhou Museum. Sustainability **12**(7), 3061 (2020)
15. Rechardt, P.: The phenomenal hyperspace: a study of the dimensional and spatio-temporal structures of phenomenal space and binding. J. Conscious. Stud. **30**(3–4), 106–131 (2023)
16. Marto, A., Gonçalves, A., Melo, M., Bessa, M.: A survey of multisensory VR and AR applications for cultural heritage. Comput. Graph. **102**, 426–440 (2022)

A Cognitive Psychoanalytic Perspective on Interaction Design in the Education of School-Age Children in Museums

Lin Lin, Lang Lu$^{(\boxtimes)}$, and Na Lin

School of Arts, Soochow University, Suzhou, Jiangsu, China
lulang@suda.edu.com

Abstract. The education of school-age children is an essential stage in the sustainable educational development of a country. As an important place in children's learning system, interactive education in museums is of practical significance in stimulating, guiding, and enhancing children's perception and thinking abilities. The focus of this paper is on how to promote a positive influence on children's cognitive ability through the interactive design of museum exhibits.

This paper focuses on the interaction design in the education of school-age children (6–12 years old) in museums from the perspective of cognitive psychoanalysis. The main research content includes: 1. Analyzing the characteristics of children's cognitive psychology at this stage; 2. Taking Suzhou Museum in China as an example, analyzing the exhibition and teaching system and interactive experience mode established by its Children's Discovery Experience Museum to educate children aged 6–12 years; 3. For the developmental characteristics of school-age children, condensing the design strategies of the museum's interactive experience to meet the needs of children's cognitive behaviors, such as strengthening the multidimensional sensory experience, optimizing the critical points of spatial experience, building the form of gamification interactive experience, etc. to create an emotional experience for children, and establish appropriate interface perception from visual elements, information hierarchy, interaction mode, etc. to promote the development of children's cognitive ability. Finally, based on the analysis and research on the interaction design of the Suzhou Museum Exploration Experience Hall, we put forward the interaction design strategy for museums to enhance the cognitive ability of children aged 6–12.

Keywords: Museums · Interaction Design · Education for School-age Children · Cognitive Psychology · Suzhou Museum

1 Introduction

With the advancement of education levels worldwide and the high-quality requirements for school-age children's education, museums, which are rich in cultural and educational resources, are becoming increasingly crucial for school-age children's education due to their unique exploratory learning mode and atmosphere [1]. According to the statistical monitoring report of *the Chinese Children's Development Program (2021–2030)*, in 2022, minors visited museums 150 million times yearly. Against the background of rapid changes in the cultural atmosphere, consumption patterns, and technical means, how can museums meet the new needs of school-age children, enhance their visiting experience, build a new service system, and give full play to the educational function of informal teaching environment has become one of the emerging hotspots that need to be researched in the design of current museum exhibition [2].

2 Cognitive Psychology of School-Age Children

Cognition is the process of individuals processing external information, and the cognitive level of individuals is affected by the complexity of external information and their knowledge, culture, interest, and other factors [3]. Psychologist Jean Piaget divided the development of children's cognitive ability into four stages: sensory-motor stage, pre-operational stage, concrete operation stage, and formal operation stage. The cognitive ability of school-age children is in the concrete operation stage [4]. At this stage, children can gradually accept the educational model of museums due to their increasing logical and cognitive abilities. Children's cognitive psychology includes three stages: receiving information, understanding information, and storing information; each stage corresponds to three experience levels of sensory, thinking, and memory respectively, i.e., children mainly receive information in the sensory experience, understand information in the thinking experience, and store information in the memory experience, which together constitute the main content of the museum children's experience design [5]. Therefore, the research on interaction design in museum schoolchildren's education is multidimensional and will be influenced by their cognitive and psychological characteristics [6].

3 Children's Exploration Experience Hall Design Practice in Suzhou Museum West Hall

Located on the first basement level of the Suzhou Museum (West Wing), the Children's Discovery Museum covers an area of 4,500 square meters. Focusing on children between 3 and 12, the museum provides an exclusive space for learning and exploration. It allows them to learn about Suzhou culture in an open, interactive, and exploratory experience, with the educational expansion function of a "museum school." Themed interactive spaces such as "Folding Time and Space," "Viewing the World from the Curiosity Cabinet," "Learning Suzhou Language at Grandma's House," and "Memories of Child-hood for Adults" are set up in the Children's Exploration Experience Hall. Various cross-media technologies are integrated into the path of "gamification," which actively promotes children's groups to acquire knowledge in the exhibitions and focuses on carrying out multi-dimensional children's education through interactive experiences.

3.1 Multi-dimensional Perceptual Design

Allowing children to accept exhibition information during the visit effectively is the primary condition for children's museums to fulfill their educational function, and visual, auditory, and tactile senses are the three sensory experiences that are more frequently used in the design of children's museum experience [7]. Regarding vision, for the color sensitivity of school-age children, the Children's Discovery Experience Museum uses bright and rich colors to attract children's attention and stimulate their emotions and sensory activity. For example, in the theme space of "Seeing Jiangnan in Gusu City," the city characteristics of Suzhou's "small bridges and flowing water" are reproduced using scenery and lighting, bringing children into the touring experience of Suzhou's famous monuments. In terms of hearing, contextualized sound helps children to recognize things, and natural sound effects and cue music can shape the exhibition atmosphere and bring children closer to the information on display so that they can immerse themselves in it and enhance the effectiveness of information dissemination [8]. For example, in the theme space of "Learning Suzhou Dialect at Grandma's House," children can imitate and sing along with Suzhou nursery rhymes and learn the authentic Suzhou dialect. In terms of tactile sensation, school-age children prefer to have contact and interaction with exhibits. After receiving tactile feedback, they will have a more profound impression of the exhibition. For example, in the "Curious Cabinets of the World" themed space, by touching the cabinets of different themes and seeing the development of different civilizations and cultures, children can intuitively feel that the world is harmonious and different, thus nurturing valuable qualities such as tolerance and openness (see Fig. 1).

Fig. 1. Children's Exploration Experience Museum Multi-Dimensional Perception Experience Scene. Source: https://mp.weixin.qq.com/s/Y8FgTsolalTj7FYvt4oUxw

3.2 Immersive Exhibit Line Design

The open exhibition line design is conducive to children's group and social activities, and at the same time, it is easy for museum educators or parents to watch over children. Therefore, the Children's Exploration and Experience Museum connects display, science popularization, and interaction into a smooth and narrative exhibition line so that children can gradually immerse themselves in the thematic atmosphere through emotional transitions, realizing children's cognitive fluency in the exhibition line design of the museum [9]. In addition, the exhibition hall minimizes partitions as much as possible. It sets up many thematic scenes according to the narrative logic of the content so that children can choose projects freely according to their aesthetic inclinations. The theme space of "My Gusu City" connects the typical scenes of Suzhou's unique characteristics, such as the

Temple of Literature and the School of Government, Shantang River, Pingjiang Road, and the gardens, according to the timeline of the development of the morning, noon, and evening. Through exhibits, sounds, and other content to stimulate children's cognitive desire to realize the initial science education and then in the interactive space through the game interaction, science and technology installations for children to understand the development of the history of Suzhou, to enhance the mood of the exhibition; and then into the experience area, children can be based on the theme of the relevant painting, handicrafts, and other activities, to increase their sense of achievement (see Fig. 2). It can be seen that the Children's Exploration and Experience Hall connects practical, sound, visual, and science education spaces in a specific color and time sequence, allowing children to perceive the relationship between exhibits and activities in a multi-dimensional way during the exhibition [10].

Fig. 2. Different Exploration and Experience Space and Mode Settings. Source: https://mp.wei xin.qq.com/s/Y8FgTsolalTj7FYvt4oUxw

3.3 Game Interaction Design

Enhancing children's understanding of information through interactive games and activities is necessary for museums to fulfill their educational function [11]. For school-age children, playful experiences can stimulate their inner self-drive and desire for exploration. In response to this psychological characteristic of children, the Children's Discovery and Experience Museum has designed and developed a guidebook around the core exhibition area "My Gusu City," which allows children to achieve the ultimate goal of in-depth learning and experience by playing games, breaking through levels, and collecting chapters in the process of visiting the museum. Using Panmen and Shantang Street as the restoration references, the guidebook simulates a day's life in Gusu City through the three units of exhibition experience in the morning, noon, and evening of a day so that children can understand the essential elements of the city's culture in a multi-temporal dimension, such as finding out the difference between ancient and modern life in the "Gusu Flourishing Map," searching for Suzhou food in the nostalgic "Grandma's House," and solving puzzles and finding treasures in the labyrinth of Pingjiang Historical District and introducing game-based thinking into the interactive experience design of children's education in museums (see Fig. 3), constructing a game-based service model that enhances children's interest in participation and sense of experience, developing the depth and breadth of the combination of service design and game-based thinking research, and promoting children's cognition of the city's history and culture [12].

Fig. 3. Tutorial Manual and Game Interaction Settings. Source: https://ticket.szmuseum.com/act ivities/0dfbd4cd45947a692c8410a149c7c489?location=1

4 Design Strategies for Children's Interactive Experiences in Museums

4.1 Enhance Multi-dimensional Sensory Experience

In the museum viewing experience, the generation of user pleasure perception is multi-dimensional, including visual, auditory, olfactory, gustatory, tactile, and other aspects. Diversified perceptual experiences can increase the attention and participation of school-age children, make them feel happy, and enhance their desire to learn. Strengthening audio-visual perception is an effective way to enhance perceptual experience. Compared with simple textual explanations of exhibits, video-type explanations strengthen the perceptual experience of "listening" and "seeing", which helps children better understand the stories behind the exhibits. In addition, audiobooks can be added around the exhibits, or audio explanations can be set up during the visit to enhance the visual and auditory experience. Most children are interested in physical models and exhibits with sound, light, and electricity. They like to lie down around the imitation exhibits to observe and occasionally reach out to touch them. This kind of conditioned reflexive active touching behavior is a way for children to perceive the world innately, and they are used to touching the texture of the material and the surface texture to know things. Therefore, adding touchable specimens or interactive experiences based on various types of screens to enhance children's tactile sensations during visits and learning can be more in line with the cognitive experience of children's groups (see Fig. 4) [13].

Fig. 4. Use a Variety of Media to Enhance Children's Multi-Dimensional Sensory Experience. Source: https://ticket.szmuseum.com/activities/0dfbd4cd45947a692c8410a149c7c489?loc ation=1

4.2 Key Points for Optimizing the Spatial Experience

A user experience map is a tool to visualize users' experience of products and services in stages based on users' needs, which intuitively shows the relationship between users and the environment and consists of experience stages, user behaviors, contact points, user emotions, pain points, and opportunity points [14]. Designers can create a museum children's experience map through the children's perspective, utilizing the data and information obtained during the research, in order to refine the children's emotions at each experience node fully and to explore their pain points and opportunity points during the visit, to enhance the children's visit experience. The experience key point is the node where users have a more profound impression of the experience process. In the museum visit experience, the complicated information can easily make children feel tired or lose interest in visiting. In this regard, tokens can be given appropriate spiritual or material rewards during the user experience to improve children's memory. In addition, when children are tired of visiting the museum, relying on the external environment to bring them a sense of ritual with inner sensual experience can give children a sense of closeness and trust and enhance their motivation to visit the museum [15].

4.3 Constructing a Gamified Form of Interactive Experience

The game creates an abstract structure that isolates itself from other environmental factors and promotes collaboration and competition among participating characters in an ideal state with a specific time frame, a specific place, and specific rules; it also constructs a miniature "world model" that accommodates the activities of various individuals [16]. In the museum, "reproducing" urban civilization and history and culture with the design framework of "gamification" enables children to follow the rhythm of the story, more interactively experience the flow of different individual destinies in historical time and space, and trace the dynamic development process of various themes and events in specific social conditions [17]. The interactive experience for children in museums can be constructed according to the operations of setting the conditions of the era, constructing the spatial scene, determining the storyline, introducing the main body of the action, visualizing the fundamental mechanisms, and embedding them into the decision-making system during the game, etc., and at the same time matching the needs of children to show them lasting attraction, further increasing their willingness to participate and loyalty [18].

5   Conclusion

Museums are public places with various functions, such as popularizing science, entertainment, etc. They have unique educational value and are important places in the learning system of school-age children. Since children's cognitive ability is still quite different from that of adults, there is a greater need to study and explore the interaction design of museums serving children's education based on children's cognitive psychology and behavior. In this paper, we analyze the Exploration Experience Hall of Suzhou Museum from the psychological process and characteristics of children's cognition, which is aimed at the age characteristics of children aged 6–12 years old, combined with Suzhou's characteristic culture, and in line with the international education concepts, to establish its unique exhibition and teaching system and interactive experience mode, which can effectively improve the cognitive ability of school-age children. On this basis, it concludes that the museum interactive experience design strategies to enhance the cognitive

ability of school-age children, such as strengthening multi-dimensional sensory experience, optimizing the critical points of spatial experience, and constructing the form of
game-based interactive experience, allow children to maintain their interest in learning
and their desire to explore in museums, to cultivate better their imagination, thinking
ability, and innovation ability (see Fig. 5).

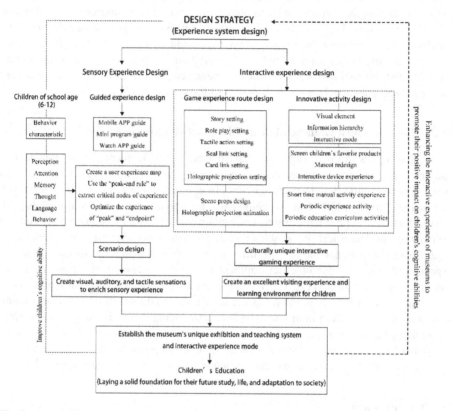

Fig. 5. A Cognitive Psychoanalytic Perspective on Interaction Design Strategies in the Education
of School-age Children in Museums

References

1. Huang, J., Lim, S., Kim, J.: A study on the empirical space characteristics of children's
   museum. J. Korea Inst. Spatial Des. **14**(7), 99
2. Chapin, D.A.: The status of special programming for minority youth and children with special
   needs: a report on the perceptions of children's museum education directors. State University
   of New York at Albany (2009)
3. Corris, A.: An enactive-developmental systems framing of cognizing systems. Biol. Philos.
   37(4), 32 (2022)

4. Vonèche, J., Vidal, F.: Jean Piaget and the child psychologist. Synthese, 121–138 (1985)
5. Foley, M.A., Johnson, M.K., Raye, C.L.: Age-related changes in confusion between memories for thoughts and memories for speech. Child Dev., 51–60 (1983)
6. Yang, H.J., Kim, N.H.: A Study on the Movements of Based on the Psychological Characteristics of Children and Analysis of Preferred Experience of Children's Museum according to Piaget's cognitive development process. Korean Inst. Interior Des. J. **19**(1), 37–45 (2010)
7. Tan, F., Gong, X., Tsang, M.C.: The educational effects of children's museums on cognitive development: Empirical evidence based on two samples from Beijing. Int. J. Educ. Res. **106**, 101729 (2021)
8. Beliveau, J.E.: Audio elements: understanding current uses of sound in museum exhibits (Doctoral dissertation) (2015)
9. Oh, S.: A study on the classifying the design of immersion exhibition in the children's museums. J. Korea Des. Knowl. **19**, 41–50 (2011)
10. Hye-Yeon, C.: The educational roles of interactive spaces for children in contemporary art museums. J. Res. Art Educ. **14**(3), 59–79 (2013)
11. Price, S., Sakr, M., Jewitt, C.: Exploring whole-body interaction and design for museums. Interact. Comput. **28**(5), 569–583 (2016)
12. Othman, M.K., Aman, S., Anuar, N.N., Ahmad, I.: Improving children's cultural heritage experience using game-based learning at a living museum. J. Comput. Cultural Heritage (JOCCH) **14**(3), 1–24 (2021)
13. Shawcroft, J.E., Gale, M., Workman, K., Leiter, V., Jorgensen-Wells, M., Jensen, A.C.: Screenplay: an observational study of the effect of screen media on Children's play in a museum setting. Comput. Hum. Behav. **132**, 107254 (2022)
14. Wang, X., Crookes, D., Harding, S.A., Johnston, D.: Stories, journeys and smart maps: an approach to universal access. Univ. Access Inf. Soc. **21**(2), 419–435 (2022)
15. Murray, C.: From maps to spatial stories: a case study to understand children's (re-) productions of art museum space. Children's Geographies, 1–17 (2023)
16. Sounderpandian, J.: Totally monotonic games and flow games. Oper. Res. Lett. **36**(2), 165–167 (2008)
17. Symeonidi, A.Z.: Games design as a curatorial intervention: Rethinking museum representation, meaning-making and agency with games design (Doctoral dissertation, UCL (University College London) (2020)
18. Beavis, C., O'Mara, J., Thompson, R.: Digital games in the museum: perspectives and priorities in videogame design. Learn. Media Technol. **46**(3), 294–305 (2021)

Enhancing Visitor Engagement: Non-Player Characters for Social Presence in Metaverse Art Museums

Sanghun Nam[⊠] 🆔

Department of Culture Technology, Changwon National University, Changwon, South Korea
sanghunnam@changwon.ac.kr

Abstract. This study delves into the creation of a metaverse art museum utilizing Unity and HMD for immersive virtual experiences. It highlights the integration of Non-Player Characters (NPCs) to foster a social atmosphere, closely mirroring the interpersonal dynamics of physical museums. This innovative approach enhances virtual visitor engagement and interaction, offering a new dimension to art appreciation and museum experiences in the digital realm.

Keywords: Metaverse Museum · NPC Interaction · Social Presence

1 Introduction

As the COVID-19 pandemic spread, people's freedom to move around was restricted, and entry to public places where many people gather was limited. In the field of culture and arts, the opportunities for people to visit cultural spaces and experience cultural content were restricted, leading to difficulties in the production and dissemination of cultural content. Authors producing cultural content found it hard to find opportunities to create and exhibit their content, and institutions in the cultural and arts sector, such as museums and concert halls, struggled with the absence of audiences. In order to overcome this situation, technical attempts were made to allow audiences to visit and participate in virtual spaces without physically visiting the actual spaces. Art projects were undertaken to convert paintings into image data and precisely model sculptures with 3D scanning, and virtual museums were created so that audiences could appreciate artworks using computers and smartphones without visiting museums [1]. Recently, gaming technology has been used to allow a large number of people to participate in concerts and exhibitions in the metaverse space simultaneously, providing interactions among audiences [2].

As the COVID-19 pandemic subsided and people began to travel freely and visit cultural spaces in person, the participation rate in metaverse museums relatively declined, causing stress in introducing new metaverse exhibition halls or maintaining existing ones. Metaverse museums were not only a substitute for museums during the COVID-19 pandemic but also an alternative that could provide a variety of user experiences

C. Stephanidis et al. (Eds.): HCII 2024, CCIS 2119, pp. 220–225, 2024.
https://doi.org/10.1007/978-3-031-61966-3_25

that physical museums cannot offer and bring cultural benefits to people who have difficulty visiting exhibitions. Many metaverse spaces have been facing the problem of audiences not revisiting over time. Initially, the metaverse utilized multiplayer game technology to allow users' avatars to move and provide information. However, for continued participation, the metaverse needs to be maintained and developed by forming virtual communities where users gather. This paper studies the elements that enable continuous visits by audiences to metaverse museums and proposes a design for metaverse museums.

2   Related Works

The metaverse is a new concept of platform and service that combines various technologies to construct a virtual world where many people can participate simultaneously and create a virtual society and culture [3]. The development of extended reality, including social network services, virtual/augmented reality technologies, and the advancement of 5G/6G wireless networks, has laid the technological foundation for the fusion of the real world with the virtual world [4]. Artificial intelligence technology, used to create virtual humans that can converse and act naturally like humans, is creating a realistic metaverse environment. The metaverse, being a space simulated by programs, has the advantage of expressing everything imaginable, regardless of the physical laws of the real world. This characteristic of the metaverse shows the potential to overcome limited situations in various fields in reality and expand, hence it is expected to be utilized in education, smart cities, culture, medicine, economy, manufacturing, and more [5]. Although the metaverse can be used in various fields, designing and producing a universal metaverse platform that can be utilized in all fields is very difficult. The metaverse must be designed according to the characteristics of the field and user tendencies to maintain and sustain an active and continuous metaverse society. This paper focuses on the metaverse in the field of culture and arts, such as metaverse museums, as its research scope.

Due to the COVID-19 pandemic, the concept of virtual museums, metaverse museums, that can eliminate time and space constraints, was rapidly applied. Many cultural heritage and artworks began to be digitalized, and visitors could access metaverse museums without the constraints of time and space to view artworks. This phenomenon should not be understood as merely substituting physical museums during the COVID-19 pandemic but as a shift towards providing an appropriate user experience for museums in the current era. New forms of user experience utilizing digital technology offer visitors sensory and easily understandable new forms of interaction. Metaverse exhibition halls can curate a variety of works from around the world and create thematic exhibitions that are difficult to produce in the real world. It helps residents in areas difficult to physically visit and people with disabilities who cannot move freely to experience culture in a way that suits them [6]. Museums using extended reality technology can be visited in new times and spaces and compose surreal exhibition spaces that cannot be expressed in offline museums, thereby maximizing the potential of storytelling and interacting with audiences in original ways [7].

When building and operating an offline museum in the metaverse world, it is necessary to secure personnel and budget for metaverse program development, operation, and content production. A method for producing a metaverse museum without complicated programming skills is to utilize commercial metaverse platforms such as Roblox, Zepeto, and GatherTown. Using commercial metaverse platforms has the advantage of easy access for existing platform users, but there is also a downside that museums must be created within the user interface and features supported by the metaverse platform, making it difficult to show originality or differentiation from other metaverse museums created on the same platform [8].

Since commercial metaverse platforms have not been around for very long, there is a need for research on user experience. However, in the gaming sector, research on user participation and sustainability has been consistently conducted for a long time. The MMORPG (Massively Multiplayer Online Role-Playing Game) sector of the gaming industry, which allows many people to connect simultaneously and build social networks within the game, showing behaviors similar to those in the real world, shares many similarities with the metaverse. Especially in multiplayer games, high user engagement is necessary for active social interaction. This paper analyzes research on game platforms similar to the metaverse, summarizes elements that can be applied to metaverse museums, and uses them in the design of metaverse art museums.

3   Revisiting Metaverse

The metaverse constructs virtual spaces where numerous users gather to form a virtual society. For this virtual society to persist, its members must engage in dialogue and cooperation to create culture, and beyond that, the society must be capable of economic activities. Initially, many users visit out of curiosity, but over time, the rate of return visits to metaverse services decreases, eventually leading to some services being discontinued. To ensure the sustainability of metaverse services, it is essential to analyze what elements can encourage users to visit regularly and incorporate these elements into the service design. Firstly, users visit the metaverse for information acquisition. Visitors to metaverse museums can gain three-dimensional access to cultural and artistic works and related information, providing an opportunity to initiate the service. However, since metaverse museums cannot change their content quickly, those that provide the same information repeatedly will see a decline in repeat visitors. Even if the same artworks are exhibited, changing the storytelling or using a gaming approach to allow users to participate actively in the metaverse space can be elements that encourage regular visits to the metaverse service.

Secondly, the reason for visiting the metaverse service is social interaction, which occurs within the social relationships formed by meeting other users. The metaverse is becoming a new playground for the younger generation, reducing loneliness in their daily lives, where social presence and interaction are crucial factors for participation. Building a multiplayer-based metaverse allows users to enjoy the fun of social interaction and influences continued use.

Thirdly, users want to feel social presence during their experiences of social interaction in the metaverse space. Ways to manifest social presence in virtual space include creating avatars and personalized content. An avatar represents a virtual body visualized and interacting in the virtual world on behalf of the real user. An avatar is a visual representation of the user and signifies the user's identity, with users often idealizing their personality traits when designing their avatars. Unique avatars that represent oneself in the virtual world can give users a social presence in the virtual society, and the ability to customize avatars can enhance user participation. Decorating one's space or creating games and inviting other users for interaction can provide a social experience that gives meaning to the user's existence in the metaverse and a sense of achievement. Owning personalized content psychologically and experiencing feedback with other users can have a positive impact on continued use.

4 Development of Metaverse Art Museum

In this study, a metaverse art museum was constructed to allow the appreciation of art works in virtual space, utilizing the Unity game engine and HMD (Head-Mounted Display) to enable users to experience the metaverse space from a first-person perspective. To mimic the environment of a museum, lighting objects were placed inside the museum. NPCs (Non-Player Characters) were deployed within the metaverse museum to enhance the social atmosphere when users log in the metaverse space. A navigation mesh was used to define walkable spaces within the museum, ensuring NPCs could move naturally around the museum without passing through walls or stairs, leveraging AI for their movements as shown in Fig. 1.

Fig. 1. Museum design with NPC

As shown in Fig. 2, NPCs were designed to mimic the movements of people entering the museum's metaverse, acting as if they were looking at artworks when near them. A box object with an invisible box collider was placed in spaces where artworks could be viewed, and when an avatar enters the box, a trigger event occurs, stopping movement and maintaining a stationary position facing the artwork for a certain period. When real users come close to NPCs in the museum, the NPCs present simple dialogues, allowing users to feel social interaction. Additionally, as shown in Fig. 3, a curator NPC was proposed. The curator NPC follows the user, explaining the artworks. A function was developed to calculate the direction of the user's gaze when admiring an artwork, ensuring the explanation does not obstruct the view. Virtual reality technology was used to make the metaverse museum appear realistic, allowing users to participate in virtual space with a real-life perspective, as shown in Fig. 3, enhancing immersion.

Fig. 2. NPC Navigation in Art Museum

Fig. 3. Curator NPC

5 Conclusion

The metaverse art museum can provide a new museum experience to users by offering information related to culture and arts and forming social relationships. Particularly, social interaction is a crucial factor that encourages active participation and return visits to the metaverse. For social relationships to be built, multiple users must connect simultaneously and feel social presence through interaction; without meeting other users, social interaction does not occur, leading to a decrease in the metaverse's revisit rate. To solve this issue, we proposed a metaverse museum that uses curator NPCs and audience NPCs to allow users to feel social presence. NPCs move around the museum and admire artworks like real users when no real users are present. When a user approaches an NPC, it is designed to enable simple interaction. Research was conducted to explore methods for sustaining visits to the metaverse museum by allowing users to feel social presence through automatic NPCs. Future research will study the user experience of the proposed metaverse museum.

Acknowledgments. This research was supported by the Basic Science Research Program through the National Research Foundation of Korea (NRF) funded by the Ministry of Education (NRF2020R1I1A3051739).

References

1. Carvajal, D.A.L., Morita, M.M., Bilmes, G.M.: Virtual museums. Captured reality and 3D modeling. J. Cultural Heritage **45**, 234–239 (2020)
2. Onderdijk, K.E., Bouckaert, L., Van Dyck, E., Maes, P.J.: Concert experiences in virtual reality environments. Virtual Reality **27**, 2383–2396 (2023)
3. Ning, H., et al.: A survey on the metaverse: the state-of-the-art, technologies, applications, and challenges. IEEE Internet Things J. **10**(16), 14671–14688 (2023)
4. Huynh-The, T., Pham, Q.V., Pham, X.Q., Nguyen, T.T., Han, Z., Kim, D.S.: Artificial intelligence for the metaverse: a survey. Eng. Appl. Artif. Intell. **117**, 105581 (2023)
5. Sun, J., Gan, W., Chao, H.C., Yu, P.S.: Metaverse: survey, applications, security, and opportunities. arXiv preprint arXiv:2210.07990 (2022)
6. Hutson, J., Hutson, P.: Museums and the Metaverse: Emerging Technologies to Promote Inclusivity and Engagement. Application of Modern Trends in Museums, IntechOpen, United Kingdom (2023)
7. Sylaiou, S., Dafiotis, P.: Storytelling in virtual museums: engaging a multitude of voices. In: Visual Computing for Cultural Heritage, pp. 369–388. Springer, Cham (2020)
8. Kang, D., Choi, H., Nam, S.: Learning cultural spaces: a collaborative creation of a virtual art museum using roblox. Int. J. Emerging Technol. Learn. **17**(22) (2022)
9. Oh, H.J., Kim, J., Chang, J.J., Park, N., Lee, S.: Social benefits of living in the metaverse: the relationships among social presence, supportive interaction, social self-efficacy, and feelings of loneliness. Comput. Hum. Behav. **139**, 107498 (2023)
10. Ducheneaut, N., Wen, M. H., Yee, N., Wadley, G.: Body and mind: a study of avatar personalization in three virtual worlds. In: Proceedings of the SIGCHI Conference on Human Factors in Computing Systems, pp. 1151–1160. ACM, Boston (2009)

Virtual Museums: State of the Art, Trends, and Challenges

Li Yang[1], Nankai Cheng[1(✉)], Puyuan Jiang[2], and Paulo Noriega[3]

[1] Faculty of Architecture, University of Lisbon, Lisbon, Portugal
nankai.cheng@edu.ulisboa.pt
[2] Faculty of Arts, University of Coimbra, Coimbra, Portugal
[3] Research Center for Architecture, Urbanism, Design and User Experience Lab (ErgoUX),
Faculty of Architecture, University of Lisbon, Lisbon, Portugal

Abstract. Virtual museums represent a significant innovation in the digital cultural heritage domain, harnessing digital technology to create immersive, interactive experiences that transcend geographical boundaries. Utilizing advanced Virtual Reality (VR) and Augmented Reality (AR) technologies, these platforms enable remote access to cultural and historical heritage, revolutionizing the way cultural artifacts are exhibited and preserved. They offer immersive experiences, enhanced interactivity through innovative entertainment like gaming, and foster interdisciplinary collaboration across various fields. Additionally, virtual museums promote cultural diversity, providing a platform for lesser-known cultures.

However, the widespread adoption and development of virtual museums face challenges, including digital disparities affecting access in regions with limited internet connectivity and the need for sustainable financial models for their development and maintenance. Moreover, user experience design is crucial in ensuring meaningful cultural engagement. Despite these challenges, virtual museums hold immense potential for preserving and educating about cultural heritage. This paper reviews the current progress in the field, examining existing solutions and identifying both novel designs and areas for improvement. It also highlights the development trends, technological advancements, and the interplay of challenges and opportunities in virtual museum design. The research aims to guide the future design of virtual museums, focusing on technological implementation and enhancing user satisfaction, contributing to the field's growth and impact.

Keywords: Virtual Museums · Digital Cultural Heritage · Augmented Reality (AR) · Virtual Reality (VR) · Immersive Experience

1 Introduction

In recent years, the emergence and evolution of virtual museums have marked a significant milestone in the domain of digital cultural heritage. Virtual museums, leveraging digital technologies such as Virtual Reality (VR) and Augmented Reality (AR), have redefined the way we interact with and experience cultural heritage. These innovative

C. Stephanidis et al. (Eds.): HCII 2024, CCIS 2119, pp. 226–237, 2024.
https://doi.org/10.1007/978-3-031-61966-3_26

platforms utilize multimedia and interactive displays to not only digitize collections but also to recreate authentic museum experiences [1]. The ability of virtual museums to transcend geographical constraints is particularly noteworthy, as it allows remote access to cultural and historical heritage from anywhere in the world, broadening the scope and reach of traditional museums [2]. This paradigm shift in the museum experience is driven by the advancement in AR and VR technologies, which provide increasingly immersive experiences. Through such technologies, virtual museums offer enhanced interactivity and a more engaging form of entertainment. This has led to a more profound connection between audiences and the cultural heritage they explore. Additionally, virtual museums foster interdisciplinary collaboration and innovation, bringing together cultural heritage preservationists, technology developers, designers, artists, and educators. This collaborative effort is pivotal in creating experiences that are not only educational but also entertaining, thereby enriching the overall value of virtual museums [3].

However, the adoption and development of virtual museums are not without challenges. One of the most significant hurdles is the disparity in digital access, particularly in regions with limited internet connectivity, which affects the widespread adoption of virtual museum resources [4]. Furthermore, sustainable development of these platforms is a concern, as many virtual museum projects depend on limited financial resources. Another critical aspect is the design of user experiences, which requires careful consideration to ensure that interfaces and interactive elements are intuitive and meaningful. Parallel to the rise of virtual museums, traditional museums continue to evolve, integrating digital technology innovations to preserve and experience cultural heritage. This process involves transforming exhibitions, organizational structures, services, and the relationship between visitors and museums. Despite the growing embrace of digital innovation in the museum world, challenges remain in achieving a seamless interaction between virtual and real content and in designing optimal content that conveys cultural significance and effectively guides visitor experiences. This study aims to explore the support of new technologies in virtual museums, with a focus on enhancing the integration of virtual and real content in museum settings. It seeks to understand how these technologies can be coordinated with spatial layouts, visitor paths, and diverse experiences, aiming to attract and guide visitors effectively. In the era of digitalization, museums are still exploring the best ways to use technological innovations to interweave virtual and real content, aiming to build a richer and more engaging visitor experience. The ultimate goal of this research is to uncover future trends in museum experiences and to provide meaningful guidance for increasing public sensitivity and engagement with cultural heritage [5].

2 Theoretical Background

Museums and cultural heritage institutions have played a key role since ancient times as guardians of civilization and transmitters of knowledge. They have evolved and transformed over centuries, adapting to the constant social, cultural and economic changes in human history [6]. With roots in the third century BC, one of the fundamental attributes of museums is to fulfill their educational mission through the sharing of knowledge. However, as times have evolved, museums have embraced technological innovations and integrated technology into their collections to create engaging experiences, enhance the wow factor, satisfy audiences' entertainment needs, and provide them with collections that are not actually on display access opportunities to provide a richer experience and information about the artifacts on display [5].

Currently, with the advent of the digital age, museums and heritage sectors are facing the challenges and opportunities of digital transformation. The International Documentation Committee (CIDOC) of the International Council of Museums (ICOM) has established "Digital Transformation of Cultural Heritage Institutions" as a research agenda for 2020, recognizing that digital tools have gradually changed the concept of documents, as well as the management of collections, Perspectives on conservation, research and dissemination[7,8]. This marks a new era. Although digitalization has been working hard to bring benefits to museums and cultural institutions in terms of preservation, dissemination, and added value, there has been no systematic review of the comprehensive transformation of museums and cultural heritage by digital virtual reality technology. Research and in-depth theoretical discussion [9]. In this context, the latest technologies, trends and challenges of virtual museums will be discussed to promote the further development of virtual museums.

2.1 State of the Art: Extended Reality (XR)

Achieving a unique and unified augmented reality (XR) experience in a virtual museum involved several technological achievements. XR technology is considered a powerful tool to promote cultural experience in museums, and its application allows people to travel through time and space virtually and experience the history and legends of various places in a fascinating way [10]. Cultural organizations and institutions engaged in or promoting humanitarian work are actively taking advantage of augmented reality (AR), mixed reality (MR) and virtual reality (VR) technologies, especially VR's empathy-inducing capabilities. The disruptive power of new realities such as virtual reality (VR), augmented reality (AR) and mixed reality (MR) are the innovations that have the greatest impact on cultural heritage and museums [11]. The physical-virtual continuum is redesigned, introducing advanced forms of human-human, human-technology, and technology-technology interaction [12].

Based on the idea of the reality-virtual continuum, the conception of the virtual reality continuum encompasses various examples of the application of cultural heritage technologies [13]. Specifically, the real environment is adjusted through mobile devices, holographic (wired/wireless) AR, mobile VR or desktop VR technology (see Fig. 1) allowing users to immerse themselves in a seamless blend of real and virtual worlds [14]. For example, existing physical exhibits can be made richer by enhancing digital information that can be displayed on mobile devices, thereby changing the user's perception of the exhibits [15]. Sometimes the user's perception can even be replaced by a virtual counterpart, or the physical exhibits can be completely virtualized and can only be accessed through VR technology [16]. These technological applications play a key role in virtual museums, enriching visitors' experience and enhancing the interactivity and depth of cultural inheritance [17, 18].

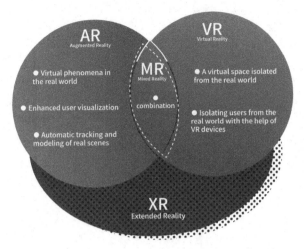

Fig. 1. The relationship between XR, AR, VR and MR.

The Fig. 1 illustrates the relationship between three types of reality technologies: augmented reality (AR), virtual reality (VR), and mixed reality (MR). Together, these technologies are encompassed by the term extended reality (XR). The main functions of AR (augmented reality) include overlaying virtual phenomena on the real world, enhanced user visualization, and automatic tracking and modeling of real scenes. VR (Virtual Reality) is characterized by creating a virtual space that is isolated from the real world. It immerses users in a completely digital environment, isolating them from the real world with the help of VR devices. MR (Mixed Reality) is a hybrid of AR and VR. It allows a combination of real-world and digital elements, and users can interact with both simultaneously. The broader category represented by XR (Extended Reality). XR is an umbrella term that covers all forms of computer-altered reality, including AR, VR and MR.

3   Research Methodology

This study applied some procedures and methods to conduct literature research on the data set with the aim of answering the research questions (see Fig. 2).

A. Research questions.

The research questions this study hopes to answer through bibliometrics are:

- Q1: What is the development trend of virtual museums?
- Q2: In the field of virtual museums, which key technologies and innovations have received widespread attention?

Bibliometric analysis of virtual museums involves collecting a large number of documents and keywords from databases and then analyzing them to identify the most prominent research themes and trends over time, as well as the most influential research in the field. Content analysis further deepens the understanding of the specific challenges and application areas of virtual museums.

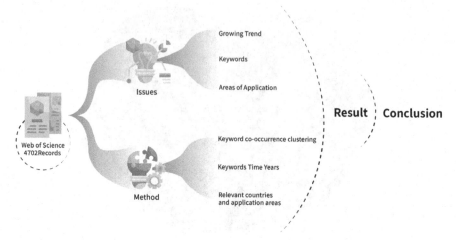

Fig. 2. Virtual museum information search process.

3.1 Literature Review Process

The following studies were selected to be searched in the Web of Science core database, the search strategy was set to "Virtual Museum", and the five major citation indexes commonly used in the WOS database, SSCI, SCI-Expanded, A&HCI, CPCI-S and CPCI-SSH, were selected as search sources. In order to collect all relevant articles, the search time span was set to all years (from 1965 to 2024). The retrieved documents were exported to txt files in the format of "full records and cited references", and a total of 4702 documents were finally obtained for further quantitative analysis (see Fig. 3).

The Fig. 3 shows the keywords and keyword importance and frequency related to virtual museums. Figure a shows the importance proportion and frequency of "virtual reality", "cultural heritage" and "assessment" as well as other keywords. This shows that these concepts appear frequently in the literature on virtual museums, highlighting the importance of the research field in virtual museums. Figure b and c show that in the field of virtual museums, "virtual reality" is very closely related to "cultural heritage", which leads to branches such as behavior, memory, and models of people. Indicates that accurate representation and modeling of cultural heritage is very important when building a virtual museum. Figure d shows "assessment" as a keyword, emphasizing words such as "evolution", "climate change" and "investigation" in the field of virtual museum research, pointing out the role of virtual museums in educating the public about natural history and environmental issues.By searching for keywords about virtual museums, the core ones are "virtual reality" and "cultural heritage", which shows that virtual museums mainly use VR technology to digitally preserve and present cultural relics and historical relics. Surrounding terms such as "3D reconstruction", "virtual exhibition", "tourism" and "design" illustrate the various components of the virtual museum (see Fig. 4).

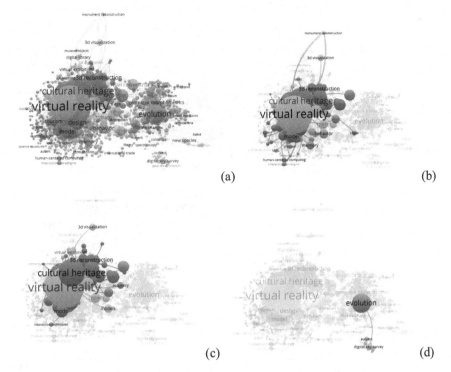

Fig. 3. Visual map based on co-occurrence keywords.

The Fig. 4 shows keywords combined with the timeline and color gradient, which allows you to analyze the historical trends of the keywords in each graph. In figure a, keywords such as "virtual reality", "cultural heritage" and "3D reconstruction" are in larger fonts and close to each other. The green color indicates that these concepts are very important and frequently discussed in the literature at a time point closer to 2020. In contrast, the lighter colors and smaller words indicate that around the year 2014, these concepts are less prominent. Figure b continues to highlight "cultural heritage" and "virtual reality", and the colors of these words also tend to be green, which further confirms that the discussion of these topics became more focused later in time. In addition, some specific regions and scientific themes emerge (e.g., "Evolution"), which may indicate an increase in interest and importance in research over time for these regions or themes. In figure c, the position and size of the terms "cultural heritage," "virtual reality," and "models" and "design" indicate that these areas have been the focus of research throughout the time period. At the same time, the appearance and color of "new species" indicates that at the back end of the timeline, near 2020, topics about biodiversity and the discovery of new species may have gained more attention within the realm of virtual museums.

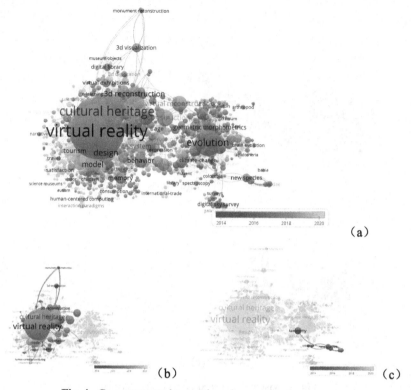

Fig. 4. Co-occurrence keywords and years visual map.

The Fig. 5 shows the participation of institutions and research institutions in relation to virtual museum applications. The names of countries are shown, among which words such as "USA", "Japan", "Canada" and "Italy" show that they may have high activity in research and applications in the field of virtual museums due to their large size and prominent position. As the time transitions from green in 2016 to yellow in 2020, we can see the continued importance of certain countries such as "USA" and "Italy", indicating that these countries are driving virtual museum technology and applications Play a leadership role. Figure b is about the application of virtual museums in institutions, including universities and companies, such as "nat hist museum" (natural history museum) and "caltech" (Caltech), indicating that these institutions have made significant progress in the research and application of virtual museums in the near future. Contribution.

3.2 Results and Discussion

According to the literature review and analysis of data and trends in the field of virtual museums, the research and application of virtual museums has shown a significant growth trend worldwide [19], especially in countries such as the United States and Italy. Keyword analysis shows that "virtual reality", "cultural heritage", and "assessment" are

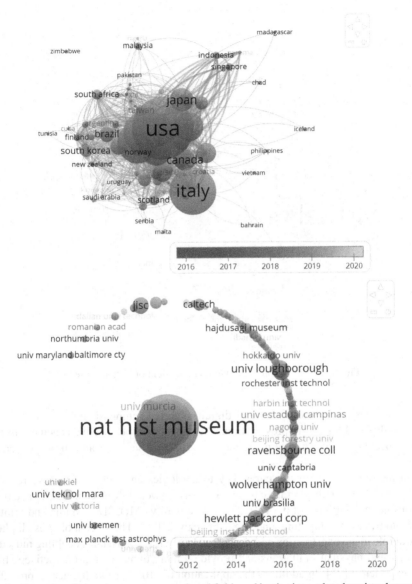

Fig. 5. Countries of virtual museum research and fields and institutions related to virtual museum applications.

the most prominent terms in the study, which reflects the hot topics and research focus in the field of virtual museums (see Fig. 6).

Based on the analysis, Q1 is answered and discussed. The development trend of virtual museums points to the importance of technological integration and innovation [20]. This includes the integration of virtual reality technology to provide users with an immersive experience; 3D reconstruction technology to accurately restore and preserve

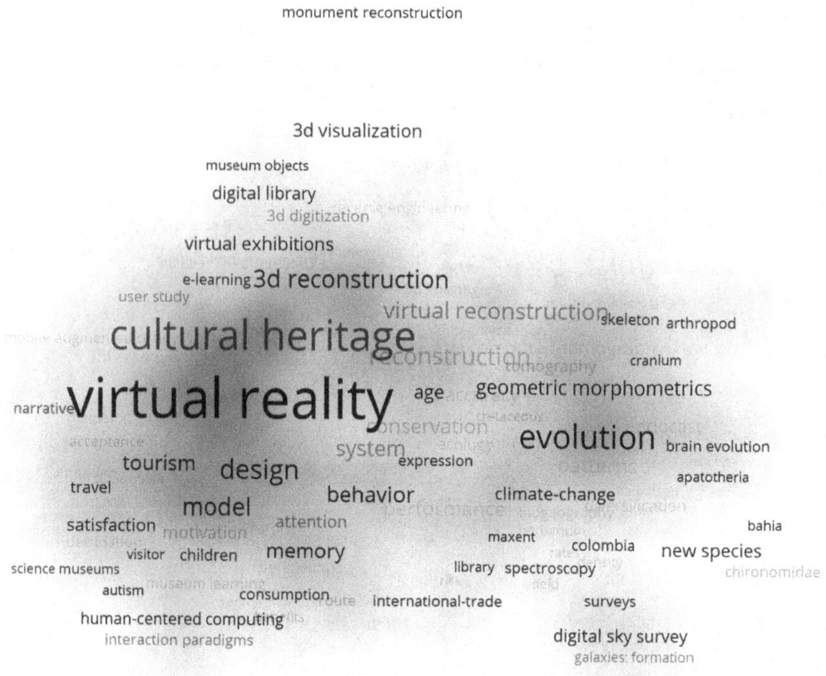

monument reconstruction

3d visualization

museum objects

digital library

3d digitization

virtual exhibitions

e-learning 3d reconstruction

user study

cultural heritage

virtual reconstruction skeleton arthropod

reconstruction

cranium

narrative virtual reality age geometric morphometrics

conservation

acceptance system expression evolution brain evolution

tourism design apatotheria

travel

model behavior climate-change

satisfaction motivation attention bahia

maxent

visitor children memory colombia new species

science museums library spectroscopy chironomidae

autism consumption international-trade surveys

human-centered computing

interaction paradigms digital sky survey

galaxies: formation

Fig. 6. Visualization of hot words in the field of virtual museums.

historical sites; and the expansion of digital materials, emphasizing the emphasis on accessibility and long-term preservation. The educational perspective is equally important, especially virtual museums as tools for distance learning and digital education [21].

In the field of virtual museums, key technologies and innovations have received attention [22]. From the literature review, Q2 was answered. Key technologies and innovations include virtual reality (VR), augmented reality (AR), 3D scanning and printing technology, cloud computing, and Big data analysis [23]. These technologies all play a central role in the construction and management of virtual museums, enabling museums to transcend physical limitations and provide a more dynamic and interactive exhibition experience [24]. In addition, the application of artificial intelligence in providing personalized access experience is also gradually increasing, which promotes the development of personalized learning and display content [25]. Research in the field of virtual museums has shown diversified development directions and technology applications, indicating great potential in the digital preservation and educational dissemination of cultural heritage in the future [26].

4 Conclusions

The comprehensive research conducted in this study, underpinned by bibliometric analysis, reveals the dynamic evolution and multifaceted potential of virtual museums. This field, propelled by advanced technologies, offers innovative solutions to cultural heritage preservation and educational dissemination. Virtual Reality (VR) technology [27] has been pivotal in providing immersive experiences, allowing users to engage with exhibitions in three-dimensional spaces. Augmented Reality (AR) [28] enriches the visitor experience by integrating digital information with the physical world. Additionally, the accuracy and preservation capabilities of 3D scanning and printing [29] are instrumental in replicating cultural relics. Cloud computing and big data analysis [30] play crucial roles in managing and personalizing the virtual museum experience. The development of virtual museums is characterized by a trend of cross-border collaboration, particularly prominent in countries like the United States, Italy, and Japan. These nations have been at the forefront, with institutions significantly contributing to the advancement and application of related technologies. The involvement of educational institutions and businesses indicates the expanding application scope of virtual museums, notably in distance learning and digital education. Despite the rapid growth and potential in the field, virtual museums face several challenges. Technical issues, such as achieving high-quality 3D restoration, managing large-scale data, and ensuring a stable user experience, are significant [31]. Cultural challenges include maintaining diversity and accuracy in representation. Furthermore, the accessibility and affordability of these technologies, along with the safeguarding of user privacy and data security, remain pressing concerns [32]. In conclusion, the field of virtual museums stands at the cusp of significant contributions to cultural heritage protection, educational outreach, and technological advancement. The findings of this study underscore the need for continuous research and innovation to support the healthy and sustained growth of this burgeoning field. The insights gained through this research not only highlight the current achievements but also chart a path for future exploration and development in the realm of virtual museums.

References

1. Fu, Y., Kim, S., Zhou, T.: Staging the 'authenticity' of intangible heritage from the production perspective: the case of craftsmanship museum cluster in Hangzhou, China. J. Tour. Cult. Chang. **13**(4), 285–300 (2015)
2. Trunfio, M., Campana, S.: A visitors' experience model for mixed reality in the museum. Curr. Issue Tour. **23**(9), 1053–1058 (2020)
3. Margetis, G., Apostolakis, K.C., Ntoa, S., Papagiannakis, G., Stephanidis, C.: X-reality museums: unifying the virtual and real world towards realistic virtual museums. Appl. Sci. **11**(1), 338 (2020)
4. Lahav, S.: Curating, Interpretation and Museums: When Attitude Becomes Form. Taylor & Francis (2023)
5. Camarero, C., Garrido, M.J.: Fostering innovation in cultural contexts: Market orientation, service orientation, and innovations in museums. J. Serv. Res. **15**(1), 39–58 (2012)
6. Falk, J.H., Dierking, L.D.: The museum experience revisited. Routledge (2016)

7. ICOM. Museums and sustainable development: How can ICOM support, in concrete terms, the museum community's sustainable development projects? Thematic Panel of the Advisory Committee, n°1 (2011)

8. ICOM, & OECD. Culture and Local Development: Maximizing the Impact. Guide for Local Governments, Communities and Museums (2018)

9. Trunfio, M., Lucia, M.D., Campana, S., Magnelli, A.: Innovating the cultural heritage museum service model through virtual reality and augmented reality: the effects on the overall visitor experience and satisfaction. J. Herit. Tour. 17(1), 1–19 (2022)

10. Ptukhin, A., Serkov, K., Khrushkov, A., Bozhko, E.: Prospects and modern technologies in the development of VR/AR. In: 2018 Ural Symposium on Biomedical Engineering, Radioelectronics and Information Technology (USBEREIT), pp. 169–173. IEEE, May 2018

11. Schaper, M.M., Santos, M., Malinverni, L., Berro, J.Z., Pares, N.: Learning about the past through situatedness, embodied exploration and digital augmentation of cultural heritage sites. Int. J. Hum. Comput. Stud. 114, 36–50 (2018)

12. Bekele, M.K., Town, C., Pierdicca, R., Frontoni, E., Malinverni, E.S.: A survey of augmented, virtual, and mixed reality for cultural heritage. J. Comput. Cultural Heritage 11(2), 1–36 (2018)

13. Flavián, C., Ibáñez-sánchez, S., Orús, C.: The impact of virtual, augmented and mixed reality technologies on the customer experience. J. Bus. Res. 100, 547–560 (2019)

14. Hudson, S., Matson-Barkat, S., Pallamin, N., Jegou, G.: With or without you? Interaction and immersion in a virtual reality experience. J. Bus. Res. 100, 459–468 (2019)

15. Bakhshi, H., Throsby, D.: Innovation in arts and cultural organisations. NESTA (2009)

16. Kim, M.J., Lee, C.K., Jung, T.: Exploring consumer behavior in virtual reality tourism using an extended stimulus-organism-response model. J. Travel Res. 59(1), 69–89 (2020)

17. Han, D.I., tom Dieck, M.C., Jung, T.: User experience model for augmented reality applications in urban heritage tourism. J. Heritage Tourism 13(1), 46–61 (2018)

18. Little, C., Bec, A., Moyle, B.D., Patterson, D.: Innovative methods for heritage tourism experiences: creating windows into the past. J. Herit. Tour. 1, 1–13 (2019)

19. Kamariotou, V., Kamariotou, M., Kitsios, F.: Strategic planning for virtual exhibitions and visitors' experience: a multidisciplinary approach for museums in the digital age. Digital Appl. Archaeology Cultural Heritage 21, e00183 (2021)

20. Kiourt, C., Koutsoudis, A., Pavlidis, G.: DynaMus: a fully dynamic 3D virtual museum framework. J. Cult. Herit. 22, 984–991 (2016)

21. Daniela, L.: Virtual museums as learning agents. Sustainability 12(7), 2698 (2020)

22. Panciroli, C., Russo, V., Macauda, A.: When technology meets art: museum paths between real and virtual. In: Proceedings, vol. 1, No. 9, p. 913. MDPI, November 2017

23. Besoain, F., Jego, L., Gallardo, I.: Developing a virtual museum: experience from the design and creation process. Information 12(6), 244 (2021)

24. Nisiotis, L., Alboul, L.: Initial evaluation of an intelligent virtual museum prototype powered by AI, XR and robots. In: Augmented Reality, Virtual Reality, and Computer Graphics: 8th International Conference, AVR 2021, Virtual Event, September 7–10, 2021, Proceedings 8, pp. 290–305. Springer International Publishing (2021)

25. Recuero Virto, N., López, M.F.B.: Robots, artificial intelligence, and service automation to the core: remastering experiences at museums. In: Robots, artificial intelligence, and service automation in travel, tourism and hospitality, pp. 239–253. Emerald Publishing Limited (2019)

26. Shaw, A., Krug, D.: Heritage meets social media: designing a virtual museum space for young people. J. Museum Educ. 38(2), 239–252 (2013)

27. Lee, H., Jung, T.H., tom Dieck, M.C., Chung, N.: Experiencing immersive virtual reality in museums. Inform. Manage. 57(5), 103229 (2020)

28. Pervolarakis, Z., et al.: Visiting Heritage Sites in AR and VR. Heritage 6(3), 2489–2502 (2023)

29. Williams, T.L.: More than just a novelty? Museum visitor interactions with 3D printed artifacts (Doctoral dissertation) (2017)
30. Yang, S., Hou, M., Huo, P., Li, A., Jiang, L.: A cloud computing platform to support digital heritage application using a service-oriented approach. Int. Arch. Photogramm. Remote. Sens. Spat. Inf. Sci. **43**, 1497–1504 (2020)
31. Anton, M., Nicolae, G., Moldoveanu, A., Balan, O.: Virtual museums-technologies, opportunities and perspectives. Romanian J. Hum.-Comput. Interact. **11**(2) (2018)
32. Sylaiou, S., Kasapakis, V., Dzardanova, E., Gavalas, D.: Assessment of virtual guides' credibility in virtual museum environments. In: Augmented Reality, Virtual Reality, and Computer Graphics: 6th International Conference, AVR 2019, Santa Maria al Bagno, Italy, June 24–27, 2019, Proceedings, Part II, pp. 230–238. Springer, Cham (2019). https://doi.org/10.1007/978-3-030-25999-0_20

User Experience Centered AR Interface Design to Ruins Museums

Jiexin Yang[✉]

Ocean University of China, Shandong, Qingdao 266000, The People's Republic of China
18333851079@163.com

Abstract. Cultural heritage has been continuously impacted in the process of globalization, and how to protect cultural ruins in an innovative and efficient way has attracted widespread attention. While ruins museums play the role of guardians and inheritors, digital intelligence technology has started to be used as an auxiliary tool for museums to disseminate knowledge and enhance user experience. Due to the continuous upgrading of users' pursuit of museum visiting experience, this paper aims to combine the ruins museums with AR multi-sensory interactive experience, and construct the AR multi-sensory experience system of ruins museums in order to improve users' experience from multiple perspectives. This method of combining ruins museums with AR technology under the principle of service experience provides new ideas for future related designs in terms of personalized experience and multi-dimensional interaction, which can enhance the attractiveness of museum-type venues to the public and promote the long-term dissemination of knowledge.

Keywords: AR · Multi-Sensory Experience · User Experience · Ruins Museums

1 Introduction

As the process of globalization continues to accelerate, the protection and transmission of cultural heritage are facing unprecedented challenges. These valuable heritages, as witnesses of human history and civilization, are under constant attack. How to protect cultural heritage innovatively and efficiently has become the focus of extensive attention worldwide. In 1982, the International Council of Museums (ICOM) [1] defined "ruins museums" as "museums established for the preservation in situ of movable and immovable natural or cultural heritage, i.e., museums built on the site where the heritage was created or discovered." As an important guardian and inheritor of cultural heritage, ruins museums have an important historical mission. They not only provide a place for people to learn about the past and perceive history, but also serve as a bridge between the present and the future, as well as a special social responsibility at the educational level. However, the traditional way of museum display in the rapid development of digital intelligent technology today has been difficult to meet the increasingly diversified user needs. The application of digital intelligent technology can make the museum exhibition form break through the traditional form of restrictions, can be more intuitive display of cultural relics information content, at the same time can improve the degree of participation and interest of visitors.

C. Stephanidis et al. (Eds.): HCII 2024, CCIS 2119, pp. 238–247, 2024.
https://doi.org/10.1007/978-3-031-61966-3_27

2   Literature Review

2.1   Analysis of the Current Situation of Museums Applying Digital Intelligence Technology

With the comprehensive development of digital intelligence technology and gradually penetrate into all walks of life, museums have also been transformed to embark on the road of digitization to use a variety of media forms to achieve the maximization of the dissemination of museum information resources. Although the digital transformation of museums is not a new proposition, but digital intelligence technology as a complementary means of museum construction is still an important way for museums to achieve cultural dissemination [2]. How to select effectively and use rationally digital intelligence technology, or will become a new challenge for museums.

At present, the application of digital intelligence technologies such as screen display, projection display, multi-touch interactive display, virtual reality display, augmented reality display, etc. in museums is becoming more and more abundant [3]. Museums based on two-dimensional/three-dimensional scanning, rendering three-dimensional digital collection models, so that off-site personnel to appreciate and study the collection becomes possible, while realizing the collection of "sustainable" preservation. The museum builds digital people based on artificial intelligence technology, which can interact with visitors in real time, act as virtual interpreters to explain the story of the collection and answer questions for different visitors.

2.2   Analysis of the Current Situation of the Application of AR Technology in Ruins Museums

For the protection of cultural relics, tourists can not directly contact the cultural relics when visiting the ruins museums, and at the same time, the cultural relics appear to be old due to time, it is difficult to completely restore the historical scene, and because the traditional display is relatively boring, resulting in a lack of interactivity between the visitors and the cultural relics, the audience can not be very good feel the deeper significance of the cultural relics. Numerous museums have launched AR APP, and visitors are able to see three-dimensional digital artifacts by scanning the QR code after opening the APP. Unlike static physical artifacts, digital artifacts are given a new life, which can interact with visitors to enhance the interest and experience [4]. China's "Dunhuang AR Intelligent Guide" brings a new immersive tour experience to the audience, where visitors only need a pair of Rokid AR glasses to experience the history and culture of the Mogao Grottoes in an immersive way under the guidance of a digital interpreter (see Fig. 1) [5]. Visitors to the National Building Museum's new exhibition, Notre-Damede Paris: the Augmented exhibition, use HistoPad touchscreen tablets to navigate the exhibition, experience an immersive and interactive tour, and travel back in time to the Notre Dame de Paris of the past (see Fig. 2) [6].

With the gradual popularization and mature development of augmented reality technology in various countries, its application fields are becoming more and more extensive, such as manufacturing maintenance, marketing and sales, construction and medical care, military field, film and television entertainment, education and teaching, exhibition and

Fig. 1. China, Dunhuang AR Intelligent Guide.

Fig. 2. American, Notre-Damede Paris: the Augmented exhibition.

display, and cultural heritage protection, etc., and is gradually becoming the main direction for the development of the next-generation human-computer interaction technology [7].

2.3 Weaknesses and Shortcomings of Existing Studies

There are many problems in the visiting experience of traditional ruins museums, which can be manifested as: single display, lack of interaction, aging obsolescence, spatial limitations and restricted knowledge channels [8]. Although a few ruins museums have begun to try to apply augmented reality technology to improve the audience's visiting experience, the current application still has many problems. Today's choice of platform devices is more in the form of easily popularized mobile devices combined with apps, and although users can get more information and visit better by being provided with free apps [9], many AR apps are still immaturely developed, resulting in them appearing rough and less realistic in presenting details and backstories of historical ruins. In addition, the popularity and compatibility problems of AR equipment also limit the breadth and convenience of its application. Augmented reality technology in the museum display needs to rely on its powerful technical characteristics, so that the exhibits have the advantages of multi-angle presentation, make up for the information gap, enrich the form of restoration display and enhance the sense of interactive experience, etc. However, in terms of people's experience of augmented reality technology, it also emerges that the form of augmented reality technology is greater than the content, the sense of immersion and interactive experience is insufficient, the sense of participation is low, etc., which needs to be further remedied and improved. These problems need to be further remedied and improved.

Furthermore, the lack of personalized AR content for different audience groups makes the visiting experience lack of diversity and attraction. Therefore, in order to more effectively use AR technology to enhance the visiting experience of ruins museums, more exploration and improvement in multi-sensory experience, diverse interaction, and personalized design are needed [3].

3   Design Cases

The Qingdao World War I Ruins Museum in Shandong, China is the richest and most comprehensive thematic museum documenting the relationship between World War I and China. The museum not only displays a large number of valuable historical artifacts and photos, but also uses 4D technology, multimedia touch screen and other modern digital exhibition methods to vividly reproduce the difficult course of Qingdao from its establishment to the return of sovereignty. Therefore, the authors took this as a case study to conduct field experience and randomly invited 62 tourists who visited the museum offline to fill out questionnaires and conduct interviews, and obtained the following analysis results.

3.1   Analysis of the Museum User Experience

A total of 62 valid data were obtained from this questionnaire, of which 30 were males and 32 were females, with the main age group being 18–30 years old.

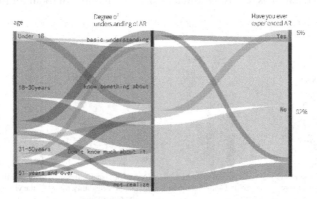

Fig. 3. Sankey Chart - Data visualization for user age, user's level of understanding of AR, whether they have experienced AR or not.

Most visitors don't know much about AR, and only 8% have experienced an AR device. The age of users is negatively correlated with their knowledge of digital intelligence technologies such as AR (see Fig. 3).

In recent years, museums have been committed to innovating methods and tools to disseminate knowledge, and interactive experiential exhibitions are one of the most common methods used. A simple way to create interactive content is to utilize digital intelligence technologies, virtual reality and augmented reality technologies can be very useful to improve the interactivity between users and exhibits. In particular, Augmented Reality technology adds additional information on top of existing content to correlate the information delivery [10]. Through data analysis, users' expectations for AR technology experience (see Fig. 4) are mainly immersion, fun and interactivity, accounting for 61.29%, 70.79% and 58.06%, respectively.

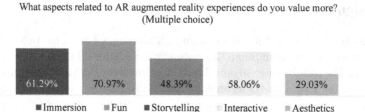

Fig. 4. User expectations of the AR experience.

Through the visitors' scores on the overall quality of the museum (see Fig. 5), calculated by the weighted average, Qingdao World War I Ruins Museum scored 7.52, 7.39, 7.45, 8.26 in the above four items respectively.

It can be concluded that Qingdao World War I Ruins Museum has deficiencies in the immersive interactive experience, the sense of integration and the degree of thought provoking is a little poor, the exhibition content is not easy to be understood intuitively, the degree of visualization is relatively low, and there is a number of room for improvement.

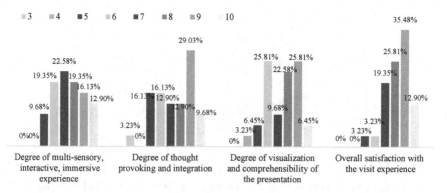

Fig. 5. Statistics on how users rated various aspects of the museum.

Through the questionnaire data analysis, if AR experience design is carried out for this museum, the users' demand for experience feedback is more for entertainment and relaxation, and at the same time, they hope to obtain souvenirs of special significance and certain knowledge and skills from the visit, and the demand for generating emotional resonance is a little weaker than the former (see Fig. 6). The study shows that AR technology applied to museums can help improve the sense of visitors' visiting experience and add some informal learning, enjoyment and interest. At the same time, it can promote the sale of museum-related goods, which can increase the desire of tourists to buy [11].

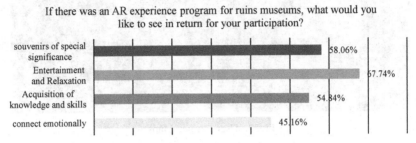

Fig. 6. User expectations of AR applied to ruins museums.

Through the user interviews, in response to the questions of "what content in the museum has triggered your thoughts" and "what suggestions do you have for the museum experience", relevant conclusions can be drawn: tourists put forward further expectations for the experience of the Jiaoji Railway carriages in the museum, and make suggestions on the display mode and story coherence of the exhibition hall. Most of the tourists said that they did not leave too much memory after the visit, which also reflects to a certain extent that the display of the museum is not interesting and it is difficult to stimulate the desire of tourists to visit the museum.

3.2 Design Methods

User Journey Maps. Based on the visitor interviews and user analysis, a user journey map (see Fig. 7) is drawn to analyze the pain points, demand points, and opportunity points of users during their visit to the museum. The analysis process is carried out in accordance with (1) looking for a guide to understand the overall situation of the museum, (2) visiting the Jiaozhou Bay Incident, (3) experiencing the Jiaoji Railway train carriages, (4) touch screen to understand the battle situation of the Japanese-German War, (5) cultural and creative stores, (6) paying tribute in front of the electronic screen, (7) Jiaoao Acceptance Monument, the seven main activities to carry out the unfolding of the analysis.

The main issues of concern are: although the museum has restored some of the scenes, the user's immersion during the visit has not been significantly enhanced due to its static and single display. The cultural and creative products in the museum lack personalization and uniqueness, and the types and styles of souvenirs are patterned. There are too many long text displays, and tourists are not willing to read them, which leads to the effect of conveying information and educational significance that cannot be realized well.

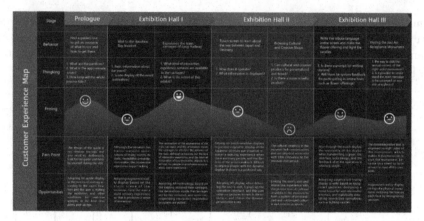

Fig. 7. User Journey Maps.

Touchpoints Matrix. The touchpoint matrix of the design case is drawn by integrating some of the features of the experience map, showing the results of different facilities, interfaces, functions and interactions, and how these elements are interrelated (see Fig. 8). Through the analysis of the touchpoint matrix, AR technology is integrated into the pavilion guide, important scene recovery, the museum's cultural and creative store and the main interactive props to enhance the visual recognition and organization, improve the sense of immersion experience and fun for visitors, to make the whole tour more meaningful for visiting and learning after the integration of AR technology.

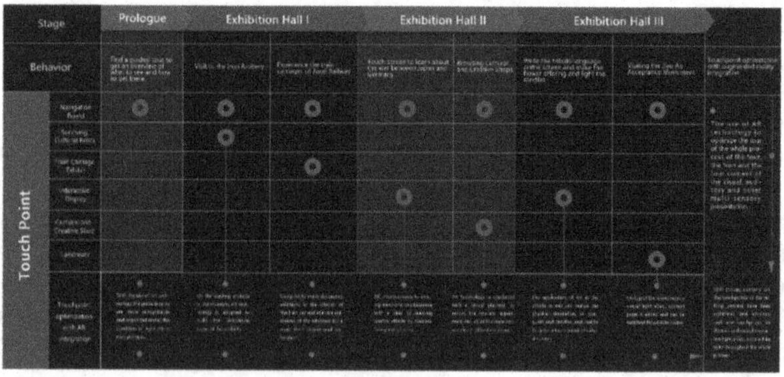

Fig. 8. Touchpoints Matrix.

Service Blueprint. By drawing the service blueprint of the case site (see Fig. 9), it is possible to establish a global viewpoint and overall service awareness, show the components and relationships of service links, analyze the line of contact between service personnel and customers, and recognize ways to improve service quality. These roles can work together to promote the improvement of service quality and tourist satisfaction. It is not difficult to understand that the user's acceptance of knowledge under multi-sensory content presentation is better than the traditional text reading experience, and the service blueprint makes plans for the interactive content of multi-sensory experience.

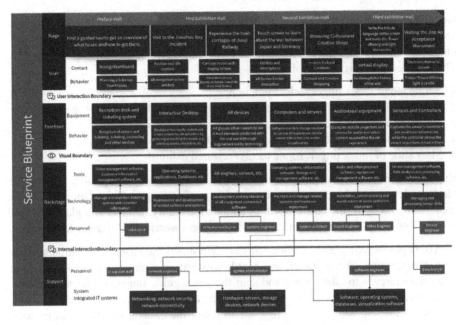

Fig. 9. Service Blueprint.

3.3 Design Content

Design Strategy. In the previous research interviews, it was also found that users thought that the text of the introduction of the exhibits in the visiting stage was too long, and the title of the picture introduction was not clear, which reflected the users' resistance to the simple text content, and required us to carry out the innovation of the interaction design in the relevant links. Meanwhile, users are most interested and active in the old object restoration and multi-sensory experience nodes, and remember the knowledge to the deepest extent. In addition, users are very much looking forward to the visual enjoyment. By analyzing the users' feelings about the interface layout and its style, it is found that the users have a strong demand for unity of style and personalization, and a more obvious demand for the aesthetics of the interface layout.

Points of attention for interface design are summarized as follows:

1. Interface layout: basic information should be displayed in real time, and augmented reality icons and animations should avoid blocking the display elements.
2. Interface style: the whole should be simple and flat, and the focus of the visit should still be based on the museum exhibits. It is necessary to appropriately increase the fun and technology elements to improve the user experience and participation. The design process should avoid inverting the subject and the object.

3. Interface color: the design color matches the exhibition environment and theme. Especially, in the ruins museum, the design color should show the sense of stability while not losing the sense of technology.

Gesture Recognition Designs. Users mainly interact through gestures in the experience scenario, mainly through actions such as clicking and swiping. Considering the large age range of visitors, the gesture design should be as simple and easy to operate as possible. The gestures are designed as follows:

1. Single tap of index finger: select function;
2. Pinch displacement of index finger and thumb: to show the scaling of the item;
3. Two consecutive taps of the index finger: start the voice guide;
4. Vertical sliding of index finger: toggle selection;
5. Slow slide of index finger: rotate the 3D restored exhibits.

Experience Flow & Interface Design. Since today's augmented reality experience platform devices are more often chosen in the form of easily popularized mobile devices combined with apps, the carrier form of augmented reality helmets and glasses is just coming into its own. This design case envisions users wearing AR glasses for a visit.

Users get the AR glasses device, the interface shows the basic information such as time, temperature, device power, and health information such as steps and heart rate. Enter the museum to take photos and start the voice guide function. During the visit, experience the old objects and scene recovery function in various aspects such as vision, hearing and touch. Slide the progress bar to select the content of interest to browse. Experience the scenes inside the Jiaoji Railway carriages and watch the restoration of the platform scenes outside the carriages. When you see a long text, you can experience the function of combining graphics and audio explanation. Entering the Cultural and Creative Shop, visitors can choose souvenirs and customize them by themselves.

Accompanied by voice explanation and multi-sensory interactive experience, visitors form a certain degree of cognitive system of the history displayed in the museum, and leave satisfied at the end of the experience. The interface experience high-fidelity design is as follows (see Fig. 10).

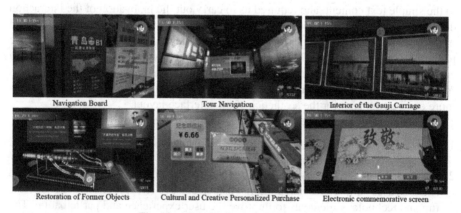

Fig. 10. High fidelity interface design.

4 Summary Analysis and Prospects

In this paper, through in-depth research on the demand characteristics of user groups for visiting experience under the conditions of applying digital intelligent technology in ruins museums, using the relevant methods of service design, carrying out the process and interface design of the case land, and summarizing the gesture recognition and other relevant design strategies of AR experience interface design.

Through literature research, it is found that there is less research on the personalized needs of users and multi-sensory experience in the process of exhibition design of ruins museums combined with AR technology. This paper prioritizes personalized design and multi-sensory experience in the design of ruins museums combined with AR technology, which can provide new ideas in the future design, and then bring a more immersive visiting experience for users to deepen the cultural communication significance of ruins museums.

This design practice also has some limitations, that is, there is no feasibility test and analysis of the final design results. However, given that there are museums that use AR devices to assist exhibitions, the results of this practice have been verified in similar studies, and we can make a preliminary judgment on the feasibility of the design results based on this. Moreover, different ruins museums need to combine the characteristics of their own pavilions and develop the design in a comprehensive way, so as to enhance the attractiveness of the ruins museum venues to the public and promote the long-term dissemination of knowledge.

References

1. The International Council of Museum (ICOM).: Archaeological Site Museum. Unesco, Paris (1982)
2. Tingshan, L.: Bringing artifacts to life: digitization helps museums' convergent communication. Mass Media **4**, 34–36 (2022). (in Chinese)
3. Ziyue, J.: Research on the Application of Augmented Reality Technology in Digital Display of Museums. Wuhan Textile University, Hubei (2023). https://doi.org/10.27698/d.cnki.gwhxj.2023.000648 (in Chinese)
4. KPMG Homepage. https://assets.kpmg.com/content/dam/kpmg/cn/pdf/zh/2023/10/kpmg-global-tech-report-2023.pdf. Accessed 12 Mar 2024
5. China Daily Homepage. https://cn.chinadaily.com.cn/a/202301/19/WS63c8c0d3a3102ada8b22c04c.html. Accessed 11 MAr 2024
6. The Historic New Orleans Collection Homepage. https://www.hnoc.org/exhibitions/notre-dame-de-paris-augmented-exhibition. Accessed 11 Mar 2024
7. Yuxi, W., Fengjun, Z., Yue, L.: Research status and development trend of augmented reality technology. Sci. Technol. Herald **36**(10), 75–83 (2018). (in Chinese)
8. Challenor, J., Minhua, M.: A review of augmented reality applications for history education and heritage visualisation. Multimodal Technol. Interact. **3**(2), 39 (2019)
9. Gitto, S., Geri, F.: The versatility of augmented reality for the enhancement of cultural heritage. IOP Conference Series: Materials Science and Engineering **949**(1), 012077 (2020)
10. Spadoni, E., Porro, S., Bordegoni, M., Arosio, I., Barbalini, L., Carulli, M.: Augmented reality to engage visitors of science museums through interactive experiences. Heritage **5**(3), 1370–1394 (2022)
11. Mohammed-Amin, R.K.: Augmented Experiences: What Can Mobile Augmented Reality Offer Museums and Historic Sites? University of Calgary, Canada (2015)

HCI in Healthcare

SmartSecur: Integrating an Empatica Watch to Enhance Patient Physical Security

Kyle Bordeaux[✉][iD], James Manning[iD], Aidan Noonan, and Mohamed Azab[iD]

Virginia Military Institute, Lexington, VA 24450, USA
{bordeauxk122,manningja25,noonanam24,azabmm}@vmi.edu

Abstract. In modern society, heart-related incidents claim a life every 33 s, underscoring the need for real-time health-tracking devices. The challenge of monitoring poses significant risks for those without access to systems capable of responding to real-time biological changes. Hence, enhancing smart monitoring and responsive devices is essential for addressing various patient supervision issues. The SmartSecur System aims to mitigate these monitoring challenges by providing timely feedback on biomarker data, a task exemplified by technologies like the EmbracePlus smartwatch in conjunction with SmartSecur. These advancements offer a holistic approach to continuous health monitoring for at-risk individuals, such as those with diabetes or a predisposition to heart attacks. Nevertheless, devices like EmbracePlus may not realize their full potential without proper data interpretation and processing. SmartSecur enhances human-computer interaction and enables potentially lifesaving automated notifications by enabling real-time in-depth analysis of collected health data. This research presents SmartSecur as an innovative solution, empowering patients to conduct daily activities without fearing their physiological conditions adversely affecting them. By combining smart wearable technologies with responsive monitoring systems, a significant shift is made towards a safer, more informed health management paradigm, effectively closing the gap between data collection and actionable health interventions.

Keywords: Post Traumatic Stress Disorder (PTSD) · Heart Rate Variability (HRV) · Photoplethysmography (PPG)

1 Introduction

The utilization of Smartwatches in the modern world is common due to the ease of use. This in turn allows the use of a plethora of tools such as heart rate monitoring, electrodermal activity, temperature, steps, and etc. With these tools it allows individuals who need constant monitoring due to various medical issues such as Post Traumatic Stress Disorder, heart disease, and those susceptible to heart disease to be able to track and monitor their bio-metric data. Although this data is readily available it may be hard for the user's to understand, collect, and monitor themselves making the data redundant due to its lack of use. The utilization of Smartwatches paired with a monitoring system allows ease of mind due to its ability to monitor the users data in real-time potentially saving their life in a moment of distress such as a diabetic episode, heart attack, or PTSD episode. This is done through the utilization of the system reacting to some sort of change in the patients normal bio-metrics initiating a response that could potentially save their life. In addition adding more sensors could potentially add more safety measures in the normal day to day life. This research shows the potential of a distinct system setting the foundation of SmartSecur, allowing patients to live ordinary lives without fear of their impediments affecting them.

The purpose of this application is to provide a way to mitigate the potential risk of heart related sources to help the user and people around the user at the time of the episode or attack occurs. This application not only provides risk management, but also provides a way to get a hold of a family member, health care provider, or even emergency services depending on the severity of the attack and the type of attack. Some attacks and episodes include but are not limited to Anxiety, PTSD, Diabetes, heart failure, and other heart diseases. These attacks or episode could potentially be fatal and even put others in danger depending on where it occurs whether that be in a car on public roads, in public in general, or even around your family in your own home making it imperative to develop an application that could help not only save the user's life, but the people around the user as well.

This is conducted through Android Studio and the utilization of the Empatica's wearable smart device EmbracePlus. In the application it will utilize a progressive algorithm utilizing the user's real time data to determine states of emergency. This done through Empatica system's portal that collects the data determining the user's normal HRV. If the application discerns an abnormality within the users data it will then utilize Artificial Intelligence to proceed to provide a warning message to the user in a timely manner to sooth the user and contact medical providers stated by the user such as family members or doctors that are supplied by the users input in the application of SmartSecur. The data that is being tracked by the biomarker that measure clinically accurate information based on the user's heart, respiratory, and a multitude of different data points to help provide a more sound determination of the user's potential emergency.

Section 2 of this paper provides an in depth review of related literature. In continuation, Sect. 3 of this paper provides a thorough overview of the problem definition and the effects on society as a whole. Section 4 continues to provide an outline of the SmartSecur framework and its intended function.

2   Related Works

2.1   Remote Patient Monitoring

Technology has been integral to the development of society and the healthcare field is no exception. The emergence of new technologies has given way to the study of remote monitoring for real-time and efficient detection of illness [7]. Remote monitoring applications have been released to the market and proven successful. One example is a fetal heart rate monitor utilizing a mobile phone. This application detects and stores data on a fetus' heart rate to be examined by a midwife [11]. This method requires a human element in combination with technology. Requiring human evaluation is the largest downfall of this technology.

2.2   Post Traumatic Stress Disorder as It Relates to Heart Rate

Post Traumatic Stress Disorder (PTSD) has been studied to show unique patterns of heart rate. Heart rates during hyper-arousal episodes has shown higher levels of variation and fluctuation compared to healthy heart rates [9]. This evidence was obtained in a study that involved self-reported hyper-arousal episodes of PTSD correlated with a heart rate monitor. The study concluded that there is substantial evidence to claim that there is a correlation between these episodes and a fluctuation in heart rate. With this evidence, the study stated that this data could be influential in just-in-time self-management, digital therapeutics, and coaching technologies.

2.3   Utilization of Heart Rate Variability to Detect

In this paper we aim to continue the study of wearable devices and finding a sound solution in determining a way to detect different episodes such as PTSD, Anxiety attacks, and even heart attacks. The utilization of a wearable smart device to detect HRV is continuously growing and collecting data, but in a literary review it was determined through 23 different studies that their is an absolute error that was found acceptable due to the ease of use [6]. Through the continuous collection of data and the improvement of technology for these wearable devices we will be able to determine a more accurate measurement of the heart rate spikes and drops or better known as the rhythm of the heart. This data will result in the detection of abnormalities or inconsistencies that are found in patients allowing our application to notify and provide timely assistance that could potentially save their life. Although through this literary review they discuss the downfall of the technology, they determined in their conclusion that the HRV detection was a reliable source [6].

2.4   Importance of Wearable Smart Watch Sensors

A major factor in making this application to work is the sensors in the devices that we utilize. These sensors are what allow us to determine the abnormalities of the heart making it the biggest factor in the application itself. Through a review on photoplethysmography sensors it was determined that the sensor has been gaining popularity due to its potential application in the monitoring patients allowing health-care providers the ability to determine different cardiovascular issues at an earlier point. This allows them to diagnose and potentially save patients lives at a higher rate in comparison to the past [2]. This popularity potentially leads to the further development of the PPG sensor allowing us to advance our applications ability to determine abnormal heart rates in patients. In the PPG sensor utilises pulsatile components through reading changes in blood volume through cardiac activity determining the heart rate allowing it to collect based on each person's age, heart condition, and physical fitness [2]. This revelation allows us for detection of the heart rhythm to further determine each individual's normal rates and compare it to data that is not in the normal for that patient.

2.5   Determining Heart Failure Through the Utilization of Heart Rate Variability

Wearable smart devices utilize HPV through the utilization of sensors that indicate an individuals heart rates while also collecting the data. In a study analyzing short term HRV and its correlation to potential heart failure determined that a lower HRV had a independent connection to heart failure through studying a multi-ethnic population [10]. This determination assists our application in showing the potentional of utilizing wearable smart devices and allowing early indication of potential heart failure with the user and notifying them to contact their health provider to determine a solution to resolve the low HRV. Through this determination the user can utilize the functionality of the application to provide a warning to proper channels to save their life.

2.6   Utilization of Commercial Wearable Devices as an Health Indicator

Although there is a lot of speculation that devices are unable to determine accurate and sound data a study on wearable smart devices was conducted and determined there was little to no difference between a commercial Fitbit Inspire HR and gold standard devices. In the study they further discuss that the utilized data collected from the Fitbit device to determine potential heart conditions and irregularities in the heart providing continuous monitoring of elderly health [8]. Although this study focuses on monitoring the elderly the utilization of the wearable smart device is not confined to just the elderly since it is a device that is available to anyone and everyone. Instead of utilizing it to continuously monitor the patient the application would be doing the monitoring on its own communicating with Artificial Intelligence APIs in the background only providing a warning if the user has an irregularity from their normal HPV. This shows the potential of the application to provide accurate and fair warnings of potential attacks or heart failure of the patient.

2.7   Smart Heart Rate Monitor

Researchers utilized an Arduino Uno and Raspberry Pi to determine a person's heart rate. The use of this technology to determine heart rate is not revolutionary as heart rate monitors have been a common occurrence in today's society. The importance of this is, as technology becomes more advanced, new applications can be developed to further the accessibility to proper healthcare monitoring. In places that certain technologies might not be as available, the production of new technologies is necessary to increase the accessibility in these areas. This paper concluded that it is relatively simple to construct these devices for more accurate heart rate monitoring [1].

2.8   The Accuracy of Wearable Photoplethysmography Sensors for Telehealth Monitoring

The use of Photoplethysmography sensors became more relevant during the COVID-19 pandemic for the management of chronic diseases and neurological disorders [5]. This posed the question of how accurate these devices are in a medical sense. This paper discussed the accuracy of these devices for heart rate and heart rate variability, atrial fibrillation, blood pressure (BP), obstructive sleep apnea, blood glucose, heart failure, and respiratory rate. It was concluded that there is a general lack of studies with a large subject size and an absence of reporting for standard accuracy metrics. This conclusion, published in 2022, shows that there might be some inaccuracy in the metrics provided by these devices, however, the use of these devices should not be discounted for early detection of certain health concerns.

3   System Overview

The proposed system provides an application for users to receive warning outputs and eventual calls for assistance in their everyday lives. This is done through the utilization of the EmbracePlus Wearable Smart device, which feeds data to the SmartSecur. In turn, through the continuous monitoring of the data, the application compares the data to the different rule sets based on different indications provided by Artificial Intelligence API of potential episodes that could occur. As noted in the design image Fig. 1, it is a continuous flow that only proceeds to the next step of providing a medical request to the user based on the potential risk that is detected by the system. As soon as a risk is detected, a medical request is generated to be sent to the help provider. The system automatically sets a timer, allowing the user to potentially stop a possible false alert. If the user is incapacitated, unable to stop the alert, or chooses to let the timer end, a medical service request will automatically be sent out.

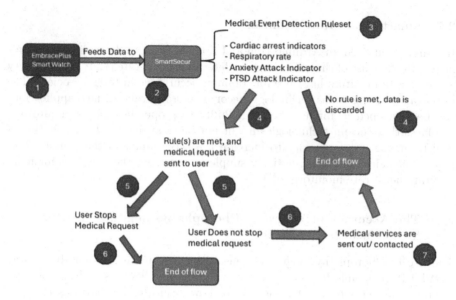

Fig. 1. Work Flow of Our System

4   Methodology

Assimilating smart watch devices to patients marks a new period of health-related data collection methodologies. As the leading cause of death in the US, heart diseases (including heart attacks) have been proven to be non-fatal with early intervention [4]. Within the realm of health monitoring devices, Empatica, the creator of EmbracePlus, has developed a series of biomarkers that can measure clinically validated measures. EmbracePlus has the ability to preemptively predict heart attacks based on biometric data and prevent mortal attacks. By responding to these data points, we also may be able to prevent fatal actions by recognizing hyperarousal events like heart rate variability and skin conductance [9].

Ultimately, we offer a novel system, SmartSecur, that monitors data fed to it via a smartwatch then responds to pre-trained events by triggering features in other devices and contacts medical services as needed. The model is affirmed on a progressive algorithm, capable of discerning medical emergencies and providing a custom response that is in accordance with the patient's medical conditions and available devices around them. In SmartSecur's ruleset, specific thresholds are entrenched with data submitted through the smartwatch that, if exceeded, trigger one or more responses from one or more SmartSecur-controlled devices. Feedback from SmartSecur is elicited when the monitor side collects enough data to determine a probable event that the user is currently experiencing. An increase in heart and respiratory rate, along with other indicators of a heart attack, will trigger a message to emergency medical services. Medical personnel will respond if the user does not intervene in a specified time frame and stop the outgoing message. Heart rate variability reactivity, which is indicative of an anxiety disorder, will trigger soothing sounds from the smartwatch, and other nearby devices that SmartSecur controls and manages to calm the patient down until their biometrics return to their baseline numbers [3]. These responses ensure an adequate timeout time for the user until they can return to their normal physiological state and continue with their day safely.

Prevailing research on a few modest medical scenarios lays a strong underpinning of research for future, more advanced, systems and monitor/response structures. As our medical comprehension of human health increases daily, so does the potential for SmartSecur to save more lives and increase its feedback accuracy.

In a smart city, the proposed system can play a major role in patient safety. It can help in stations where a driver might be able to pull over safely after experiencing an epileptic seizure because SmartSecur will activate self-driving or automatic parking of the car and cautiously pull over until medical assistance arrives.

5   Discussion

The application of a device of this nature would be useful for individuals with diagnoses, whether physical or neurological, that affect heart rate variability. A device that can consume data on a patient and make predictions to allow for early warnings for life-threatening or non-life-threatening episodes has the potential to improve, if not save, lives. The largest downfall of this technology is the reliability of the data obtained and the reliability of the interpretation. Testing and controls would mitigate the concern for unreliable functionality.

Users of this technology would have the ability to carry out normal day-to-day activities. If the device detects that the user has the potential to be entering an episode the device would provide a warning stating that the user should be prepared. This could also allow the user an opportunity to provide the device with additional data based on the user's current activity. Activities such as physical training have been shown to increase heart rate and increase variability rapidly. If the user is engaging in such activity, the user could provide that data to the device and cease warnings.

Allowing users to receive an early warning of episodes gives them the ability to prepare themselves and possibly prevent the episode in its entirety. Future research is needed to refine the data processed by the device and the reliability of its functionality.

6   Conclusions and Future Work

This paper provides a framework for a device designed to detect heart rate variability to provide warnings to users. SmartSecur aims to allow users to continue with their normal lives while the device enables the user to be more aware of their conditions whether physical or neurological. A device of this nature, with full implementation, could provide many patients a greater sense of security and awareness. Utilizing Empatica's EmbracePlus, the user could have the reassurance that their condition is being monitored with the ease of just wearing a smart watch. In future work, a full implementation with thorough testing and evaluation is necessary. Development of the software and testing the hardware combined with the software is the next step in the development process.

Acknowledgements. This study was conducted at Virginia Military Institute as a part of an Independent Study over two semesters. A great many thanks to Doctor Azab for mentoring me and my fellow Cadets who helped Co-Author this paper. This study is sponsored by CyDef, a Department of. Defense (DoD), NSA grant, and in part by the Commonwealth Cyber Initiative, an investment in the advancement of cyber R&D, innovation, and workforce development. For more information about CCI, visit: www.cyberinitiative.org.

Disclosure of Interests. The authors have no competing interests to declare that are relevant to the content of this article.

References

1. Bansal, P., Malik, M., Kundu, R.: Smart heart rate monitoring system. In: 2018 IEEMA Engineer Infinite Conference (eTechNxT), pp. 1–4. IEEE (2018)
2. Castaneda, D., Esparza, A., Ghamari, M., Soltanpur, C., Nazeran, H.: A review on wearable photoplethysmography sensors and their potential future applications in health care. Int. J. Biosensors Bioelectron. **4**(4), 195 (2018)
3. Cheng, Y.C., Su, M.I., Liu, C.W., Huang, Y.C., Huang, W.L.: Heart rate variability in patients with anxiety disorders: a systematic review and meta-analysis. Psychiatry Clin. Neurosci. **76**(7), 292–302 (2022)
4. Fang, J., Luncheon, C., Ayala, C., Odom, E., Loustalot, F.: Awareness of heart attack symptoms and response among adults-united states, 2008, 2014, and 2017. Morb. Mortal. Wkly Rep. **68**(5), 101 (2019)
5. Knight, S., Lipoth, J., Namvari, M., Gu, C., Hedayati, M., Syed-Abdul, S., Spiteri, R.J.: The accuracy of wearable photoplethysmography sensors for telehealth monitoring: a scoping review. Telemed. e-Health **29**(6), 813–828 (2023)
6. Li, K., Cardoso, C., Moctezuma-Ramirez, A., Elgalad, A., Perin, E.: Heart rate variability measurement through a wearable device: another breakthrough for personal health monitoring? (2023)
7. Malasinghe, L.P., Ramzan, N., Dahal, K.: Remote patient monitoring: a comprehensive study. J. Ambient. Intell. Humaniz. Comput. **10**, 57–76 (2019)
8. Rodrigues, E., et al.: HRV monitoring using commercial wearable devices as a health indicator for older persons during the pandemic. Sensors **22**(5), 2001 (2022)
9. Sadeghi, M., Sasangohar, F., McDonald, A.D., Hegde, S.: Understanding heart rate reactions to post-traumatic stress disorder (PTSD) among veterans: a naturalistic study. Hum. Factors **64**(1), 173–187 (2022)
10. Shah, S.A., Kambur, T., Chan, C., Herrington, D.M., Liu, K., Shah, S.J.: Relation of short-term heart rate variability to incident heart failure (from the multi-ethnic study of atherosclerosis). Am. J. Cardiol. **112**(4), 533–540 (2013)
11. Silva, B.M., Rodrigues, J.J., de la Torre Díez, I., López-Coronado, M., Saleem, K.: Mobile-health: a review of current state in 2015. J. Biomed. Inform. **56**, 265–272 (2015)

How to Consider Health Literacy in Digital Health Interventions?

Kerstin Denecke[1]([✉]) [iD], Beatrice Kaufmann[2] [iD], Daniel Reichenpfader[1] [iD], and Carolyn Petersen[3] [iD]

[1] Bern University of Applied Sciences, Institute Patient-Centered Digital Health, Quellgasse 21, 2502 Biel, Switzerland
{kerstin.denecke,daniel.reichenpfader}@bfh.ch

[2] Institute of Design Research, Bern Academy of the Arts HKB, Fellerstrasse 11, 3027 Bern, Switzerland
beatrice.kaufmannvatter@hkb.bfh.ch

[3] Department of Artificial Intelligence and Informatics, Mayo Clinic, Rochester, MN, USA
Petersen.Carolyn@mayo.edu

Abstract. Digital health interventions (DHIs) are designed to prevent, manage or treat health conditions using evidence-based methods. Ensuring that these interventions are both accessible and that the content is understandable to diverse user groups, regardless of their digital, data and health literacy, is critical to reducing health inequalities and achieving optimal health outcomes. This paper aims to synthesize information essential for the development of inclusive DHIs by conducting a literature review to identify best practices in patient communication skills and strategies. These practices emphasize the importance of tailoring information to patients' knowledge, needs, preferences, and literacy levels; simplifying language and reducing medical jargon; breaking information down into manageable chunks to facilitate patient engagement and understanding; and checking patient understanding. To embody these principles, DHIs must have adaptable content delivery mechanisms, language simplification options, and the ability to segment information based on individual user needs. The use of artificial intelligence (AI) can enhance these aspects by enabling personalized content delivery and simplifying complex language. Incorporating health literacy and accessibility considerations from the outset of DHI design and development is critical to promoting equitable and effective digital health solutions, ultimately leading to improved health outcomes. Future research should on the one hand explore the specific support mechanisms, such as visual aids or explanatory content, that users need to fully understand the information presented by DHIs, and on the other hand develop applicable metrics to measure inclusive design.

Keywords: Healthcare communication · digital health intervention · health literacy · inclusive design · user-centered digital health

C. Stephanidis et al. (Eds.): HCII 2024, CCIS 2119, pp. 259–267, 2024.
https://doi.org/10.1007/978-3-031-61966-3_29

1 Background and Motivation

Low health literacy and poor accessibility of health information lead to negative consequences for patients' health and well-being, such as misunderstandings or medication errors [1]. As digitalization progresses, patients increasingly need to navigate digital health interventions (DHI) independently. DHI are evidence-based tools designed to prevent, manage, or treat a medical condition. To prevent or reduce health inequalities and achieve the desired outcomes, it is essential that information about DHI is accessible and understandable to a wider range of users. However, accessibility, health literacy and health numeracy are often overlooked in the development and delivery of DHI.

The American Medical Association considers a health literate person as having "a constellation of skills, including the ability to perform basic reading and numerical tasks required to function in the health care environment. Patients with adequate health literacy can read, understand, and act on health care information" [2]. These skills are necessary for patients to be able to follow instructions related to care and treatment or engaging appropriate activities of disease and self-care management. The connection between health literacy, numeracy, and health equity is crucial, especially for delivering personalized and equitable care across diverse populations [3]. Studies show varying levels of health literacy across Europe, with nearly half of citizens included in an eight-country survey showing insufficient levels [4]. Researchers identified a need to focus on digital health literacy and engagement [5, 6], including efforts designed specifically for virtual care environments [7], to improve health outcomes and reduce health disparities. The rise of health technology increases the risk of health inequities, particularly for older, less educated, and lower socioeconomic groups [8], so initiatives that address digital health literacy are critical to success. We believe that considering health literacy in DHI is essential for mitigate the digital divide and contribute to health equity and that DHI should be designed in a way that health literacy is increased. When designed appropriately, technology has the potential to increase access to information, treatment, improving communication between patient and healthcare professional [9]. Tailoring DHIs to patients' health literacy promotes inclusiveness, effectiveness and patient-centered care, leading to better health outcomes and more efficient treatment [10].

Inclusive design aims to create products, services, and environments that are usable by people with a diverse range of abilities, characteristics, and needs [11, 12]. It can thus help in considering health literacy in designing DHI. Inclusive design encompasses inclusivity, accessibility and usability and considers the full range of human diversity including age, gender, culture, and abilities [13, 14]. In the context of DHI, 'inclusive design' refers to the deliberate creation of technology-based solutions that meet the diverse needs of all patients, considering differences in technological and health literacy, ability and cultural background [15, 16]. Inclusive design ensures that patients can effectively use and benefit from these solutions [17]. Patient-centered research guidelines such as those from the Patient-Centered Outcomes Research Institute [18] emphasize patient involvement in research processes to ensure relevant outcomes. Another guide to developing eHealth interventions for people with low socio-economic status advises professionals on the development, adaptation, evaluation and implementation of such interventions [19]. However, there are currently no specific guidelines for the design of inclusive DHI in healthcare, but their development should incorporate existing standards, address diverse user needs, and prioritize effective, ethical, and empathetic communication.

In this paper, we study how health literacy could be considered in designing and developing DHI. We answer on the following three questions:

- How do healthcare providers consider health literacy in patient-provider communications?
- Which technologies could contribute to inclusive design of DHI?
- Which best practices or guidelines are already available for inclusive design of DHI?

To answer these questions, we collected literature related to patient-provider communication, design guidelines for health information technology (health IT) and inclusive design. Based on this literature review and our experience in developing DHI, we collect technologies that could support inclusive design. All this collected information is aggregated into recommendations.

2 Results

In the following we describe the results of our literature search.

2.1 Health Literacy in Patient-Provider Communication

Best practices in patient-provider communication during medical encounters emphasize the importance of tailoring information to the patient's existing knowledge, needs, preferences and level of literacy [20]. They advocate simplifying the language used, minimizing medical jargon, and structuring information into digestible chunks that allow patients time to process and respond [21]. They also emphasize the need to test patients' understanding by teach-back, a step that is critical to ensuring effective communication and engagement in their healthcare [20]. The teach-back method, where patients are asked to summarize or explain back the information provided, is a practical tool for confirming understanding.

Other recommendations from literature for patient-doctor encounters include creating a safe and respectful environment, and actively engaging the individual in the conversation [20]. In addition, the use of memory aids or notes, and the provision of written summaries of encounters, can further support patients' understanding and retention of information. The use of multiple teaching channels - such as visual aids, written summaries, video and audio media, graphics and pictures - enhances the understanding by addressing health literacy levels, readability skills or cognitive abilities [21, 22].

2.2 Best Practices and Guidelines for Inclusive Design

In this section, we collect best practices and guidelines for inclusive design in health IT. Basic concepts reported in the literature focus on user-centered design as a prerequisite for inclusive design, language accessibility, and the inclusion of cultural relevance. User-centered design is a fundamental principle of inclusive design, emphasizing the importance of involving users in the development process to tailor DHI to their specific needs and contexts [23]. Needs of users of DHI may be different among the broader public resulting from structural and social factors, culture, language, and other factors.

Lyles et al. as well as Eichner and Dullabh have highlighted the critical need for language accessibility, advocating the simplification of language complexity and ensuring that content is understandable at a sixth grade reading level or below [24, 25]. In addition to these principles, it is important to make information clear and actionable, and complement written text with icons to aid comprehension and engagement.

Additionally, the cultural backgrounds and linguistic nuances of the users have to be considered when designing DHI. It is essential that content is relevant to different racial and ethnic groups and that it is iteratively tested and revised to improve usability. The guidelines for health IT proposed by Eichner et al. [25] take this further by recommending the use of simple and clear language, content that is relevant to a diverse audience with minimal presumed prior knowledge, and formats that support easy reading and comprehension.

Apple Inc., Google LLC and Microsoft Corporation provide guidelines for ensuring inclusivity and equity in digital solutions. As an example, we considered the Microsoft Inclusive Design Toolkit (https://www.inclusivedesigntoolkit.com) and the Microsoft Inclusive Design for Cognition Toolkit that provide valuable insights into a design process that prioritizes user involvement, co-creation, and an understanding of user diversity. The recommendations from these resources suggest considering three key aspects when targeting inclusive design: preserve, direct, and adapt [26]. "Preserve" focuses on ensuring that communications from the digital solution are controllable, actionable, concise, and relevant, coupled with clear navigation and transparent, easily controllable privacy settings to build trust. "Direct" emphasizes the importance of maintaining momentum through clear, accessible and logical flows, providing guidance and information as needed. "Adapt" allows users to adjust readability and appearance, including filtering information and setting preferences to enhance personalization.

2.3   Technologies for Supporting Inclusive Design

There are already some technologies available that can be considered for ensuring inclusive design of DHI. Just-in-time adaptive intervention (JITAI) design represents an application of Artificial Intelligence (AI) and machine learning in health technology [27] to dynamically adjust application's behavior in response to the user's changing needs. By assessing various factors such as the user's preferred communication channel (e.g. SMS, email, phone call), their reading and health literacy levels, and the most desired content type (text, video, voice), JITAI can offer personalized interactions that significantly improve user engagement and comprehension [27]. When designing JITAI, an initial assessment of a user's health literacy level is necessary and could be realized during the onboarding process. This step allows for immediate customization of the DHI experience, ensuring that the information and interventions presented are aligned with the user's understanding and preferences.

Deep learning and machine learning algorithms are critical to the personalization of DHIs. By analyzing user data and interactions, these technologies can tailor health information and interventions to individual preferences and literacy levels. The potential of large language models, such as GPT-3, has been recognized for their ability to simplify complex health information into plain language, making it more accessible to users with varying levels of literacy. Ayre et al. have noted that output from models such as ChatGPT can serve as an initial draft of health information, which can then be refined by human experts to ensure accuracy and comprehensibility [28].

Visual tools, such as pictograms and videos, improve health literacy and medication adherence, especially among low-literate people [29]. The use of medical graphic narratives has been shown to be an effective tool for improving patient understanding, particularly in the context of informed consent [30]. Studies by Brand et al. demonstrated that visual narratives significantly improve comprehension by presenting medical information in an engaging and digestible format [30, 31]. This approach highlights the importance of visual aids in communicating complex information to users with varying levels of literacy.

The content provided through DHI should consider the recommendations on patient-provider communication. One basic approach is to check the language and language use in a DHI. The Sydney Health Literacy Lab provides a health literacy editor tool to help assess and improve the readability and simplicity of text-based health information (https://www.sydneyhealthliteracylab.org.au/health-literacy-editor). This tool assesses language complexity, use of unusual words and overall readability, and provides suggestions for improving the text to make it more accessible to a wider audience. It could be applied to improve texts used in a DHI.

3 Discussion

This paper highlights the indispensable role of health literacy in the design and implementation of DHIs. Based on the synthesis of best practices, guidelines, and technological advances relevant to addressing health literacy through inclusive design in DHI, we formulated recommendations for embedding health literacy considerations from the outset of DHI development to ensure these tools are accessible and effective for a diverse user group. They are aggregated in Fig. 1. The recommendations underscore the necessity for continuous refinement of DHIs through user feedback and iterative design, emphasizing that inclusivity and patient-centeredness are key to overcoming health disparities through digital health solutions. To realize this, it is important to collaborate across disciplines, including health professionals, designers, technologists and end-users. Such collaboration can foster innovative solutions that are more likely to meet the diverse needs of users.

In Europe, the European accessibility law (Directive (EU) 2019/882 on the accessibility requirements for products and services) will apply from June 2025. Among other things, it will require products and services to adopt practices, policies and procedures to meet the needs of people with disabilities. Although these guidelines basically consider individuals with disabilities, we believe that it is important to ensure accessibility also in terms of understandability of content provided. Nevertheless, the accessibility law demonstrates the need for solutions that meet the needs of a diverse population.

We are only aware of studies that evaluate DHI usability and ease of use (besides effectiveness) [32]. Although related, understanding of content provided in DHI remained unconsidered. Beyond cognitive diversity and health literacy, cultural competence in DHI design can play a critical role in ensuring that digital health solutions are

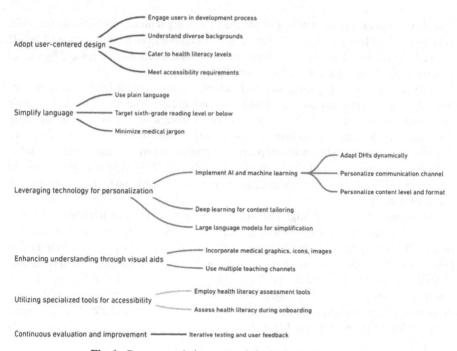

Fig. 1. Recommendations towards inclusive design of DHI

accessible and effective across different cultural backgrounds. Incorporating cultural considerations could increase the relevance and acceptability of DHIs among diverse populations. Spanhel et al. provided already a taxonomy of components of cultural adaptation of internet- and mobile-based interventions for mental disorders [33]. Considering these aspects might be of relevance for inclusive design. Additionally, developing a taxonomy for inclusive design may help developers and researchers in the inclusive design of DHI.

Furthermore, metrics to measure inclusive design are still unavailable and future research should focus on this. Questions that could be addressed to study inclusiveness comprise:

- How does the DHI supports cognitive diversity of users and makes them feel?
- How does the DHI considers health literacy and supports understanding of content provided?
- What support does the design incorporate to reduce cognitive demands?
- Are individual's goals understood and facilitated by design?

Future research should also explore the specific support mechanisms, such as visual aids or explanatory content, that users need to fully understand the information presented by DHIs.

This research must be considered preliminary, since no systematic review was conducted. Best practices could also be derived from a systematic assessment of existing

DHIs. However, this requires the ability to identify DHIs that are already designed in an inclusive manner.

4 Conclusion

Translating the identified recommendations into the digital realm, DHIs should be designed to offer tailored information delivery, allowing content to be adapted to the needs of the individual user. Such customization includes not only simplification of language and thoughtful portioning of information, but also the flexibility to adjust these elements based on user feedback and understanding. Technical strategies and design requirements to achieve these goals include the use of plain language and the incorporation of visual aids or videos, which can significantly reduce the reliance on textual explanations and make information more accessible, especially to users with varying levels of health literacy.

Applying the identified recommendations enables the development of DHIs that not only deliver information effectively, but also empower users by improving their ability to engage with and understand their health information. This approach to inclusive design recognizes the diverse needs and preferences of users and ensures that digital health interventions are accessible, understandable and useful to all, regardless of their health literacy level.

Transparency Statement. The draft of this paper was refined using the AI tools ChatGPT and DeepL Write to increase clarity and comprehensibility of the text.

Disclosure of Interests. The authors declare no conflicts of interest.

References

1. Shahid, R., Shoker, M., Chu, L.M., Frehlick, R., Ward, H., Pahwa, P.: Impact of low health literacy on patients' health outcomes: a multicenter cohort study. BMC Health Serv. Res. **22**, 1148 (2022). https://doi.org/10.1186/s12913-022-08527-9
2. Gazmararian, J.A.: Health literacy among medicare enrollees in a managed care organization. JAMA **281**, 545 (1999). https://doi.org/10.1001/jama.281.6.545
3. Toward Health Equity and Patient-Centeredness: Integrating Health Literacy, Disparities Reduction, and Quality Improvement: Workshop Summary; National Academies Press: Washington, D.C., 2009; p. 12502; ISBN 978-0-309-12749-3
4. Sørensen, K., et al.: Health literacy in Europe: comparative results of the European health literacy survey (HLS-EU). Eur. J. Public Health **25**, 1053–1058 (2015). https://doi.org/10.1093/eurpub/ckv043
5. Jackson, D.N., Trivedi, N., Baur, C.: Re-prioritizing digital health and health literacy in *Healthy People 2030* to affect health equity. Health Commun. **36**, 1155–1162 (2021). https://doi.org/10.1080/10410236.2020.1748828
6. Jaworski, B.K., et al.: Advancing digital health equity: directions for behavioral and social science research. Trans. Behav. Med. **13**, 132–139 (2023). https://doi.org/10.1093/tbm/ibac088

7. Budhwani, S., et al.: Challenges and strategies for promoting health equity in virtual care: findings and policy directions from a scoping review of reviews. J. Am. Med. Inform. Assoc. **29**, 990–999 (2022). https://doi.org/10.1093/jamia/ocac022

8. Rivera-Romero, O., Gabarron, E., Miron-Shatz, T., Petersen, C., Denecke, K.: Social media, digital health literacy, and digital ethics in the light of health equity: imia participatory health and social media working group. Yearb. Med. Inform. **31**, 082–087 (2022). https://doi.org/10.1055/s-0042-1742503

9. Dunn, P., Hazzard, E.: Technology approaches to digital health literacy. Int. J. Cardiol. **293**, 294–296 (2019). https://doi.org/10.1016/j.ijcard.2019.06.039

10. Walters, R., Leslie, S.J., Polson, R., Cusack, T., Gorely, T.: Establishing the efficacy of interventions to improve health literacy and health behaviours: a systematic review. BMC Public Health **20**, 1040 (2020). https://doi.org/10.1186/s12889-020-08991-0

11. John Clarkson, P., Coleman, R.: History of inclusive design in the UK. Appl. Ergon. **46**, 235–247 (2015). https://doi.org/10.1016/j.apergo.2013.03.002

12. Waller, S., Bradley, M., Hosking, I., Clarkson, P.J.: Making the case for inclusive design. Appl. Ergon. **46**, 297–303 (2015). https://doi.org/10.1016/j.apergo.2013.03.012

13. Interaction Design Foundation - IxDF. What Is Inclusive Design? Interaction Design Foundation – IxDF, 16 Aug 2016. https://www.interaction-design.org/literature/topics/inclusive-design

14. Lawton Henry, S.: WCAG 2 Overview. https://www.w3.org/WAI/standards-guidelines/wcag/. Accessed 24 Feb 2024

15. Borg, K., Boulet, M., Smith, L., Bragge, P.: Digital Inclusion & health communication: a rapid review of literature. Health Commun. **34**, 1320–1328 (2019). https://doi.org/10.1080/10410236.2018.1485077

16. Motta, I., Quaresma, M.: Increasing transparency to design inclusive conversational agents (CAs): perspectives and open issues. In: Proceedings of the Proceedings of the 5th International Conference on Conversational User Interfaces; ACM: Eindhoven Netherlands, July 19 2023, pp. 1–4 (2023)

17. Lee, J., Kim, J.: Can menstrual health apps selected based on users' needs change health-related factors? a double-blind randomized controlled trial. J. Am. Med. Inform. Assoc. **26**, 655–666 (2019). https://doi.org/10.1093/jamia/ocz019

18. Patient-Centered Outcomes Research Institute PCORI Methodology Standards. https://www.pcori.org/research/about-our-research/research-methodology/pcori-methodology-standards. Accessed 21 Feb 2024

19. Faber, J.S., et al.: Guide development for ehealth interventions targeting people with a low socioeconomic position: participatory design approach. J. Med. Internet Res. **25**, e48461 (2023). https://doi.org/10.2196/48461

20. Coleman, C.: Health Literacy and Clear Communication Best Practices for Telemedicine. HLRP: Health Literacy Research and Practice 2020, 4. https://doi.org/10.3928/24748307-20200924-01

21. Murugesu, L., Heijmans, M., Rademakers, J., Fransen, M.P.: Challenges and solutions in communication with patients with low health literacy: perspectives of healthcare providers. PLoS ONE **17**, e0267782 (2022). https://doi.org/10.1371/journal.pone.0267782

22. Norman, C.D., Skinner, H.A.: EHealth literacy: essential skills for consumer health in a networked world. J. Med. Internet Res. **8**, e9 (2006). https://doi.org/10.2196/jmir.8.2.e9

23. Bridging the Digital Health Divide Series. California Health Care Foundation

24. Lyles, C.R., Aguilera, A., Nguyen, O., Sarkar, U.: Bridging the Digital Health Divide: How Providers and Plans Can Help Communities Better Adopt Digital Health Tools. California Health Care Foundation (2022)

25. Eichner, J., Dullabh, P.: Accessible Health Information Technology (Health IT) for Populations with Limited Literacy: A Guide for Developers and Purchasers of Health IT.; 2007; Vol. AHRQ Publication No. 08-0010-EF, MD Agency for Healthcare Research and Quality (2007)

26. Microsoft Inclusive Design Team: Inclusive Design for Mental Health (2024)

27. Nahum-Shani, I., et al.: Just-in-Time Adaptive Interventions (JITAIs) in mobile health: key components and design principles for ongoing health behavior support. Ann. Behav. Med. **52**, 446–462 (2018). https://doi.org/10.1007/s12160-016-9830-8

28. Ayre, J., et al.: New frontiers in health literacy: using ChatGPT to simplify health information for people in the community. J. Gen. Intern. Med. (2023). https://doi.org/10.1007/s11606-023-08469-w

29. Garcia-Retamero, R., Okan, Y., Cokely, E.T.: Using visual aids to improve communication of risks about health: a review. Sci. World J. **2012**, 1 (2012). https://doi.org/10.1100/2012/562637

30. Brand, A., et al.: Medical graphic narratives to improve patient comprehension and periprocedural anxiety before coronary angiography and percutaneous coronary intervention: a randomized trial. Ann. Intern. Med. **170**, 579 (2019). https://doi.org/10.7326/M18-2976

31. Brand, A., et al.: Medical graphics to improve patient understanding and anxiety in elderly and cognitively impaired patients scheduled for transcatheter Aortic Valve Implantation (TAVI). Clin. Res. Cardiol. (2023). https://doi.org/10.1007/s00392-023-02352-8

32. Patel, S., et al.: The acceptability and usability of digital health interventions for adults with depression, anxiety, and somatoform disorders: qualitative systematic review and meta-synthesis. J. Med. Internet Res. **22**, e16228 (2020). https://doi.org/10.2196/16228

33. Spanhel, K., Balci, S., Feldhahn, F., Bengel, J., Baumeister, H., Sander, L.B.: Cultural adaptation of internet- and mobile-based interventions for mental disorders: a systematic review. NPJ Digit. Med. **4**, 128 (2021). https://doi.org/10.1038/s41746-021-00498-1

Creation of a "Lean Manufacturing" System for Outpatient Scanning of Malignant Neoplasms

Natalia Guryeva$^{(\boxtimes)}$ (ID), Vasily Orel (ID), Andrey Kim (ID), Victoria Smirnova (ID),
Vasily Sereda (ID), Lyubov Sharafutdinova (ID), Andrey Kulev (ID), Tatiana Buldakova (ID),
Alexander Ushkats (ID), Zinaida Roslova (ID), Dmitry Chentsov (ID), Alexander Kakanov (ID),
and Sergey Lytaev (ID)

Saint Petersburg State Pediatric Medical University, Litovskaya, 2, 194100 Saint Petersburg,
Russia
spb@gpmu.org

Abstract. Malignant neoplasms are socially significant diseases, as they occupy one of the leading positions in the structure of morbidity and mortality of the population in the Russian Federation, therefore, the fight against these diseases is a priority task of the domestic healthcare system. The article provides indicators of the prevalence and structure of oncological pathology among the population. Based on the study of the existing system of organization of medical care for patients with malignant neoplasms, the substantiation of the expediency of taking measures to improve the organization of outpatient oncological care centers in terms of dispensary monitoring of patients with malignant neoplasms is presented. An analysis of the work of outpatient oncological care centers has been carried out and an action plan has been developed aimed at increasing the coverage of dynamic dispensary monitoring of patients with malignant neoplasms, in accordance with the methods of "Lean Manufacturing". This work consisted of two successive stages: 1) assessment of the current state of the process and 2) development of an action plan taking into account the identified problems in achieving the targets. The basic methods of lean manufacturing were used to obtain the necessary data: mapping, root cause analysis and standardization.

Keywords: Malignant Neoplasms · Dispensary Supervision · Lean Manufacturing

1 Introduction

The degree of well-being of society is usually judged by the level and state of health of the population. Negative trends in public health indicators are a serious socio-political problem. A number of diseases that pose the greatest threat to the well-being of the population, characterized by massive, high annual growth rates in the number of patients, and restriction of the full functioning of a person in society, are classified as a group of socially significant diseases [1, 2, 7, 12, 19].

C. Stephanidis et al. (Eds.): HCII 2024, CCIS 2119, pp. 268–276, 2024.
https://doi.org/10.1007/978-3-031-61966-3_30

The top three in this group include malignant neoplasms, which represent one of the most difficult medical and social problems in healthcare due to the high prevalence among the population [4, 6].

Experts of the World Health Organization predict a steady growth trend in oncological diseases in the world: at the beginning of the century, about 10 million new cases of cancer and more than 6 million deaths from it were registered annually in the world, the number of cases was expected to reach 15 million per year by 2020, up to 24 million and deaths up to 16 million by 2050, but Already in 2018, the number of cases exceeded 18 million new cases of cancer and more than 9.6 million deaths from it [5, 11].

The annual growth rate of malignant neoplasms is about 2%, which exceeds the growth of the world population by 0.3–0.5%. Malignant neoplasms are the second most common cause of death in the Russian Federation after diseases of the circulatory system [9].

According to Rosstat in 2022, 624,835 cases of malignant neoplasms were detected in the Russian Federation for the first time in their lives, of which 283,179 in male patients and 341,656 in female patients. The increase in this indicator compared to 2021 amounted to 7.6%. The "rough" indicator of the incidence of malignant neoplasms per 100,000 population of Russia was 428.4, which is 8.1% higher than the level of 2021, 16.6% higher than the level of 2012, but 1.8% lower than the level of 2019 [11, 16].

The prevalence of malignant neoplasms in the Russian population in 2022 amounted to 2,758.3 per 100,000 population, which is higher than in 2012. (2,091.9) by 31.9%. The growth of this indicator is due to both an increase in morbidity and detectability, and an increase in the survival rate of cancer patients [8, 16].

In 2022, every third malignant neoplasm was detected in stage I, every fourth in stage II, and every fifth in stage IV. The proportion of patients who died within the first year after diagnosis was 19.1% [1, 16].

In the structure of this pathology, depending on the localization of the process, the top five include malignant neoplasms of the breast (19.1%), skin (except melanoma) (10.8%), prostate (7.2%), uterine body (7.1%), colon (6,0%) [2, 16].

Among patients under dynamic dispensary supervision for 5 years or more, a greater proportion are patients with tumors of the breast (21.0%), uterine body (8.0%), skin (except melanoma) (6.8%), lymphatic and hematopoietic tissue (6.1%), prostate (6.0%) [16, 18].

The number of years of life lost as a result of the disease of one of the forms of malignant neoplasms is on average 7.5 years in men and 10 years in women [10, 17].

The most important component of ensuring the duration of active life for patients with malignant neoplasms is the rational routing of patient data and effective dynamic follow-up. Advanced technologies, in particular "Lean manufacturing", should be included in the activities to improve these processes" [3, 13–15, 20].

The research was aimed to analyze the organization of dispensary observation of outpatients with malignant neoplasms and develop measures based on the principles of lean manufacturing to improve this area of activity.

2 Methods

The organization of the process of dynamic dispensary observation of patients with malignant neoplasms in one of the administrative districts of St. Petersburg was analyzed. The main methods of lean production were used: mapping, root cause analysis and standardization. The study consisted of two consecutive stages: 1) assessment of the current state of the process and 2) development of an action plan taking into account the identified problems in achieving the targets.

3 Outcomes

At the end of the main treatment, the patient should be taken under medical supervision at the district Center. In each administrative district of St. Petersburg, such outpatient oncological care centers are organized, where the entire complex of therapeutic and diagnostic measures is implemented within the framework of primary specialized medical care in the field of "oncology", including dynamic dispensary monitoring.

In accordance with the order of the Ministry of Health of the Russian Federation dated June 4, 2020 No. 548n "On approval of the procedure for dispensary supervision of adults with oncological diseases", the recommended frequency of dispensary appointments of a patient by a doctor: during the first year - once every three months, during the second year - once every six months, in the future – once once a year (if the course of the disease does not require a change in the patient's management tactics).

In order to increase the coverage of dispensary monitoring of patients with malignant neoplasms, an analysis of the organization of the process of dynamic dispensary monitoring of patients using lean manufacturing technologies was carried out: mapping, root cause analysis and standardization. The analysis was carried out in two stages. At the first stage, an assessment of the current state was carried out using mapping. Mapping is a tool for visualization and analysis of material and information flows in the process of value creation, which makes it possible to identify losses and, after analyzing them, make the right management decisions to improve the process [13].

The assessment of the current state was carried out by collecting complete information about all operations at the place of execution of the workflow and allowed reflecting the actual flow indicators. Based on the analysis of all sequential operations of the process, the patient's route was analyzed, the time spent on conducting research and the entire process within the framework of dispensary observation were studied.

During the analysis of the Center's activities: statistical indicators of morbidity and mortality, the order of work of oncological offices, the maintenance of medical documentation, the organization of preventive areas of work (dispensary supervision and sanitary and educational work), the implementation of intra- and interdepartmental interaction in the provision of outpatient medical care to patients with malignant neoplasms, problems affecting the process of dispensary supervision of patients with oncological profile have been identified.

Based on the results of the current state and analysis of the root causes, a number of organizational problems were identified:

Process map "Increasing the coverage of patients with malignant neoplasms with dispensary observation" (current status)

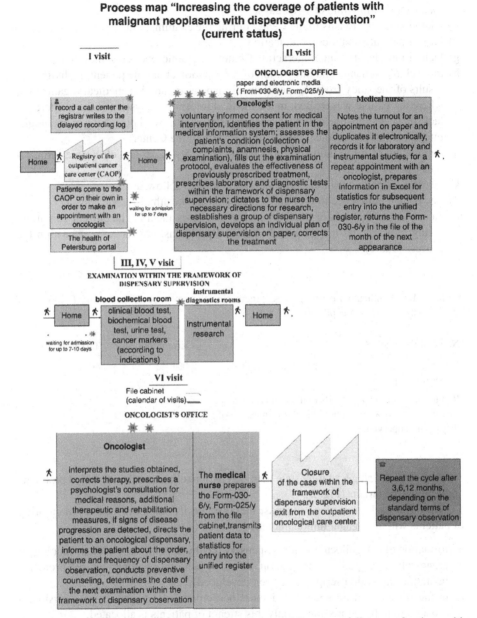

Fig. 1. The map of the process "Increasing the coverage of dispensary follow-up of patients with malignant neoplasms" (current status).

a) lack of an appointment with an oncologist as part of a dispensary observation (an appointment is provided only for the initial appointment);

b) mixing of flows (primary, repeat, dispensary admission);

c) long waiting time for an appointment with an oncologist up to 7 days;

d) long examination time of 7–10 days;
e) a large number of visits to the Center during the examination;
f) lack of patient-Center communication;
g) lack of interdepartmental interaction Center-polyclinic-oncological dispensary;
h) the lack of exchange and integration of information about the patient, including the results of the study from the oncological dispensary, another medical organization where the patient was treated, in the medical information system of the Center;
i) lack of access to the unified cancer registry at the workplace of an oncologist integrated into the medical information system of the Center;
j) duplication of information on three media (F.-025/y paper and electronic form, F.-030/y paper form);
k) insufficient patient awareness of the importance of follow-up;
l) low patient adherence to preventive measures and healthy lifestyle (Fig. 1).
m) According to the data of the first stage of the assessment of the current condition, taking into account mapping and identified problems, targets were set within the process (Table).

Table 1. Target indicators of the process "Increasing the coverage of dispensary follow-up of patients with malignant neoplasms"

Name of the goal	Current indicator	Target indicator
Coverage of patients with malignant neoplasms by dispensary supervision	60%	80%
Reducing the number of visits to the outpatient cancer care center for examination within the framework of dispensary supervision	6 visits	3 visits

At the second stage, a target state map was built to eliminate the identified problems and achieve the targets (Fig. 2).

The developed action plan to increase the coverage of dynamic dispensary monitoring of patients with malignant tumors included:

- formation of lists, allocation of a dispensary day by appointment with an oncologist;
- organization of patient registration for a dispensary appointment by proactive invitation (invitation scripts have been developed);
- in the schedule of all specialist doctors participating in dispensary supervision, a separate time for admission of only this stream of patients is allocated;
- communication with the patient via e-mail, mobile communication, SMS mailing is organized;
- the nurse is informed in the medical information system of the Center about the need for a patient under dispensary supervision to see an oncologist with an indication of the time of appearance;
- a unified medical information system has been created for interdepartmental interaction between the Center and medical organizations of the district;

Process map "Increasing coverage of patients with malignant neoplasms with dispensary observation" (target condition)

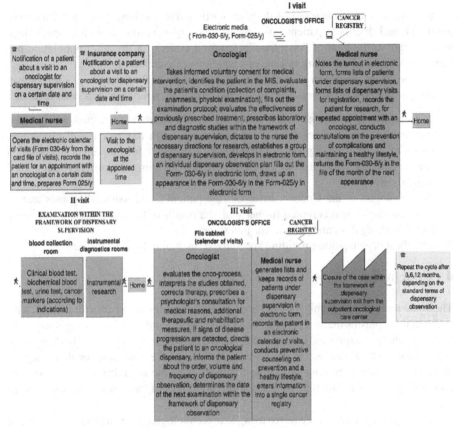

Fig. 2. The map of the process "Increasing the coverage of dispensary follow-up of patients with breast cancer" (target condition).

- an electronic calendar of dispensary visits has been created in the medical information system;
- the possibility of forming a list of dispensary visits in the medical information system for inclusion in the unified anti-cancer register has been created;
- access from the automated workplace of an oncologist to the unified cancer registry is provided;
- the program module "Dispensary supervision" has been introduced, which allows you to create an individual patient management plan in electronic form, enter F-030/y data in electronic form;
- the standard operating procedure "Dispensary appointment by an oncologist of a patient with a malignant neoplasm in the Center of the district" has been developed;
- cooperation with the city center for Medical Prevention has been organized to conduct an information and communication campaign aimed at increasing adherence to

treatment and prevention, including dispensary supervision and maintaining a healthy lifestyle.

In order to detect oncological diseases early, reduce waiting times for diagnosis, treatment, and distribute patient flows to medical organizations providing specialized medical care in the field of "oncology", a routing system for the adult population has been formed in St. Petersburg in case of suspicion or detection of cancer.

As part of the provision of specialized medical care in St. Petersburg, a three-level system for diagnosing patients with suspected malignant neoplasms has been formed.

1. An outpatient specialist/general hospital doctor, if a patient is suspected or diagnosed with an oncological disease, shall, in accordance with the established procedure, refer him within one day for consultation to the center for outpatient oncological care (hereinafter referred to as the Center) to provide him with primary specialized medical care.
2. The oncologist of the Center carries out the patient's admission, diagnosis and, if indicated, the patient is routed further with the results of the examinations. No more than 7 working days are allowed for this stage.
3. A medical organization providing specialized, including high-tech care.

4 Conclusion

The assessment of the organization of the dispensary monitoring process for patients with malignant neoplasms made it possible to identify "key points" for improving the quality of work, which is expressed in an increase in the timeliness of admission to dispensary supervision and an increase in the coverage of preventive measures for this category of patients. When preparing proposals for improving the organization of dispensary monitoring of patients with breast cancer, the principles of "lean manufacturing" were used.

The implementation of measures using lean technologies made it possible to achieve the following targets: increase the coverage of dispensary supervision of patients with malignant neoplasms from 60% to 80%, reduce the number of visits to the Center for examination from 6 to 3 visits. Quarterly audits by the Internal quality Control Department are planned to assess the monitoring and control of the achieved results.

Thus, the use of lean manufacturing methods made it possible to improve the management process of the organization of dispensary supervision of patients with malignant neoplasms, increase the coverage of dispensary supervision, increase the efficiency of dispensary supervision and ensure automation of the work processes of medical workers of the Center at all stages of dispensary supervision.

References

1. Anufrieva, E.V., et al.: A project approach to the organization of colorectal cancer screening as a basis for improving public health. Public Health Habitat **31**, 7–14 (2023)
2. Chigrina, V.P., Khodakova, O.V., Tyufilin, D.S., et al.: Analysis of the dynamics of morbidity in the population of the Russian Federation, taking into account factors affecting the availability of primary health care. Healthcare Russian Federation **67**, 275–283 (2023)

3. Fedoskina A.K., Fedoskina L.A.: Implementation of a lean approach in the context of a new model of a medical organization: results and prospects. I.P. Pavlov Russian Med. Biol. Herald **30**, 39–50 (2022)
4. Garkavenko, F.V., et al.: Analysis of factors of effectiveness of oncological care at the level of the subject of the Russian Federation using multiple linear regression. Medical technologies. Eval. Selection **45**, 9–26 (2023)
5. Khil'ko, V.A., et al.: The topographic mapping of evoked bioelectrical activity and other methods for the functional neural visualization of the brain. Vestn. Ross. Akad. Med. Nauk **3**, 36–41 (1993)
6. Linnik, S.A.: Analysis of the accessibility of patients with malignant neoplasms to drug provision at the outpatient stage of treatment in the Russian Federation. Healthcare Russian Federation **67**, 97–105 (2023)
7. Lytaev, S., Vatamaniuk, I.: Physiological and medico-social research trends of the wave P300 and more late components of visual event-related potentials. Brain Sci. **11**, 125 (2021)
8. Lytaev, S.: Modern neurophysiological research of the human brain in clinic and psychophysiology. Lect. Notes Comput. Sci. **12940**, 231–241 (2021)
9. Lytaev, S.: Psychological and neurophysiological screening investigation of the collective and personal stress resilience. Behav. Sci. **13**, 258 (2023)
10. Lytaev, S.: Short time algorithms for screening examinations of the collective and personal stress resilience. Lect. Notes Comput. Sci. **14017**, 442–458 (2023)
11. Marchenko, B.I., et al.: Malignant neoplasms in an industrial city: epidemiology, current trends and prognosis. Public Health Habitat **31**, 17–26 (2023)
12. Orel, V., Nosyreva, O, Buldakova, T., et al.: Differences in the structure of infectious morbidity of the population during the first and second half of 2020 in St. Petersburg. Book of Abstracts ASMDA 2021 and Demographics 2021 Workshop, pp. 535–543 (2021)
13. Orel, V., Smirnova, V., Guryeva, N., et al.: Ways of economical production in medical institution risk management. In: Duffy, V.G. (eds.) Digital Human Modeling and Applications in Health, Safety, Ergonomics and Risk Management. Health, Operations Management, and Design. HCII 2022.LNCS, vol. 13320, pp. 237–248 (2022). Doi: https://doi.org/10.1007/978-3-031-06018-2_17
14. Orel, V.I., Guryeva, N.A., Rubezhov, A.L., et al.: Lean manufacturing technologies as a way to improve the organization processes in a dental clinic. Med. Healthcare Organization **7**, 36–45 (2022)
15. Orel, V.I., Smirnova, V.I., Chentsov, D.V., et al.: Organization of the workplace according to the principle of 5C in medical organizations: educational and visual aid. St. Petersburg: Federal State Budgetary Educational Institution of the Ministry of Health of the Russian Federation. (2021)
16. The state of cancer care for the population of Russia in 2022. Edited by A.D. Kaprin, V.V. Starinsky, A.O. Shakhzadova – M.: P.A. Herzen Moscow State Medical Research Institute – branch of the Federal State Budgetary Institution "NMIC of Radiology" of the Ministry of Health of the Russian Federation, 2022, 239 (2023)
17. Timurzieva, A.B., Lindenbraten, A.L.: On the factors influencing the interaction of participants in the therapeutic and diagnostic process and effectiveness in the healthcare system (literature review). Healthcare the Russian Federation **66**, 336–341 (2022)
18. Yesaulenko, I.E., Petrova, T.N., Tolbin, A.A., et al.: Optimization of the system of early detection of oncological diseases in outpatient medical organizations. I.P. Pavlov Russian Med. Biol. Herald **31**, 635–642 (2023)

19. Zadvornaya, O.L.: Conceptual approaches to advanced training of personnel for the implementation of lean manufacturing technologies in medical organizations providing primary health care. Medical technologies. Eval. Selection **39**, 48–54 (2020)
20. Uspenskaya, I.V., Selyavina, O.N.: The use of "lean" technologies in the process of medical examination of the adult population of the Ryazan region. I.P. Pavlov Russian Med. Biol. Herald **30**, 159–166 (2022)

Web System for the Prediction of Type II Diabetes Based on Machine Learning

Erika Hernández-Rubio[1]([✉]), Carlos A. Jaimes Mackay[2],
Paula G. Robles Sosa[2], and Rubén Galicia-Mejía[2]

[1] Instituto Politécnico Nacional, SEPI-ESCOM, Ciudad de México, Mexico
ehernandezru@ipn.mx
[2] Instituto Politécnico Nacional, ESCOM, Ciudad de México, Mexico
rgalicia@ipn.mx

Abstract. Diabetes is a chronic disease, which is characterized by high levels of glucose in the blood and by too little insulin production or when it cannot be used effectively. The number of people who develop type 1 diabetes is increasing every year, it usually appears in the childhood or youth, and can develop during the development of the fetus in the womb, feeding during the first years of life, etc. Regarding type 2 diabetes, it occurs mostly from forty years and people suffering from obesity or other chronic diseases. This work presents the development of a web system application to support the pre-diagnosis of type II diabetes, with a precision acceptable using classification machine learning algorithms. The detection and diagnosis process will be facilitated with the use of machine learning algorithms for this, a framework will be developed using information based on health databases to anticipate whether the patient presents symptoms of diabetes or not, providing a basic diagnosis to anticipate the level threat with greater accuracy.

Keywords: Classification · Diabetes · machine learnig · prediction

1 Introduction

Diabetes is a chronic disease, which is characterized by high levels of glucose in the blood and by too little insulin production or when it cannot be used effectively. There are four types of diabetes; type 1 diabetes mellitus, type 2 diabetes mellitus, Latent Autoimmune Diabetes in Adults (LADA) type diabetes and gestational diabetes, without however, type 2 diabetes mellitus is the most common because, according to the Mexican diabetes federation, it includes between 85% and 90% of total cases. Any type of diabetes, if not treated or controlled, can produce complications in many parts of the body and increase the risk of premature death [5].

The number of people who develop type 1 diabetes is increasing every year, it usually appears in the childhood or youth, and can develop during the development of the fetus in the womb, feeding during the first years of life, etc. Regarding type 2 diabetes, it occurs mostly from forty years and people suffering from obesity or other chronic diseases [17].

C. Stephanidis et al. (Eds.): HCII 2024, CCIS 2119, pp. 277–285, 2024.
https://doi.org/10.1007/978-3-031-61966-3_31

Machine learning algorithms are pieces of code, which help analyze data and search one meaning. The goal is to detect patterns so that they can be used to make predictions or classify information [3]. Based on the figures for the year 2020 that have been released in recent years by the INEGI, in Mexico, the Diabetes is the third leading cause of death. If diabetes is diagnosed early, it can help people to manage their illness [14].

In this sense, machine learning acts in a way that does not need to be explicitly programmed and actually works with the data exposed to it, using two types of algorithms: learning supervised and unsupervised learning. The supervised learning model is one in which they learn functions, relationships that associate inputs with outputs, so they fit a set of examples of which we know the relationship between the input and the desired output. In the case of the model unsupervised learning, are those in which we are not interested in adjusting pairs (input, output), but in increasing the structural knowledge of the available data (and possible future data that come from the same phenomenon), for example, giving a grouping of the data according to their similarity (clustering), simplifying their structure while maintaining their fundamental characteristics (as in dimensionality reduction processes), or extracting the internal structure with which it is they distribute the data in its original space (topological learning) [1,9].

2   Related Work

The scientific article "Bayesian System for Diabetes Prediction" [6] and the "CDC Prediabetes" web application [8] are related to the project that is being developed. The differences against the project are: the scientific article is only a proposal so it has not yet been developed and the web application only makes the pre-diagnosis of type II diabetes and does not explain how it makes that pre-diagnosis. However, the project that is being developed also makes the pre-diagnosis of type II diabetes using machine learning algorithms to have better precision.

3   Diabetes in México

Diabetes is a condition that affects the body's ability to transform food into energy. Insulin helps you get energy from food. Part of what you eat is transformed into sugar called glucose. Glucose travels through your body in the blood. Your body stores glucose in cells to use for energy. Insulin is the key that opens the door to cells [2].

3.1   Type I Diabetes

Although type I diabetes can develop in adults, it is characterized by the fact that it has a higher incidence among young people and children. In this type of diabetes, the patient's own immune system destroys the beta cells of the pancreas, causing a total insulin deficiency. Insulin is the hormone that allows glucose from food to pass into the body's cells [4].

3.2   Type II Diabetes

Although type II diabetes can affect people of any age, even children, it develops more frequently in adults and older people. Obesity and a sedentary lifestyle are, among others, some of the factors that can cause this type of diabetes. Most people with type 2 diabetes can produce insulin, but not in sufficient quantities that the body needs for proper functioning. In many cases, and in clear difference with type 1 diabetes, type 2 diabetes can be prevented by maintaining healthy eating habits and are combined with moderate physical activity [4].

4   Machine Learning Algorithms

Machine learning techniques can be defined as a set of methods capable of automatically detecting patterns in data. Under this definition, the concept of machine learning has existed at least since the 1950s, a period in which various statistical methods were discovered and redefined and applied to machine learning through simple algorithms, although limited almost exclusively to the academic field [16]. This concept of machine learning has since included the use of detected patterns to make predictions, or to make other types of decisions in uncertain environments.

4.1   Supervised Learning

In supervised learning, an algorithm is given a set of data that is labeled with corresponding output values on which it can be trained and define a prediction model. This algorithm can then be used on new data to predict its corresponding output values [7].

Support Vector Machine. They are classification models that try to resolve the difficulties that complex data samples can pose, where the relationships do not have to be linear. That is, it is intended to classify the observations into several groups or classes, but these are not separable via a hyperplane in the dimensional space defined by the data. To do this, the data set is embedded in a higher dimensional space through a function that allows the data to be separated in the new space through a hyperplane in said space [13].

Classification Trees. Classification trees (when the target variable is categorical) and regression trees (when the target variable is continuous) are analysis techniques that allow predicting the assignment of samples to predefined groups based on a series of predictive variables. The predictive power of this algorithm may be more limited than that of other models, because they perform an orthogonal partition of the space, which turns the sample into silos and limits the predictive capacity because this algorithm tends to overtrain. Classification and regression trees are machine-learning methods for constructing prediction models from data. The models are obtained by recursively partitioning the data space and fitting a simple prediction model within each partition. As a result, the partitioning can be represented graphically as a decision tree [12].

Neural Networks. Artificial neural networks are massively parallel intercon-
nected networks of simple elements (usually adaptive) and with hierarchical
organization, which attempt to interact with real-world objects in the same way
that the biological nervous system does. They are able to learn from experience,
to generalize from previous cases to new cases, to abstract essential features from
inputs that represent irrelevant information, etc. [11].

KNN Algorithm. The K-nearest neighbors (KNN) algorithm is a Machine
Learning algorithm that belongs to the simple and easy-to-apply supervised
learning algorithms that can be used to solve classification and regression problems. A disadvantage What it has is that the algorithm becomes slower as the
number of observations increases and the independent variables increase [7].

4.2   Unsupervised Learning

In this type of learning, the construction sample does not have information on
a variable that you want to predict. The goal of this type of problem is to
find patterns or relationships in the data. For this reason, it is also known as
knowledge discovery (the process of identifying patterns in data that are valid,
new, potentially useful and understandable) [16].

Clustering. Clustering is an unsupervised model that is used to identify groups
(clusters) or patterns of similar observations in a data set. One of the most
used techniques is the k-means method, which consists of defining a central
reference point for each cluster (called centroid) and assigning each individual
to the cluster of the closest centroid based on the distances between the input
attributes. The algorithm starts by setting k centroids randomly and, through an
iterative process, each point is assigned to the cluster with the closest centroid,
proceeding to update the value of the centroids. This process ends when a certain
convergence criterion is reached [16].

Data Analysis. Dimensionality reduction methods aim to reduce the number of
dimensions of the analysis space, determined by the set of explanatory variables.
One of the techniques is principal component analysis (principal component
analysis or PCA), which converts a set of correlated variables into another (with
a smaller number of variables) without correlation, called principal components.
The main disadvantage of applying PCA on the data set is that they lose their
interpretability [16].

5   Design

In this system, a Dataset from the Behavioral Risk Factor Surveillance System
(BRFSS) is used. The BRFSS is a health-related survey, collected annually via
telephone. The survey has more than 400,000 responses from Americans with

health-related risk behaviors, chronic disease conditions and use of preventive services. This survey has been conducted annually since 1984 [10].

The variables selected from the BRFSS 2020 dataset are divided into two types, the dependent variables, which allow us to know the result of the evaluation, and the independent variables, which present different values that provide the final result and allow us to obtain a evaluation index.

The classification algorithms were obtained from the scikit-learn library within Python. The use of this library facilitates the use of classification algorithms and after the data evaluation process, precision statistics can be obtained. Such as the Matthews correlation coefficient. The algorithms used in this system are: KNN classifier, decision tree and neural networks [15].

For the presentation of the application, an intuitive and minimalist user interface was planned, to highlight the important aspects, and to be able to meet the objective of raising users' awareness about the importance of keeping their health situation in mind, as well as performing the test. So that they can receive guidance based on their results. As shown in Fig. 1, we have the following design of the first interaction with the user. For login, shown in Fig. 2, the use of modals is used for an intuitive user experience.

Figure 3 shows one of the questions in the questionnaire.

6   Test and Results

Based on the performance tests, it can be stated that it is an optimal classification system with an accuracy above 85% based on the accuracy scores of all the algorithms together.

6.1   Execution of Tests with Users

Based on the performance tests, it can be stated that it is an optimal classification system with an accuracy above 85% based on the accuracy scores of all the algorithms together.

Tests were carried out with 67 people (Fig. 4), who provided their data to make usage graphs. It was observed that one of the variables that most affects the risk factor is family history with diabetes since users who answered "yes" to this variable see an increase of 15% to 20% compared to those who do not and who have similar lifestyles (Fig. 5).

Another variable that demonstrated a high impact was physical activity. Within the data bank, a format of 2 possible responses could be used for this variable, simplifying the calculation that is carried out.

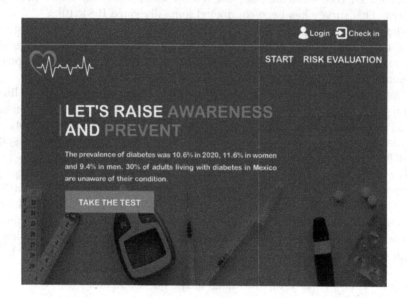

Fig. 1. Homepage

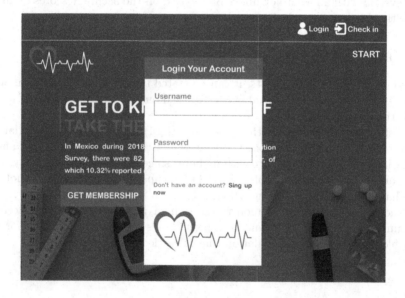

Fig. 2. Log in

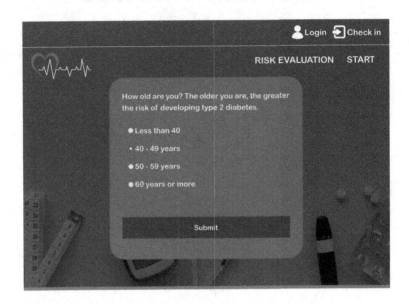

Fig. 3. Questionnaire

NUMBER OF REGISTERED PEOPLE

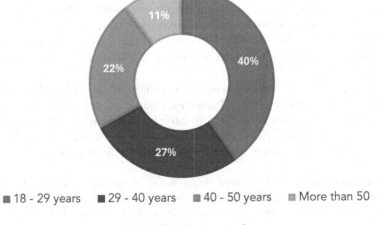

Fig. 4. People surveyed

RISK FACOR PERCENTAGE

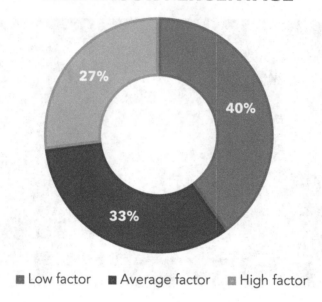

Fig. 5. Risk factor percentage

7 Conclusions

To train the algorithms, information could be extracted from a database of 118,000 records. Of the machine learning algorithms existing in the literature, 5 algorithms were selected: Nearest Neighbor, Decision Tree, Random Forest, Naive Bayes and Neural Networks. The reason for this selection was because they are algorithms commonly used in classification and prediction through data banks. The combination of the 5 allows increasing the precision and reliability of the prediction. The third specific objective was met by creating a method with these machine learning algorithms generating a mathematical model to achieve diabetes prediction.

A web page was developed where the user registers and performs the risk assessment, answering a series of questions based on the information that we can reference in the data bank and validated by a general practitioner. Once the questions are answered, the system compares the user's input with the mathematical model and responds with the evaluation of the risk factor.

Acknowledgements. The authors thank financial support given by the Instituto Politénico Nacional trough SIP program with the project number 20231330. The authors thank to Daira Aguilar for her support with the edition of the images.

References

1. Aguirre Ascona, Y.D.: Métodos de aprendizaje supervisado para la predicción de diabetes: una revisión sistemática de la literatura (2019)
2. A. D. Association. qué es la diabetes? (2022)
3. Azure, M.: Algoritmos de aprendizaje automático (2023)
4. Care, B.D.: Diferencias basicas entre la diabetes tipo 1 y diabetes tipo 2 (2022)
5. Castellanos, J.L.V., Cerda, A.P.: Diabetes mellitus tipo 2: un problema epidemiológico y de emergencia en méxico. Investigación en Salud **150**(99), 18–26 (2001)
6. Castrillón, O.D., Sarache, W., Castaño, E.: Sistema bayesiano para la predicción de la diabetes. Información tecnológica **28**(6), 161–168 (2017)
7. DataScientest. qué es el algoritmo knn? (2024)
8. C. for Disease Control and Prevention. take the test - prediabetes (2023)
9. Iyer, A., Jeyalatha, S., Sumbaly, R.: Diagnosis of diabetes using classification mining techniques. arXiv Preprint arXiv:1502.03774 (2015)
10. Kaggle. Behavioral risk factor surveillance system 2020 survey data (2020)
11. Krogh, A.: What are artificial neural networks? Nat. Biotechnol. **26**(2), 195–197 (2008)
12. Loh, W.-Y.: Classification and regression trees. Wiley Interdisciplinary Rev. Data Mining Knowl. Discovery **1**(1), 14–23 (2011)
13. Noble, W.S.: What is a support vector machine? Nat. Biotechnol. **24**(12), 1565–1567 (2006)
14. G.E. D. N. I. Y. (s. f.). Prevalencia de obesidad, hipertensión y diabetes para los municipios de méxico (2018)
15. scikit learn. Supervised learning (2024)
16. Solutions, M.: Machine learning, una pieza clave en la transformacion de los modelos de negocio (2018)
17. van Wilpe, R., Hulst, A.H., Siegelaar, S.E., DeVries, J.H., Preckel, B., Hermanides, J.: Type 1 and other types of diabetes mellitus in the perioperative period. what the anaesthetist should know. J. Clin. Anesthesia **84**, 111012 (2023)

Human-Centered Design of Cadre: A Digital Platform to Support Cardiac Arrest (Co-) Survivorship

Gabrielle M. Jean-Pierre[1,2], Angel Rajotia[1,2(✉)], Enid Montague[1,2],
Damyen Henderson-Lee Wah[3], Raima Lohani[4], Quynh Pham[3,4,5],
and Katie N. Dainty[3,6]

[1] Faculty of Applied Science and Engineering, University of Toronto, Toronto, Canada
angel.rajotia@mail.utoronto.ca
[2] Wellness and Health Enhancement Engineering Laboratory, University of Toronto, Toronto, Canada
[3] Institute of Health Policy, Management and Evaluation, University of Toronto, Toronto, Canada
[4] Centre for Digital Therapeutics, University Health Network, Toronto, Canada
[5] Toronto General Hospital Research Institute, University Health Network, Toronto, Canada
[6] North York General Hospital, Toronto, Canada

Abstract. Life after sudden cardiac arrest (SCA) encompasses multifaceted challenges pertaining to the psychological, financial, lifestyle, and cognitive aspects of both the survivor and their family's recovery. Current health services do not address their complex and evolving needs once they return home, leaving them to navigate (co-)survivorship on their own with limited support. In this study, we describe the process of developing user-centered requirements for a digital healthcare intervention, called Cadre. The goals were to address the limitations of equitably providing services and support to cardiac arrest survivors. In Phase I, user journey mapping and Scenario-Based Design methods, supported by Actor-Network Theory, were used to analyze focus group interview data and develop user personas and problem scenarios. Phase II involved the ideation of application features for Cadre. Phase I results include the emergence of a new theme – *every cardiac arrest survivor experience is unique* – and the creation of personas and scenarios that reflect this theme. The identified needs (validation, guidance, and lack of emotional support) were translated into a vision for Cadre that will be evaluated via iterative prototype development and usability testing in the future. This project addresses a critical opportunity in the field of SCA survivorship as it not only advances the design of a comprehensive support solution for survivors and their families but also represents a crucial move toward equitable post-discharge care for all.

Keywords: Digital healthcare · Out-of-hospital cardiac arrest · Survivorship · Co-survivorship · Human-centered design · Scenario-Based Design · Actor-Network Theory · User Journey Mapping

---

Gabrielle M. Jean-Pierre and Angel Rajotia are co-first authors on this paper.

© The Author(s), under exclusive license to Springer Nature Switzerland AG 2024
C. Stephanidis et al. (Eds.): HCII 2024, CCIS 2119, pp. 286–298, 2024.
https://doi.org/10.1007/978-3-031-61966-3_32

1 Introduction

Sudden cardiac arrest (SCA) is characterized by an abrupt disruption in cardiac activity, onset by fibrillating heart ventricles that neither contract nor relax. As such, perfusion is no longer possible and interventions like cardiopulmonary resuscitation (CPR) and defibrillation are required to escape death [1]. Each year, more than 60,000 Canadians suffer an out-of-hospital cardiac arrest (OHCA): that's one every 9 min, and only one in ten people survive [2]. Nonetheless, advancements in prehospital response and critical care over the last decade have improved SCA diagnosis and increasingly effective and timely interventions occur earlier [3].

Despite the improved survival rates of SCA, the Canadian healthcare system falls short in targeting the multifaceted emotional, physical, social, and economic challenges associated with life after cardiac arrest. The recently published American Heart Association Scientific Statement on survivorship makes a direct call for attention to quality of life, survivorship, and rehabilitation. It recommends a shift from the language of survival to a discourse of recovery, as it acknowledges that SCA survivorship is more than just having clinically survived a near-death experience [4]. With a significant proportion of survivors experiencing varying degrees of neurocognitive and psychosocial impairment due to brain damage from oxygen deprivation, survivors are recognized as both cardiac and brain injury survivors. Two-thirds of cardiac arrest survivors suffer from cognitive deficits, particularly memory, planning, problem-solving, and attention; two-thirds experience symptoms of anxiety and depression; one-third develop post-traumatic stress symptoms and only half return to their previous occupations [5–9]. Additionally, family members of SCA survivors experience a similar range of challenges as they navigate the complexity of the co-survivorship journey which involves understanding the new "normal" and providing ongoing support to the survivor [10, 11].

The contemporary shift to digital-first healthcare [12] coupled with the complex needs of cardiac arrest survivors and their families presents an urgent opportunity to position digitally mediated care as a viable solution for personalized management of their (co-)survivorship journeys. Digital health has been described as the secure and cost-effective utilization of information communication technologies in support of health and health-related fields, including healthcare services, health surveillance, health information, education, and research [13]. The use of digital health in supportive care is a potential route to optimize the provision and coordination of services [14], overcome barriers to ongoing support and improve poorer outcomes for those living in remote and underserved areas, [15, 16] or as a lower-cost alternative in which access to healthcare is not universal [17, 18].

In recognition of the critical intersection of digital health and cardiac arrest survivorship, our team began the development of a remote management platform, called Cadre, to support survivors and caregivers throughout their recoveries. Ideally, Cadre would have been co-designed alongside these user groups, however, limited access to interactions with the community caused us to pivot to a method that temporarily helps us advance into the design process. To center our end-users (patients, caregivers, clinicians) in the platform design, user-centered service design frameworks guided our design activities, including user journey mapping and Scenario-Based Design (SBD). User journey mapping is a tool in user experience (UX) that captures a person's interactions with a system over time to reveal insights into areas that can be improved. SBD is an approach used in human-centered design where stakeholder stories, termed scenarios, are created to summarize the current lived experiences of the users and highlight how they currently overcome challenges related to the design opportunity. Solutions to the latter challenges are then brainstormed from the stories to ensure the ideation of a product that inserts itself well into the lived experience of its target users. Additionally, Actor-Network Theory (ANT) was employed in conjunction with SBD during the scenario development process. This theory states that all things are a result of the networks that form them and that to truly understand an actor's behaviours, it is crucial to understand how other actors influence their actions. Using this approach provided a deeper perspective of the stakeholders' experiences such that meaningful personas and scenarios could be designed. Our overall efforts resulted in the establishment of a recovery timeline via user journey mapping, the creation of seven realistic persona scenarios supported by ANT, and a strong user-centered vision for Cadre. Our research contributes to the generation of a novel healthcare intervention for the cardiac arrest survivorship community while also advancing methods of engineering healthcare initiatives.

2   Related Works

2.1   Worldwide In-Person SCA Interventions

Attempts at bridging the transition from acute care to life after cardiac arrest have been implemented as in-person clinical interventions outside of Canada in the Netherlands, United States, and United Kingdom, with notable work recently conducted in Denmark [12–14, 19]. Wagner et al. [20] conducted focus group interviews with Danish SCA survivors attending a tailored rehabilitation program who mentioned "feeling understood for the first time" after a year or more of very little post-discharge support. Since then, Wagner [13, 21, 22] has been involved in documenting a range of (co-)survivorship aspects (fatigue, return-to-work) as stakeholders engage with interventions (SCARF, ROCK, respectively), with their most recent contribution being the development of a concrete follow-up pathway for SCA called the "Copenhagen framework." This framework encompasses steps to be taken pre-discharge, such as diagnostic evaluation and screening of both the SCA survivors and their family members, as well as checkpoints for post-discharge follow-up. Although in-person "clinic" interventions have been reported as effective for both SCA survivors and their families, they come with significant resource requirements and often exacerbate existing inequities in access to care for those outside of large academic centers. This is of high relevance to the geographically diverse Canadian landscape, where rural communities continue to experience barriers to secondary and tertiary care, including challenges associated with poor health professional recruitment and retention [15, 16]. To the best of our knowledge, no digital interventions tailored to sudden cardiac arrest (co-)survivorship have been developed, making Cadre the first of its kind.

2.2   Designing Interventions: Insights from SCA Survivors and Family

Underpinning our work is research conducted by Damyen Henderson-Lee Wah, under the supervision of Dr. Katie Dainty, titled *"Grounding the Design of a Supportive*

Intervention in the Experiences and Perspectives of Sudden Cardiac Arrest Survivors and Family Members." This study aimed to gain an in-depth understanding of (co-)survivorship experiences during the first year of recovery from the perspectives of OHCA survivors and close family members. During focus groups interviews, survivors and family reflected on different periods during the first year after hospitalization and where they felt they could have used support. As an additional means of triangulation, interviews were conducted among a variety of clinicians with experience caring for OHCA survivors and/or family members as well as interviews among researchers with experience developing survivorship interventions in other condition contexts such as stroke and cancer.

The data collected was analyzed via qualitative methods to identify major themes that encompass key aspects of the (co-)survivorship journey. For example, the theme of *"Challenges navigating new territory without a map"* addresses the gaps around expectation setting and information resources described by the participants. Additionally, *"The impact of time and evolution of needs"* delineates how those expectations and information needs evolve continuously over time. Henderson-Lee Wah et al. further highlight the connection between these two major themes and the patterns and key turning points that represent opportunities to enhance the recovery experience.

Supported by literature, Henderson-Lee Wah describes the potential for a digital solution for OHCA survivors and family members navigating survivorship, stating that as mobile devices become more universal, supportive technologies and information dissemination pathways used in healthcare should evolve accordingly [23]. Moreover, evidence exists to support the effectiveness of digital health interventions to enhance self-management [24], and that collaborative design approaches have previously been applied to develop mobile health applications [24–27]. Henderson-Lee Wah et al.'s work is in the process of being submitted for publication.

3 Design Methods

Human-centered service design was applied in the conception of Cadre, specifically Scenario-Based Design (SBD). Developed by Rosson and Carroll [28], SBD places user experiences at the forefront of the ideation process, emphasizing the creation and analysis of user personas and problem scenarios. These personas and scenarios are then used to introduce the product being developed to key stakeholders and assess how it would fit into the lives of users. This approach contrasts with a solution-first design approach, which, while faster, can introduce bias by not fully understanding the design context, potentially hindering future implementation.

With the objective to create an intervention that meaningfully facilitates survivorship well-being with minimal burden for end-users, our initial design phase focused on the first two phases of SBD: Requirements Analysis and Activity Design. Cadre's design methodology is unique in the tools used conjointly with SBD, namely, user journey mapping and Actor-Network Theory (Fig. 1).

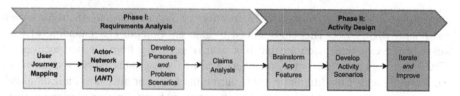

Fig. 1. A flowchart of the Cadre design methodology, with tools of interest **bolded**.

3.1 Qualitative Data Analysis

The aim of Requirements Analysis is to develop a preliminary understanding of stake-holder needs [29]. We did so by conducting a qualitative data analysis of the focus group transcripts provided by Henderson-Lee Wah, from which themes analogous to the study's two themes were extracted. Since the interviews covered their experiences across a year post-discharge, with notable timepoints at 3, 6, and 12 months, user journey mapping was used to summarize the data. We viewed the recovery journey of SCA survivors and their family caregivers as a long and dynamic process, with challenges evolving over time, and user journey mapping could capture that. The following categories were evaluated within the journey maps: *Feelings, Needs & Pains, Resources Used, What would have helped, What helped.* Summarizing data pertaining to those topics provided a holistic overview of the survivorship journey and the SCA survivor user journey map is shown in Fig. 2. An emotion graph component is also included to highlight the highs and lows of the journey. Henderson-Lee Wah had already extracted major themes that encompassed our own observations; however, we suggested a third theme: *The importance of adapting to different experiences while building on commonalities.* This theme arose upon realizing how each column in every row contained similar words as well as contrasting ones. For instance, at the 6-month mark, some survivors were developing confidence in themselves, while others were experiencing psychological challenges. Experiences can differ due to the nature of the incident (causes of arrest, impairments) and a victim's identity (area of residence, personal connections), which are factors we aimed to keep in mind for the subsequent design stages.

3.2 Problem Scenario Development

Following journey mapping, personas and problem scenarios were developed to encompass the main themes identified. User personas are fictional stakeholders and problem scenarios showcase how they currently navigate challenges. The degree of detail for each persona and scenario varies across projects; our goal was to create elaborate and detailed stories that reflect the complexities of (co-)survivorship experiences. Doing so was our way of honoring the third theme presented above. To translate journey maps back into stories, Actor-Network Theory (ANT) was used.

Briefly, ANT postulates that an actor (person, object, business, government, etc.) behaves, thrives, struggles, or exists due to the other actors that influence it. Used mainly in Sociology, ANT is employed to understand the power that a given actor holds within a network and to pinpoint the reasons for which they hold it by breaking down the smaller

Journey Timeline	Before Hospital Discharge	After Hospital Discharge	6-Months After Discharge	1-Year After Discharge	Many Years Later
Feelings	• Anxious • Afraid to leave hospital • Traumatized • Confused • Unheard	• Lucky to have survived • Fear of recurrence • Anxiety • Insecurity • Lost trust in body • Scared of being away from hospital • Fear of missing any symptoms • Helplessness • Felt weak but loved and supported • Angry • Shocked • Disappointed about not being able to work normally	• Clinical depression and PTSD • Insecurity episodes • Gaining back trust on body • Took time to be comfortable living far from hospital • Found it hard to interact with people in rehab of different age groups and conditions • Overwhelmed and stressed • Worried about impact on family • Discouraged & frustrated by arising cognitive impairments (aphasia, hypoxia) • More confident (driving, work, etc.)	• PTSD and being triggered and reminded of pain and fear • Excited • Felt invisible • Discriminated against for being a trauma survivor because looked young/healthy • Lucky • Felt they were in better shape now than ever • Discouraged about not having the best physical health • Focus shifted back on personal life problems	• Overall physical improvements, but lingering psychological and emotional impacts • PTSD and being triggered by SCA stories
Needs and Pains	• Validation • Help with making important decisions • Answer to "What next?" • Emotional attention • Rehab information	• Resources for rehab, psychologist etc. • Artificial heart pump • Looking young/healthy should not cause negligence or discrimination • 24-hour care • Open conversations about emotions	• Need validation ("nothing is wrong with you") • Mental support for trauma • Physical independence • Timely follow-ups by doctors and support staff • Timely and regular cognitive assessment • No access to GP/cardiologist for a while due to living in a rural area	• Extreme treatment by others (too disabled/fragile or not enough disability) • Panic attacks • Lack of emotional and financial help • Doctor fragmentation (no communication among practitioners) • Make sure there was AED nearby at all times	• Has to reside near hospitals with specialists that can attend to their condition (restricted establishments) • Can't have babies without risking death • Denied benefits of many programs due to the invisibility/internal nature of cardiac arrest recovery
Resources Used	• Physiotherapy • Conversation with Cardiologist • Validation and timely attention	• Cardiac rehab programs • Personal mental health resources • Care from family • Follow-up with cardiologist a month later	• Mental health care • Physiotherapy • Cardiac rehab programs	• Psychologist • Nutritionist • Kinesiologist	• Mental health care for their families
What would have helped?	• Professional emotional support • Reassurance	• Psychologist/Emotional support • Knowing what to expect • Having personalized care/rehab • More relevant rehab groups • Follow-ups	• Someone to talk to • Emotional support for family too (a heads up would have been nice) • Help not limited to cardio	• Affordable care • Customized rehabilitation programs • Peer group support • Regular cardio check-ins • More people trained in LVAD	• Sensitization of general population to be more understanding and empathetic of SCA survivor's needs and condition • Access to immediate care in case of emergency without the dear of being away from the hospital
What helped?	• Acute care was good • Personal connections • Being in a group of people with similar health conditions and familiar background	• Receiving validation about healing from an invisible traumatic injury • Cardiac rehabilitation helped with establishing routine and structure	• Mental health care • Physiotherapy • Validation that nothing is wrong with them • Finding your own way to heal (writing things down to consolidate emotions, for example)	• Teaching CPR to family members • Joining facebook groups to support others who were recovering for cardiac arrest (helping others helped them) • Sharing their story • Personal accomplishments	• Training family members to conduct CPR
Emotions *Very emotional* High *Not emotional* Low					

Fig. 2. Example of a user journey map that represents the recovery journey of a SCA survivor.

networks that are the source of the power [30]. An understanding of the latter prepared us for the creation of meaningful scenarios.

Stakeholder networks were drawn from the summarized data in the user journey maps. The network for a *"Survivor as they recover"* is demonstrated below in Fig. 3 and the sub-networks of greatest importance are partitioned into *"Feelings"*, *"Support System"*, *"Resources"*, *"Time"*, and *"Multi-dimensionality."* The first three became the key foci in scenarios, with each being explored deeply through one persona. With regards to the latter two sub-networks, each persona was assigned a different recovery time point and multi-dimensional identity. Networks for *"Caregivers as they recover"* and *"Clinicians as they treat"* were also made and the sub-themes that originated from them were *"Responsibilities & Mental Well-being"* and *"Navigating the system & patient interactions"* respectively. Overall, 7 personas were created: 3 survivors, 2 family caregivers and 2 clinicians. Conventionally, fewer than 7 personas are made for SBD, however we found that fully exploring one challenge per scenario granted a thorough representation of each key need. The persona names and scenario themes are summarized in Table 1.

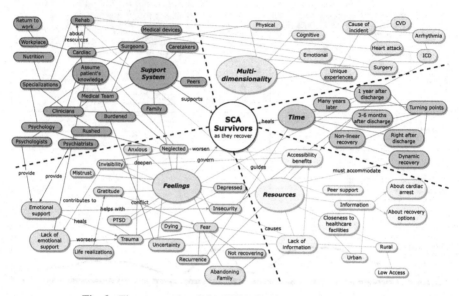

Fig. 3. The actor network for "SCA Survivors as they recover."

Table 1. The seven personas, their summarized profiles, and associated problem scenario themes.

Persona	Summarized Profile	Main Theme of Scenario
Walter	A retired clinical laboratory technician from Victoria, British Columbia, who survived SCA **a year ago** onset by his arrhythmia (supraventricular tachycardia)	Struggling **support system**
Em	A 32-year-old sales associate living in rural Binbrook, Ontario, who survived SCA **6 months ago** onset by stress-related myocardial infarction	Declining **mental well-being**
Kiara	A first-year international law student from Bangkok, Thailand, now residing in Hamilton, ON, who survived a SCA **2 months ago** onset by an unknown cause	Limited **resources**
Alyssa	Kiara's mother	Overwhelming **responsibilities**
Shirley	Walter's wife	Declining **mental well-being**
Dr. Mandel	Walter's cardiologist	Challenging **patient-clinician** interactions
Dr. Kent	Kiara and Em's cardiologist	**Healthcare system** limitations

Interestingly, tracing along the nodes and branches of the network formed a story outline for a scenario, introducing a secondary purpose of ANT in our methodology. See the example of the traces for Walter's scenario in Fig. 4. In the end, ANT facilitated the persona and problem scenario development, and its implementation in the context of SBD yielded rich stories and realistic characters. The final stage of Requirements Analysis, Claims Analysis, was carried out herein. This involved extracting important aspects of the scenarios that have a considerable impact on the personas' experiences [29]. Upsides and downsides of those aspects were noted and served as the basis for upcoming brainstorming processes.

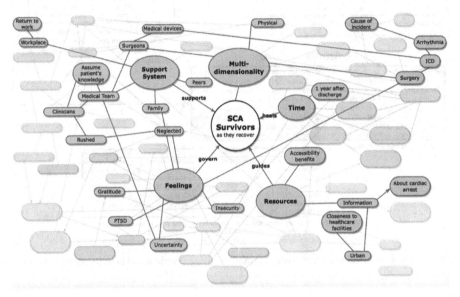

Fig. 4. The story outline for Walter's scenario.

3.3 Activity Design and Cadre App Features

Activity design (AD) is the next step in Scenario-Based Design. At this stage, the problem scenarios are modified to include the personas' use of Cadre. Application features were brainstormed from claims analysis where a viable feature is meant to capitalize on the upsides of a claim, while diminishing its downsides [31]. Following the brainstorming process, multiple features were introduced into the scenarios to assess their viability, feasibility, and impact against real-life experiences. The final ideas that were converged to were hence ones that suited the activity scenarios, and the ideas that seemed promising during brainstorming but could not be well integrated into scenarios, were omitted. Shown in Fig. 5 is a flowchart of the framework used. In Table 2, the Cadre vision that resulted from AD is summarized into its three main components: *Healthcare, Support, Personal Tracking*, and application feature examples.

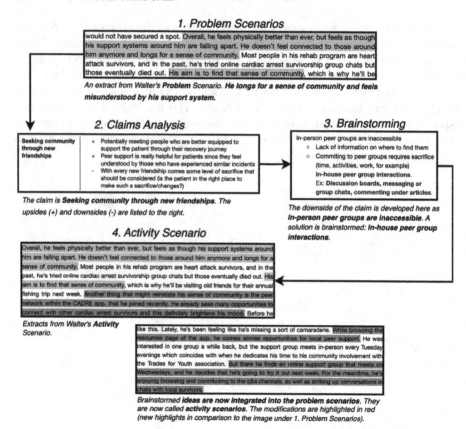

Fig. 5. The activity design framework summarized using problem and activity scenario extracts.

Table 2. The Cadre vision: Healthcare, Support, and Personal Tracking. The values for each component are **bolded** under *Description* and potential application features are listed under *Feature Examples*.

Component	Description	Feature Examples
Healthcare	**Accessibility, Equity** Virtual pipeline connecting survivors to their medical team	• Asynchronous patient tasks • Doctor's notes • Appointment scheduling
Support	**Empowerment** Empower survivors and caregivers throughout their journeys, by facilitating access to learning and health resources and community-building	• Education: Frequently Asked Questions (FAQ) • Resources: Links to external resources • Community: Chats, Question-and-Answer channels
Personal Tracking	**Self-management** Where survivors and caregivers track their well-being and progress over time	• Wellness assessments • Graphed scores • Activity logging

4 Discussion and Conclusion

The Cadre application will be the first of its kind for sudden cardiac arrest and has the potential to be a significant resource for survivors and their family members. The vision for the initial prototype has been developed according to a Scenario-Based Design (SBD) framework which was complemented with an Actor-Network Theory (ANT) approach to scenario writing. These tools are the topics of discussion in this section.

SBD has been successfully applied in healthcare design in the past and has proved to be effective in addressing complex healthcare challenges. Reeder and Turner [32] investigated the usefulness of SBD for understanding complex healthcare information by creating user personas and problem scenarios. Another study, conducted by Göttgens et al. [33], revealed that problem-driven strategies are most impactful in healthcare innovation, and identified a need for the incorporation of power dimensions, agency, and intersectionality in healthcare design, which is possible via use of SBD. Overall, the use of SBD in healthcare is a well-supported idea; however, our use of it was out-of-bounds in terms of co-design. For instance, Reeder and Turner [32] also went on to iteratively validate the personas and scenarios with study participants belonging to the target user group. The value of scenario validation and co-design is further demonstrated by Loomis and Montague's [34] work, where they developed problem scenarios alongside clinicians to inform the design of an automated feedback technology in primary care. The additional step of co-design is powerful and given greater access to survivor groups, we would have chosen a similar approach. Nonetheless, at this stage, SBD is a satisfactory user-centered design tool.

ANT was leveraged to meaningfully capture the complex reality of SCA experiences in the scenarios. Although not prevalent in healthcare implementation studies, ANT has previously shown to be useful in improving information technology (IT) implementations in the healthcare sector or understanding why these systems were rejected by users. When Cresswell et al. [35] sought to uncover why a £12.7 billion initiative for transitioning from paper records to electronic health records (EHRs) in English hospitals was ultimately abandoned, they turned to ANT. By drawing the network and replacing the paper records with EHR, they noticed a shift in connections between actors. This shift explained the difficulty faced by users to adapt to a new system that was compromising their social interactions with one another.

It has been argued that ANT is not a robust theory as it mainly supports a reflective analysis and lacks the explanatory nature of a traditional theory, as well as the ability to offer predictions. Nonetheless, this project's scope did not require a prediction, only a direction. ANT was sufficient for its purpose of inspiring the scenarios outlined in this research. A next step in applying ANT to subsequent Cadre design would be to modify the networks by inserting a node for the Cadre platform and determining how this new technology would affect the network. As such, ANT would provide insight and guidance into the successful implementation of Cadre in the future.

Another limitation in our methodology resulted from our initial framing of Cadre. A primary reference design for Cadre was the *Ned* ("No Evidence of Disease") platform, a prostate cancer survivorship digital intervention developed by the Centre of Digital Therapeutics (CDTx) at the University Health Network in Toronto, Canada. Its framework involves shifting patient-clinician interactions to an asynchronous remote management care model where patients and clinicians asynchronously manage the cancer survivorship journey. Specifically, the *Ned* care model leverages a web-based patient application and clinician dashboard that allows users to access clinical information (i.e. lab results), virtually complete patient reported outcomes on their quality of life and have asynchronous follow-ups with their clinician. Initially, we imagined Cadre as an adaptation of *Ned* for the SCA community. This vision was further solidified by the focus group data, where the survivors had generally positive outcomes and good connections to specialized practitioners. The persona and scenario development process that ensued resulted in profiles and stories that closely reflect the original qualitative data, where all survivors had a cardiologist that dedicated time to a digital platform, despite their busy schedules; this is not realistic. To add, we did not develop a co-survivor persona who administered CPR at the time of the arrest, nor a general practitioner persona, both of which are people we would commonly find in survivorship stories. It was only after Activity Design when we identified the biases we had adopted, along with the limitations that a siloed healthcare system, like Canada's, posed for the initial Cadre architecture. We underestimated the challenge of integrating digital health and the system by assuming it could be done in the future. As of now, we've modified the Cadre vision shown in Table 2, to a self-management framework that avoids system integration for the time being. We believe this approach is more realistic, hence more promising. Ultimately, when conducting SBD, the personas and scenarios undoubtedly form invaluable artefacts for design, however it is crucial that the data upon which it is based presents varied outcomes, and if that is not possible, an additional step should be taken to determine who is being left behind.

In conclusion, the initial stages of developing Cadre, a digital intervention for supporting cardiac arrest survivors and their family members through the disorienting recovery process, have been very successful. Scenario-Based Design and Actor-Network Theory were crucial tools to ensure that stakeholder experiences drove the design process despite the missing consultations with user groups. Next steps involve finalizing the first iteration of an interactive prototype and conducting several rounds of usability testing and expert heuristic evaluation. Success in the latter rounds would lead to the implementation of Cadre which will be supported by the University Health Network's CDTx. Our project aims not only to bring value to the development of a guiding tool for survivors and co-survivors, but our implementation of SBD combined with ANT presents a design framework that can be applied to other digital healthcare interventions in rehabilitation and survivorship care, with appropriate modifications tailored to stakeholder and healthcare system needs.

Acknowledgments. This research was supported by the Natural Sciences and Engineering Research Council (NSERC), TransformHF at the Ted Rogers Centre for Heart Research, and the University Health Network's Centre for Digital Therapeutics. Damyen Henderson-Lee Wah et al.'s work served as the foundation upon which our research was based.

References

1. Patel, K., Hipskind, J.E.: Cardiac Arrest. In: StatPearls. StatPearls Publishing, Treasure Island (FL) (2024)

2. Heart & Stroke 2024 Cardiac Arrest report. https://issuu.com/heartandstroke/docs/cardiac_a rrest_report_feb_2024
3. Buick, J.E., et al.: Rescu investigators: improving temporal trends in survival and neurological outcomes after out-of-hospital cardiac arrest. Circ. Cardiovasc. Qual. Outcomes **11**, e003561 (2018). https://doi.org/10.1161/CIRCOUTCOMES.117.003561
4. Sawyer, K.N., et al.: On behalf of the American Heart Association Emergency Cardiovascular Care Committee; Council on Cardiovascular and Stroke Nursing; Council on Genomic and Precision Medicine; Council on Quality of Care and Outcomes Research; and Stroke Council: Sudden Cardiac Arrest Survivorship: A Scientific Statement From the American Heart Association. Circulation **141** (2020). https://doi.org/10.1161/CIR.0000000000000747
5. Agarwal, S., et al.: Psychological distress after sudden cardiac arrest and its impact on recovery. Curr. Cardiol. Rep. **24**, 1351–1360 (2022). https://doi.org/10.1007/s11886-022-017 47-9
6. Presciutti, A., et al.: Posttraumatic stress and depressive symptoms characterize cardiac arrest survivors' perceived recovery at hospital discharge. Gen. Hosp. Psychiatry **53**, 108–113 (2018). https://doi.org/10.1016/j.genhosppsych.2018.02.006
7. Evald, L., et al.: Younger age is associated with higher levels of self-reported affective and cognitive sequelae six months post-cardiac arrest. Resuscitation **165**, 148–153 (2021). https://doi.org/10.1016/j.resuscitation.2021.04.009
8. Whitehead, L., Tierney, S., Biggerstaff, D., Perkins, G.D., Haywood, K.L.: Trapped in a disrupted normality: survivors' and partners' experiences of life after a sudden cardiac arrest. Resuscitation **147**, 81–87 (2020). https://doi.org/10.1016/j.resuscitation.2019.12.017
9. Christensen, J., Winkel, B.G., Eskildsen, S.J., Gottlieb, R., Hassager, C., Wagner, M.K.: Return-to-work and rehabilitation needs in cardiac arrest survivors: an exploratory cross-sectional study. Eur. J. Cardiovasc. Nurs. **22**, 328–331 (2023). https://doi.org/10.1093/eurjcn/zvac039
10. Bohm, M., et al.: Caregiver burden and health-related quality of life amongst caregivers of out-of-hospital cardiac arrest survivors. Resuscitation **167**, 118–127 (2021). https://doi.org/10.1016/j.resuscitation.2021.08.025
11. Rojas, D.A., DeForge, C.E., Abukhadra, S.L., Farrell, L., George, M., Agarwal, S.: Family experiences and health outcomes following a loved ones' hospital discharge or death after cardiac arrest: a scoping review. Resuscitation Plus. **14**, 100370 (2023). https://doi.org/10.1016/j.resplu.2023.100370
12. Mion, M., et al.: Follow-up care after out-of-hospital cardiac arrest: a pilot study of survivors and families' experiences and recommendations. Resuscitation Plus **7**, 100154 (2021). https://doi.org/10.1016/j.resplu.2021.100154
13. Joshi, V.L., et al.: Promising results from a residential rehabilitation intervention focused on fatigue and the secondary psychological and physical consequences of cardiac arrest: the SCARF feasibility study. Resuscitation **173**, 12–22 (2022). https://doi.org/10.1016/j.resusc itation.2022.02.002
14. Moulaert, V.R.M., et al.: Early neurologically-focused follow-up after cardiac arrest improves quality of life at one year: a randomised controlled trial. Int. J. Cardiol. **193**, 8–16 (2015). https://doi.org/10.1016/j.ijcard.2015.04.229
15. Jesus, T.S., Landry, M.D., Dussault, G., Fronteira, I.: Human resources for health (and rehabilitation): Six Rehab-Workforce Challenges for the century. Hum. Resour. Health **15**, 8 (2017). https://doi.org/10.1186/s12960-017-0182-7
16. Tran, D., et al.: Identification of recruitment and retention strategies for rehabilitation professionals in Ontario, Canada: results from expert panels. BMC Health Serv. Res. **8**, 249 (2008). https://doi.org/10.1186/1472-6963-8-249
17. Cafazzo, J.A.: A digital-first model of diabetes care. Diabetes Technol. Ther. **21**, S252–S258 (2019). https://doi.org/10.1089/dia.2019.0058

18. Global strategy on digital health 2020–2025. World Health Organization, Geneva. Licence: CC BY-NC-SA 3.0 IGO (2021)
19. Mion, M., et al.: Care after REsuscitation: implementation of the United Kingdom's first dedicated multidisciplinary follow-up program for survivors of out-of-hospital cardiac arrest. Ther. Hypothermia Temp. Manag. **10**, 53–59 (2020). https://doi.org/10.1089/ther.2018.0048
20. Ellen, M.E., Shach, R., Balicer, R.D.: Helping patients help themselves: supporting the healthcare journey. Patient Educ. Couns. **101**, 1708–1711 (2018). https://doi.org/10.1016/j.pec.2018.04.005
21. Guhl, E.N., et al.: Rationale and design of the Atrial Fibrillation health Literacy Information Technology Trial: (AF-LITT). Contemp. Clin. Trials **62**, 153–158 (2017). https://doi.org/10.1016/j.cct.2017.09.005
22. Amann, J., Fiordelli, M., Brach, M., Bertschy, S., Scheel-Sailer, A., Rubinelli, S.: Co-designing a self-management app prototype to support people with spinal cord injury in the prevention of pressure injuries: mixed methods study. JMIR Mhealth Uhealth **8**, e18018 (2020). https://doi.org/10.2196/18018
23. Schnall, R., et al.: A user-centered model for designing consumer mobile health (mHealth) applications (apps). J. Biomed. Inform. **60**, 243–251 (2016). https://doi.org/10.1016/j.jbi.2016.02.002
24. Neubeck, L., et al.: Development of an integrated e-health tool for people with, or at high risk of, cardiovascular disease: The Consumer Navigation of Electronic Cardiovascular Tools (CONNECT) web application. Int. J. Med. Informatics **96**, 24–37 (2016). https://doi.org/10.1016/j.ijmedinf.2016.01.009
25. Rosson, M.B., Carroll, J.M.: Scenario-based design. In: The Human-Computer Interaction Handbook: Fundamentals, Evolving Technologies and Emerging Applications, pp. 1032–1050. L. Erlbaum Associates Inc., USA (2002)
26. Rosson, M.B., Carroll, J.M.: Chapter 2 - Analyzing requirements. In: Rosson, M.B., Carroll, J.M. (eds.) Usability Engineering, pp. 37–78. Morgan Kaufmann, San Francisco (2002)
27. Law, J.: Notes on the theory of the actor-network: ordering, strategy, and heterogeneity. Syst. Pract. **5**, 379–393 (1992). https://doi.org/10.1007/BF01059830
28. Rosson, M.B., Carroll, J.M.: Chapter 3 - Activity design. In: Rosson, M.B., Carroll, J.M. (eds.) Usability Engineering. pp. 79–II. Morgan Kaufmann, San Francisco (2002)
29. Reeder, B., Turner, A.M.: Scenario-based design: a method for connecting information system design with public health operations and emergency management. J. Biomed. Inform. **44**, 978–988 (2011). https://doi.org/10.1016/j.jbi.2011.07.004
30. Göttgens, I., Oertelt-Prigione, S.: The application of human-centered design approaches in health research and innovation: a narrative review of current practices. JMIR Mhealth Uhealth **9**, e28102 (2021). https://doi.org/10.2196/28102
31. Loomis, A., Montague, E.: Scenario-based methods for hard-to-reach populations in healthcare. In: Kurosu, M. (ed.) Human-Computer Interaction. Theoretical Approaches and Design Methods, pp. 264–273. Springer, Cham (2022). https://doi.org/10.1007/978-3-031-05311-5_18
32. Cresswell, K.: Using actor-network theory to study health information technology interventions. In: Applied Interdisciplinary Theory in Health Informatics, pp. 87–97. IOS Press (2019)

Proposal of a Fetal Movement Sharing System Using a Pressure Sensor Array

Takayuki Kosaka$^{(\boxtimes)}$ (ID)

TOKAI University, Hiratsuka, Kanagawa, Japan
kosaka@kosaka-lab.com

Abstract. We propose a novel fetal movement sharing system employing a pressure sensor array-based fetal movement scanner and a display device. The proposed system aims to bridge the gap between subjective fetal movements experienced by pregnant women and objective shareable fetal movement data that enable fathers and other family members to strengthen their bond with the fetus. The system can be easily mounted on the abdomen of a pregnant woman, allowing the scanner to capture detailed data about the location and intensity of fetal movements; the display device visually and tactilely reproduces these movements and makes them available for viewing. Experiments conducted on pregnant women demonstrate the system's ability to measure and reproduce fetal movements, thus providing insights into the fetus's health and activity patterns. Feedback from individuals with and without childbirth experience has indicated the system's potential to promote emotional connections and strengthen family bonds. This innovative approach not only contributes to the scientific understanding of fetal movements but also provides a new aspect of prenatal care that emphasizes the emotional and psychological well-being of the whole family.

Keywords: Fetal Movement Sharing System · Pressure Sensor Array · Prenatal Care · Objective Measurement of Fetal Movement · Emotional and Psychological Well-being

1 Introduction

Pregnancy and childbirth are essential for the continuation of human life, which starts within the maternal womb. The fertilization of an ovum by sperm creates the fetus, which grows over time. After a certain period, fetal movements occur and can be perceived, eventually leading to childbirth.

Timor-Tritsch [1] states that "Quickening is the first maternal perception of fetal activity and is often a useful index of gestational age. It is through this fetal movement that a mother first becomes acquainted with her fetus, and with time the activity becomes reassuring to both mother and physician."

The timing of fetal movement perception varies. Typically, it starts at ~20 weeks into pregnancy; however, in some cases, it starts as early as 16 weeks into pregnancy, whereas it may occur as late as 22 weeks into pregnancy. Furthermore, women who

C. Stephanidis et al. (Eds.): HCII 2024, CCIS 2119, pp. 299–309, 2024.
https://doi.org/10.1007/978-3-031-61966-3_33

already have experienced pregnancy tend to feel fetal movements earlier than those who become pregnant for the first time [2, 3]. For pregnant women, fetal movement is an important indicator of the fetus's health [4].

Several fetal movement observation methods have been proposed [5–8]. Among them, the "count-to-ten" method can be easily implemented. This method involves recording the time required to perceive 10 fetal movements each day and checking the number of movements per gestational week. Although there are individual differences in the pattern and frequency of fetal movements, a reduced fetal movement activity or its absence can be a precursor to fetal death [9].

However, it is unclear whether the fetal movement count method is effective in reducing fetal mortality. Some studies have reported that fetal movement counting combined with support from medical institutions, has reduced fetal mortality [10]. According to Mangesi [11], there is no solid evidence of the effectiveness of the fetal movement count method. However, it has been reported that this method allows pregnant women to self-assess the health of their fetus outside of regular checkups. Therefore, the fetal movement count method is considered useful.

Nevertheless, checking the number of fetal movements daily can be a complicated and time-consuming process. Additionally, since many fetal movements are subjective, first-time pregnant women may need some time to perceive fetal movements. Therefore, there is an increasing need to record fetal movements objectively rather than subjectively.

Previous fetal movement count methods have only considered the presence and frequency of movements without considering their specific locations on the abdomen. We conducted a survey on the location of fetal movements perceived by pregnant women. Specifically, we collected information about specific locations of fetal movements along with their strength and pattern. The results showed that their location varies each gestational week, providing important information for the early detection and treatment of fetal abnormalities.

Furthermore, fetal movements can be considered a means of physical communication between a pregnant woman and her fetus that increases her affection. Condon [12], reported that a woman's attachment to her fetus rapidly increases after she experiences fetal movements for the first time. Additionally, viewing ultrasound images can reduce stress and anxiety levels in parents [13]. This quasi-experimental/control study reported that parents who were able to view the ultrasound screen experienced lower levels of stress and anxiety compared which those who could not view the screen.

According to Reissland Nadja [14], it was reported that when fathers view ultrasound images and experience fetal movements, their bond to the fetus is improved. The study highlighted that "seeing their baby helps them to bond," potentially enhancing prenatal attachment and encouraging positive health behaviors. This is very important because fetal movements not only promote positive maternal behavior and mood during pregnancy but also allow fathers and other family members to strengthen their affection for the fetus. However, since fetal movements occur within the womb of a pregnant woman, it is impossible for the father and other family members to directly perceive them. If they could perceive them, their affection for the pregnant woman and the fetus would be strengthened.

In this study, we propose a system that displays and shares fetal movements using a fetal movement scanner. This scanner can objectively measure the location and strength of fetal movements by employing a pressure sensor array mounted on the abdomen of a pregnant woman. Then, a fetal movement display can artificially reproduce fetal movements.

2 Related Studies

Methods for assessing a fetus's health include ultrasound diagnostics, where an ultrasound probe is applied to the abdomen of a pregnant woman to monitor the fetus's health [9, 15]. Recently developed 3D and 4D ultrasound diagnostics provide 3D and moving images for fetus monitoring [16, 17]. However, these methods require expensive medical devices that can only be used in medical institutions.

The fetal movement acceleration measurement recorder has been proposed for objectively and easily monitoring fetal movements at home over a long period [18, 19]. This device monitors fetal movements in a pregnant woman, even during her sleep. It records the vibrations caused by fetal movements and captures them via an electrostatic capacitance acceleration sensor. Bloom life [20] developed a system with a wearable device, which measures the heartbeat of the mother and fetus as well as uterine contractions at home during pregnancy and shares these data with the attending physician via a smartphone app. However, currently, this system only records the presence and frequency of fetal movements and not their specific locations.

Aiming at recording and sharing fetal movements, the diaper manufacturer Huggies released a video of the Hug Belt in 2013 [21]. However, no technical documentation on the measurement and reproduction details of fetal movements are available, indicating that Hug Belt is possibly a concept video. Fibo [22] is a bracelet device that provides fetal movement data to the father. It detects the presence of fetal movements using an inertial measurement unit and eight acoustic sensors that to detect vibrations caused by fetal movements; these sensors are mounted on the abdomen of a pregnant woman. The bracelet, which is mounted on the father's wrist, contains beads of different sizes; these are activated when the fetus kicks or moves, allowing the father to perceive these movements as pressure or beats on his wrist. Although the bracelet is a convenient wearable device for sharing fetal movement data, it is desirable that these movements are perceived by the mother's abdomen rather than the father's wrist.

3 Proposed Fetal Movement Sharing System

Fetal movements can only be perceived by pregnant women. Other family members cannot directly perceive them. Therefore, we considered the possibility for the father and other family members to perceive fetal movements; this would strengthen the affection for the unborn child. For this purpose, we propose a fetal movement sharing system, which consists of a fetal movement scanner and a fetal movement display. The scanner records the location and strength of fetal movements objectively; this is achieved by mounting a pressure sensor array on the abdomen of a pregnant woman. The fetal movement display artificially reproduces the recorded movements. The proposed system is shown in Fig. 1.

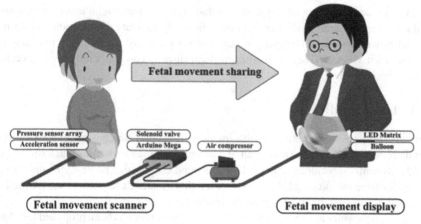

Fig. 1. Diagram of the proposed Fetal Movement Sharing System Configuration

3.1 Fetal Movement Scanner

The fetal movement scanner detects the presence and location of fetal movements. By mounting a pressure sensor array on a belt, which is placed on the abdomen of a pregnant woman, it is possible to detect fetal movements appearing on the woman's abdomen skin. For this purpose, we employed the FSR406 sensor (Interlink Electronics); its dimensions are 43.7 mm × 43.7 mm. The sensor features a pressure-sensitive area of 40 mm × 40 mm. Its force sensitivity range is 0.2 N–20 N. Eleven FSR406 sensors were mounted on the belt in all directions at equal distances among them (Fig. 2).

Fig. 2. Layout of the Fetal Movement Scanner Pressure Sensor

An Arduino MEGA 2560 microcontroller was used in the measurements. By employing a 25-Hz sampling rate, the microcontroller converts the analog signals obtained from the pressure sensor into digital signals in the 0–1023 value range via a 10-bit analog-to-digital converter and records them on a secure digital card. During measurements, the pregnant woman was in a resting state; however, we also considered the impact of her unintended movements on the pressure sensors by employing a 3-axis accelerometer. If the movements detected by the accelerometer exceeded a predefined threshold, they were excluded from the pressure sensor readings. The fetal movement scanner was built using inexpensive devices with a total cost of ~$150.

3.2 Experimental Procedure Using the Proposed Fetal Movement Scanner

We conducted experiments on four pregnant women (33-week, 34-week, 36-week, and 39-week pregnant, respectively) to investigate the possibility of measuring fetal movements using the developed fetal movement scanner. The participants were informed both verbally and in writing about the purpose of the study, the experimental method, their free will to participate and withdraw at any time during the experiments, and their privacy protection. During the experiments, a midwife was always present. In case the participants experienced any discomfort or other problems, the experiment would be stopped. This study was approved by the ethics review board for human research at Kanagawa Institute of Technology.

During the experiments, the participants were instructed to sit on a chair to eliminate any noise except that produced by fetal movements. No specific instructions were given about their sitting posture. The participants were also informed that pressure sensors would be mounted on their abdomen and instructed not to touch their abdomen. During the experiments, they were instructed to refrain from talking, moving, and other activities, except in an emergency. The fetal movement scanner was mounted on their abdomen, and the participants held a push-button switch on their hands. When they perceived fetal movements, they were instructed to press the switch. By analyzing the information obtained from the switch and the sensors, we investigated the possibility of measuring fetal movements using the proposed fetal movement scanner.

Normally, a fetus repeats REM and non-REM sleep cycles. At 7 months of pregnancy, there are 40–50 min periods of reduced fetal movement during non-REM sleep and 20–30 min periods of intense movement during REM sleep. At 9 months of pregnancy, the corresponding periods are ~20 min during both non-REM and REM sleep. In the fetal movement count method, the time required to measure 10 fetal movements for early-pregnancy women is ~15–20 min; the average time of all pregnancy stages is ~30 min [3, 4]. Based on the above, the time was set to 40 min in the experiments (Fig. 3).

3.3 Fetal Movement Scanner Results and Discussion

We obtained measurement data (with noise removed) by applying the proposed fetal movement scanner on a 34-week pregnant woman. The data obtained from 11 pressure sensors are shown in Fig. 4, and their average values are shown in Fig. 5. In Figs. 4 and 5, Switch ON corresponds to the time a participant perceives fetal movements and presses the push-button switch.

The data obtained from the pressure sensors exhibit a cyclic pattern with a cycle period of ~3 s. According to the survey by Miyamoto et al. [21], the number of breaths per min of the pregnant women was 19.9; consequently, the cycle duration per breath was ~3 s. This indicates that the cyclic pattern of the sensor values was affected by breathing (Fig. 5).

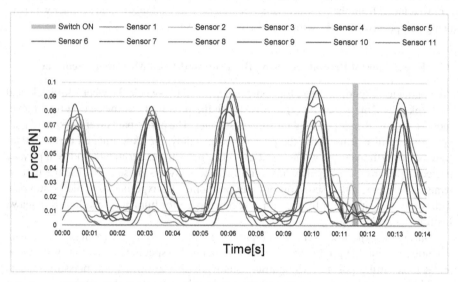

Fig. 3. Fetal Movement Scanner Results Obtained from Each Sensor

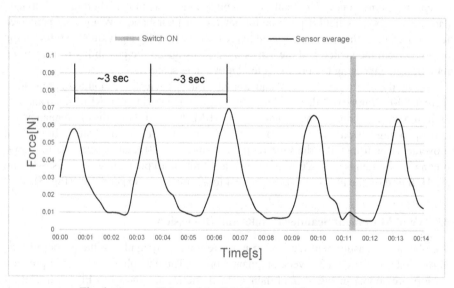

Fig. 4. Average Values of the Fetal Movement Scanner Results

For sensors 5, 6, 7, and 8, a pressure change different from the breathing cycle was identified before and after the participant had perceived fetal movements and pressed the push-button switch (Fig. 6). We observe that the measured data vary differently from the

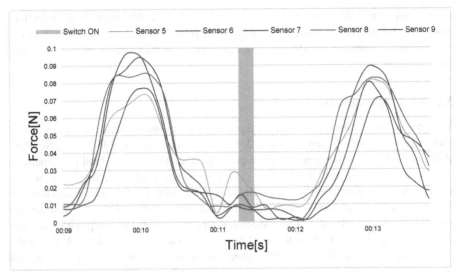

Fig. 5. Measurement Data Obtained from Sensors 5, 6, 7, 8, and 9 Near the Time the Switch Was Pressed

breathing cycle data, indicating that the participants recorded the fetal movements that appeared on their abdomen skin; however, the impact of participants' movements on the measured data cannot be ignored. However, since we observe no significant change in the measured data, it is highly possible that the fetal movement scanner measured actual fetal movements. A visualization fetal movement map of a 3D abdomen model is shown in Fig. 7.

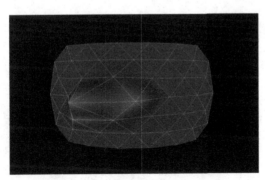

Fig. 6. Fetal Movement Mapping of Data Obtained from Sensors 5, 6, 7, 8, and 9 Near the Time the Switch Was Pressed

Not all experimental data were analyzed; however, the use of the proposed fetal movement scanner indicates the possibility of objectively measuring fetal movements on the abdomen skin. We only measured fetal movements that appeared on the abdomen skin (it is possible that internal movements that did not appear on the abdomen skin were not measured); therefore, further data analysis is required. Additionally, the data obtained from the fetal movement scanner included noise related to participants' breathing and movements; consequently, advanced data processing is required to extract only fetal movement data.

3.4 Fetal Movement Display

The fetal movement display artificially reproduces the measured fetal movements on the abdomen by expanding them. A full-color LED matrix (2 × Flexible 8 × 32 NeoPixel RGB LED Matrix) was mounted on the participant's belt to enable fetal movements to be visually expanded and observed (Fig. 8). Low-pressure areas are displayed in blue, whereas high-pressure areas are displayed in red. Additionally, fetal movement data can be mapped on a 3D abdomen model and displayed on a monitor (Fig. 9). These devices do not only display already measured fetal movement data but also reproduce the fetal movement data obtained from the fetal movement scanner in real time. Additionally, they can reproduce a day's fetal movement data in one minute within a specific time frame.

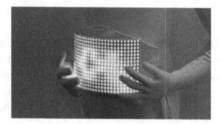

Fig. 7. Fetal Movement Display (LED Matrix Diagram)

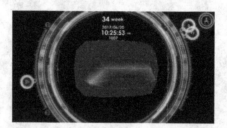

Fig. 8. Fetal Movement Display Mapping on the Abdomen 3D Model

3.5 Fetal Movement Sharing System Results and Discussion

Characteristic fetal movement data obtained from subject A (a 34-week pregnant woman) using the fetal movement scanner were processed by the fetal movement display to reproduce one minute of significant fetal movements. The reproduced data were viewed by visitors at a school festival held at Kanagawa Institute of Technology.

Women with childbirth experience provided positive comments such as "cute," "nostalgic," and "I want to experience pregnancy again." On the other hand, many women who had perceived fetal movements during their pregnancy provided comments such as "It felt more intense when I was pregnant." We attributed this inconsistency to the large differences in fetal movements experienced by different people.

Conversely, those who had not experienced childbirth expressed surprise regarding the intensity of movements and provided comments such as "Does it move this much?" "Cute," and "(Since it's displayed via LEDs) it's fun to watch because you can see the fetal movements." The novelty of the artificially reproduced fetal movements probably surprised those who had never experienced fetal movements. Additionally, children probably asked their mothers "Did I move like this too?"

Furthermore, we conducted an experiment to reproduce fetal movements in real time using the proposed fetal movement sharing system. Unfortunately, noise from participants' breathing and movements was also reproduced in the fetal movement display. A married couple of Japanese comedians (the woman was 35-week pregnant) participated in the experiment and published their experience on their YouTube channel (in Japanese) [23]. No fetal movements were observed for the first 5 min of the experiment. When the fetus was exposed to music, active fetal movements were observed [24]. The father reported a significant increase in the frequency of fetal movements especially during the chorus performance and commented very positively. He stated that this experience had an impact on him and could not be perceived by just explaining. Additionally, it generated compassion and strengthened the communication between partners. Before experiencing fetal movements, the father had a sense of exclusion such as being "left out." The experience resolved this issue, making him feel part of the family, and he expressed the desire to share it with other people. Furthermore, it increased his affection for his wife. This experiment demonstrates the potential of the fetal movement sharing system to increase fathers' involvement in pregnancy experiences and strengthen the bond between partners.

4 Conclusion

In this study, we developed a system for objectively measuring and sharing fetal movements. The system consists of a fetal movement scanner, which employs multiple pressure sensors mounted on the abdomen of a pregnant woman, and a fetal movement display, which artificially reproduces the recorded fetal movements. The proposed system not only allows pregnant women but also fathers and families to strengthen their bond with the fetus. It should be mentioned that the fetal movement scanner can be constructed at a relatively low cost (~20,000 yen), making it affordable for average-income households and research institutions. Consequently, the proposed system is expected to be employed in a wide range of applications. Additionally, it could be used in fetal health monitoring in regions or environments with limited medical resources. Furthermore, the reproduction of fetal movements via the fetal movement display strengthens the communication between partners during pregnancy and their affection for the unborn child.

The results showed that conducting objective measurements using the proposed system is possible, and fetal movement reproduction via a fetal movement display strengthens family bonds. Consequently, the proposed system exhibits significant potential for pregnant women and their families to share fetal movements as well as for monitoring the health of the fetus.

In a future study, we will attempt to resolve the noise problem in the data measured by the fetal movement scanner and improve the reproduction quality of the fetal movement display, thus developing a more practical system. Overall, this study provided new insights into fetal movement sharing, enabling pregnant women, fathers, and their families to strengthen their bond with the fetus. In the future, we hope that the proposed, relatively inexpensive system will be widely used to enhance the pregnancy experience and strengthen family bonds.

References

1. Timor-Tritsch, I.L., Zador, I., Hertz, R.H., Rosen, M.G.: Classification of human fetal movement. Am. J. Obstet. Gynecol. **126**, 70–77 (1976). https://doi.org/10.1016/0002-9378(76)90467-1
2. Sadovsky, E., Yaffe, H.: Daily fetal movement recording and fetal prognosis. Obstet. Gynecol. **41**, 845–850 (1973)
3. Rayburn, W.F., McKean, H.E.: Maternal perception of fetal movement and perinatal outcome. Obstet. Gynecol. **56**, 161–164 (1980)
4. Barros, J.G., Rosado, R., Ayres-de-Campos, D.: Glob. libr. women's med. ISSN: 1756 2228. https://doi.org/10.3843/GLOWM.411783
5. Leader, L.R., Baillie, P., Van Schalkwyk, D.J.: Fetal movements and fetal outcome: a prospective study. Obstet. Gynecol. **57**, 431–436 (1981)
6. Harper, R.G., Greenberg, M., Farahani, G., Glassman, I., Kierney, C.M.: Fetal movement, biochemical and biophysical parameters, and the outcome of pregnancy. Am. J. Obstet. Gynecol. **141**, 39–42 (1981)
7. Pearson, J.F., Weaver, J.B.: Fetal activity and fetal wellbeing: an evaluation. BMJ **1**, 1305–1307 (1976)
8. Valentin, L., Maršál, K.: Subjective recording of fetal movements. II. Screening of a pregnant population; methodological aspects. Acta Obstetricia et Gynecologica Scandinavica **65**, 639–644 (1986)
9. Jouppila, P.: Diagnosis of fetal movements in early pregnancy. Acta Obstetricia et Gynecologica Scandinavica Supplementum **47**, 52 (1975)
10. Moore, T.R., Piacquadio, K.: A prospective evaluation of fetal movement screening to reduce the incidence of antepartum fetal death. Am. J. Obstet. Gynecol. **160**, 1075–1080 (1989)
11. Mangesi, L., Hofmeyr, G.J., Smith, V.: Fetal movement counting for assessment of fetal wellbeing. In: Cochrane Database of Systematic Reviews, p. 1 (2007). https://doi.org/10.1002/14651858.CD004909.pub2
12. Condon, J.T.: The parental-fetal relationship—a comparison of male and female expectant parents. J. Psychosom. Obstet. Gynaecol. **24**, 313–320 (1985)
13. Kovacevic, M.: The impact of fetus visualization on parents' psychological reactions. Pre-Peri-natal Psychol. J. **8**, 83–93 (1993)
14. Hata, T., Uematsu, R., Reissland, N., Austen, J.M.: The potential use of the fetal observable movement system in clinical practice. Donald Sch. J. Ultrasound Obstet. Gynecol. **9**, 426–433 (2015). https://doi.org/10.5005/jp-journals-10009-1430

15. Hata, T., Manabe, A., Aoki, S., Miyazaki, K., Yoshino, K., Yamamoto, K.: Three-dimensional intrauterine sonography in the early first-trimester of human pregnancy: preliminary study. Hum. Reprod. **13**, 740–743 (1998)
16. Hata, T., Kanenishi, K., Sasaki, M.: Four-dimensional sonographic assessment of fetal movement in the late first trimester. Int. J. Gynecol. Obstet. **109**, 190–193 (2010)
17. Yagel, S., Cohen, S.M., Shapiro, I., Valsky, D.V.: 3D and 4D ultrasound in fetal cardiac scanning: a new look at the fetal heart. Ultrasound Obstet. Gynecol. **29**, 81–95 (2007)
18. Nishihara, K., Ohki, N., Kamata, H., Ryo, E., Horiuchi, S.: Automated software analysis of fetal movement recorded during a pregnant woman's sleep at home. PLoS ONE **10**, e0130503 (2015). https://doi.org/10.1371/journal.pone.0130503
19. Ryo, E., Nishihara, K., Matsumoto, S., Kamata, H.: A new method for long-term home monitoring of fetal movement by pregnant women themselves. Med. Eng. Phys. **34**, 566–572 (2012). PMID: 21962570
20. Bloomlife: Announces FDA Clearance of Bloomlife MFM-Pro. PR Newswire, 16 January 2024. https://www.prnewswire.com/news-releases/bloomlife-announces-fda-clearance-of-bloomlife-mfm-pro-302035052.html. Accessed 17 Jan 2023
21. Mitchell, E.S.: Huggies Pregnancy Belt for Men Lets Dads Feel Their Babies Kicking. Adweek (2013). https://www.adweek.com/performance-marketing/huggies-pregnancy-belt-for-men-lets-dads-feel-their-babies-kicking/
22. Fibo by First Bond Wearables. WekfareTech (2005). https://forcetechnology.com/-/media/force-technology-media/pdf-files/5001-to-5500/5042-fibo-by-first-bond-wearables.pdf
23. Shiratori, T., Yoshitake, C.: [Fetal Movement Challenge!] Cherry is moved by feeling fetal movement for the first time! [Video]. YouTube, 9 June 2021. https://www.youtube.com/watch?v=FCG2Yh-xtNA
24. Priest, J.: Research review: fetal responses to music. Perspect. J. Early Child. Music Mov. Assoc. **5**, 20–24 (2010)

Replay, Revise, and Refresh: Smartphone-Based Refresher Training for Community Healthcare Workers in India

Arka Majhi[1]([envelope])[ID], Aparajita Mondal[2][ID], and Satish B. Agnihotri[1][ID]

[1] Indian Institute of Technology Bombay, Powai, Mumbai 400076, India
{arka.majhi,sbagnihotri}@iitb.ac.in
[2] Tampere University, Kalevantie 4, 33100 Tampere, Finland
aparajita.mondal@tuni.fi
https://arkadesignstudio.in

Abstract. In India, community healthcare workers are the primary touchpoints between the state and the beneficiaries, such as pregnant mothers and children. Their healthcare knowledge directly impacts the quality of care they provide through home visits and community activities. Classroom in-person or traditional ways of training are found ineffective in imparting knowledge and render poor knowledge retention, which needs reinforcements through short, frequent revisions. Smartphone games on healthcare topics could be a promising solution as a refresher, as they can be scaled and tailored as per players' requirements. This study aims to check the differences in knowledge gain, pre and post-intervention, and, secondly, to check knowledge retention after six months. 270 CHWs or participants were recruited to evaluate different modes of refresher training and assigned into three equal groups of 90 each. The control group (CG) (n = 90) was trained using the standard classroom method, which is usually followed. Intervention Group-1 (IG1) (n = 90) was trained in a physical card game format, and Intervention Group-2 (IG2)(n = 90) was trained in a smartphone game format. 4 sets of questionnaires were made by shuffling 45 questions based on immunization of equal weightage. The questionnaires were filled out by CHWs by hand and collected, evaluated, and analyzed. Paired t-tests were conducted to compare pre-post knowledge increments and repeated measure ANOVA to check for differences in knowledge retention. Results suggest a significant difference in scores in all three groups. A significant difference was observed between the physical and digital gameplay modes. Pre-post knowledge increment was higher in the digital mode (p < 0.05), but knowledge retained was not significantly different (p = .4) in digital and physical card versions. Card games confirm their effectiveness in gaining knowledge when compared to classroom training. Through this research, we found that the gamified way of learning has an improved retention rate compared to the traditional training method.

C. Stephanidis et al. (Eds.): HCII 2024, CCIS 2119, pp. 310–320, 2024.
https://doi.org/10.1007/978-3-031-61966-3_34

Keywords: Community Healthcare Workers · ASHA Workers · Anganwadi Workers · Card Game

1   Introduction

There are two main cadres of community healthcare workers (CHWs) with overlapping and sometimes complimentary job roles: Accredited Social Health Activists (ASHAs) and Anganwadi Workers (AWWs). The ASHAs bridge the gap between citizens and government by facilitating access to healtWhile services and receiving performance-based incentives [4]. While the AWWs handle mother and child nutrition, early education, and overall development. They are forced to work in challenging conditions, with incomplete information, low compensation, and unrecognized or invisible efforts [25]. Their caregiving nature is motivated not only by their salary or incentive but also by the desire to earn respect, familiarity, and trust from the community [25]. Evaluation-based research highlights inadequate training and supervision as the primary challenges to the performance of CHWs [3,6].

According to the National Family Health Survey-5 (NFHS-5; 2019-20) [11], immunization coverage for children aged 12–23 is 62.2%, a marginal improvement from the last round, NFHS-4 60% [10], despite efforts from the government to provide free vaccinations through Universal Immunization Program (UIP) and mission Indradhanush. The Mother and Child Protection Card (MCPC) is given to pregnant women when they first register for pregnancy. It contains the child's immunization schedule and the necessary information for mothers. The CHWs' lack of sound knowledge of immunization, service schedules, and related information on MCPC reduces the effectiveness of their services [1,2]. Partial understanding of immunization schedules by CHWs often leads to partial child immunization in the community [14]. Hence, it becomes trivial for CHWs to understand the immunization schedule. Therefore, we chose the timeline or content of the child immunization schedule, which is derived from the Indian Academics of Paediatrician (IAP) guidelines [13] (referred in Table 1), Ante-Natal Care (ANC) or during pregnancy and Post-Natal Care (PNC) or after the birth of a baby, as the learning material.

Classroom in-person or traditional ways of training are found ineffective in imparting knowledge and render poor knowledge retention, which needs reinforcements through short, frequent revisions. The adoption of smartphones in India [23] is fast increasing. Smartphones are being given to the CHWs to maintain records of mothers and children. Smartphone-based games on healthcare topics could be a promising solution as a refresher training for the CHWs. Digital or smartphone-based games engage players through gameful interactions, are customizable according to the player's learning requirements, are playable by low-literate and less tech-savvy players, and reach a large audience by listing in app stores.

The study tries to answer the following research questions:

- **RQ1:** Are games an effective alternative to in-person, traditional classroom refresher training?
- **RQ2:** Do physical and digital gameplay modes differ significantly in knowledge gains?
- **RQ3:** Do physical and digital gameplay modes differ significantly in long-term (after three weeks) knowledge retention?

Table 1. Child Immunization schedule

Vaccine name	Birth	$1\frac{1}{2}$ months	$2\frac{1}{2}$ months	$3\frac{1}{2}$ months	9 months	$1\frac{1}{2}-2$ years
BCG	✓					
Hepatitis-B	✓					
OPV	✓	✓	✓	✓		✓
IPV		✓		✓		
Pentavalent		✓	✓	✓		
PCV		✓		✓	✓	
Rota		✓	✓	✓		
MR					✓	✓
JE					✓	✓
DPT						✓

1.1   Related Works

Previous researchers conducted different methods of training CHWs. A group of researchers suggested using community radio to broadcast training materials to the masses [15–17,26,28–30]. Researchers created and collected short informative videos on community healthcare and distributed them to CHWs through memory cards for mobile phones for offline viewing [12,21]. After watching the short videos, researchers conducted quizzes through phone calls [22] and quiz apps on their smartphones [19] to refresh their knowledge, followed by an incentive of talk time in the form of cell phone balance. Instructional illustrations were also tried to impart procedural knowledge to the CHWs [24]. Playful activities based on Augmented Reality were tested for collaborative play and refresher training on immunization [18].

2   Methodology

2.1   Physical and Digital Card Game

A deck of 60 cards is designed to represent all the vaccines and services related to mother and child care. The cards are divided into four silos or foundations:

Children below one year, Children above one year, Antenatal care and Postnatal care. The game aims to sequence the cards as per their schedule. Each player takes turns putting their card from hand to the foundations, towards completing the sequence forward or backward, starting from a point in each of the four foundations. The player emptying their hand first wins the game. A digital version of the game with the same rules was designed to compare the effectiveness of both modalities through user testing. The details of the game are not in the scope of this paper.

Fig. 1. Physical card Decks

2.2 Participants

The sample size was calculated using G-Power [5]. T-test with independent means was chosen as the statistical test (d = 0.5, $1 - \beta = 0.95$, and $\alpha = 0.05$). The required sample or number of participants for each group was calculated to be 88. Considering attrition, 95 were recruited for each group. However, post-attrition, 90 participants from each group were retained till the end of the study, totaling 270 participants across three groups.

2.3 Ethical Consideration

The Institute Review Board, Indian Institute of Technology Bombay, India [9], approved the ethical conduct of the study (Approval No: IITB-IRB/2022/051),

Table 2. A. Participants' Demography and B. & C. Study Results

A. Participants' Demography

	Intervention Group-1 Digital Card Game (n = 90)		Intervention Group-2 Physical Card Game (n = 90)		Intervention Group-3 Classroom In-Person training (n = 90)	
Parameters	ASHAs(%) (n = 45)	AWWs(%) (n = 45)	ASHAs(%) (n = 45)	AWWs(%) (n = 45)	ASHAs(%) (n = 45)	AWWs(%) (n = 45)
Age group (years)						
Less than 30	1 (2.22%)	0 (0%)	1 (2.22%)	1 (2.22%)	2 (4.44%)	2 (4.44%)
30–40	22 (48.89%)	19 (42.22%)	22 (48.89%)	20 (44.44%)	23 (51.11%)	19 (42.22%)
40–50	21 (46.67%)	25 (55.56%)	20 (44.44%)	24 (53.33%)	20 (44.44%)	24 (53.33%)
No information	1 (2.22%)	1 (2.22%)	2 (4.44%)	0 (0%)	0 (0%)	0 (0%)
Education (schooling grade)						
Below 8th	3 (6.67%)	2 (4.44%)	1 (2.27%)	2 (4.44%)	1 (2.22%)	2 (4.44%)
8th–10th	9 (20%)	11 (24.44%)	9 (20.45%)	14 (31.11%)	10 (22.22%)	12 (26.67%)
10th–12th	29 (64.44%)	28 (62.22%)	29 (65.91%)	23 (51.11%)	29 (64.44%)	27 (60%)
Graduate and above	4 (8.89%)	4 (8.89%)	4 (9.09%)	5 (11.11%)	5 (11.11%)	4 (8.89%)
No information	0 (0%)	0 (0%)	1 (2.27%)	1 (2.22%)	0 (0%)	0 (0%)
Experience as CHWs (years)						
0–5	2 (4.44%)	2 (4.44%)	4 (8.89%)	3 (6.67%)	4 (8.89%)	2 (4.35%)
5–10	18 (40%)	17 (37.78%)	16 (35.56%)	16 (35.56%)	19 (42.22%)	17 (36.96%)
10–15	18 (40%)	18 (40%)	18 (40%)	19 (42.22%)	17 (37.78%)	18 (39.13%)
Above 15	7 (15.56%)	8 (17.78%)	7 (15.56%)	6 (13.33%)	4 (8.89%)	8 (17.39%)
No information	0 (0%)	0 (0%)	0 (0%)	1 (2.22%)	1 (2.22%)	1 (2.17%)
Experimental Study Results	**Intervention Group-1 Test Scores**		**Intervention Group-2 Test Scores**		**Intervention Group-3 Test Scores**	
Test phase	Mean (SD)	Median (min–max)	Mean (SD)	Median (min–max)	Mean (SD)	Median (min–max)
Pre-test scores	24.85 (3.34)	24.16 (18–33)	24.28 (2.88)	24.13 (19–30)	25.02 (3.19)	24.69 (19–32)
Post-test scores	35.62 (3.57)	35.56 (28–42)	31.86 (4.1)	31.48 (24–42)	30.01 (4.32)	29.71 (19–39)
Long Post-test scores (After three weeks)	31.75 (4.69)	32.23 (22–41)	30.62 (4.1)	30.82 (21–40)	26.46 (3.54)	26.75 (19–34)

B. Between-group comparisons of total scores according to the three points of assessment

	Pre-test	Post-test	Long-term Post-test
IG-1 × IG-2 × IG-3	$F_{2,45} = 0.84, p = .44$	$F_{2,45} = 22.96, p < .00001$	$F_{2,45} = 20.62, p < .00001$

C. Within-group comparisons of total scores according to the three points of assessment

Paired t-test results Points of Assessment	Intervention Group-1 (p-value)	Intervention Group-2 (p-value)	Intervention Group-3 (p-value)
Pre-test × Post-test	0	0	1×10^{-7}
Pre-test × Long-term Post-test	2×10^{-10}	0	0.04
Post-test × Long-term Post-test	6×10^{-5}	0.12 (Not Significant at $p < .05$)	6×10^{-5}

D. Between-group comparisons of total scores according to the three points of assessment

Paired t-test results (All groups combined) Point of Assessment	Intervention Group-1 (p-value)
Pre-test × Post-test	0
Pre-test × Long-term Post-test	2×10^{-20}
Post-test × Long-term Post-test	7×10^{-7}

which adheres to the guidelines of the Declaration of Helsinki [27]. All participants were verbally informed about the objective and procedure of the study. Written consent with a signature was obtained every time a survey was conducted with the participants and included in the questionnaire. The results of the surveys and study findings were provided to the CHW supervisors so that they could understand the overall knowledge gained and retention of the CHWs. However, the names and other identifiers of the participants were masked.

2.4 Evaluation

The knowledge of CHWs is assessed through questionnaire surveys in three points. Initially, a baseline survey is conducted to check the prior knowledge. Then, as per the allotted groups, they either get a deck of cards or install the app on their phones. Then, the CHWs either play the card game on their smartphones (IG1) or the physical card game (IG2) or attend regular in-person classroom training (IG3). Then, another assessment is conducted to check the immediate knowledge gained after the refresher training. Then, CHWs are encouraged to play and attend classes according to their allotted groups for the next three weeks. Previous researchers suggest two or more weeks for retention tests [8,20]. After that, a long-term post-test survey is conducted to check the knowledge retention of the CHWs.

The questionnaire starts with consent to participate in the evaluation study by filling in demographic details and putting in a signature. It contains 45 multiple-choice, single-correct questions of equal weightage and is shuffled for each assessment point. CHWs are usually given 30 min to fill out the questionnaire. Researchers and volunteers check the answers against a solved questionnaire and calculate the score for each participant. They are then analyzed to check for trends in knowledge gain and retention.

Fig. 2. Left: Photo of CHW holding her smartphone during gameplay session; Right: CHWs filling questionnaire survey form

All group scores were checked for normality before conducting parametric tests. Paired t-tests were conducted within groups and between groups. Repeated Measure ANOVA and multiple One-Way ANOVA were performed to check if there was an overall difference in scores within groups and between groups and with points of assessment.

3   Findings

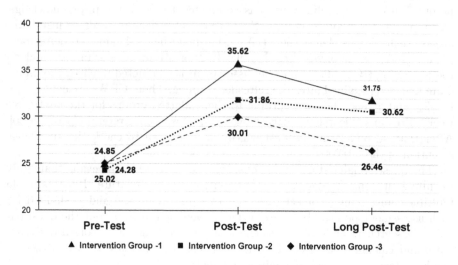

Fig. 3. Line chart showing trends of change of mean value in the pre-test, post-test, and long post-test

Between Group (Table 2 B):

Pre-test scores: No significant differences were found between groups ($F = 0.84, p = .44$) at $p < .05$. We found that the baseline or prior knowledge was not significantly different across the three groups.

Post-test scores: Significant differences were found between groups ($F = 22.96, p < .00001$) at $p < .05$. Tukey's HSD test shows pairwise significant difference ($Q_{.05} = 3.35$) between IG1 and IG2 ($Q = 6.36$ ($p = .00004$)) & IG3 ($Q = 9.39$ ($p < .000001$)) and no significance between IG2 and IG3 ($Q = 3.03$ ($p = .085$)). IG1, or smartphone app intervention group, scored exceptionally better than IG2, or physical card game, and IG3, or in-person training.

Long-term Post-test scores: Significant difference between groups ($F = 20.62, p < .00001$) at $p < .05$. Tukey's HSD test shows pairwise significant difference ($Q_{.05} = 3.35$) between IG3 and IG1 ($Q = 8.62$ ($p < .000001$)) & IG2 ($Q = 6.78$ ($p = .00001$)) and no significance between IG1 and IG2 ($Q = 1.84$ ($p = .4$)).

Within Group (Table 2 C): A significant difference was observed between all three groups across all assessment points except IG2 while comparing post-test and long-term post-test ($p = .12$, $p > .05$)

Between Group (Table 2 D): Pre-test scores were significantly lower compared to post-tests and long-term post-tests. A significant difference was observed between all three groups across all assessment points. A decline in knowledge retention across the groups confirms the pattern of depleting knowledge over time. Comparing digital and physical card game outcomes, it's interesting to note that the immediate knowledge gained post-intervention in smartphone mode or digital one (IG1) is significantly higher compared to physical card play mode (IG2). However, the long-term post-test scores showed lower knowledge retention in all three groups. IG2 had the highest retention rate, and the loss of knowledge was minimal compared to the baseline or pretest scores. After three weeks, the retained knowledge or long-term post-test scores were similar or not significantly different between digital and physical play modes or IG1 and IG2. The knowledge graph of the three groups (Fig. 3) also reflects the findings.

4 Discussion

In this study, we compared two modes of refresher training for CHWs: traditional in-person refresher training and training through games (RQ1). Also, we compared if there is a difference in knowledge acquisition between physical and digital card play (RQ2). Also, we compared if there is a difference in knowledge retention between physical and digital card play (RQ3). The study evaluates the efficacy of three refresher training methods. It provides objective evidence to curriculum designers and decision-makers on implementing the method and the expected short- and long-term deployment outcome.

After the study, we interviewed some CHWs for feedback. Some CHWs expressed their preference for printed study materials over the phone app. They said that the printed materials improve their knowledge and act as a vetted brochure to show to mothers during counseling sessions or home visits. Some said the printed brochure lets them relax and study independently, at their own pace. Some reported distractions when playing smartphone games for refresher training compared to reading class notes or printed brochures.

5 Limitations

This is a field-based study and was conducted in government institutions like government hospitals and training centres. Some CHWs might feel intimidated by their supervisor's presence while giving feedback on the play experience. Often, one smartphone was shared by multiple CHWs. Some felt uncomfortable using someone else's devices due to the possessiveness and affordances that users grow using their own devices. Conducting a true experiment is impossible in this case because it does not fulfill the condition of a true experiment [7]. So, we conducted a quasi-experimental study. The drawback of such a study lies in lower internal and higher external validity, as the effectiveness is judged through the outcome [7].

6   Novelty

As far as we know, this research attempted to explore the effects of combining two CHW cadres, ASHAs and AWWs, as a team to play physical and digital card games for their refresher training for the first time.

7   Conclusion

The study results show that the digital play mode enhanced knowledge better than the physical mode. However, the digital mode has shown a marginal improvement in long-term knowledge retention compared to the physical mode. The latter finding is more important, as knowing the long-term effects of an intervention is required for curriculum development, implementation, policy recommendations, and future decision-making. It is important to note that the gamified training method is not intended to replace the initial in-person training of the CHWs but to act as a voluntary refresher training for the CHWs to help them revise the child immunization schedule and other services.

7.1   Future Works

Further studies need to be conducted, considering other variables that might affect the intrinsic and extrinsic motivation of playing the game. Longitudinal studies need to be undertaken to check improved learning outcomes, with more arms for checking variations in learning effectiveness and a larger sample size for a more balanced and better representation of CHWs in India.

Acknowledgments. This study was jointly funded by SERB, FICCI, and UNICEF India. We thank all the Community Healthcare Workers (Accredited Social Health Activists and Anganwadi Workers) and their supervisors who actively participated in this study. We also thank the anonymous reviewers for providing feedback.

Disclosure of Interests. The authors have no conflicts of interest.

References

1. Bag, S., Datta, M.: Evaluation of mother and child protection card entries in a rural area of West Bengal. Int. J. Commun. Med. Public Health **4**(7), 2604 (2017). https://doi.org/10.18203/2394-6040.ijcmph20172867
2. Bashingwa, J.J.H., et al.: Examining the reach and exposure of a mobile phone-based training programme for frontline health workers (ASHAs) in 13 states across India, August 2021. https://doi.org/10.1136/bmjgh-2021-005299
3. Burger, O., et al.: Facilitating behavioral change: a comparative assessment of ASHA efficacy in rural Bihar. PLOS Global Public Health **2**(8), e0000756 (2022). https://doi.org/10.1371/journal.pgph.0000756

4. Farah, N.F., Mohan, R., Kiruba, S.V., Aditi, K., Ananthkumar, S.R., Prem, K.M.: Assessment of 'Accredited Social Health Activists'-A National Community Health Volunteer Scheme in Karnataka State, India (2015). https://www.ncbi.nlm.nih. gov/pmc/articles/PMC4438657/

5. Faul, F., Erdfelder, E., Lang, A.G., Buchner, A.: G*Power 3: a flexible statistical power analysis program for the social, behavioral, and biomedical sciences. In: Behavior Research Methods, vol. 39 (2007). https://doi.org/10.3758/BF03193146

6. Gopalan, S.S., Varatharajan, D.: Addressing maternal healthcare through demand side financial incentives: experience of Janani Suraksha Yojana program in India. Technical report (2012). http://www.biomedcentral.com/1472-6963/12/319

7. Harris, A.D., et al.: The use and interpretation of quasi-experimental studies in medical informatics. J. Am. Med. Inform. Assoc. 13(1), 16–23 (2006). https://doi. org/10.1197/jamia.M1749

8. Haynie, W.J.: Effects of multiple-choice and short-answer tests on delayed retention learning. Technical Report 1 (1994)

9. IIT Bombay: Institutional Review Board, IIT Bombay, India, May 2020. https:// rnd.iitb.ac.in/institute_review_board

10. Indian Institute Population Sciences and Ministry of Health and Family Welfare: National Family Health Survey-4 India Fact Sheet. Indian Institute Population Sciences and Ministry of Health and Family Welfare (2016). http://rchiips.org/ NFHS/NFHS-4Reports/India.pdf

11. Indian Institute Population Sciences and Ministry of Health and Family Welfare: National Family Health Survey-5 India Fact Sheet. Indian Institute Population Sciences and Ministry of Health and Family Welfare (2021). http://rchiips.org/ nfhs/factsheet_NFHS-5.shtml

12. Javaid, M., Fatima, B., Batool, A.: Bridging the knowledge gaps in lady health visitors through video based learning tool. In: ACM International Conference Proceeding Series, vol. Part F1320 (2017). https://doi.org/10.1145/3136560.3136603

13. Kasi, S.G., et.al.: Indian Academy of Pediatrics (IAP) Advisory Committee on Vaccines and Immunization Practices (ACVIP): Recommended Immunization Schedule (2020–2021) and update on immunization for children aged 0 through 18 years. Indian Pediatrics 58(1), 44–53 (2021). https://doi.org/10.1007/s13312-021-2096-7

14. Kizhatil, A., Reshma, Hariharan, H.C., John, A., Thomas, A.M., Padmanabhan, G.: Assessment of immunization coverage and associated factors among children in Paravur Taluk of Ernakulam district, Kerala. Int. J. Commun. Med. Public Health 6(8), 3594 (2019). https://doi.org/10.18203/2394-6040.ijcmph20193494

15. Kumar, N., Anderson, R.: Mobile phones for maternal health in rural India. In: Conference on Human Factors in Computing Systems - Proceedings, April 2015, pp. 427–436 (2015). https://doi.org/10.1145/2702123.2702258

16. Kumar, N., et al.: Projecting health: community-led video education for maternal health. In: ACM International Conference Proceeding Series, vol. 15 (2015). https://doi.org/10.1145/2737856.2738023

17. Kumar, N., Rangaswamy, N.: The mobile media actor-network in urban India. In: Conference on Human Factors in Computing Systems - Proceedings, pp. 1989–1998 (2013). https://doi.org/10.1145/2470654.2466263

18. Majhi, A., Agnihotri, S., Mondal, A.: Physical and augmented reality based playful activities for refresher training of ASHA workers in India. In: Conference on Human Factors in Computing Systems - Proceedings (2022). https://doi.org/10. 1145/3516492.3558788

19. Majhi, A., Joshi, A., Agnihotri, S.B., Mondal, A.: Refresher training through Quiz App for capacity building of Community Healthcare Workers or Anganwadi Workers in India. In: 5th Asian CHI Symposium 2021 (2021). https://doi.org/10.1145/3429360.3468186
20. Nungester, R.J., Duchastel, P.C.: Testing versus review: effects on retention. J. Educ. Psychol. **74**(1), 18–22 (1982). https://doi.org/10.1037//0022-0663.74.1.18
21. Ramachandran, D., Canny, J., Das, P.D., Cutrell, E.: Mobile-izing health workers in rural India. In: Conference on Human Factors in Computing Systems - Proceedings, vol. 3, pp. 1889–1898 (2010). https://doi.org/10.1145/1753326.1753610
22. Shah, M.P., Kamble, P.A., Agnihotri, S.B.: Tackling child malnutrition: an innovative approach for training health workers using ICT: a pilot study. In: IEEE Region 10 Humanitarian Technology Conference 2016, R10-HTC 2016 - Proceedings (2017). https://doi.org/10.1109/R10-HTC.2016.7906811
23. Telecom Regulatory Authority of India: TRAI Press Release No. 03/2024. Technical report (2024). https://www.trai.gov.in/sites/default/files/PR_No.03of2024_0.pdf
24. Tulaskar, R.: Study of instructional illustrations on ICTs: considering persona of low-literate users from India. In: ACM International Conference Proceeding Series, pp. 53–56 (2020). https://doi.org/10.1145/3391203.3391217
25. Verdezoto, N., et al.: The invisible work of maintenance in community health: challenges and opportunities for digital health to support frontline health workers in Karnataka, South India. Proc. ACM Hum. Comput. Interact. **5**(CSCW1), 1–31 (2021). https://doi.org/10.1145/3449165
26. Ward, V.C., et al.: Impact of Mhealth interventions for reproductive, maternal, newborn and child health and nutrition at scale: BBC Media Action and The Ananya Program in Bihar, India. J. Global Health **10**(2), 021005 (2020). https://doi.org/10.7189/jogh.10.021005
27. World Medical Association: WMA Declaration of Helsinki - Ethical Principles for Medical Research Involving Human Subjects. Technical report (2013). https://www.med.or.jp/dl-med/wma/helsinki2013e.pdf
28. Yadav, D., Bhandari, A., Singh, P.: LEAP: scaffolding collaborative learning of community health workers in India. Proc. ACM Hum. Comput. Interact. **3**(CSCW), 1–27 (2019). https://doi.org/10.1145/3359271
29. Yadav, D., et al.: Sangoshthi: empowering community health workers through peer learning in rural India. In: 26th International World Wide Web Conference, WWW 2017 (2017). https://doi.org/10.1145/3038912.3052624
30. Yadav, D., et al.: FeedPal: understanding opportunities for chatbots in breastfeeding education of women in India. Proc. ACM Hum.-Comput. Interact. **3**(CSCW), 1–30 (2019). https://doi.org/10.1145/3359272

Investigating Employee Acceptance of Automated Technologies in Healthcare: A Case Study on Automated Bed Washing Systems

Lukas Niemann Frandsen, Hans-Henrik Lundvang, Máté Hidegföldi, and Justina Karpavičė[⊠]

Aarhus University, 7400 Herning, Denmark
justina@btech.au.dk

Abstract. The transition from manual to automated processes has become a central challenge that hinders the successful adoption of technologies, resulting in heightened resistance and anxiety among employees regarding technological changes. Therefore, this research aims to investigate individuals' perceptions of automated technologies and identify variables impacting technology adoption. The research is based on a cross-sectional case study that examined the employees' acceptance of the automated bed washer at three regional hospitals within the Midtjylland region in Denmark. This study extends the TAM by incorporating facilitating conditions, self-efficacy, social influence, anxiety, and trust. A mixed-method approach was applied for data collection, including insights from observations and results from interviews, complemented with a TAM-based questionnaire. Drawing from the results, facilitating conditions, self-efficacy and trust were identified as the key determinants impacting PU and PEOU.

Keywords: Technology Acceptance Model · Automated Technologies · Employees Acceptance · Healthcare

1 Introduction

In today's work environment, the shift from manual to automated processes stands as a central challenge for successful adoption of technologies, leading to increased employee resistance and anxiety towards technological changes [1]. The implementation and use of digital and automated technologies leads to new organizational, technical, and social considerations and significantly impacts the working environment [2]. Concerns regarding technological unemployment represent a major obstacle in the widespread implementation of new technologies in conventional labor sectors [3]. Employees often experience uncertainty and fear about their job security, unwillingness to rely on self-operating solutions, and concerns about whether they will be able to adapt to new work processes [4]. Given these challenges, the efficient transition from manual to automated operations highly depends on employees' willingness to accept and adopt these changes [3].

Enhancing employees' intention to utilize automated systems in their everyday work tasks is essential for increasing productivity, reducing the likelihood of errors, ensuring consistent quality of products and services that lead to substantial cost savings [4–6].

While numerous studies have delved into technology acceptance across different sectors, such as IT/IS [7–9], process automation [5, 10, 11], human-robot collaboration [3, 6, 12] and digital technologies in healthcare [13, 14], a notable research gap exists in research concerning technology acceptance in the context of automated cleaning services within the healthcare industry. Thus, this research aims to examine the peculiarities of the process automation by identifying the influential factors impacting employees' acceptance of automated bed washers (ABW) in hospitals across the Midtjylland region in Denmark. The study utilizes the technology acceptance model (TAM) to investigate the employees' perception of the automated solution.

2　Research Model and Hypotheses

2.1　Automated Bed Washer

Automated washers for hospital beds are a relatively new technology, introduced at regional hospitals in the Midtjylland region in Denmark since 2018. The ABWs were implemented by the hospitals' service partners, responsible for laundry, washing, and servicing of hospital beds and assistive devices. The objective of the implementations was to continuously support hygienic efforts at hospitals and reduce infections and cross contaminations within the healthcare system. Technology replaced locally placed manual washing stations by centralizing the cleaning process around the new machine. The solution greatly improved process efficiency, reducing the unnecessary movement of staff and equipment. Before implementing the automated solution, the washing processes were performed by hand, involving spraying beds with a hose, and scrubbing with cloths. Consequently, the technological change also had a positive impact on the work environment and ergonomics. The system is worked through a human-machine interface screen, where the different sections of the machine can be supervised and controlled accordingly by the dedicated machine operators.

2.2　Technology Acceptance Model

Overall, technology acceptance is generally understood as "an individual's psychological state regarding his or her voluntary or intended use of a particular technology" [15]. In the field of information systems, extensive research has been focused on identifying, developing, and predicting constructs that influence individuals' adoption of technologies and innovations [7]. This has resulted in the development of diverse models and theories dedicated to understanding technology acceptance, such as Theory of Reasoned Action [16], Technology Acceptance Model [17], or Unified Theory of Acceptance and Use of Technology [18].

TAM aims to explain technology acceptance by proposing that the acceptance and use of technologies are driven by individuals' perceptions of their usefulness and ease of use. TAM suggests that a user's attitude towards technology affects their intention to use it, and this behavioral intention in turn influences the actual usage of the technology [17]. The model is designed to predict acceptance of new technologies by individuals, offering a robust tool for understanding their perceptions, as well as identifying potential improvements in technology or process development [19].

This model has been substantially utilized in a variety of domains, including such sectors as the physical process automation and healthcare, consistently explaining the variability in usage intentions, and solving difficulties in technology adoption [20, 21]. The following studies have assessed the acceptance of automation utilizing TAM methodology, within the topics as RPA [22], industry 4.0 [23], robotics [1], collaborative robots [24], and others. Furthermore, since the use of ICT across the health sector is increasing, several studies have been conducted towards the technology acceptance of a broad spectrum of IT and automated systems in this area, including telemonitoring [25], digital health technologies [26], automated medication dispensing cabinets [27], electronic hand hygiene sinks [19], mHealth [20], artificial intelligence [13].

While extensive research has been conducted within the domains of automation and healthcare, to the best of our knowledge, none of the studies explore the adoption of automated bed washers in hospitals. Since the capability to identify, forecast, and manage an individual's acceptance of technology is expected to alleviate the implementation efforts [28], there is a need to carry out an empirical study to identify the most influential factors impacting employees' adoption of an ABW.

2.3 Research Hypotheses

Despite its widespread application, the TAM model exhibits limitations in capturing other individual, motivational, and organizational aspects of technology acceptance [26]. As a result, the original model has been subject to various incremental expansions aiming to enhance its predictive power by adding new variables [29]. Some of the extensions are particularly complementary to the research regarding process automation in healthcare. [30] presented TAM3 with the appended variables of trust and perceived risk of technology. Subsequently, TAM2 proposed by [31], included social influence and cognitive instrumental processes. Another modification of TAM is UTAUT, introduced by [18], which provides a more holistic view of acceptance by adding facilitating conditions as direct determinant of behavioral intention. Consequently, this research expands the TAM by aggregating the factors proposed by other studies as potential antecedents of an ABW acceptance. Overall, 146 constructs were gathered from the selected 17 studies, which were subsequently classified into 40 variables, grouped into 13 categories. Table 1 provides a summary of the investigated studies.

Figure 1 displays the distribution of classified variables that appear more than once across the selected papers. Drawing from the findings of investigated studies, this research has incorporated Facilitating Conditions, Self-efficacy, Social Influence, Anxiety, and Trust as external variables to the original TAM for analyzing the employees' acceptance of an ABW. The descriptions of selected variables are provided below.

Trust. In general, trust is understood as a behavioral component that relates to the user's intention to act in a specific way and reflects the security one has in the other [7]. In human-technology interaction, trust goes beyond the traditional concept of social relationships and expands its definition by referring to it as a users' general confidence in

Table 1. A summary of seventeen investigated studies.

Source	Context	Variables
[32]	Technology acceptance in healthcare	PU, PEOU, INT, ATT, USE, Facilitating Conditions, Social Influence, Self-efficacy, Innovativeness, Anxiety, Trust
[26]	Adoption of digital health technologies among healthcare professionals	PU, PEOU, INT, Perceived Availability, Resistance to Change, Perceived Physical Condition, Technology Anxiety, Social Influence, Technical Skills, Personal Innovativeness
[33]	Barcode technology acceptance in Hospitals	PU, PEOU, ATT, INT, Ease of Learning, Capabilities
[19]	Acceptance of a new automated sink at the hospital	PU, PEOU, INT, Confident of Use, Satisfaction of Use
[34]	User perception of electronic hand hygiene monitoring systems	PU, PEOU, INT, ATT, Trust in Technology, Self-efficacy, Facilitating Conditions, Anxiety, Social Influence
[25]	Healthcare professionals' adoption of a new telemonitoring system	PU, PEOU, INT, ATT, Habits, Compatibility, Facilitators, Subjective Norm
[27]	Acceptance of automated medication dispensing cabinets by nurses	PU, PEOU, ATT, Perceived Usefulness to enhance Control Systems, Training, Perceived risks, Experience Level
[20]	Technology acceptance and user adoption of mHealth	PU, PEOU, ATT, INT, Technology Anxiety, Trust, Social Influence, Resistance to Change, Perceived Risk, Perceived Physical Condition
[15]	Acceptance of breast tumor registry system	PU, PEOU, INT, ATT, Anxiety, Resistance to change
[28]	Technology acceptance of ICT in health	PU, PEOU, INT, ATT, USE, Social Influence, Compatibility, Computer Anxiety, Organizational Facilitating Conditions, Computer Self-efficacy
[21]		PE, PU, ATT, INT, USE, Compatibility, Trust
[11]	The extension of TAM to assess the acceptance of automation	PU, PEOU, INT, IT infrastructure, Subjective Norm, Top management support, Financial Support, Training, Readiness, Efficacy, Reliability, Security, Anxiety, Productivity

(continued)

Table 1. (*continued*)

Source	Context	Variables
[1]	Adoption of robotics and automation among transformational companies	PU, PEOU, INT, Job Relevance, Innovativeness, Optimism, Discomfort, Insecurity, Computer Self-efficacy, Anxiety, Perception of External Control
[35]	Adoption of industrial automation technologies in manufacturing	ATT, Fear, Perceived Social Benefits, Advantages, Dehumanisation, Disadvantages, Innovative Personality, Social Influence, Technological skills, Professionalism, Job automatability
[24]	Employees perception of the automation	Cognitive Workload, User Acceptance, Perceived Stress, Trust
[23]	User acceptance and trust in collaborative robots	Resilience, Goal Orientation, Information/Training, Technology acceptance, Work Engagement
[22]	Employees acceptance of innovative systems (industry 4)	PU, PEOU, INT, Social Influence, Job relevance, Result Demonstrability, User Involvement, Trust, Computer Self-efficacy, Innovation Joy, Facilitating conditions, Hedonic Motivation

* PU – Perceived Usefulness, PEOU – Perceived Ease of Use, INT – Behavioural Intention to Use, ATT – Attitude towards technology; USE – Usage of technology

technology systems, influencing their intention to use the technology [36]. Trust is significantly influenced by the level of experience with the technology, as it evolves gradually through continuous interactions over time [20]. Authors [21] indicate that inadequately calibrated trust can result in either misuse or disuse of technology, corresponding to inappropriate levels of reliance, which could potentially affect operator's ability to identify failures in automated systems. [20] noted that individuals are more likely to trust technologies if it aligns with their expectations, especially in terms of safety and security. Since the increase in trust might lead to positive intentions to adopt, various researchers used the trust variable to assess technology acceptance. In their review, [32] focused on TAM in healthcare and identified trust as a recurring significant factor affecting technology acceptance. [20] depicted trust as a catalyst for adopting technologies in healthcare services, implying its positive impact on the perceived usefulness and perceived ease of use.

Self-efficacy. The adoption of new technologies requires individuals to maintain corresponding competences, as it entails engaging with various and ever-evolving technological systems [26]. Consequently, this necessitates a focus on self-efficacy in technological adaptability, examining individuals' technological proficiencies to navigate complex environments, where technologies are being used [26]. Self-efficacy is defined as "the degree to which an individual believes that he or she has the ability to perform a specific

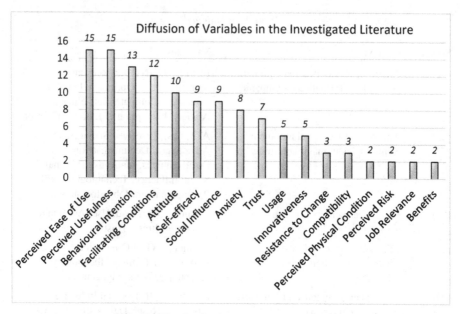

Fig. 1. The distribution of classified variables.

task/job using the computer" [37]. When people are interacting with technologies, their confidence in their own knowledge and skills has a substantial impact on determining the ease of use of the new technology [37]. The person's confidence in successfully achieving tasks with technological systems increases satisfaction, and, in turn, impacts the behavioral intention to use them. Self-efficacy as a determinant was proposed by [30] and has already been examined as an influential factor by other automation technology studies [1, 22, 28, 32, 34].

Facilitating Conditions. Literature related to technology acceptance highlights that ongoing support should be accessible to employees, throughout their interaction with automated technologies, including training sessions, detailed documentation, and user manuals for successful operation with technological systems [22]. The acquired competence and availability of essential resources positively influence attitudes towards technologies and their adoption [38]. As a result, facilitating conditions have been identified as one of the most significant predictors of the acceptance of automated technologies [22]. In general, facilitating conditions refer to "the degree to which an individual believes that an organizational and technical infrastructure exists to support the use of the system." [18]. A research study by [25] concludes that facilitating conditions are the primary contributor in determining the high likelihood of behavioral intention to use digital technologies. Results supporting the positive influence of facilitating conditions are present in digital and automated technologies [27, 28, 34] telemonitoring systems [25], robots and automation [11, 22], innovative systems [23] literature.

Social Influence. Social influence, as defined by authors [8], is the extent to which individuals perceive that people who are important believe they should use particular technologies. Similarly, [26] argues that social influence refers to both intentional and unintentional efforts by others to impact a person's thoughts, emotions, or intentions. The capacity of social influence to shape and alter the perception of an individual turns this determinant into a critical factor whether to embrace or reject new technology [20]. Considering the significant role of the social environment in facilitating attitudes and intentions to adopt technologies, people tend to adhere to the dominant norms within their surroundings, especially when the actors in the environment govern level of respect and knowledge [26]. Consequently, peer opinions and views of social circles in the workplace can have a substantial impact on decision-making [20]. A number of technology acceptance studies in digital technologies and healthcare have demonstrated a direct impact of social influence on perceived usefulness, perceived ease of use, and behavioral intention [20, 26, 28, 32, 34].

Anxiety. Anxiety is defined as an emotional condition marked by feelings of fear and perceived frustration, especially prevalent in circumstances that include challenging tasks or elements of uncertainty [26]. The fear or dislike of new or complex innovations originates from a lack of familiarity with technology and perceived complexities in its use, leading to negative attitudes, thoughts, and apprehension [26]. The transition from manual to automated operations might lead to employees' discomfort and frustration, thereby reducing motivation and fostering negative perceptions of the work environment. Particularly in situations where individuals do not have any control over the adoption process, anxiety becomes more evident [15]. Extensive research in IS field [1, 11, 28, 34] has examined negative effect of anxiety on perceived usefulness, perceived ease of use, and behavioral intention.

3 Methodology

This research is built on a descriptive cross-sectional case study that performs a comprehensive examination of the employees' acceptance of the automated bed washer at hospitals within Midtjylland in Denmark. The selection of external variables was based on the technology acceptance models established in prior studies within the healthcare and automation technologies literature. Consequently, a qualitative meta-analysis was employed to provide a consistent and comprehensive collection of findings across primary studies within the same research topic [39]. As a result, this study accumulated a group of 17 studies in healthcare and automation to identify the most commonly occurring variables for technology acceptance. The selection of prior studies was based on a narrative literature review followed by the keyword-based search in the Scopus and Web of Science databases. Several combinations of keywords were used in relation to digital technologies and automation in healthcare and employees' technology acceptance.

The research was conducted at three regional hospitals within the Midtjylland region in Denmark, that had implemented the automated bed washers for their cleaning operations. Utilizing the purposive sampling technique, which is characterized by the identification and selection of individuals or groups possessing specialized knowledge and experienced with a phenomenon of research interest [40], this study encompassed all machine operators and technicians actively engaged in the operation and maintenance of

ABWs. In total, the study involved interviewing 17 machine operators and 2 technicians from three distinct hospitals, ranging from 20 to 61 years (average age = 44 years), and consisting of 10 females and 9 males. Average experience in working with an ABW was three years with a minimum of one-year experience. The data gathering occurred over the period of three consecutive days in March 2024, with each day dedicated to visiting a different hospital.

A mixed-method approach has been applied for data collection, including insights from controlled observations, and results from unstructured interviews complemented with a TAM-based questionnaire. First, controlled observations were conducted by observing operator's behavior during the interactions with automated machines at one of the investigated hospitals. Second, interactive sessions with participants were conducted, beginning with the questionnaire to evaluate their perception of an ABW. The questionnaire was composed of eight sub-sections, with the first seven related to the main variables of the model and the last one focused on demographic characteristics. Overall, the questionnaire comprised 43 items (40 for the variables and 3 for demographics) designed to assess the constructs and relationships proposed in the research model. The survey utilized measures derived from existing literature, where their validity and reliability were confirmed as well as their relevance to the research model, primarily from those employed by [22, 26, 35]. A seven-point Likert-type scale was used to rate items, ranging from 1 (strongly disagree) to 7 (strongly agree). After completing the questionnaire, unstructured interviews were conducted to form a guided conversation with participants and gather rich, in-depth data about impactful determinants for ABW adoption without imposing any restrictions on the topic.

A two-phase method was employed to analyze the empirical data gathered from the questionnaire. First, the measurement model was examined using descriptive statistics to provide insight into the general patterns and distribution of the participants' answers. Second, Pearson's correlation was performed to measure the strength and direction of the linear relationships between two variables.

4 Results

The statistical analysis results confirm the validity and reliability of the measurement model. Table 2 presents questionnaire items alongside their respective descriptive statistics. Additionally, it includes the Cronbach's Alpha values for each variable. Overall, the results validate the reliability of the survey instrument, with all Cronbach's Alpha values exceeding the 0.7 threshold, indicating a strong internal consistency, particularly for Behavioral Intention, Anxiety, and Perceived Ease of Use.

Based on calculated mean and standard deviation values, participants feel quite confident in their ability to use ABWs and they generally believe that their workplace provides adequate support and resources for using ABWs. Moreover, the low mean scores (1.842 to 2.842) suggest that the participants generally do not feel anxious or distressed about using ABWs. However, while participants moderately trust the functionality and safety of ABWs, less consensus is observed in their reliability.

Pearson's correlation results demonstrate self-efficacy as a central construct, suggesting that individuals with higher self-efficacy tend to experience less anxiety and find

Table 2. Questionnaire items and descriptive statistics.

Variables and Questionnaire Items	Mean	St. dev.
Social Influence (Adapted from [26, 35], Cronbach's Alpha 0.731)		
People who I am acquainted with influence my opinion about ABW	3,895	2,158
My colleagues and peers think it is a good idea to use an ABW	6,158	0,898
People who influence my behavior think I should use an ABW	6,526	0,697
My peers use an ABW and have encouraged me to accept the technology	6,000	1,374
I trust other people's opinions about an ABW	5,158	1,425
Anxiety (Adapted from [12, 15, 26, 35], Cronbach's Alpha 0.898)		
Using an ABW makes me feel distress and unease	1,842	1,463
I am anxious that the use of an ABW on my current job will require knowledge and skills that I do not have	2,842	2,410
I feel that an ABW make my competency and skills useless and obsolete	1,895	1,595
I feel that an ABW make my role redundant and unneeded	1,737	1,447
I am anxious that I might lose my current job due to automation technologies within the next 5 years	1,842	1,675
Self-efficacy (Adapted from [26, 30, 35], Cronbach's Alpha 0.789)		
I have knowledge and skills to use an ABW	6,105	1,049
I am confident that I can use an ABW successfully	6,368	0,761
It is not hard for me to learn to use an ABW	6,316	1,057
I could complete the given task using ABW if someone showed me how to do it first	6,316	1,250
I am confident that I can use an ABW if I receive formal training	6,684	0,820
Facilitating conditions (Adapted from [22, 25 and self-developed], Cronbach's Alpha 0.850)		
My workplace offers sufficient training to learn how to use an ABW	5,526	2,091
There is adequate technical support available for issues from an ABW use	5,421	1,539
My workplace has the necessary infrastructure to support use of an ABW	5,526	1,744
I have the resources necessary to use an ABW	6,000	1,155

(continued)

Table 2. (*continued*)

Variables and Questionnaire Items	Mean	St. dev.
There is a clear managerial support for adopting automated technologies	6,056	1,110
Trust (Adapted from [3, 22, 24] and self-developed, Cronbach's Alpha 0.798)		
I trust an ABW to deliver the desired results	5,526	2,010
I trust that an ABW will function as intended without frequent breakdowns	3,737	1,790
I trust that an ABW perform tasks effectively	6,053	1,580
I feel safe working with an ABW	6,053	1,615
I feel that an ABW is controllable	5,684	1,668
Perceived Usefulness (Adapted from [26, 33, 36], Cronbach's Alpha 0.857)		
Using an ABW increases my productivity at work	6,000	1,328
Using an ABW enhances my effectiveness at work	6,333	1,188
Using an ABW improves my job performance	6,111	1,367
Using an ABW reduces workload and work pressure	5,579	1,742
Using an ABW is useful for my job	6,167	1,098
Perceived Ease of Use (Adapted from [15, 20, 22, 33], Cronbach's Alpha 0.891)		
I find the ABW easy to use	5,895	1,487
An ABW has an understandable interface	5,474	1,926
I find an ABW easy to learn	5,000	1,633
It is easy to remember and use commands when working with an ABW	5,842	1,675
I find it easy to get an ABW to do what I want it to do	5,526	1,611
Behavioral Intention (Adapted from [3, 15, 26], Cronbach's Alpha 0.934)		
I intend to use an ABW in my workplace in the future	6,444	1,042
If given a choice, I would always use an ABW instead of manual work	6,263	1,240
I am willing to accept an ABW in my workplace	6,684	0,820
If I have the resources, knowledge, and ability, I will use an ABW	6,789	0,713
I would recommend others to use the system	6,421	1,121

technology easier to use (Table 3). Furthermore, facilitating conditions strongly correlate with trust and PEOU, suggesting that when employees perceive favorable facilitating conditions, they are more likely to trust the system and find it easier to use. However, social influence shows less significant correlation with other variables, potentially indicating its influence might be limited or context-dependent in this research.

Table 3. Pearson's correlation.

	SI	AX	SE	FC	T	PU	PE	IN
SI		r=0,05	r=0,41	r=0,13	r=0,29	r=-0,11	r=0,03	r=0,26
		p=0,84	p=0,08	p=0,59	p=0,22	p=0,64	p=0,89	p=0,29
AX	r=-0,05		r=-0,67	r=-0,3	r=-0,41	r=-0,08	r=-0,51	r=-0,21
	p=0,84		p=0,00	p=0,22	p=0,08	p=0,74	p=0,03	p=0,39
SE	r=0,41	r=-0,67		r=0,59	r=0,53	r=0,35	r=0,66	r=0,38
	p=0,08	p=0,00		p=0,01	p=0,02	p=0,14	p=0,00	p=0,11
FC	r=0,13	r=-0,3	r=0,59		r=0,77	r=0,48	r=0,79	r=0,57
	p=0,59	p=0,22	p=0,01		p=0,00	p=0,04	p=0,00	p=0,01
T	r=0,29	r=-0,41	r=0,53	r=0,77		r=0,22	r=0,78	r=0,49
	p=0,22	p=0,08	p=0,02	p=0,00		p=0,37	p=0,00	p=0,03
PU	r=-0,11	r=-0,08	r=0,35	r=0,48	r=0,22		r=0,35	r=0,48
	p=0,64	p=0,74	p=0,14	p=0,04	p=0,37		p=0,14	p=0,04
PE	r=0,03	r=-0,51	r=0,66	r=0,79	r=0,78	r=0,35		r=0,37
	p=0,89	p=0,03	p=0,00	p=0,00	p=0,00	p=0,14		p=0,11
IN	r=0,26	r=-0,21	r=0,38	r=0,57	r=0,49	r=0,48	r=0,37	
	p=0,29	p=0,39	p=0,11	p=0,01	p=0,03	p=0,04	p=0,11	

5   Conclusion

To conclude, this study utilized TAM to investigate the employees' perception of ABWs and identify influential determinants for technology adoption. Drawing from the findings of investigated studies, five external variables were selected for extended TAM, including facilitating conditions, self-efficacy, social influence, anxiety, and trust. Based on statistical analysis, the data indicated a generally positive perception towards ABWs with high self-efficacy, perceived usefulness, and behavioral intention to use the technology. The main area of concern appeared to be related trust, especially regarding the reliability of the technology.

References

1. Bakar, M.A., Razali, N.A.M., Wook, M., Ismail, M.N., Sembok, T.M.T.: Exploring and developing an industrial automation acceptance model in the manufacturing sector towards adoption of Industry 4.0. Manuf. Technol. **21**(4), 434–446 (2021)
2. Bardmann, M.M., Ruiner, C., Künzel, L., Klumpp, M.: In control or out of control? Work Organ. Labour Globalisation **17**(1), 136–152 (2023)
3. Çiğdem, Ş., Meidute-Kavaliauskiene, I., Yıldız, B.: Industry 4.0 and industrial robots: a study from the perspective of manufacturing company employees. Logistics **7**(1), 17 (2023)
4. Fernandez, D., Aman, A.: The influence of robotic process automation (Rpa) towards employee acceptance. Int. J. Recent Technol. Eng. **9**(5), 295–299 (2021)
5. Cao, D., et al.: Acceptance of automation manufacturing technology in China: an examination of perceived norm and organizational efficacy. Prod. Plan. Control **31**(8), 660–672 (2020)
6. Eimontaite, I., et al.: Dynamic graphical instructions result in improved attitudes and decreased task completion time in human–robot co-working: an experimental manufacturing study. Sustainability **14**(6), 1–19 (2022)

7. Dutot, V.: Factors influencing Near Field Communication (NFC) adoption: an extended TAM approach. J. High Technol. Manag. Res. **26**(1), 45–57 (2015)

8. Venkatesh, V., et al.: Consumer acceptance and use of information technology: extending the unified theory of acceptance and use of technology. MIS Q. **36**, 157–178 (2012)

9. Defty, T.W., Kruger, K., Basson, A.H.: Possibilities and challenges for human-system integration in the South African manufacturing context. In: Smart, Sustainable Manufacturing in an Ever-Changing World: Proceedings of International Conference on Competitive Manufacturing, pp. 301–313 (2023)

10. Filgueiras, L.V.L., et al.: Working with robotic process automation: user experience after 18 months of adoption. Front. Comput. Sci. **4**, 936146 (2022)

11. Aldossari, M., Zin, A.M.: A conceptual framework for adopting automation and robotics innovations in the transformational companies in the Kingdom of Saudi Arabia. Emerg. Trends Intell. Comput. Inform. **4**, 894–905 (2020)

12. Cappuccio, M.L., Galliott, J.C., Eyssel, F., Lanteri, A.: Autonomous systems and technology resistance: new tools for monitoring acceptance, trust, and tolerance. Int. J. Soc. Robot. 1–25 (2023)

13. Labrague, L.J., Aguilar-Rosales, R., Yboa, B.C., Sabio, J.B., de Los Santos, J.A.: Student nurses' attitudes, perceived utilization, and intention to adopt artificial intelligence (AI) technology in nursing practice: a cross-sectional study. Nurse Educ. Pract. **73**, 1–7 (2023)

14. Foglia, E., et al.: Digital technology and COVID-19 pandemic: feasibility and acceptance of an innovative telemedicine platform. Technovation **130**, 1–11 (2024)

15. Özdemir-Güngör, D., Camgöz-Akdağ, H.: Examining the effects of technology anxiety and resistance to change on the acceptance of breast tumor registry system: evidence from Turkey. Technol. Soc. **54**, 66–73 (2018)

16. Fishbein, M., Ajzen, I.: Belief, Attitude, Intention and Behavior: An Introduction to Theory and Research. Addison-Wesley, Reading (1975)

17. Davis, F.D.: Perceived usefulness, perceived ease of use, and user acceptance of information technology. MIS Q. **13**(3), 319–340 (1989)

18. Venkatesh, V., Morris, M.G., Davis, G.B., Davis, F.D.: User acceptance of information technology: toward a unified view. MIS Q. **27**, 425–478 (2003)

19. Dawson, C.H., Mackrill, J.B., Cain, R.: Assessing user acceptance towards automated and conventional sink use for hand decontamination using the technology acceptance model. Ergonomics **60**(12), 1621–1633 (2017)

20. Rajak, M., Shaw, K.: An extension of technology acceptance model for mHealth user adoption. Technol. Soc. **67**, 1–17 (2021)

21. Ghazizadeh, M., Lee, J.D., Boyle, L.N.: Extending the technology acceptance model to assess automation. Cogn. Technol. Work **14**, 39–49 (2012)

22. Wewerka, J., Dax, S., Reichert, M.: A user acceptance model for robotic process automation. In: 2020 IEEE 24th IEDOC Conference, pp. 97–106 (2020)

23. Molino, M., Cortese, C.G., Ghislieri, C.: The promotion of technology acceptance and work engagement in industry 4.0: from personal resources to information and training. Int. J. Environ. Res. Public Health **17**(7), 1–15 (2020)

24. Panchetti, T., Pietrantoni, L., Puzzo, G., Gualtieri, L., Fraboni, F.: Assessing the relationship between cognitive workload, workstation design, user acceptance and trust in collaborative robots. Appl. Sci. **13**(3), 1–14 (2023)

25. Gagnon, M.P., Orruño, E., Asua, J., Abdeljelil, A.B., Emparanza, J.: Using a modified technology acceptance model to evaluate healthcare professionals' adoption of a new telemonitoring system. Telemed. e-Health **18**(1), 54–59 (2012)

26. Edo, O.C., Ang, D., Etu, E.-E., Tenebe, I., Edo, S., Diekola, O.A.: Why do healthcare workers adopt digital health technologies—a cross-sectional study integrating the TAM and UTAUT model in a developing economy. Int. J. Inf. Man. Data Insights **3**(2), 100186 (2023)

27. Elkady, T., Rees, A., Khalifa, M.: Nurses acceptance of automated medication dispensing cabinets. In: ICIMTH, pp. 47–50 (2019)
28. Schaper, L.K., et al.: ICT and OTs: a model of information and communication technology acceptance and utilisation by occupational therapists. Int. J. Med. Inf. **76**, 212–221 (2007)
29. Brooksbank, R., Scott, J.M., Fullerton, S.: In-store surveillance technologies: what drives their acceptability among consumers? Int. Rev. Retail Distrib. Consum. Res. **32**(5), 508–531 (2022)
30. Venkatesh, V., Bala, H.: Technology acceptance model 3 and a research agenda on interventions. Decis. Sci. **39**(2), 273–315 (2008)
31. Venkatesh, V., Davis, F.D.: Theoretical extension of the Technology Acceptance Model: four longitudinal field studies. Manage. Sci. **46**(2), 186–204 (2000)
32. AlQudah, A.A., Al-Emran, M., Shaalan, K.: Technology acceptance in healthcare: a systematic review. Appl. Sci. **11**(22), 1–40 (2021)
33. Ehteshami, A.: Barcode technology acceptance and utilization in health information management department at academic hospitals according to technology acceptance model. Acta Informatica Medica **25**(1), 4–8 (2017)
34. Druckerman, D.G., et al.: Healthcare worker perceptions of hand hygiene monitoring technologies: does technology performance matter? Infect. Control Hosp. Epidemiol. **42**(12), 1519–1520 (2021)
35. Ivanov, S., Kuyumdzhiev, M., Webster, C.: Automation fears: drivers and solutions. Technol. Soc. **63**, 101431 (2020)
36. Dirsehan, T., Can, C.: Examination of trust and sustainability concerns in autonomous vehicle adoption. Technol. Soc. **63**, 101361 (2020)
37. Blut, M., Wang, C., Schoefer, K.: Factors influencing the acceptance of self-service technologies: a meta-analysis. J. Serv. Res. **19**(4), 396–416 (2016)
38. Chen, K.Y., Chang, M.L.: User acceptance of 'near field communication' mobile phone service: an investigation based on the 'unified theory of acceptance and use of technology' model. Serv. Ind. J. **33**(6), 609–623 (2013)
39. Timulak, L.: Meta-analysis of qualitative studies: a tool for reviewing qualitative research findings in psychotherapy. Psychother. Res. **19**(4–5), 591–600 (2009)
40. Palinkas, L.A., et al.: Purposeful sampling for qualitative data collection and analysis in mixed method implementation research. Adm. Policy Mental Health Mental Health Serv. Res. **42**, 533–544 (2015)

Communication Skills for Future Doctors and Health Professionals: Developing Student Personas for an Interdisciplinary Digital Course on Complementary and Alternative Medicine (CAM) and Health Communication

Monika Pröbster[1]([⊠]) [iD], Helena Pagiatakis[2], Sarah Salomo[2] [iD], Cord Spreckelsen[2], Martin Haag[1] [iD], Jutta Hübner[2], and Nicola Marsden[1] [iD]

[1] Heilbronn University, Max-Planck-Str. 39, 74081 Heilbronn, Germany
{monika.proebster,martin.haag,nicola.marsden}@hs-heilbronn.de
[2] Friedrich-Schiller-University Jena, 07737 Jena, Germany
{Helena.Pagiatakis,Sarah.Salomo,Cord.Spreckelsen,
jutta.huebner}@med.uni-jena.de

Abstract. Wide segments of the population express interest in what they believe are alternatives to evidence-based therapies, leading to increasing challenges in the care provided by doctors and other professionals such as nutritionists, pharmacists, and psychologists. Regarding the field of Complementary and Alternative Medicine (CAM), there is a multitude of digital health information that patients base their opinions on. Education confronts the dual challenge of updating teaching concepts to keep pace with progressing digitalization and equipping students to manage digital health information in future patient interactions. In our project, we transfer the concept of medical case conferences into the digital space and develop an interdisciplinary and collaborative blended-learning course with a unique method of competence impartation. We report on the construction of a set of student personas based on the data of the target group gathered in three iterations. These personas are available for further use in the adaption of the blended-learning course that equip future health professionals with the knowledge to advocate evidence-based practices within interdisciplinary teams and communicate effectively with patients about CAM.

Keywords: Personas · blended learning · interdisciplinary collaboration · Complementary and Alternative Medicine

1 Introduction

In light of growing public interest in what is perceived as alternatives to evidence-based therapies, healthcare faces new challenges. This shift impacts various professions, including doctors, nutritionists, pharmacists, and psychologists. In the field of Complementary and Alternative Medicine (CAM), there is a multitude of digital health information that influences patient opinions. To address this in the education of healthcare

C. Stephanidis et al. (Eds.): HCII 2024, CCIS 2119, pp. 334–343, 2024.
https://doi.org/10.1007/978-3-031-61966-3_36

professionals, we develop a project for medical university education to scientifically illuminate the topics of CAM [1] and educate on the handling of digital health information in this sensitive area.

We report on this project, in which we transfer the concept of medical case conferences into the digital space and develop an interdisciplinary and collaborative blended-learning course with a unique method of competence impartation.

The research goal of this paper is to enhance the design of blended-learning modules for medical education. Specifically, we aim to transform in-person medical case conferences into a hybrid format that effectively integrates theoretical and practical knowledge Complementary and Alternative Medicine (CAM) in the light of evidence-based medicine, considering potential evidence and risks. To achieve this, we have developed student personas as a foundational tool for the design process. Personas are fictionalized representations of different user groups, based on empirical data of these user groups. They are used to avoid applying one's own assumptions onto a design [2]. These student personas will guide the creation of e-learning modules, ensuring they equip future healthcare professionals—doctors, nutritionists, pharmacists, and psychologists—with the knowledge to advocate evidence-based practices within interdisciplinary teams and communicate effectively with patients about CAM.

2 Related Work

The persona development described in this paper took place in the context of the design of a blended-learning course on CAM. In the following section, we elaborate the concept and the structure of the course and introduce personas as a tool for the design process.

2.1 The Concept and Structure of the Course

Complementary medicine garners considerable interest among cancer patients, with about 50% of them using these approaches [3]. A main motivation comes from wanting to take an active role in their health enhancement. It's crucial to acknowledge these endeavors while carefully considering the balance of risks and benefits [4]. For treatments involving substance administration, the issue of potential drug interactions looms large. Conversely, for non-substance-based modalities, safeguarding patients from unproven methods—where time and money are invested—is paramount [4]. Especially since it has been shown that patients who have experienced positive outcomes through ineffective methods, often due to placebo effects, may initially favor such approaches even in the face of serious cancer diagnoses, potentially delaying effective treatment [5]. Moreover, increasingly complex health requirements render interdisciplinary education and collaborations in the health sector more important [6]. Against this background, it is essential to prepare future health professionals for dealing with patients considering or seeking CAM.

Interdisciplinary case conferences are an established method used in medical practice e.g. for complex health conditions such as cancer, where professionals of different disciplines come together to discuss the treatment of a patient [7]. In a past research project, the method of interdisciplinary case conferences was systematically integrated into a course at the medical school at a German university, open to students from different health disciplines.

The shift to digital education at German universities has been accelerated during the COVID-19 pandemic. This transition involved a swift move from on-campus classes to technology-enhanced formats, emphasizing video conferencing and multimodal learning [8]. However, failures regarding the state of digitalization at German universities became also apparent and after the lockdown was over, often new digital methods as well as efforts to improve digitalization became abandoned again [9]. So, there is still a considerable potential for fostering and improving digital education to enhance students' digital competencies as well as making use of the specific benefits of digital formats [9, 10].

The present paper reports on our transfer of the concept of in-person interdisciplinary case conferences into a digital format, enabling long-term collaboration among students from different disciplines with incompatible curricula in face-to-face instruction. Moreover, the digital format offers the possibility of collaborations between universities from different cities, and thus extending the course to remote students who otherwise would not have been able to participate.

In the beginning, we developed a repository of digital "knowledge nuggets" for students to acquire the necessary knowledge and skills. Along with collaborative learning steps and assigned test task(s), these "knowledge nuggets" constitute a unit referred to as a "Micro Collaboration" (MiCo). In total, there are 11 MiCos, referring to different subjects. More precisely, each MiCo consists of materials on a subject (for self-study) in different formats such as texts, videos, quizzes, tasks etc., i.e. the asynchron part (a module), as well as interdisciplinary group tasks and group discussions related to the specific subject which are conducted during the 4 online-sessions (i.e. the synchronous part).

The media and the digital didactic design are based on principles of effective learning and the promotion of multi-professional cooperation and are tailored to the heterogeneous predispositions and levels of knowledge to ensure accessibility for students from different disciplines. Methods and approaches from design science research (such as personas, third-space workshops, etc.) are employed, and a participatory and iterative process ensures that MiCos are continuously formatively evaluated in the design process. The didactic approach of MiCos is uniformly applied and is the focus of the technical implementation.

In terms of content, MiCos address several relevant areas: As knowledge nuggets, existing materials are integrated (e.g., guidelines, glossaries, and patient guidelines). Different methods of complementary and alternative medicine are presented in texts, videos, interviews, practical examples, quizzes, etc. Additionally, preparation for a scholarly engagement with the different concepts of CAM is provided, highlighting the significance of evidence-based medicine and its approach in dealing with CAM through typical examples (e.g., homeopathy, anthropology, cancer diets).

MiCos also include questions and tasks that require students to engage in critical thinking, reflect on the patient perspective, apply their disciplinary knowledge, clinical skills, and professional attitudes. Tasks include searching for evidence and assessing it, handling CAM in discussions within their own professional group, interdisciplinary, and across professional groups.

In total, the course consists of 11 eLearning modules as part of the 11 MiCos, 4 online sessions and one concluding intensive, 3-day block seminar.

At the end of the semester, the students should be familiar with an array of different methods of CAM and know to which extents these methods are based on scientific evidence or not. Further, they should have gathered and deeper understanding in interdisciplinary collaboration and communication strategies to address patients requesting CAM.

For developing these MiCos and to further guide our process as well as support future lecturers, we gathered extensive data and constructed a set of personas in three iterations.

2.2 Personas

Personas are fictional representations of individuals created to embody users or target groups during the design phase. Originating from "goal-centered design" [11], personas have been integrated into user-centered approaches and methodologies, including the human-centered design process [12] and the contextual design methodology [13], among others. Moreover, personas are extensively employed in the development of novel technologies [2]. Personas are constructed based on collected user data, which may include surveys, interviews, field observations, or workshops facilitated by design teams. As people connect more easily with other people than abstract data, personas make data more tangible, but have also been criticized for being too simplistic and foster stereotypes [2, 14, 15]. We will describe our methods of data collection, the construction of our personas, and re-evaluation with members of the target groups in the following.

3 Methods

The personas were developed in three iterations. In total, 23 students participated in the course in the first iteration (in 2023), 33 students in the second and 25 students in the third iteration (in 2024). The course is part of the studies in "Integrative Oncology" at the medical department of the Friedrich-Schiller-University Jena.

In a first iteration, student data was collected as the basis for persona development. All students were students at Friedrich-Schiller-University Jena (either bachelor, master or state exam), studying medicine ($N = 8$), nutritional sciences ($N = 5$), pharmacy ($N = 2$), psychology ($N = 3$) or communication sciences ($N = 5$).

After each eLearning module that the students worked on individually and after each online session, they filled out a short questionnaire dealing the present subject (in total, 11 subjects) or the online session at hand (in total, three sessions) featuring open questions and rating questions.

The questionnaire administered at the end of each module as well as the online sessions consisted of a mixture of open questions and ratings, requesting answers on the following: Which aspect appeared particularly important to me? What did I stumble over? Where do I feel particularly supported in implementing the topic discussed today? Where do I personally see myself particularly challenged in implementing the discussed topic? What positive outcomes do I expect from implementing what I learned today? Moreover, we asked about anticipated difficulties and positive effects when applying what they learned, pros and cons regarding the methods used, and general potential improvements. Additionally, we collected the assessment of the materials, content, structure, perceived learning gain, perceived usefulness, preparation time, and appropriateness of the methods on a 4-point Likert scale (ranging from "does not apply" to "fully applicable").

As filling out the short feedback questions was voluntary, students participated irregularly, and we could not gather demographical information as it would have forfeited the students' anonymity. However, some demographical data could be gathered at the evaluation at the end of the semester, as 17 students (14 female, 3 male) took part.

A total of 994 information snippets were extracted from the feedback sessions (of 2023), further structured as an affinity diagram and clustered using the methods of contextual design [13].

Several topics emerged in the process: the different disciplinary backgrounds and specific previous knowledge, the methods used, different interests, usability issues, aspects of digital literacy, and expectations for further use. We decided to represent four different disciplines with one persona each to consider the range of degrees of the students, i.e. medicine, nutritional science, communication science and psychology.

After an additional short feedback session with one of the lectures, we finished a first draft of four personas and thus, the first iteration.

In the second and third iterations, students were confronted with the personas that had been developed in the previous iteration and participated in co-design workshops to improve the personas.

The students of the second iteration studied medicine ($N = 10$), nutritional sciences ($N = 6$), psychology ($N = 3$), health communication ($N = 1$), pharmacy ($N = 3$) and social work ($N = 10$), the latter at a partner university in Germany. The students of the third iteration studied medicine ($N = 9$), psychology ($N = 5$), pharmacy ($N = 1$) and social work ($N = 10$).

The co-design workshops took place online. After a short introduction on personas in general, the students went into breakout sessions that were facilitated by a researcher. They evaluated the personas (the draft of the first iteration) by answering questions and giving open feedback. Questions referred to "first impressions", "Which aspects of the persona do you find applicable", "With which aspects can you not identify?", "If applicable: What confuses you?", "What do you find successful (content-wise/graphically)?" and "other suggestions for improvement".

Based on the input from the co-design workshop, the personas were adjusted, e.g. the quote of one persona was changed and for three personas, their preferences of topics and methods were refined. Additionally, the headlines of some sections were altered and some adjustments of the fonts were made.

These updated personas (the draft of the second iteration) were again presented to another group of students in the third iteration, which repeated the steps of the co-design workshop of the second iteration. Based on the results, we further modified parts of the background stories of two personas, two headlines and the preferences regarding certain contents and methods.

4   Results

In the following, we will present all four personas in their final state, (i.e. after all three iterations) focusing on the disciplines nutritional science, medicine, communication science, and psychology.

The first persona, Darian, is a 25-year-old nutritional science student with a background in the hospitality industry and a passion for both nutrition counseling and hobby cooking. He seeks a comprehensive understanding of various nutritional approaches and values active participation and open communication in educational settings (see Fig. 1).

The second persona, Nihan, 23, is a medical student who is keen on discerning evidence-based procedures in her studies, emphasizing the necessity for clarity in whether course literature is evidence-based or anecdotal. Her educational journey is also marked by a desire for practical communication skills and a thorough examination of course subjects, aiming for an education that mirrors the rigor of medical practice (see Fig. 2).

The third persona, Anna is a 24-year-old communication sciences student intent on mastering strategies for open patient engagement and understanding the genesis of their health beliefs. Her academic focus is complemented by an interest in Mind-Body Medicine, nutrition, and the need for clear communication (see Fig. 3).

The fourth persona, Alexander, 23, is a psychology student with aspirations to work as a psychotherapist and is interested in the backgrounds of Anthroposophy and Eastern martial arts. He is engaged in understanding the differences between alternative, integrative, and complementary medicine and takes a holistic approach to psychological wellness (see Fig. 4).

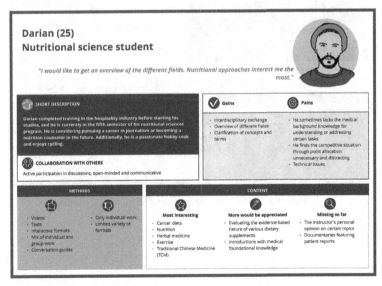

Fig. 1. Persona "Darian" (translated from German by the authors)

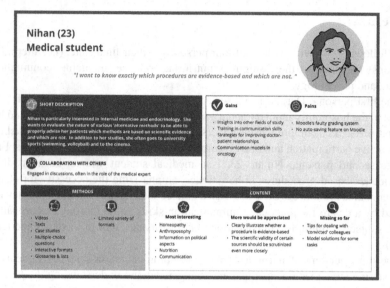

Fig. 2. Persona "Nihan" (translated from German by the authors)

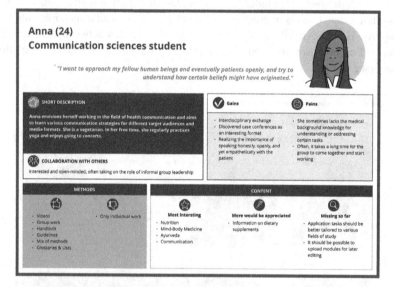

Fig. 3. Persona "Anna" (translated from German by the authors)

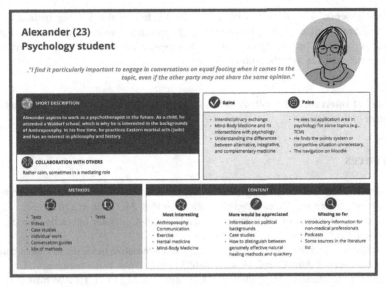

Fig. 4. Persona "Alexander" (translated from German by the authors)

5 Conclusion

The iterative development and application of student personas in our project have enriched the design and implementation process of our blended-learning modules focused on Complementary and Alternative Medicine within medical education. This approach not only enabled us to distill critical insights from student feedback but also to refine the development of the Micro Collaborations (MiCos), including the e-learning modules and modalities of the course.

Regarding the topic at hand, it is important to account for the diversity of the students in terms of professional background knowledge. Moreover, even though the answers in our questionnaires were extensive, the second and third iteration with co-design workshops with the students were instrumental in mitigating the risk of embedding discipline-related stereotypes and assumptions into the course content, thereby ensuring a more inclusive and representative educational experience. Considering plans to expand the project and course, the student personas will provide future instructors who are implementing the course with their students with background information and orientation. The student personas can thus provide a nuanced understanding of student profiles, which is essential for adapting the course content and pedagogical approaches to diverse learner groups.

In conclusion, this project not only advances our understanding of how to effectively integrate digital and blended-learning strategies in healthcare education but also highlights the critical role of student-centered design in creating more effective, engaging, and inclusive learning environments.

Acknowledgments. This work has been partially funded by the Stiftung Innovation in der Hochschullehre (Foundation Innovation in Higher Education) under Grant Number FRFMM-284/2022 as part of the project "Querschnitt12 - Kompetenz interfakultär!". The responsibility for all content supplied lies with the authors.

Disclosure of Interests. The authors have no competing interests to declare that are relevant to the content of this article.

References

1. Huebner, J., et al.: Counseling patients on cancer diets: a review of the literature and recommendations for clinical practice. Anticancer Res. **34**(1), 39–48 (2014)
2. Nielsen, L.: Personas - User Focused Design (Human–Computer Interaction Series, vol. 15 Springer, Cham (2013)
3. Molassiotis, A., et al.: Use of complementary and alternative medicine in cancer patients: a European survey. Ann. Oncol. **16**(4), 655–663 (2005)
4. Hübner, J., Beckmann, M., Follmann, M., Nothacker, M., Prott, F.J., Wörmann, B.: Complementary medicine in the treatment of cancer patients. Dtsch. Arztebl. Int. **118**(39), 654 (2021)
5. Huebner, J., et al.: User rate of complementary and alternative medicine (CAM) of patients visiting a counseling facility for CAM of a German comprehensive cancer center. Anticancer Res. **34**(2), 943–948 (2014)
6. W. H. Organization, Framework for action on interprofessional education and collaborative practice, World Health Organization (2010). https://iris.who.int/handle/10665/70185
7. Wright, F., De Vito, C., Langer, B., Hunter, A.: Multidisciplinary cancer conferences: a systematic review and development of practice standards. Eur. J. Cancer **43**(6), 1002–1010 (2007)
8. Skulmowski, A., Rey, G.D.: COVID-19 as an accelerator for digitalization at a German university: establishing hybrid campuses in times of crisis. Hum. Behav. Emerg. Technol. **2**(3), 212–216 (2020)
9. Dittler, U., Kreidl, C.: Kurzinterviews mit Expert: innen aus dem Hochschulmanagement und aus Organisationsabteilungen zum Lehren und Lernen. In: Dittler, U., Kreidl, C. (eds.) Wie Corona die Hochschullehre verändert: Erfahrungen und Gedanken aus der Krise zum zukünftigen Einsatz von eLearning 2023, pp. 209–230. Springer, Cham (2023). https://doi.org/10.1007/978-3-658-40163-4_13
10. Thillosen, A., Kehrer, M.: Hochschulbildung seit Corona–ein (erneutes) Plädoyer für Vernetzung, Zusammenarbeit und Diskurs. In: Dittler, U., Kreidl, C. (eds.) Wie Corona die Hochschullehre verändert: Erfahrungen und Gedanken aus der Krise zum zukünftigen Einsatz von eLearning, pp. 55–76. Springer, Cham (2023). https://doi.org/10.1007/978-3-658-40163-4_4
11. Cooper, A.: The Inmates are Running the Asylum: Why High-Tech Products Drive Us Crazy and How to Restore the Sanity. Sams, Indianapolis (1999)
12. DIN, Ergonomie der Mensch-System-Interaktion - Teil 210: Prozess zur Gestaltung gebrauchstauglicher interaktiver Systeme (ISO 9241-210:2010); Deutsche Fassung EN ISO 9241-210:2010 (2010)
13. Holtzblatt, K., Beyer, H.: Contextual Design: Design for Life. Morgan Kaufmann, Boston (2017)

14. Nielsen, L.: Engaging personas and narrative scenarios. Ph.D. series, vol. 17 (2004)
15. Marsden, N., Haag, M.: Stereotypes and politics: reflections on personas. In: Proceedings of the SIGCHI Conference on Human Factors in Computing Systems (CHI 2016), pp. 4017–4031 (2016)

An Architecture to Support Graduated Levels of Trust for Cancer Diagnosis with AI

Olya Rezaeian[1]([⊠]) [iD], Alparslan Emrah Bayrak[2], and Onur Asan[1]

[1] Stevens Institute of Technology, Hoboken, NJ 07030, USA
orezaeia@stevens.edu
[2] Lehigh University, Bethlehem, PA 18015, USA

Abstract. Our research addresses the critical challenge of building trust in Artificial Intelligence (AI) for Clinical Decision Support Systems (CDSS), focusing on breast cancer diagnosis. It is difficult for clinicians to trust AI-generated recommendations due to a lack of explanations by the AI especially when diagnosing life threatening diseases such as breast cancer. To tackle this, we propose a dual-stage AI model combining U-Net architecture for image segmentation and Convolutional Neural Networks (CNN) for cancer prediction. This model operates on breast cancer tissue images and introduces four levels of explainability: basic classification, probability distribution, tumor localization, and advanced tumor localization with varying confidence levels. These levels are designed to offer increasing detail about diagnostic suggestions, aiming to study the effect of different explanation types on clinicians' trust in the AI system. Our methodology encompasses the development of explanation mechanisms and their application in experimental settings to evaluate their impact on enhancing clinician trust in AI. This initiative seeks to bridge the gap between AI capabilities and clinician acceptance by improving the transparency and usefulness of AI in healthcare. Ultimately, our work aims to contribute to better patient outcomes and increased efficiency in healthcare delivery by facilitating the integration of explainable AI into clinical practice.

Keywords: Explainablity · Clinical Decision Support Systems (CDSS) · Breast Cancer · Trust · Artificial Intelligence (AI)

1 Introduction

Clinical Decision Support Systems (CDSS) leveraging Artificial Intelligence (AI) utilize extensive healthcare data and machine learning to support clinicians in diagnosis [8,12,13,15], treatment planning [11], and symptom checking [23]. These AI-powered tools hold the potential to transform healthcare by reducing diagnostic errors and improving patient care [7,20,24], potentially leading to better patient outcomes and early-stage treatment cost savings [6].

However, the successful deployment of CDSS faces hurdles such as technical complexities, potential disruptions in clinical workflows, and changes in clinician behavior and judgment [10]. A critical challenge is building trust between users and AI systems, which is essential for their widespread adoption in the medical field.

Our study focuses on the pivotal role of explainability in fostering trust between clinicians and AI-powered Clinical Decision Support Systems (CDSS), especially in the realms of oncology and radiology for cancer diagnosis. Recognizing the intricate nature of cancer diagnosis, where each decision significantly impacts patient care, we emphasize the importance of explainability in AI systems. This approach facilitates a deeper understanding of AI-generated recommendations, addressing the critical need for clinicians to grasp the "why" and "how" behind these suggestions. By highlighting various levels of explanation-from basic interpretations to more detailed insights-we illustrate the potential of these mechanisms to enhance clinician trust and reliance on CDSS [16].

We propose exploring these explainability mechanisms through future human subject experiments, aiming to assess their effectiveness in real-world clinical settings. This forward-looking approach will allow us to evaluate the impact of different explanation depths on clinician decision-making and trust in AI systems. Our intention is not to present a fully developed CDSS, but to outline the foundational elements for a research platform that could significantly contribute to the design of such systems. By acknowledging individual differences among clinicians, including their experience and decision-making styles, our study seeks to pave the way for AI applications in healthcare that are both transparent and adaptable to user needs. The ultimate goal is to enhance patient outcomes by bridging the gap between advanced AI capabilities and the practical requirements of healthcare professionals, ensuring that CDSS can be trusted and effectively integrated into medical practice.

2 Literature Review

The review article [21] explores the factors affecting users' trust in AI. This review article considers the frequency of use of these factors in both qualitative and quantitative studies to be a key indication of their significance. Among many human factors, explainability consistently emerges as the foremost factor influencing trust in numerous studies [4, 19, 21]. Muir [14] suggests that users' experience with a system can influence their trust levels, and observing the predictability of a system's behavior can foster greater trust.

The challenge of interpreting black-box ML models has led to the development of explainable AI (xAI) methods like LIME [17] and SHAP [9] to mitigate decision-making risks. There's growing research on xAI's role in decision-making, including studies on trust calibration within AI systems. Wang et al. [22] evaluated established xAI methods in AI-assisted decision tasks, finding their effectiveness varies by the user's domain expertise, offering insights into effective xAI design for human decision support.

Example-based explanations, such as those tested on the QuickDraw platform, show how normative and comparative examples can enhance or reveal system limitations, indicating the nuanced benefits of example types [5]. Another study explored the impact of re-diagnosis by an AI system and different explanation types on user satisfaction and trust, suggesting richer explanations improve patient outcomes at crucial junctures [3].

Evans et al.'s work [6] on digital pathologists' interaction with xAI tools provides insights into preferences for understandable AI guidance but does not quantify the impact on trust and decision-making reliance. This gap underscores the importance of further investigating how various xAI tools and explanation levels influence professional trust and usage in medical contexts.

While existing research has studied the effectiveness of various xAI methods, a significant gap in the literature exists when it comes to quantifying the impact of different levels of explainability on trust, reliance, and their subsequent influence on clinical decisions. As a first step to bridge this knowledge gap, this paper answers the following research question (RQ):

- **RQ:** What are the mechanisms to build explainability into AI recommendations to make diagnosis decisions?

3   Research Methodology

3.1   Baseline AI Model

In this section, we present our approach to develop an AI system that combines a U-Net architecture for image segmentation with an established Convolutional Neural Network (CNN) for cancer prediction, as referenced in the existing literature [1]. This AI system integrated in a CDSS generates the diagnostic suggestions for breast cancer application.

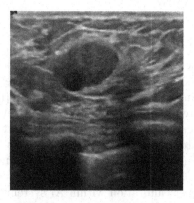

Fig. 1. A sample of mammogram image

Our study utilizes a de-identified, publicly available breast cancer dataset [2], which contains 780 ultrasound images from a diverse group of 600 female patients aged 25 to 75 years. A sample ultrasound image is shown in Fig. 1. These images are classified into healthy, benign, and malignant categories, based on a process overseen by expert radiologists from Baheya Hospital. The distribution of images within each class is listed in Table 1.

Image Segmentation Using U-Net: Ronneberger et al. [18] developed the U-Net architecture for precise biomedical image segmentation, crucial for segmenting breast cancer tissue images into detailed areas, including cancerous and non-cancerous parts, through semantic segmentation. Here, every pixel in an image is categorized, rather than just identifying objects and their outlines.

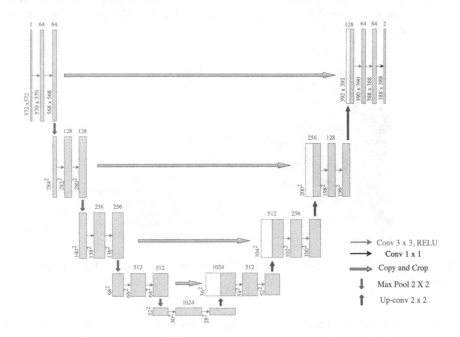

Fig. 2. U-Net architecture [18]

The U-Net, named for its U-shaped structure as you can see in Fig. 2, consists of a contraction path and an expanding path. Our application of U-Net provides a segmentation map where each pixel's value indicates the likelihood of belonging to a specific class.

Cancer Prediction Using CNN: The second stage of our system employs a Convolutional Neural Network (CNN) to analyze cancer from segmented images (Fig. 3), utilizing a structure of four convolutional layers followed by two dense

Table 1. Number of Images for Each Category in the Dataset

Image Category	Number of Images
Healthy	133
Benign	487
Malignant	210

layers. Each convolutional layer employs Conv2D filters for feature extraction. Batch normalization follows each convolutional layer, normalizing activations, while dropout layers reduce overfitting by randomly deactivating neuron activations. The network uses LeakyReLU activation. After convolutional processing, the data is prepared for dense layers, concluding with an output layer of three neurons employing a softmax function to classify images into healthy, benign, or malignant categories.

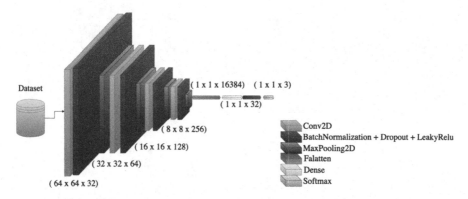

Fig. 3. Schematic representation of the CNN architecture employed for image-based cancer detection.

Data preparation involved reserving a portion for segmentation, with the majority split between training and testing phases, adhering to standard practices for model evaluation. The model demonstrated an 81% diagnostic accuracy on a test set, indicating its potential as a decision-support tool with cautious interpretation of its recommendations.

3.2 Explanation Mechanisms

There are four types of diagnostic suggestions provided by our AI model, each providing doctors with more information than the previous one:

Type I: Classification: The model's first level of output is a direct diagnosis suggestion. After feature extraction through convolutional layers, the model provides the classification corresponding to the image as Healthy, Benign, or Malignant.

Type II: Probability Distribution: The model calculates the likelihood of each diagnostic category using a softmax layer. Then, the model presents the probabilities, as well as the final classification.

Type III: Tumor Localization: The U-Net processes input images to segment the regions of interest, focusing on identifying potential tumor areas within the tissue. After segmentation, the model applies a threshold of 0.5 to the segmented outputs to classify pixels as cancerous or non-cancerous. This binary classification of pixels enables the model to localize the tumor by delineating the area where the likelihood of cancerous pixels are above the threshold (Fig. 4).

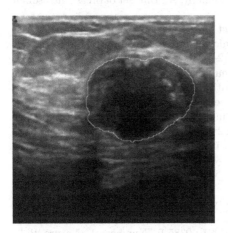   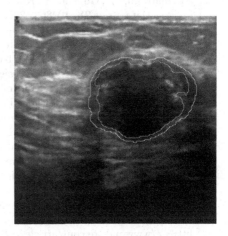

Fig. 4. Tumor Localization   **Fig. 5.** Enhanced Tumor Localization

Type IV: Enhanced Tumor Localization with Confidence Level: The model extends its localization capability by introducing two thresholds. If the probability of a pixel being cancerous is above 0.9, it is classified with high confidence. If the probability is between 0.5 and 0.9, it is classified with a lower confidence level (Fig. 5).

4   Conclusions

Throughout this paper, we outline a novel framework for developing explanation mechanisms for elucidating the inner workings of machine learning (ML) models that are used to make AI recommendations. These mechanisms aim to enhance transparency and foster trust in AI systems by making their decision-making processes more understandable to users. While we've laid the theoretical groundwork and proposed a variety of explanation types, practical assessment of these mechanisms through human-subject experiments is planned for future research. This next step is crucial for evaluating the effectiveness of our approach in improving user trust and comprehension of AI systems across different contexts. Such empirical validation will guide the refinement of explanation mechanisms to better meet user needs, marking a significant advancement in the field of explainable AI.

References

1. Breast Cancer Image Segmentation|Unet Model. https://kaggle.com/code/radwahashiesh/breast-cancer-image-segmentation-unet-model
2. Al-Dhabyani, W., Gomaa, M., Khaled, H., Fahmy, A.: Dataset of breast ultrasound images. Data Brief **28**, 104863 (2020)
3. Alam, L., Mueller, S.: Examining the effect of explanation on satisfaction and trust in AI diagnostic systems. BMC Med. Inform. Decis. Making **21**(1), 178 (2021). https://doi.org/10.1186/s12911-021-01542-6
4. Bernardo, E., Seva, R.: Affective design analysis of explainable artificial intelligence (xAI): a user-centric perspective. Informatics **10**, 32 (2023). MDPI
5. Cai, C.J., Jongejan, J., Holbrook, J.: The effects of example-based explanations in a machine learning interface. In: Proceedings of the 24th International Conference on Intelligent User Interfaces, pp. 258–262 (2019)
6. Evans, T., et al.: The explainability paradox: challenges for xAI in digital pathology. Futur. Gener. Comput. Syst. **133**, 281–296 (2022). https://doi.org/10.1016/j.future.2022.03.009, https://www.sciencedirect.com/science/article/pii/S0167739X22000838
7. Gaube, S., et al.: Do as AI say: susceptibility in deployment of clinical decision-aids. NPJ Digit. Med. **4**(1), 1–8 (2021). https://doi.org/10.1038/s41746-021-00385-9, https://www.nature.com/articles/s41746-021-00385-9. Number: 1, Nature Publishing Group
8. Janowczyk, A., Madabhushi, A.: Deep learning for digital pathology image analysis: a comprehensive tutorial with selected use cases. J. Pathol. Inform. **7**(1), 29 (2016). ISBN: 2153-3539, Elsevier
9. Lundberg, S.M., Lee, S.I.: A unified approach to interpreting model predictions. In: Advances in Neural Information Processing Systems, vol. 30 (2017)
10. McIntosh, C., et al.: Clinical integration of machine learning for curative-intent radiation treatment of patients with prostate cancer. Nat. Med. **27**(6), 999–1005 (2021). https://doi.org/10.1038/s41591-021-01359-w, https://www.nature.com/articles/s41591-021-01359-w. Number: 6, Nature Publishing Group
11. McIntosh, C., Purdie, T.G.: Voxel-based dose prediction with multi-patient atlas selection for automated radiotherapy treatment planning. Phys. Med. Biol. **62**(2), 415 (2016). ISBN: 0031-9155, IOP Publishing
12. McKinney, S.M., et al.: International evaluation of an AI system for breast cancer screening. Nature **577**(7788), 89–94 (2020). ISBN: 0028-0836, Nature Publishing Group UK London
13. Micocci, M., et al.: Attitudes towards trusting artificial intelligence insights and factors to prevent the passive adherence of GPs: a pilot study. J. Clin. Med. **10**(14), 3101 (2021). ISBN: 2077-0383, MDPI

14. Muir, B.M.: Trust between humans and machines, and the design of decision aids. Int. J. Man Mach. Stud. **27**(5–6), 527–539 (1987)
15. Nahata, H., Singh, S.P.: Deep learning solutions for skin cancer detection and diagnosis. In: Jain, V., Chatterjee, J.M. (eds.) Machine Learning with Health Care Perspective. LAIS, vol. 13, pp. 159–182. Springer, Cham (2020). https://doi.org/10.1007/978-3-030-40850-3_8, ISBN: 3030408493
16. Naiseh, M., Al-Thani, D., Jiang, N., Ali, R.: How the different explanation classes impact trust calibration: the case of clinical decision support systems. Int. J. Hum Comput Stud. **169**, 102941 (2023)
17. Ribeiro, M.T., Singh, S., Guestrin, C.: "Why should i trust you?" Explaining the predictions of any classifier. In: Proceedings of the 22nd ACM SIGKDD International Conference on Knowledge Discovery and Data Mining, pp. 1135–1144 (2016)
18. Ronneberger, O., Fischer, P., Brox, T.: U-Net: convolutional networks for biomedical image segmentation. In: Navab, N., Hornegger, J., Wells, W., Frangi, A. (eds.) Medical Image Computing and Computer-Assisted Intervention–MICCAI 2015: 18th International Conference, Munich, Germany, 5–9 October 2015, Proceedings. LNCS, Part III 18, pp. 234–241. Springer, Cham (2015). https://doi.org/10.1007/978-3-319-24574-4_28
19. Shin, D.: The effects of explainability and causability on perception, trust, and acceptance: implications for explainable AI. Int. J. Hum Comput Stud. **146**, 102551 (2021)
20. Topol, E.J.: High-performance medicine: the convergence of human and artificial intelligence. Nat. Med. **25**(1), 44–56 (2019)
21. Tucci, V., Saary, J., Doyle, T.E.: Factors influencing trust in medical artificial intelligence for healthcare professionals: a narrative review. J. Med. Artif. Intell. **5**(4) (2022)
22. Wang, X., Yin, M.: Are explanations helpful? A comparative study of the effects of explanations in AI-assisted decision-making. In: 26th International Conference on Intelligent User Interfaces, pp. 318–328 (2021)
23. Woodcock, C., Mittelstadt, B., Busbridge, D., Blank, G.: The impact of explanations on layperson trust in Artificial Intelligence-driven symptom checker apps: experimental study. J. Med. Internet Res. **23**(11), e29386 (2021). ISBN: 1438-8871, JMIR Publications, Toronto, Canada
24. Čartolovni, A., Tomičić, A., Mosler, E.L.: Ethical, legal, and social considerations of AI-based medical decision-support tools: a scoping review. Int. J. Med. Inform. **161**, 104738 (2022). ISBN: 1386-5056, Elsevier

More than Words: Visualizing AI-Based Analysis of Human-to-Human Communication Training in Healthcare Education

Fabian Samek(✉) [ID], Markus Dresel [ID], and Nicole Jochems [ID]

Institute of Multimedia and Interactive Systems (IMIS), University of Luebeck, Ratzeburger Allee 160, 23562 Lübeck, Germany
f.samek@uni-luebeck.de
https://www.imis.uni-luebeck.de

Abstract. This paper presents the interface development of an AI-based analysis tool for communication training in healthcare contexts as part of higher education. The key functionality consists of a visualization of communication features for students and lecturers, which is based on audio recording and AI-based analyzing of roleplays. The output contains a transcription as well as charts showing each speaker's speaking time, pitch, loudness, and speech rate. In terms of methodology, a human-centered approach was followed to construct the interface by designing usage scenarios and iteratively engaging stakeholders in the process. Formative evaluations significantly contributed to the emerging web-based system that visualizes communication analysis data to complement the retrospective discussion. The system also assists in pre-configuring and recording the communication training. First qualitative results based on preliminary use in practice indicate high user acceptance and positive interest. Skepticism and uncertainties have scarcely been observed. Moreover, users perceive the effort of usage to be in good proportion to the resulting benefit. This paper comprises the essence of the product's evolution as well as its most recent version with its key features concerning visualization, and first evaluation results that point to its added value.

Keywords: Communication Training · Healthcare Education · Human-Computer Interaction · Visualization · Interactive Systems · User Interface Design · Artificial Intelligence

1 Introduction

Scientific research indicates that effective communication plays a key role in healthcare (i.e. [1, 11]) as it delivers valuable and sometimes life-saving information. Examinations show that 50% of diagnoses are derived from the spoken content exchanged in doctor-patient conversations [2]. Practicing such communication situations has gained a growing emphasis within healthcare education in the last decades, particularly focusing on empathy and communication skills [10]. An increasingly common approach involves experiential learning through the simulation of communication scenarios. In

C. Stephanidis et al. (Eds.): HCII 2024, CCIS 2119, pp. 352–362, 2024.
https://doi.org/10.1007/978-3-031-61966-3_38

these courses (see Sect. 3), students participate in roleplay exercises, acting in the roles of healthcare professionals engaging in communication scenarios with fellow students or professional actors. Typically, these exercises begin with a briefing outlining the context and respective roles. And afterwards a feedback discussion gives space for the students to reflect on the roleplay, sharing their perceptions, thoughts, and feelings. Both the roleplay and the reflective feedback discussion are valuable for the learning process.

Our project consists of multidisciplinary institutes in fields of computer science (signal processing, telematics, human-computer interaction) as well as health sciences (i.e. medicine, psychology, nursing, midwifery, or health care sciences). The overall objective is to investigate potential benefits and problems of an AI-based assistance system used in the process of communicational training. While the involved domain experts focus on didactic concepts, social implications as well as usage requirements, the development team works on flexible audio processing, performant AI calculations as well as an adequate user interface. Concerning the user interface, the following research question can be posed to address the main goals of usability and user experience factors: How should the data be visualized, so that the communication training is augmented by objective data, enriching the feedback discussion?

While there is existing research on situational and more abstract feedback assistance given during medical conversations [9], the web-based "CoSy" (Communication Support System) functions by recording and analyzing conversations without intervening in between. It rather gives the opportunity to retrospectively use this output in the feedback discussion [6]. The output includes a visualized transcription of the conversation and various charts showing communication features (CF) such as pitch, loudness, speech rate, speaking times, and speech pauses. These objective measures can complement and enrich the subjective experience and perception of the roleplay. However, given the conversation's sensitive health context, the development process and adherence to data protection requirements present significant challenges.

The study was conducted to determine usable visualization methods for the generated analysis data, balancing didactic value with minimal disruption to existing workflows. This paper specifically addresses the process of the system's interface design, including methodology (see Sect. 2), scenario development (see Sect. 3), and two iterations (see Sects. 4 and 5) including the interface development and evaluations.

2 Methods

Following the human-centered design process, our system development was guided by user characteristics, contextual information, and workflow requirements. The analysis was particularly shaped by the scenario-based design approach [3] and included observations in real communication courses as well as interviews focusing on user needs and preferences. These findings served as the basis for constructing and discussing usage scenarios (see Sect. 3) with lecturers and stakeholders. The design process followed an iterative approach, with multiple workshops held to define and refine system requirements. Regular consultations with project stakeholders and lecturers ensured ongoing user involvement throughout the development process.

In the initial iteration (see Sect. 4.1), we designed the first prototype, which was formatively evaluated through qualitative usability testing (N = 16). In the second iteration, we improved our design prototype based on the results, and implemented the web application (see Sect. 4.2). The interdisciplinary project team provided valuable feedback on system features, information architecture, and usability aspects. To identify and address potential usability issues, we conducted heuristic evaluations with usability experts and usability tests with lecturers (see Sect. 5.1).

3 Usage Scenario

This chapter presents a selection of visual and textual sketches illustrating the observed contexts of system usage, which is rooted in interviews and observations. These scenarios serve as valuable tools for understanding the practical application and workflow of our system within real-world contexts. The context of communication courses as described before (see Sect. 1) can be divided into three distinct phases.

3.1 Visual Sketches

Introduction and Briefing. The first phase of the course involves an introduction (see Fig. 1, left), providing organizational details about the course, including learning goals and specific content relevant to upcoming communication practices. Prior to commencing roleplays, a student is selected and briefed for their assigned role. If professional actors are involved, they ideally receive pre-briefing instructions. Additionally, the CoSy system must be set up for the upcoming recording.

Roleplay. The *roleplay* (see Fig. 1, center) is the key phase where the communication practice is taking place. Other students are observing the situation in the same or a different room. Meanwhile the presented system's recording must be initiated at the start and stopped at the end.

Feedback Discussion. After a roleplay the communication situation is being discussed in the *feedback discussion* (see Fig. 1, right) with everyone. Depending on the subject and objectives, the observation and reflection of emotions, thoughts and conflicts is the focus of discussion. At this point the system's analysis output is meant to be conducted. At the end, another briefing session can be held to prepare for the next cycle.

Fig. 1. From left to right: 1) *Introduction & Briefing*, 2) *Roleplay* and 3) *Feedback Discussion* are common phases in communication courses.

3.2 Textual Sketches

The objective was to manifest a basis for discussion and common understanding. Thus, a textual scenario was developed offering rich and concrete contextual information. The following excerpt shows an example from the information scenario.

'The lecturer takes the floor and asks Tom: "How are you?". He replies: "Quite okay, but my heart is still beating very hard. I found the conversation very intense. I felt totally helpless at first when the patient wouldn't stop talking. It was super difficult to move the conversation forward." When an observer comments that she feels Tom was speaking very quickly, the lecturer first shows the analysis of the voices. The most important features are roughly visualized: Summaries and salient points are shown over time: Speech rate (compared to the patient; with indication of variability), loudness (with indication of variability; compared to the patient or an average), pitch (recognized baseline; progression including deviations), speech flow (pauses within words and sentences, filler words).'

3.3 Claims

In the scenario-based design process, claims are traits associated with the scenario that have a positive or negative impact on the user or the user experience [3] (see Table 1). As a usability claim they can also describe specific aspects of usability (see Table 2). These can be used as a requirement base for further designing.

Table 1. A selection of claims based on the scenario-based design [3].

1) The feedback discussion (see Fig. 1, right) is a key component of the learning process
+ The system can bring valuable insights to verify observations
+ The system can generate discussion material
– The system might prejudice the participants in terms of their perception
2) Visual overviews can quickly and easily create an insight into the situation's key aspects and attributes
+ An arbitrary navigation over the time axis is possible
+ The user can change the scope of the analyzed segment
– Statistics, approximations, and interferences might distort the generated data
– Comparisons with average data or reference groups might provoke unintended validations or judgements
– Highly complex or non-transparent charts and visualizations might induce confusions or/and wrong deductions

Table 2. A selection of usability claims [3].

3) The user in the teaching context is given an overview and details of analyzed communication features (CF)
• The given amount of information must be appropriate to the teaching task • Every screen view must be simple and clear
4) Different CF have different importances depending on the specific situations and objectives
• Different amounts of detail must be obtainable
• The navigation system must be easy to understand and execute
5) The usage context itself includes high consume of time and effort
• The system usage must bring a positive benefit-cost ratio • Long loading times must be avoided • Usage errors must quickly be solved or handled

4   First Iteration

The first iteration resulted in an interactive prototype that, while not fully functional, generates preliminary discussion material to facilitate early evaluation. The prototype comprises a comprehensive menu structure, although the focus of this paper is on the visualization aspect of the AI-based analysis.

4.1   Prototype Development

A modular design approach was adopted to provide the users with the flexibility to access specific analysis features without provoking biases as the reflective classroom discussion should not be unintendedly anticipated.

The transcript serves as a central component, offering users an overview of the conversation. Structured sequentially akin to a chat, the transcript occupies the right side of the screen, allowing simultaneous interaction with analysis features on the left side. An audio replay tool enables users to navigate through the audio recording. Furthermore, the prototype encompasses the following features:

1. *Voice Analysis.* Based on a line chart (see Fig. 2, left), users can observe time-based data of voice features such as speech rate, pitch, and loudness for each speaker. The visualization includes average metrics and reference lines, aiding the deduction of the speakers' emotional states and interactions with their collocutors.
2. *Pauses.* Tracking and displaying pauses (see Fig. 2, right) offers insight into conversation fluency and individual speaker dynamics. The prototype includes total counts, average metrics, and visualizations of pauses over time to facilitate analysis of conversation flow and speaker engagement.
3. *Speaking Times.* Visualized through pie charts (see Fig. 3, left), it gives insight into each speaker's quantitative contribution to the conversation. A stacked line chart displays the accumulated speaking times over time, revealing distinctive conversation phases.

4. ***Overlaps and Interruptions.*** This feature highlights interferences in the conversation, particularly simultaneous speech (see Fig. 3, right). Total counts and visualizations of speaking times over time might provide additional context.
5. ***Filler Words.*** Counting of filler words (see Fig. 4, right) reflects individual communication habits, shedding light on conversational patterns and styles.
6. ***Word Cloud.*** Representing the semantic content of conversations, the word cloud lists frequently used terms (see Fig. 4, left). Further categorization of words may enhance the analysis.

Fig. 2. Left: The feedback analysis view; right: Pause widget as a CF

Fig. 3. Left: The Analysis view with the transcript; right: Interruptions widget as a CF

Fig. 4. Left: Word cloud widget as a CF; right: Filler words as a CF

4.2 Formative Evaluation

To identify usability issues and assess the alignment with user and context requirements, a semi-structured interview evaluation was conducted. Participants used the thinking aloud method [4] to vocalize their thoughts and feelings. Observations were documented to capture user feedback comprehensively. Sixteen participants took part in the study, comprising lecturers (N = 3) and students (N = 13) from diverse disciplines (medicine, psychology, physiotherapy, nursing, and health science programs). Most had prior communication course experience (N = 14), with some engaging in simulated role plays (N = 10). Participants' average technology affirmation score [5] was slightly above average (M = 3.84, SD = 0.85, α = -0.5). Each evaluation session began with a general and scenario-related introduction for the participant. They were then presented with the system's home view and guided through the CF one by one, where they interacted with the prototype while verbalizing thoughts or answering open questions. The following findings have been made.

1. *Voice Analysis:* Participants correctly identified the speech rate feature on the initial chart and matched colors with speakers accurately. However, some participants (N = 3) found it difficult to assess the chart due to lack of context. Suggestions were made to emphasize the student's data.
2. *Speaking Times:* All participants understood the pie chart and expressed positive impressions. A minor improvement leaned towards level pie chart segments. However, the feedback on the stacked line chart was polarized, with several participants (N = 8) finding it confusing or less "intuitive".
3. *Overlaps and Interruptions:* Participants were generally positive about the counts' objectivity and ease of understanding (N = 12). However, some participants found the counts complex or mistakable (N = 3) and questioned the definition of overlaps or interruptions (N = 5). While the visual chart received mostly positive feedback (N = 14), it also elicited confusion and criticism from some participants (N = 3). Suggestions included providing contextual information and identifying signals of active listening not defined as interruptions.
4. *Filler words:* This feature caused a broad positive reaction (N = 16), with comments like "clear," "interesting," or "important". Though, some noted that filler words are

generally not negative but can be used stylistically (N = 3). The suggestion for another word cloud showing filler words and their appearances emerged.

5. *Word cloud:* The frequency-based visualization of expressed words was correctly understood (N = 16). However, opinions regarding a leaner, less chaotic visualization of words was divergent (N = 6). Suggestions included incorporating other categories, such as positive and negative, relevant and irrelevant, or context words instead of key words. Displaying words that should have been mentioned but were not, was another suggestion (N = 3), or tracking when a technical term has been explained (N = 2). Participants emphasized that the classification strongly depends on the conversation context and interlocutor.

6. *Pauses:* The number and duration of pauses, as well as the visualization via bubbles in the progression diagram were understood correctly (N = 13). Feedback was mixed, with some participants viewing it as "important information" and others as "unclear." The bubble-based representation over time was de-scribed as "helpful" and "didactical," but also "irritating" and "not intuitive".

5   Second Iteration

Building upon the findings from the first iteration, a functional web application was set up to explore specific functionalities of communication analysis. The implementation involved simultaneous integration of the audio system and AI processing [6], although these aspects are not the focus of this paper. Due to interdisciplinary project constraints, a reduced set of features was implemented to facilitate evaluative testing in both laboratory and field settings.

The feedback analysis view underwent several changes based on user feedback (see Fig. 5). However, the general architecture of the view was well-received and adopted in the implementation. Notable enhancements include:

- Addition of detailed elements to the transcript, such as colored bars representing the duration of spoken content, labels indicating speakers, and timestamps
- Replacement of generic labels with specific roles chosen for the case.
- Inclusion of pauses between spoken chunks.
- Individual cards for voice analysis features (pitch, loudness, and speech rate), enabling simultaneous observation, with interactive linking between transcript and charts for contextualizing data.
- Each analysis feature is focusable, allowing for a more detailed view through an overlay.

5.1   Second Formative Evaluation

Heuristic Evaluation. This evaluation asking usability experts (N = 6) aimed to identify common usability issues such as system status visibility, consistency, standards adherence, and flexibility. Each session lasted between 1 to 1.5 h. Initially, the ten heuristics [7] were presented on a prepared Miro board for further elaboration. Participants explored the user interface via predefined usage tasks. Throughout the evaluation, participants noted usability issues and proposed solutions on the Miro board.

Fig. 5. This view represents an example feedback analysis view. While the CF are displayed on the left, the opened transcript is placed on the right.

Usability Testing. Additionally, lecturers were acquired for qualitative usability tests (N = 5) to do a holistic evaluation of the implemented interface considering usability issues and user experience factors. Again, the interview and the thinking aloud methods were used to gain transparent insights into the user interaction. Each session lasted one hour and revealed several positive and negative aspects concerning the user interface.

Results. The heuristic expert evaluation generated the following results.

- *Help and Documentation:* Participants observed that the charts did not indicate the ability to zoom in and out on data. An information button providing interaction advice was recommended.
- *Match between system and real world*: Some participants found the paragraphing in the transcript confusing, particularly when the respective speaker did not change. Another highlighted aspect was the lack of opportunity to identify parts of the conversation spoken extraordinarily loud or fast. A suggestion was to implement a hovering interaction to highlight corresponding data points in the voice analysis charts.
- *Aesthetics*: Inconsistencies in card sizes were noted, affecting the visual alignment.
- *Error Prevention*: Participants found it challenging to identify the roles of conversation participants. It was suggested to globally display the speakers' roles.

The usability tests with lecturers resulted in the following findings.

- *General Impression:* Participants generally had positive impressions of the system, noting its ability to concretize discussions about communication. Specifically, they appreciated the system's navigational capabilities through different communication features (CF), describing it as "nice," "clear," and "simple."
- *Data Interpretation Challenges*: A recurring concern was the classification and contextualization of data. Participants expressed uncertainty about data interpretation due to a lack of comparable reference values. Especially, the speaking times were perceived to lack context. It was also questioned if pitch constancy equals speech monotony and if recorded voice differs from recorded background noises.
- *Suggestions*: Following optimizations or new features were proposed.

    1. Additional information to explain data in relation to conversation context, either through textual explanations or reference data.
    2. Documenting and displaying learning objectives to enhance data review.
    3. Globally displaying the role play's speaker roles and case information.
    4. Adding a counting feature for technical terms in *speaking times*, with the ability to pre-configure relevant terms.
    5. Displaying *pauses* in the transcript based on configurable duration thresholds.
    6. Showing average values and variances in *voice analysis*

6   Conclusion and Next Steps

This project explores the application of an AI-based assistance system in healthcare communication courses, aiming to analyze and visualize communication features to enhance retrospective feedback discussions. The iterative development process has led to the creation of a sophisticated web application, enabling lecturers to prepare and control recordings to eventually access the analysis results. Qualitative findings based on formative evaluations, engaging real users and usability experts uncovered several usability issues. Above all, it was found out that the system is giving new insights into (simulated) communication situations that, on one hand, are seen to enrich the feedback discussion, and on the other hand, bear challenges in contextualizing and interpreting the data. Consequently, interpretation guidance should be considered. A final iteration will integrate latest evaluations (see Sects. 4 and 5) for a summative evaluation of the final prototype. Additional usability measures should also be considered in these future investigations, i.e. acceptance or more objective metrics like usage-errors or task-completion-times. This could shed more light on the incorporation of AI-based technologies in communication analysis and especially the visual presentation.

Acknowledgements. This work is funded by the German Federal Ministry of Education and Research (BMBF) and the regional government of the state of Schleswig-Holstein, Germany under project number 16DHBKI075.

Disclosure of Interests. The authors have no competing interests to declare that are relevant to the content of this article.

References

1. Abdullatif Alnaser, F.: Effective communication skills and patient's health. CPQ Neurol. Psychol. **3**(4), 01–11 (2020)
2. Egger, J.W.: Fakten zur Bedeutung der Arzt-Patient-Kommunikation. JAMA **298**, 993–1001 (2007)
3. Rosson, M.B., Carroll, J.M.: Usability Engineering: Scenario-Based Development of Human-Computer Interaction. Morgan Kaufmann (2002)
4. Jørgensen, A.H.: Thinking-aloud in user interface design: a method promoting cognitive ergonomics. Ergonomics **33**(4), 501–507 (1990)
5. Franke, T., Attig, C., Wessel, D.: A personal resource for technology interaction: development and validation of the affinity for technology interaction (ATI) scale. Int. J. Hum.-Comput. Interact. **35**(6), 456–467 (2019)
6. Samek, F., Eulers, M., Dresel, M., Jochems, N., Schrader, A., Mertins, A.: CoSy-AI enhanced assistance system for face to face communication trainings in higher healthcare education: AI enhanced assistance system for face to face communication trainings in higher healthcare education. In: Proceedings of the 16th International Conference on PErvasive Technologies Related to Assistive Environments, pp. 457–460 (2023, July)
7. Nielsen, J., Molich, R.: Heuristic evaluation of user interfaces. In: Proceedings of the ACM CHI 1990 Conference, Seattle, pp. 249–256 (1990)
8. Samek, F.: Development of a Prototypical User Interface of an AI-based Assistance System for Retrospective Feedback in Communication Training in Health Degree Program, [Unpublished master's thesis in German]. University of Luebeck, Institute of Multimedia and Interactive Systems (2022)
9. Patel, R.A., Hartzler, A., Pratt, W., Back, A., Czerwinski, M., Roseway, A.: Visual feedback on nonverbal communication: a design exploration with healthcare professionals. In: 2013 7th International Conference on Pervasive Computing Technologies for Healthcare and Workshops, Venice, pp. 105–112 (2013)
10. Stamer, T., Essers, G., Steinhäuser, J., Flägel, K.: From summative MAAS global to formative MAAS 2.0–a workshop report. GMS J. Med. Educ. **40**(1) (2023)
11. Stamer, T., Steinhäuser, J., Flägel, K.: Artificial intelligence supporting the training of communication skills in the education of health care professions: scoping review. J. Med. Internet Res. **25**, e43311 (2023)
12. Egger, J.W., Pieringer, W., Wisiak, U.V.: Das Lehrprogramm zu Medizinischer Psychologie, Psychosomatik und Psychotherapie in der aktuellen Diplomstudienordnung Humanmedizin an der Medizinischen Universität Graz. Psychol. Med. **18**(1), 44–52 (2007)

Progress in Computer Aided Surgery and Future Challenges

Kazuhiko Shinohara(✉)

School of Health Sciences, Tokyo University of Technology, Tokyo 1448535, Japan
kazushin@stf.teu.ac.jp

Abstract. The computer aided surgery (CAS) is a new interdisciplinary field that emerged in the 1990s. In the field of medical images, three-dimensional reconstruction of CT images, virtual endoscopy, surgical navigation has been put into practical use and they are widely used in clinical surgery. In the field of surgical manipulation, active forceps for endoscopic surgery and surgical robots have been developed and used in clinical surgery. Recently, there has also been research into automatic recognition of surgical procedure, risk warning, and surgeon skill evaluation using artificial intelligence (AI). CAS requires further human-computer interface improvements in the following areas. In the imaging field, it is necessary to improve the human-computer interface to enable rapid and intuitive image construction. The burden of eye strain must also be solved when wearing a head mounted display. Surgical robots enable intuitive surgical operations inside the patient's body. However, burdens on human resources and required time required for preparation, tidying-up and sterilization of surgical robots remains unresolved. Also, the problem of sudden computer freezes during surgery remains unresolved. Furthermore, the interface for integrated control of various medical equipment in the operating room, such as imaging equipment and energy devices, has not yet been completed. The CAS is also expected to be applied to advanced anatomical research, medical device development, hospital management by using a large amount of surgical information in the Big Data.

Keywords: Computer aided surgery · Surgical robotics · Image guided surgery

1 Introduction

Computer Aided Surgery (CAS) is a new interdisciplinary field that emerged in the late 20th century. The progress of CAS was driven by the demands of endoscopic surgery, which requires remote manipulation under the limitations of stereoscopic vision and tactile sensation. TThe themes of CAS include the research and development of surgical support systems such as robotics, imaging, navigation, and endoscopy. As a surgeon who has conducted research and development in computer surgery, the outline and problems of CAS are investigated [1, 2].

C. Stephanidis et al. (Eds.): HCII 2024, CCIS 2119, pp. 363–368, 2024.
https://doi.org/10.1007/978-3-031-61966-3_39

2   Computer Aided Imaging

Three dimensional CT images, along with virtual endoscopy, are one of the results of CAS, which was developed by utilizing advances in Information and Computer Technology (ICT) and medical imaging equipment such as CT and MRI. Doi and Hashimoto have also been working on re-constructing three-dimensional CT images of the liver since the 1980s, supporting laser treatment of liver cancer using ultrasound-guided puncture. Before the advent of high-performance Multi-Detector helical CT, the liver surface was constructed using Christiansen's Triangular Face Representation method based on 10 mm slice CT images. In addition, the vessels were constructed three-dimensionally using the Generalized Cylinder Representation method. Hashimoto used the surface rendering method, which depicts the surface shape as a collection of triangular patches, as a method to depict the surface shape of an organ [3] Fig. 1.

With the development of ICT, other methods such as volume rendering methods have also come into use. Then, in the early 2000s, functions such as the calculation of residual liver volume, portal vein branch perfusion area, and hepatic vein perfusion area were put into practical use. Surgical simulations that include functional aspects and virtual hepatectomy are also used in daily clinical practice. At the same time, advances are being made to more advanced surgical navigation during the operation.

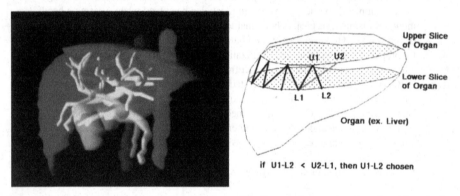

Fig. 1. Three dimensional reconstructed images of the liver and reconstruction algorithms in the early days of CAS [3]

3   Surgical Navigation System

Surgical navigation has been researched and developed mainly in the area of endoscopic surgery due to limitations of surgical field and spatial recognition with complex anatomical structures such as the liver and brain. Surgical navigation consists of the process of acquiring image data from various diagnostic imaging devices as DICOM data, extracting and positioning organs, and presentation as the integrated information for surgeons.

Segmentation is the process of identifying organs and lesions from medical images and extracting them as three-dimensional information. Registration technology is essential for integrated display of different types of medical images such as CT, Ultrasonography and MRI, as well as for responding to the displacement and deformation of organs due to body position and surgical maneuvers during surgical procedures. Various algorithms for registration have been used in recent years, including methods using artificial intelligence (AI).

Registration is easy in the field of orthopedic surgery, which targets bones and joints, as there is little deformation. But registration of the liver, bile ducts, pancreas, and gastrointestinal tract fields, where organs are significantly displaced and deformed during surgical operations are highly difficult (non-rigid registration).

As methods for creating organ deformation models for non-rigid registration, methods such as the finite element method and sphere-filled model have been developed [4, 5] (Fig. 2).

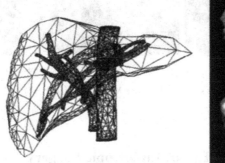
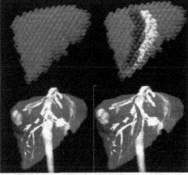

Finite element method for liver deformation simulation [4]   Sphere-filled model for liver incision simulation [5]

Fig. 2. Methods of deformation simulation

Three-dimensional position measurement of the surgical field is important for accurate registration during intraoperative navigation. Today, two methods are commonly used. The optical three-dimensional position measuring method, which measures the position of an infra-red reflective marker attached to a surgical instrument. The magnetic three-dimensional position measuring method, which uses a sensor to measure the magnetic field intensity from a magnetic field generator outside the body.

The optical measuring method has the limitation that it cannot measure markers in positions that cannot be observed by the camera. While the magnetic measuring method suffers from noise and errors due to electro-magnetic interference with other medical equipment. In recent years, advances in computer vision have been utilized to develop methods for automatically extracting feature points from living organs and measuring the three-dimensional shape of objects. All systems must be non-contact and sterilizable to be suitable for intraoperative use. Furthermore, since image accuracy depends on the performance of the position sensor, further improvements in sensing technology are required.

In this way, surgical navigation has progressed from the simple three-dimensional image reconstruction to the image processing and integration of preoperative and intra-operative images obtained from multiple medical imaging devices such as CT, MRI, and ultrasonography. We have now reached the stage where the real image and virtual image of the surgical site are integrated, augmented, and presented as a superimposed image to the surgeon and the surgical field. In addition to stereoscopic glasses and head mounted displays (HMDs), various presentation methods such as holograms, projection onto the real surgical field and the display system of a surgical robot have been developed in recent years [2] Fig. 3.

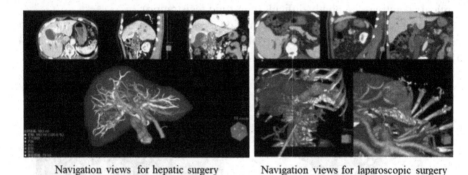

Navigation views for hepatic surgery   Navigation views for laparoscopic surgery

Fig. 3. Computer navigation images for surgery: Synapse Vincent (FUJIFILM)™ [2]

4 Development of CAS in the Era of Endoscopic Surgery and Robot-Assisted Surgery

Endoscopic surgery in Japan has rapidly spread since its inception in 1990, but surgeons are burdened with manual manipulation under two-dimensional images in a narrow working space under pneumoperitoneum. In order to improve the safety of endoscopic surgery and reduce the burden on surgeons, various research and developments have been carried out, ranging from active forceps to surgical support robots. The surgical robot system da Vinci™ dominated the global market over 20 years after its release. Now, many other surgical robots such as hinotori™ were also released.

In endoscopic surgery, it is essential to provide visual information from the surgical field. Stereoscopic endoscopes have been on the market since the 1990s, but they did not become popular because the unnaturally enhanced stereoscopic images caused a severe eye strain. Humans obtain a sense of perspective and stereopsis by using various visual cues, such as convergence, binocular disparity and accommodation. In Japan, research results such as stereoscopic endoscopes that utilize binocular disparity other than convergence have been reported, efforts have been made to improve displays to reduce eye strain, and sales of stereoscopic endoscopes have continued. These experience in developing stereoscopic endoscopes is also being utilized in surgical robotics system (Fig. 4).

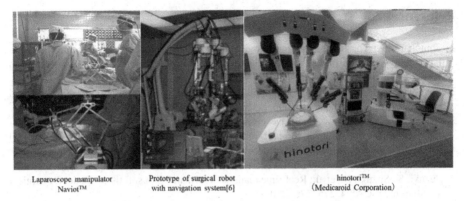

Laparoscope manipulator   Prototype of surgical robot   hinotori™
Naviot™   with navigation system[6]   (Medicaroid Corporation)

Fig. 4. Development of Surgical robotics system in Japan

5 Challenges and Prospects

Research and developments of CAS targets not only surgical support systems but also problem solving such as surgical education and medical safety. Research is underway to automatically analyze surgical videos and evaluate surgeon's technic using AI. Today's young surgeons, who were born after the advent of endoscopic surgery, have experience performing routine surgeries such as appendectomy, cholecystectomy, gastrointestinal resection, and pneumothorax under endoscopic guidance without experience of conventional open surgeries. Although surgical robots can be operated more intuitively than conventional endoscopic surgery, there is a need to emergent transfer technique from endoscopic surgery to open-surgery in case of massive bleeding and fatal damage of tissues. So, high-functional simulator for surgical training and a technology evaluation AI system are developed. These are also new targets for CAS. CAS is also expected to be applied to advanced anatomical research, medical device development, hospital management by using a large amount of surgical information data in the Big Data.

Surgical robots enable intuitive surgical operations inside the patient's body. However, burdens on human resources and required time required for preparation, tidying-up and sterilization of surgical robots remains unresolved. Also, the problem of sudden computer freezes during surgery remains unresolved.

In addition to improving the usability of navigation systems, it is also important to take further ergonomic considerations to prevent eye strain and neck-shoulder fatigue when using displays, HMDs and holograms. Until now, navigation system development efforts have been made only to accurate superimpose and display of a large amount of information. However, AI can select and present essential information for surgeons that is truly necessary to reduce the burden on surgeons.

Furthermore, the interface for integrated control of various medical equipment in the operating room, such as imaging equipment, energy devices and electronic medical record system, has not yet been completed. ICT technology is also important for improving the ergonomics of the entire surgical system.

References

1. Shinohara, K.: The feasibility of ontological description of medical device connectivity for laparoscopic surgery. In: Lightner, N. (ed.) Advances in Human Factors and Ergonomics in Healthcare and Medical Devices, pp. 88–95. Springer, Heidelberg (2019)
2. Shinohara, K.: Current status and prospects of computer aided surgery in hepatobiliary and pancreatic surgery (in Japanese). Operation **76**, 1645–1650 (2022)
3. Hashimoto, D., Dohi, T., et al.: Development of a computer-aided surgery system: three-dimensional graphic reconstruction for treatment of liver cancer. Surgery **109**, 589–596 (1991)
4. Chen, X., Sakuma, I., et al.: Liver deformation simulation using nonlinear finite element method. JJSCAS **4**, 279–280 (2002)
5. Suzuki, S., Suzuki, N., et al.: Real-time realistic deformations of soft tissue model for surgical simulation. JJSCAS **4**, 275–276 (2002)
6. Sakuma, I.: Development of surgical robotic system –JSPS research for the future program (in Japanese). J. Robot. Soc. Japan **23**, 535–537 (2005)

A Comparative Literature Study on the Persuasive Impact of Animation, Live-Action Film and Static Image in Healthcare Science Communication

Yi Su[✉]

Tongji University, 1239 Siping Road, Shanghai 200092, China
suyi2018@tongji.edu.cn

Abstract. In the digital age, animation is increasingly being used in healthcare science communication to present scenes which is difficult to shoot by camera and to visualize movements. However, the correlation between animation's attributes and its effectiveness is unclear, and related studies have often investigated the functions of multimedia without distinguishing between animation and other media. This leads designers and healthcare information providers to have an ambiguous understanding of the function of animation and to be unable to make the appropriate utilization of it. A continuation of my earlier research on animation as a persuasive tool in healthcare communication, this paper reviews the healthcare science communication literature and compares the functions of animation, live-action film, and static image within the framework of rhetorical appeal: Logos, Ethos, and Pathos. Through comparison and analysis, it is found that besides the functions and creative methods common to visual media, animation also has a unique time-reality communication function, as well as broad and flexible temporal and spatial rhetorical dimensions. It prompts the creators of medical animation to explore its potential fully.

Keywords: Animation · live-action film · static image · Healthcare Science Communication

1 Introduction

Visual media is used in healthcare scientific communication to present knowledge and ideas. Animation, as non-documentary, can visualize changes and scenes that are difficult to record by camera [1]. Its effectiveness in disseminating scientific knowledge and advice has been repeatedly demonstrated. As media properties are the basis for information dissemination [10], the nature of animation determines the form it is designed and has an important impact on meaning production and effective communication.

However, the conjunctive function of animation with other media is viewed as proof of animation's effectiveness in many studies [4, 27]. At the same time, contradictory results of the functional superiority of animation and other media are shown in different studies [4, 5, 8]. This reflects the ambiguous knowledge of the relevance and the influence factor of animation and the healthcare science communication context [3]. This will prevent healthcare science animation from fully achieving its superiority, which is of significant task in the digital age.

To distinguish the functions of animation from other media, this article reviews the literature on the function of animation, live-action film, and static image in healthcare science communication and makes a comparison. This paper aims to help health science information providers and animators recognize the uniqueness of animation from other media and choose more proper use of it.

In previous research, I defined the function of animation in conveying information, and changing viewer attitudes and behaviors as persuasive impact [6]. The persuasive impact is more complicated than simply completing an information transmission. Persuasion is determined by trust, individual experience, emotion, etc., of the intended viewer. This study continues the exploration of the function of persuasion, and adopts rhetoric as the theoretical framework. Rhetoric is the art of persuading. Aristotle proposed three rhetorical appeals (Logos, Ethos, and Pathos) that influence persuasion. The persuasive nature of media is inextricably reflected in the rhetorical appeal it produces.

The live-action film is a documentary motion image, and the static image represents a flat illustration without a timeline. They contrast with animation in both temporal and spatial dimensions, respectively. Animation's rhetorical appeals are compared with those of live-action film and static images to demonstrate the relation of the persuasive impact with the nature of media.

This article searches for literature on Google Academic Database using keywords of animation, live-action film, static image, graphic, healthcare science communication, etc. Then, literature is selected based on relevance, citation count, and impact factors of published journals. The rhetorical appeals of each medium are reviewed and compared. The commonalities and uniqueness of media in the context are analyzed and discussed sequentially.

This paper will improve the awareness of animation's unique persuasive function in healthcare science communication. It will contribute to digital healthcare, and animation's shift from film and television art to design, which promotes the creation of images in the digital age to improve real life.

2   Method

2.1   Literature Selection

Google Scholar is the main search database. In terms of scope, the research topic of the selected article is the function of relevant visual media in the field of medical science. Keywords include animation, live-action film, illustration, medical/healthcare science communication, etc. In terms of quality evaluation, the number of citations and the impact factors of publishing platforms are used to evaluate the quality of articles and select the best ones. Finally, 30 articles were selected, some articles involve multiple media.

2.2 Theoretical Framework

The rhetorical appeal refers to the *Logos, Ethos, and Pathos* of an argument that determines the effectiveness of persuasion. *Logos* is the logical structure of the argument [7]. The Logos of a healthcare science visual communication tool is how the visual materials are organized. It is closely related to the nature of the visual media. The Logos of the animated film consists of temporal and spatial elements and the form they are composited. A live-action film has a similar form of temporal narrative to an animated film, but its documentary scene differs from animation's non-documentary scene. It provides a **documentary & non-documentary spatial form comparison**. Static image has a similar spatial form to animated films, but static images don't contain a sequential timeline. The timeline of a static image is formed by the time and order of the viewer's viewing. Static images provide a **sequential & non-sequential timeline comparison.** The viewer's rational thinking, such as comprehension, recalling, etc., is seen as the performance of Logos.

Ethos refers to the trustworthiness of the author. The healthcare information provider and visual artist are the authors of a healthcare science communication work [7]. The viewer's influences on Ethos are noticed, too. Media-related Ethos are reviewed and compared.

Pathos refers to the emotional reflection of the viewer [7]. The media-related emotional reactions are identified and compared.

2.3 Analysis Procedural

Figure 1 shows the procedural of the review, sequentially including (1) the three media as the objects, (2) the rhetorical appeal as the theoretical framework, (3) the temporal and spatial character of animation's persuasive impact as the results, and (4) the advantages and disadvantages of animation as a tool of healthcare science communication as the reflection of the results.

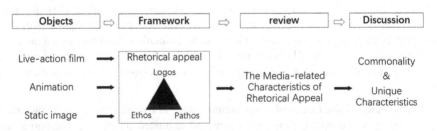

Fig. 1. The aspects of each stage of the review.

3   The Media-Related Persuasive Impact and Comparison

3.1   The Logos

The Character of the Logos of Medical Animation. Animation is non-documentary. It relies on the animation artist to present the envisioned motion picture. The flexibility of not being constrained by the physical condition and the rich temporal and spatial expressive space is the basis of its Logos.

Not constrained by the physical environment allows animated images to show microscopic organs, abstract relationships, movement, etc. [3]. At the same time, it can explain the image by adding text, labels, changing colors, adding special effects, etc. Animated images can be adapted between realism and abstract depending on the needs of the context, e.g., highly realistic animated images can be applied in contexts where organ details need to be observed [2], while abstract images are more inclusive when oriented toward complex preferences [28]. Ostherr K., similarly, suggests that when animated images selectively emphasize the main content and ignore secondary details, this not accurate and can instead give the surgeon viewing them the best training [22].

But the flexibility of visual presentation needs to be constrained by the specific nature. Corine S Meppelink, Julia CM van Weert, Carola J Haven, and Edith G Smit's research suggests that effective animation needs to avoid presenting content that is irrelevant to the subject matter [4]. This means that some decorative animations need to be examined to see whether they are impeding the dissemination of information. Ostherr K., similarly, suggests that when animated images selectively emphasize the main content and ignore secondary details, this *not accurate* and can instead give the surgeon viewing them the best training [22].

Multiple interpretations of a single animated image often exist. Animation needs to be combined with multiple media such as narration and text to improve accuracy. Mayer R. E. and Moreno R. et al. summarized effective multimedia pairings, including animation, confirming that a proper combination of animation with captioning and narration improves learners' comprehension [21]. Studies have shown that a combination of animation and voice-over narration can bridge the cognitive gap between viewers with high and low levels of health literacy to achieve equal levels of comprehension and memorization [4].

This hints at the strengths and weaknesses of animation. Image derives its meaning from the imitation of real visual experience and is a symbolic form of non-literal language, therefore animated works is interpreted based on an individual's visual experience. It has the advantage of being communicated across textual language. However, as scientific content requires precise communication, animation, and other visual language as well, needs to be carefully scrutinized in scientific communication, building on its figurative strengths, avoiding ambiguity and superfluous embellishments, and ensuring accuracy.

The Character of the Logos of Live-Action Film. A live-action film is characterized by recording a real scene. Both live-action and animated images have temporal and spatial dimensions, and their difference stems from the fact that in both dimensions, a live-action film is a documentary, while animation is non-documentary and fictional. In Per Erik Eriksson & Yvonne Eriksson's research on web video through macro-technical teaching (not for healthcare), four affordances of video are proposed, including verifiability, comparability, recordability, and these characteristics derive from following the basic principle of cinematic storytelling: "show, don't tell" and making full use of the camera to show performances and behaviors [29].

Ostherr K. claims that animation extends the picture of a live-action film by providing unfilmable content [22]. This reflects the limitations of live-action film in medical communication scenarios: it cannot show scenes that cannot be captured by a physical camera (e.g., when it is necessary to look through the surface to see the interior), and at the same time it cannot avoid capturing intrusive details [22]. However, the documentary nature of live-action filming gives the image strong credibility and reliably presents details.

Live-action film inevitably captures a real-world scenario that is rich in cultural and social information that may bring about additional effects on the viewer, such as gender, religion, race, etc., over and above the rational scientific content. These factors need to be circumvented or utilized in terms of the impact they may have on the viewer.

The Character of the Logos of Static Image.   The static image presents a visual space without an autonomous continuous timeline. It is used to present time by arranging static elements to guide the viewer's reading order and duration, creating a timeline formed by the viewer's autonomous reading. It is for readers who need to control their own reading time and sequence. Static images can also present a visual space with rich content, including photos, icons, illustrations, and other visual elements.

A study by Delp and Jones found that nursing instructions with images captured patients' attention [12]. Carney and Levin demonstrated that pictures can significantly enhance the comprehension level of students with low prior knowledge [15]. In a broader perspective, static images can have a more significant communication effect on viewers with lower levels of cognitive power [14]. Peter S. Houts et al. concluded that images are effective in all forms, whether abstract or cartoonish [12]. However, pictures are more helpful for interpretation when aided by text [15]. Experiments by Austin et al. showed that text with pictures allowed subjects to answer questions correctly at a rate (1.5 times more) than text only [13]. Pictures have been shown to aid long-term memory [20].

These studies confirm that static image is an effective health communication tool, which, like animation and live-action film, can bridge cognitive power differences, attract attention, help viewers to understand autonomously through visualization, and contribute to their adaptation to cross-cultural and long-distance communication via the Internet. Despite differences in timeline and documentability, static images can fulfill communication needs by being designed appropriately. However, the influence of the viewer's perceptions [15] suggests that the success of the Logos of static images is inextricably linked to the individual factors of the viewer, also.

3.2   The Ethos

Healthcare science information is a matter of personal safety for the viewer, and its accuracy, scientific validity, and integrity are the basis of the viewer's trust. Regardless of the medium, the healthcare communication authors include visual artists, healthcare information providers, and intended viewers. They engage and influence healthcare communication products' Ethos in a variety of ways.

Marsh C. M. et al. found that decorative animation is not conducive to learning, suggesting that the aesthetic expression of the visual artist needs to be constrained by the scientific nature of the image [9]. Diverse interpretations in artistic expression cannot be at the expense of scientific consequences. Ostherr K.'s study mentions "an expert medical director" on the creative team of a medical film, who is responsible for overseeing the professionalism of the film [22].

Involving the intended viewer in the development process of a visual product is a commonly recognized creative approach [16, 17]. When the intended group collaborates, the more effective pictograms are at conveying information about that group [17]. Under the concept of user-centered design, the intended user is essentially the most important co-creator. The provider of scientific information and the visual artist determines the form of the visual content based on the needs, preferences, and social attributes provided by the intended user. Kelly, C., Templeton, M. et al. invited young male inmates to co-create sex education animated shorts and received positive comments from them [24]. Co-creation puts the animator, the scientific information provider, and the intended viewer on the same page, ensuring that the interests of the intended viewer of the visual product are aligned, making the intended viewer more receptive to the subject conveyed in the film.

3.3 The Pathos

The Character of the Pathos of Animation. Healthcare sciences animations can elicit rich emotional responses. Kim's study showed that an animated vertical bar can be encouraging and emotionally supportive [25]. Andraka Christou's study showed that medical animation was favored among the student population because its graphics were "abstract enough to represent a range of students" [28]. The animation format emphasizes the communication of information and also affects the viewer's emotions. According to the previously mentioned, when filtering useful image content [4], by reducing the fear of facing human organs directly and increasing aesthetic pleasure, we can speculate that animation can reduce the negative impact of healthcare science information.

Kriegerd's study showed that virtual health assistants increased participants' willingness to talk about colorectal cancer screening information [26]. The viewer used the fictional animated "doctor" as an object of communication. On the one hand, this suggests that animated characters can create a communicative relationship with patients, and on the other hand, patients' preference for communicating with an animated "doctor" suggests that the animation design avoids the stress associated with a live doctor.

The Character of the Pathos of Live-action Film. Live-action videos is effective in increasing viewers' knowledge of the treatment process when used to deliver treatment plan presentations to patients, which in turn helps to dissipate their anxiety [30]. At the same time, the visual presentation of the content of the medical program and the team through the video has helped patients and their families to increase their confidence and reduce stigma [31]. According to the Logos section, the decisive difference between live-action video and animation is the documentation of real scenes. Although each medium can generate positive emotions in the viewer through the effective dissemination of information, the impact of live-action video on the viewer should be derived from the characteristics of the actual footage.

The Character of the Pathos of Static Image. A study by Delp and Jones found that nursing instructions with images captured patients' attention and made them more likely to read, understand, and act on the instructions [12]. In contrast to Walchtl and Ledesma et al.'s study [11], having patients and their families willing to turn their attention to medical information when they are in a generalized state of anxiety is a positive influence.

Associations and similarities between the image and the target viewer enhance the image's impact on the viewer's subsequent health behaviors [18]. Socio-cultural attributes of image content (e.g., gender relations [19]) can trigger different behaviors in viewers. The results of these studies can be extended to other visual media, suggesting that images derived from real life have an impact on viewers.

4 Discussion

Taken together, animation has both commonalities and important differences with live-action film and static image in terms of rhetorical appeals in healthcare communication. The differences between animation and live-action film and static image should be used to match appropriate contexts, but at the same time, their commonalities can be borrowed from each other.

4.1 Commonalities of Between Animation and Live-Action Film and Static Image

Animation, live-action film, and static image are effective Healthcare communication tools. They can effectively communicate information and influence the viewers' thoughts, emotions, and behaviors. There is a knowledge gap between professionals and viewers caused by medical terminology [12]. Animation, live-action image and static image can serve the purpose of illustrating terminology so that medical information can catch attention, be understood, memorized, and implemented [12].

The three visual media follow similar creative approaches. For example, there is a need to minimize the presentation of redundant visual information, to base the design on the cognitive style of the viewer, and to increase the accuracy of the information with text and narration [15]. The Logos of healthcare visual communication requires a balance between aesthetic presentation and rigor, which conflicts with the concept of artistic animation creation. Decoration and expression are often encouraged in artwork. But on a healthcare issue, as soon as a certain aesthetic expression interferes with the accuracy of the scientific information and the viewer's reception, it needs to be discarded. As Ostherr K. elucidates, although science and art seem to pursue different values, one must rely on the collaboration of the medical expert and the artist to best visualize the scientific content, which in turn translates into some rhetorical strategy [22].

The viewer is no longer passive, but an important participant in the development of content. The viewer's factors to the visual content have a decisive impact on their acceptance. Therefore, effective healthcare communication relies on the participation and evaluation of the target viewer.

Animations, static image, and live-action film can generate meaning through their visual similarity to human life so that they are not limited by textual boundaries. This is the basis on which imagery facilitates the dissemination of medical science knowledge globally and in different linguistic environments. Visual experience evocation is both rational and emotional. The use of evocative emotion to promote viewer acceptance of arguments is also a way to increase the effectiveness of scientific communication, provided that the accuracy of the rational content is ensured. There needs to be a balance between rationality and emotion.

4.2   Characteristics of Animation in Healthcare Communication

The advantage of animation over the other two mediums is its plasticity. Animation is better than live-action film at showing images that are difficult to capture; it can visualize dynamics better than still images. Reiser's research suggests that too much detail in medical images can make patients subjectively want to stay away [23]. To properly influence the viewer, animation allows for the retention of what is most important and the omission of what is irrelevant, in image and action. This constitutes a flexible rhetorical space for the author to construct a persuasive argument.

Supported by computer technology, animated characters are interactive, can be molded into personalities and appearances as needed, and generate continuous, real-time feedback as they interact with the viewer. It constructs a communicative relationship between real people and fictional personalities. It removes the bias that the socio-cultural context of real human beings may carry. This is impossible with live-action films and static images. A live-action image is a record of past time and cannot communicate with the present in "real-time". The static image does not have an ongoing timeline and like-wise cannot communicate with the present in "real-time". Therefore, among the three media, animation is the only one that can allow the viewer to communicate with the virtual world in a time-realized way.

This is a new possibility given to animation in the digital age. When an artificial personality and a real human can communicate, animation becomes a vehicle that can deeply influence human thoughts and emotions, and the potential for functionality in the communication of medical science could be enormous.

5   Limitations and Future Works

This paper is limited in space and covers only a limited amount of literature, so there may be more attributes of animation in Healthcare Science Communication that have not been revealed. Based on the existing findings, the influence of the viewer's socio-cultural background on the communication effectiveness of animation in healthcare science, and the characterization of animation as a time-real communication tool need to be further investigated.

6   Conclusion

This paper compares the characteristics of animation, live-action film, and static image in healthcare science communication from the perspective of rhetorical appeals. On the one hand, it clarifies the effectiveness and common creating methods of the three visual media in healthcare science communication and compares how animation differs from the other two media. Animation's plasticity allows it to adapt to the intended viewer's backgrounds and makes medical science communication potentially more persuasive. Digital interactive technology platforms allow animation to show its most prominent and unique potential, which is its ability to be used to create personable, real-time communication agents that generate deeper connections with patients in the healthcare field. With these findings, we can realize the dominant role of animation in healthcare science communication to use it wisely and do forward-looking development.

References

1. Preim, B., Meuschke, M.: A survey of medical animations. Comput. Graph. **90**, 145–168 (2020)
2. Habbal, O.A., Harris, P.F.: Teaching of human anatomy: a role for computer animation. J. Audiov. Media Med. **18**(2), 69–73 (1995)
3. Ruiz, J.G., Cook, D.A., Levinson, A.J.: Computer animations in medical education: a critical literature review. Med. Educ. **43**, 838–846 (2009)
4. Meppelink, C.S., van Weert, J.C., Haven, C.J., Smit, E.G.: The effectiveness of health animations in viewers with different health literacy levels: an experimental study. J. Med. Internet Res. **17**(1), e3979 (2015)
5. Tversky, B., Morrison, J.B., Betrancourt, M.: Animation: can it facilitate? Int. J. Hum Comput Stud. **57**(4), 247–262 (2002)
6. Su, Y.: The persuasive impact of animation in health care sciences services: a rhetoric-based literature study. In: Stephanidis, C., Antona, M., Ntoa, S., Salvendy, G. (eds.) HCII 2022. CCIS, vol. 1654, pp. 458–465. Springer, Heidelberg (2022)
7. Aristotle. On Rhetoric: A Theory of Civic Discourse. Oxford University, New York (2007)
8. Garg, A., et al.: Do virtual computer models hinder anatomy learning? Acad. Med. **74**(10), S87–S89 (1999)
9. Marsh, C.M., et al.: Design and effectiveness of a computer-based continuing education program for orthodontists. Angle Orthodontist **71**(1), 71–75 (2001)
10. McLuhan, M.: Understanding Media: The Extensions of Man. MIT Press (1994)
11. Wachtl, M., Ledesma, F., Malcolm, H., et al.: Animation supported communication on intensive care; a service improvement initiative. J. Intens. Care Soc. **23**(4), 433–438 (2022)
12. Houts, P.S., Doak, C.C., Doak, L.G., et al.: The role of pictures in improving health communication: a review of research on attention, comprehension, recall, and adherence. Patient Educ. Couns. **61**(2), 173–190 (2006)
13. Austin, P.E., Matlack, R., Dunn, K.A., Kosler, C., Brown, C.K.: Discharge instructions: do illustrations help our patients understand them? Ann. Emerg. Med. **25**, 317–320 (1995)
14. Michielutte, R., Bahnson, J., Dignan, M.B., et al.: The use of illustrations and narrative text style to improve readability of a health education brochure. J. Cancer Educ. **7**(3), 251–260 (1992)
15. Carney, R.N., Levin, J.R.: Pictorial illustrations still improve students' learning from text. Educ. Psychol. Rev. **14**, 5–26 (2002)
16. Roter, D.L., Rudd, R.E., Keogh, J., et al.: Worker produced health education material for the construction trades. Int. Q. Commun. Health Educ. **7**(2), 109–121 (1986)
17. Dowse, R., Ehlers, M.S.: The evaluation of pharmaceutical pictograms in a low-literate South African population. Patient Educ. Couns. **45**(2), 87–99 (2001)
18. Ngoh, L.N., Shepherd, M.D.: Design, development, and evaluation of visual aids for communicating prescription drug instructions to nonliterate patients in rural Cameroon. Patient Educ. Couns. **31**(3), 245–261 (1997)

19. Labranche, E.R., Helweg-Larsen, M., Byrd, C.E., et al.: To picture or not to picture: levels of erotophobia and breast self-examination brochure techniques 1. J. Appl. Soc. Psychol. **27**(24), 2200–2212 (1997)
20. Houts, P.S., Bachrach, R., Witmer, J.T., et al.: Using pictographs to enhance recall of spoken medical instructions. Patient Educ. Couns. **35**(2), 83–88 (1998)
21. Mayer, R.E., Moreno, R.: Animation as an aid to multimedia learning. Educ. Psychol. Rev. **14**, 87–99 (2002)
22. Ostherr, K.: Operative bodies: live action and animation in medical films of the 1920s. J. Vis. Cult. **11**(3), 352–377 (2012)
23. Reiser, S.J.: Technological Medicine: The Changing World of Doctors and Patients (2009)
24. Kelly, C., Templeton, M., Allen, K., Lohan, M.: Improving sexual healthcare delivery for men in prison: a nurse-led initiative. J. Clin. Nurs. **29**(13–14), 2285–2292 (2020)
25. Kim, S., Trinidad, B., Mikesell, L., Aakhus, M. Improving prognosis communication for patients facing complex medical treatment: a user-centered design approach. Int. J. Med. Inf. **141**, 104147 (2020)
26. Kayler, L.K., Dolph, B., Ranahan, M., Keller, M., Cadzow, R., Feeley, T.H.: Kidney transplant evaluation and listing: development and preliminary evaluation of multimedia education for patients. Ann. Transp. **26**, e929839–e929841 (2021)
27. Ghavami, A., et al.: Effects of observing real, animated and combined model on learning cognitive and motor levels of basketball jump shot in children. Biomed. Hum. Kinet. **14**(1), 54–60 (2022)
28. Andraka-Christou, B., Alex, B., Madeira, J.L.: College student preferences for substance use disorder educational videos: a qualitative study. Subst. Use Misuse **54**(8), 1400–1407 (2019)
29. Eriksson, P.E., Eriksson, Y.: Live-action communication design: a technical how-to video case study. Tech. Commun. Q. **28**(1), 69–91 (2019)
30. Dunbar, M., Paton, G., Singhal, A.: An educational video improves consent in pediatric lumbar puncture: a randomized control trial. Pediatr. Neurol. **100**, 74–79 (2019)
31. Talbot, R., Malas, N.: Addressing mental health stigma: a pilot educational video intervention for caregivers to facilitate psychiatric consultation in inpatient pediatric care settings. Clin. Child Psychol. Psychiatry **24**(4), 754–766 (2019)

Accuracy Improvement of Game Based Shoulder Joint ROM Measurement System for Preventive Care

Tomoji Toriyama[✉], Naoya Matsusaka, Tasuku Hanato, Yuto Minagawa,
Shin Morishima, and Akira Urashima

Toyama Prefectural University, Toyama, Japan
{toriyama,morisima,a-urasim}@pu-toyama.ac.jp

Abstract. We are developing a game-based care prevention system, which promotes physical exercise among the elderly by inducing them to wipe or clean virtual windows displayed on a screen. This game can measure the range of motion (ROM) of the shoulder joint, which is one of the main measurement items for activity of daily life (ADL) evaluation. In order to improve the calculation accuracy of the automatic ROM calculation system that is part of this game, we conducted an experiment in which we measured the shoulder ROM by a professional and captured the subject's movements with a sensor parallelly. The shoulder ROM obtained from sensors and the one obtained by professional measurements were compared and analyzed, in many cases we found that ideal movement was not induced. This suggests that shoulder ROM measurement by professionals does not actually guide ideal measurement movements, and that professionals use their previous experience to correct shoulder ROM. Therefore, when we performed shoulder ROM measurement again as ideal measurement can be induced, we confirmed that in many cases, ideal movement guidance was induced and the difference between the shoulder ROM obtained from sensors and the one obtained by professional measurements are decreased.

Keywords: Preventive Care System · Game Based Design · ROM Measurement

1 Background

The growing number of elderly people is resulting in an increased number of care-receivers, which leads to the higher overall cost of nursing care and the shortage of caregivers. In order to tackle this issue, the Japanese government is actively implementing preventative measures to maintain the health condition of the elderly so that they do not become care-receivers. It is important to understand the ADL for the elderly population and to support them in maintaining ADL so that they can remain socially active. Recently, some local communities have approached this issue through "Kayoi-no-ba" or community of connection, social gatherings that practiced physical exercises [1]. ROM of the shoulders is one of the major standards for assessing ADL. However, this assessment requires specialist knowledge and implementation, meaning that regular

© The Author(s), under exclusive license to Springer Nature Switzerland AG 2024
C. Stephanidis et al. (Eds.): HCII 2024, CCIS 2119, pp. 379–387, 2024.
https://doi.org/10.1007/978-3-031-61966-3_41

assessments would be difficult without the constant availability of professional assessors. As a method to automatically measure shoulder ROM without relying on professionals, a care prevention support method that uses E-sports to promote exercise for the purpose of care prevention and to guide shoulder movement have been devised [5, 6]. In these studies, ROM is calculated using an automatic ROM measurement system that uses a depth sensor to acquire body joint coordinates. These studies raise several prerequisites including the inducement and guidance of player actions suitable for assessment, and the ability to measure with accuracy. However, it is difficult to induce movements suitable for measurement through this E-sports, and ideal movement guidance has not been sufficiently performed [7]. In order to clarify the effectiveness of motion guidance, we acquired the guided motion performed by professionals using an automatic ROM measurement system, and verified the accuracy of the ROM calculated by the system.

2   Related Works

2.1   Measurement of Shoulder ROM

Figure 1 shows the method of measuring shoulder ROM (abduction, flexion). As shown in Fig. 1, shoulder abduction is the angle between the arm and vertical line drawn through shoulder joint. Flexion is the angle captured between the arm raised forward and vertical line through the shoulder. These angles are measured in this study [2].

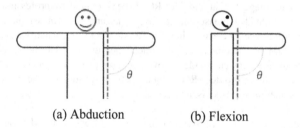

(a) Abduction   (b) Flexion

Fig. 1. Angles of measuring abduction and flexion on shoulder joint

2.2   Shoulder ROM Measurement Using Sensors

Several measurement methods using sensors are proposed, mainly with the methods of applying wearable contact sensors and non-contact depth sensors [3, 4]. When comparing these methods, contact sensors are highly accurate, as Qi et al. achieved its accuracy within ±5% to the results of measurement on shoulder and elbow ROM for 80% of subjects [3]. On the other hand, non-contact depth sensors have the benefit of relieving its subjects from unnecessary physical burden. Nan et al. achieved its accuracy within ±13.5% to the test result of measuring shoulder ROM with Microsoft's Kinect angle gauge as one of the depth sensors [4]. Nan et al. gamified some parts of their measuring process and at the time of measurement.

2.3 Shoulder ROM Measuring System with Game

Shoulder ROM measurement system emulating a window cleaning game, called "window wiping game" is proposed [5]. This system consists of a screen to show the game, depth sensors Kinect, and a computer. Player sit in front of Kinect and plays the game in their seats. Figure 2 shows that the screen shows a player's own image overlaid with yellow paint as an imitation of a grimy window. The overlaid yellow paint becomes clear when players move their arms to "clean" the window. Once the first window becomes clean, the next one appears, and this process continues until the time limit. This game seeks to measure shoulder ROM by capturing cleaning movements as well as counting how many windows a player can clean in a given amount of time. This game has a function to adjust the window frame size to fit the limit of the player's arm before the main part of game. As players try to clear the windows to the edges, they are prompted to stretch their arms outwards, which induces movements at the maximum ROM. In this game, the player's joint angles are measured, therefore the elevation angle of their arms can be calculated based on its joint angles. Figure 3 is a picture of the major upper body joint positions that Kinect V2 can capture. As thick lines indicate, the elevation angle of arms is calculated by setting up the vector that goes through neck and spine center, and one that goes through the right or left shoulder and the elbow. This system succeeded in measurement with average 21.6 degrees error compared to the measurement conducted by professionals on shoulder abduction and flexion.

Fig. 2. Screen of "window wiping game"

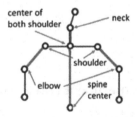

Fig. 3. Joint positions by Kinect v2

2.4 Shoulder ROM Measurement Conducted as E-Sports for the Elderly

It is common to compete and gain points or beat other teams, or watch someone play and defeat others as part of regular E-sports. However, it is difficult to simply apply the common E-sports principles to elderly players for reasons such as varied cognitive capacity. Therefore, one study loosened the competitive elements of E-sports, and measured shoulder ROM as a means of facilitating social interaction and communications among the elderly through E-sports.

Interaction through E-sports includes conversations as follows; advice given when playing games, cheering and exchanging comments after games. In our study, we boosted these conversations and signs of communications by assigning groups, requiring each member of the group to take turns to play a game, and also by encouraging others to participate through viewing or watching another group play. Participants could see the score counted by the number of windows they cleaned at the end of the game. The elderly who gathered in a venue could exchange ideas and communicate as a member of community through E-sports and developed a competitive spirit.

3 Method of Shoulder ROM Measurement

In this research, we use an automatic ROM measuring system (Fig. 4) developed using Microsoft's Kinect v2, based on the method shown in existing research [5–7]. However. The calculation method of shoulder ROM is different from that of existing research [7]. In this system, the elevation angle of the arms is calculated by setting up the vector that passes through the neck and spine center shown in Fig. 3, and one that passes through the right or left shoulder and the elbow shown in Fig. 3. This is because we believe that shoulder ROM can be calculated more accurately when the left and right shoulder located unbalanced.

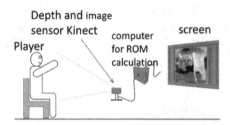

Fig. 4. Automatic ROM measuring system

4 Experiment and Result

4.1 Measurement Experiments by the Professionals

We conducted an experiment on elderly people aged 65 and older who voluntarily visited local governments or health facilities for the purpose of preventive care under the name of "Experiencing E-sports". At these experiments, shoulder ROM was measured by two physical therapists who specialize in measuring shoulder ROM. These experiments were conducted six times between June and September 2024, with 10 to 20 elderly participants each time, and a total of 100 participants. When the shoulder ROM is measured by professionals, the shoulder ROM is also measured using the shoulder ROM measurement system. Movement guidance by professionals on shoulder ROM measurement was performed using verbal instructions, and the specialist was careful not to step in front of the subject to prevent the sensor from malfunctioning. These experiments have been approved by the ethics board composed of on and off-campus members in Prefectural University of Toyama, to consider privacy protection.

Measurement Environment. Shoulder ROM was measured by two professional physical therapists using the method described in Sect. 3. One professional's role is mainly to give movement guidance instructions to the subject, and the other one's role is mainly to make measurements. After guiding the movements, both professionals worked together to determine the suitable timing of measurements.

Result. Figures 5 and 6 shows examples of experimental results when measuring the abduction/flexion angle. The figure on the left/right shows the movement of the left/right hand respectively. The horizontal axis of the figure shows the angle at which the subject's arm opens laterally with the front of the subject as 0 degrees. And the vertical axis indicates the angle at which the subject's arm opens upward with the front of the subject as 90 degrees. Abduction/flexion angle is the maximum elevation angle when lateral/forward elevation performed. This figure shows that the movement guidance provided by professionals during shoulder ROM measurement is not monotonous lateral/forward elevation.

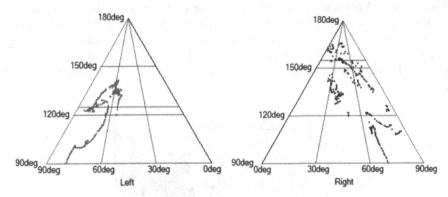

Fig. 5. Abduction angle

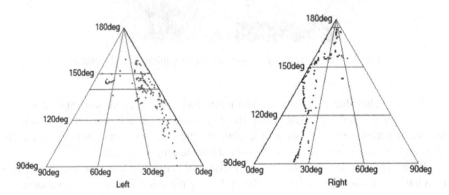

Fig. 6. Flexion angle

The horizontal green lines shown in Figs. 5 and 6 are shoulder ROM measurement angles measured by professionals. There are some significant differences on these two values.

4.2 Measurement Experiments by Professionals for Ideal Movement

After discussing these results with the professional who carried out the measurement, it becomes clear that when measuring shoulder ROM for elderly, ideal movement guidance may not be induced because they may have a hunched posture due to spinal deformity or decreased trunk muscle strength, and there is a limit to give them accurate measurement instructions verbally. Physical therapists, who are professionals, adjust these behaviors to minimize the difference from the true shoulder ROM based on their previous experience and knowledge. Therefore, in order to confirm whether the measurement accuracy improves on ideal guidance, we made tools that allow ideal movements to be performed.

Measurement Environment Including Guiding Tools. Figure 7 shows a screen covered with a transparent acrylic plate used for lateral elevation guidance (left) and the scene where this board was used during the experiment (right). It was set at the back of an elderly person so that it touches their shoulders, and the elderly person can be instructed to raise the board laterally with the back of their hand always in contact with the board.

Fig. 7. Transparent acrylic plate screen for guiding lateral elevation

Figure 8 also shows the bar used to guide forward elevation (left) and shows the scene where this rod was used during the experiment (right). It was set to the side of an elderly person so that it touches the arm, and the elderly person can be instructed to raise the arm forward with part of the arm always touching the bar.

By using these devices, elderly can perform movements while perceiving that their own hands are touching the board or bar, allowing more ideal movement guidance.

Result. The measurement results of the abduction angle and flexion angle are shown in Fig. 9 and Fig. 10, respectively. From these figures, it appears that the professional's

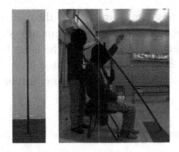

Fig. 8. Bar for guiding forward elevation

movement guidance on shoulder ROM measurement involves monotonous lateral elevation. However, in this experiment as well as in the one conducted in Sect. 4.1, when measuring shoulder ROM by professionals, it is obvious that these were not ideal movements
for measurement.

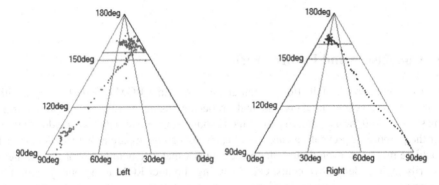

Fig. 9. Abduction angle

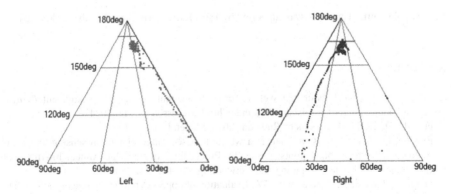

Fig. 10. Flexion angle

Table 1 shows the mean absolute errors between the values measured by professionals and the calculated values obtained by this measurement system. The experiment shown in Sect. 4.1 and ones in Sect. 4.2 indicates that the latter has improved measurement accuracy. Since the latter error is equal to or lower than that shown in the existing research in Sect. 3.2, it is assumed that ideal measurement behavior was obtained in this measurement.

Table 1. Mean absolute error between professional measurement and our system.

	Left Abduction [deg]	Right abduction [deg]	Left flexion [deg]	Right flexion [deg]
Without the guiding tool	12.8	12.7	10.4	13.2
With the guiding tool	11.2	11.3	9.6	6.8

5   Conclusion and Future Work

In order to obtain the abduction/flexion angle of shoulder ROM of elderly people with high accuracy, we measured professional's procedure using the automatic ROM measuring system. And the system is a part of the E-sports game system that we are developing for the purpose of preventing care. As a result, it become apparent that shoulder ROM could be measured even though the professional's measurement behavior did not necessarily induce ideal movements. On measuring shoulder ROM using our system, it is suggested that its mean absolute error can be about 10% when the ideal motions are guided.

Acknowledgment. This work was supported by JSPS KAKENHI Grant Number 23K11964.

References

1. Ministry of Health, Labour and Welfare. https://www.mhlw.go.jp/stf/seisakunitsuite/bunya/hukushi_kaigo/kaigo_koureisha/yobou/index.html. Accessed 11 Mar 2024
2. Fukuda, O.: ROM Measurement, 2nd edn. Miwa Shoten Ltd. (2010)
3. Bozhao, Q., Suman, B.: GonioSense: a wearable-based range of motion sensing and measurement system for body joints: poster. In: Proceedings of the 22nd Annual International Conference on Mobile Computing and Networking, pp. 441–442 (2016)
4. Peng, N., Amnad, T., Theeraphong, W.: Evaluation of upper limb joint's range of motion data by Kinect sensor for rehabilitation exercise game. In: Proceedings of the Third International Conference on Medical and Health Informatics 2019, pp. 92–98 (2019)
5. Li, M., Tsuchiya, T., Urashima, A., Morishima, S., Toriyama, T.: A game-based upper limb AROM measurement system for older adults. J. Inf. Commun. Eng. **5**(1), 294–300 (2019)

6. Morishima, S., Souna, K., Ofusa, R., Toriyama, T.: Automatic measurement of shoulder joint ROM conducted on elderly eSports. IEICE Technical Report, vol.121, no. 203, WIT2021-19, pp.12–17 (2021)
7. Toriyama, T., et al.: Guidance method of Arm Movement for Care Prevention on Game based Shoulder Joint ROM Measurement, Communications in Computer and Information Science, pp. 175–183. Springer, Cham (2023). https://doi.org/10.1007/978-3-031-35992-7_25

Application Study of Interactive Picture Books in Alleviating the Fears of Medical Experience Among Pediatric Patients

Ziyang Wang and Yuanfang Zhao[(⊠)] [iD]

College of Art and Design, Shenzhen University, Shenzhen 518060, People's Republic of China
zhaoyuanfang@szu.edu.cn

Abstract. Relative to adult patients, pediatric patients usually exhibit poorer self-control and psychological fortitude, rendering them more prone to fear, which could potentially have adverse effects on the treatment outcomes. The fears of medical experience in pediatric patients are often manifested through crying and restlessness among other psychological and behavioral traits. This study aims to explore the capability of interactive picture books and their art therapy efficacy in aiding pediatric patients to become acquainted with the examination and treatment procedures, thereby alleviating their emotional burden. Interactive picture books, a novel media interactive design, integrate illustrations, text, music, and virtual elements, enabling interaction between electronic devices and patients, and providing a child-friendly method to introduce and explain medical procedures. Additionally, the interactive experience can effectively offer social companionship and emotional support, alleviating the unfamiliarity and fear pediatric patients may harbor towards the hospital environment and surgical processes.

Through survey methods and comparative evaluation experiments, the study validated the potential benefits of interactive picture books. The research findings indicate that preoperative interactive picture books for children piqued the interest of more pediatric patients, garnering longer usage durations. Moreover, these pediatric patients were more inclined to actively cooperate with medical staff in completing the examinations and treatment procedures, no longer exhibiting common anxious emotions and resistant behaviors. By introducing interactive picture books, the research team aspires to contribute to improving medical care, alleviating the fears of medical experience, enhancing overall treatment efficacy, providing more personalized care, thereby improving treatment compliance and patient satisfaction. This study provides robust guidance for future medical practices to promote the health and recovery of pediatric patients.

Keywords: Interactive Picture Books · New Media Interactive Design · Pediatric Patients · the Fears of Medical Experience · Art Therapy

1 Introduction

As a form of books that are easy for children to read, picture books have been active in the literary and art market since the 20th century. Since the 20th century to the present, this form of books designed specifically for children has always occupied a place in the literary and art market, attracting readers with its unique charm. Traditional picture book creation requires the author to use text, color, lines, shapes and other elements to organically integrate images and text on paper, thereby guiding readers to understand the text information and stimulating their imagination. However, traditional picture books are expensive to produce and bind, are easily damaged, and difficult to preserve for a long time, which limits their dissemination scope and application scenarios to a certain extent.

Compared with traditional picture books, modern interactive picture books use the client as a platform and are more environmentally friendly, easy to share, and portable. "Rich media" is an information dissemination method that integrates animation, sound, video and interactivity, making the expression forms of modern interactive picture books more and more diverse. Through the deep integration of computer application technology and artistic design, modern interactive picture books incorporate rich animation, visual special effects and audio, allowing readers to interact with the picture books through finger control, key presses and other methods. This immersive reading experience allows readers to immerse themselves more deeply into the pictures and storyline of the picture book, thereby greatly improving their participation and reading pleasure.

Pediatrics is an important department in the hospital. Children are younger and have poor cooperation and treatment compliance. The compliance of hospitalized children with treatment refers to the children's cooperation with the doctor's treatment plan during their hospitalization. The compliance of hospitalized children determines the treatment effect of the children during their stay in the hospital [1]. Therefore, how to alleviate children's medical fears and improve children's treatment compliance has become a crucial issue.

2   Literature Review

2.1   Medical Fear

For children and adolescents, common fears generally relate to death, danger, the unknown, school and social pressure, and medical fears [2]. Medical fears are an important aspect of children's fears. Relevant research shows that medical procedures are the content that children fear most [3]. Medical fear refers to the emotional response to medical experiences and related events, including fear of medical environment, fear of medical procedures, fear of interpersonal relationships and fear of itself [4]. From the perspective of the children, the hospital is filled with the smell of disinfectant and staff and patients in special clothes, symbolizing coldness and pain. Medical fear has become a serious psychological barrier for children during the treatment process. This barrier is not conducive to the physical and mental health of children and affects the results of diagnosis and treatment.

Fear of Medical Environment. In view of the fear of children in the medical environment, this study uses the Biophilia concept proposed by Edward Wilson in the book "Biophilia" to create interactive picture books. Biophilia theory profoundly reveals the inherent emotional bond between humans and natural creatures (see Fig. 1), pointing out that closeness to nature is the innate nature of human beings. Subsequently, the design community developed the Biophilic Design concept based on this, advocating the integration of human's biophilic attributes into design practice, and actively affecting the physiological and psychological state of individuals through more use of natural elements.

In order to more effectively reduce children's fear of the medical environment, this study introduced animal images from nature into the character design of the picture book. These friendly animals not only enrich the visual expression of the picture book, but also serve as an important guide to the plot. Throughout the picture book story. Through this design, children can have in-depth communication and interaction with the natural ecology in interactive picture books, thereby effectively relieving their nervousness [5].

Fig. 1. An interactive picture book interface with animal images as the protagonists.

Fear of Medical Procedures. In order to effectively reduce children's fear of medical procedures, this study designed a plot showing courage and perseverance in the creation of an interactive picture book. By letting the children take on the roles in the picture books and experience the characters' bravery and strength during the medical process, the children's own positive emotions can be mobilized. In the narrative process of the picture book, we fully considered the diversity of children's conditions, so we designed differentiated story lines for children with different conditions to fully cover various types of medical operations. For example, in the interactive picture book, the needle tube is depicted as a paintbrush, and the injection is depicted as a small sun painted on the arm to reduce the child's fear (see Fig. 2).

The interactive picture book in this study reduces children's fear and anxiety of unknown environments by actively guiding them to experience medical operations in advance. At the same time, the interactive picture book explains medical knowledge to children in a relaxed, pleasant and easy-to-understand way, helping them better understand and accept medical operations.

Fig. 2. Interactive interface for children before injection

Fear of Interpersonal Relationships. Hospitalized children often suffer from fear of interpersonal relationships while facing illness and treatment. This fear may stem from incompatibility with unfamiliar environments, fear of medical staff, and barriers to communication with patients of the same age. In response to this problem, the interactive picture book in this study designed a corresponding solution.

Interactive picture books can create a safe and friendly interpersonal atmosphere for children with warm and friendly pictures and stories. The colors, lines and characters in the picture books should be in line with children's aesthetic habits, and at the same time incorporate elements of medical treatment and hospitalization, so that children can more easily resonate and identify with them. In the story, you can describe the plot of patients helping each other and growing together, thereby helping children to establish positive expectations for interpersonal communication. Preschool children are still unable to distinguish the difference between the real world and the virtual world, and are prone to imitate the screen content in electronic products [6]. Therefore, the storyline of interactive picture books can guide children to actively overcome their fear of crying in interpersonal relationships. The interactive design of interactive picture books can also stimulate children's curiosity and desire to explore, and encourage them to actively participate in the process of interpersonal communication. For example, picture books can be set up with some interactive links that need to be completed by children and medical staff or patients, such as page-turning mechanisms, jigsaw puzzles, etc. These interactive sessions not only allow children to relax while playing, but also allow them to enhance friendship and build trust through cooperation and communication.

Self-fear. According to the definition of medical fear, self-fear includes injury, bleeding, vomiting, crying when hurt, etcetera [7]. Interactive design is the core of interactive picture books. By adding interactive elements such as page turning, pulling, and rotating, children can be actively involved in the reading process, thus enhancing their reading experience. For example, you can design some links that require children's hands-on operations, such as pulling bandages to bandage the wounds of characters in the story, or rotating medicine bottles to take medicine for characters. Such a design not only allows children to feel their importance in the medical process, but also allows them to reduce their fear of actual medical actions through simulated operations.

2.2 Multimodal Learning Theory

Multimodal learning theory aims to emphasize the importance of mobilizing multiple senses in the process of absorbing knowledge. People use vision, hearing, touch, etc. at the same time. Multimodal learning theory emphasizes the mutual integration and integration of different modal information in the learning process. Synergy believes that human learning and understanding are based on the comprehensive processing of multiple sensory information. In the design of the interactive picture book, we made full use of the principle of multi-modal learning and presented a rich and vivid learning experience to children by combining text, images, sounds, animations and other modal information.

In this study, text, as the basic element of the picture book, provides children with basic information about medical knowledge and operations. However, for children who are younger or have limited cognitive abilities, simple text information may be difficult to understand and accept. Therefore, we use visual modal information such as images, colors, and shapes to present complex medical operations in an intuitive and easy-to-understand way, helping children better understand and accept them.

3   Method

3.1   Research Object

The research subjects selected by this research team are children aged 5–10 years old. They have active mental activities and relatively explicit emotional expressions. Children of this age group already have the ability to internalize acquired behaviors and skills into their own life experiences.

3.2   Measurement Method

This study aimed to evaluate the practical application effect of interactive picture books in the medical care of pediatric patients. To this end, we designed an experiment to test whether interactive picture books can effectively reduce children's medical fears and improve their treatment compliance.

Before the experiment began, we collected basic information about the two groups of child patients and assessed their initial medical fear and cooperation. Among the eligible children, we selected a certain number of pediatric patients and randomly divided them into two groups: the control group and the experimental group. The control group received routine medical care, while the experimental group received routine care and additional intervention using interactive picture books. We have made a self-made patient satisfaction survey form, which includes four dimensions: Interesting, rereadability, Operational difficulty suitability, and Shareability. Children need to choose whether they are satisfied, relatively satisfied, generally satisfied, or dissatisfied based on their own experience. At the same time, we also collected feedback from medical staff and parents on the effectiveness of interactive picture books through interviews (see Fig. 3).

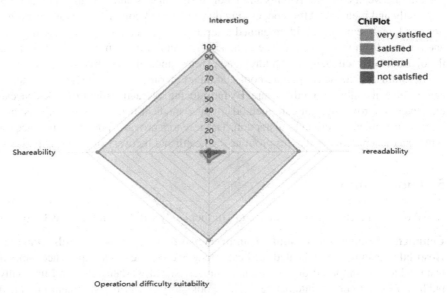

Fig. 3. Patient satisfaction radar chart

It can be seen from the above figure that hospitalized children still very much recognize the interest and shareability of picture books, but the re-readability of interactive picture books must be paid attention to. Children's novelty for new things is time-sensitive, and they may feel tired and bored after experiencing the treatment introduction and story plots in interactive picture books. In response to this problem, we plan to continue to improve the playability and story lines of interactive picture books, make the plots and interactions richer and more diverse, and carry out more innovations and optimizations in gameplay.

4   Conclusion

Interactive picture books can significantly reduce the medical fear of child patients, and medical staff and parents have also given positive comments on the effectiveness of interactive picture books. They believe that this innovative approach can not only reduce the fear of child patients, but also improve their understanding and trust in the medical process, helping to establish a good doctor-patient relationship. The interactive picture book in this study personifies related items through character introduction, simulation process, character interaction and other links. Under the guidance of nursing staff, children and parents can complete simulated treatments and examinations together, so as to gain full experience before relevant diagnosis and treatment. After the role experience, the children's pride is stimulated and their cognition related to diagnosis and treatment is improved, and the children's anxiety, crying, resistance and other emotions are reduced or relieved. Under the guidance of medical staff, children and their parents undergo diagnosis, examination and treatment together. The story-telling plot adds a sense of fun. The empathy between children, parents and medical staff makes children and parents relax physically and mentally. After cooperating during sleep to complete relevant examinations and treatments, the children gained a sense of pride and received encouragement and rewards from medical staff. The intimacy and familiarity of medical staff shortens the distance between them and children and parents, and enhances trust.

In summary, interactive picture books, as an art therapy tool, have significant application value in children's medical care. By introducing interactive picture books, we can effectively improve medical care methods, reduce medical fears of child patients, and improve treatment effects and satisfaction. This research provides powerful guidance for future medical practice and helps promote the health and recovery of pediatric patients.

5 Future Study

Based on the current experimental design, further study will be conducted as follows.

Complete Longer-Term and Comprehensive Cooperation with Partner Hospitals. Establish a dedicated medical interactive picture book experience support team, which is composed of pediatricians, nurses, social workers, etc., and internally publishes recruitment of interactive picture book story scenario assignment tasks and conducts short-term unified training to familiarize nursing members with relevant operating procedures and guidance techniques. An interesting and clear interactive picture book operation procedure was produced and pasted on the wall of the inpatient hall to facilitate children and parents to follow the instructions. Afterwards, pediatric patients who met the experimental requirements were recruited from collaborating hospitals and randomly divided into groups according to their age, gender and disease type to ensure that there was no significant difference in basic characteristics between the two groups of patients. Team members will guide the children in an orderly manner and explain the process, participation methods, and precautions for interactive picture book interaction. Pay attention to monitoring the vital signs of the children, and interact if the condition permits.

Baseline Assessment. The standardized Children's Medical Fear Scale (CMFS) was used to conduct a baseline assessment of the medical fear of the two groups of pediatric patients to ensure the reliability of the experimental results. Intervention implementation: Children in the experimental group began to use interactive picture books while receiving routine care. We have arranged dedicated personnel to assist and provide guidance to ensure that child patients can fully understand and utilize the content of the picture books.

Data Collection and Analysis. During the experiment, we must regularly collect and record relevant data, including psychological and behavioral changes of child patients, feedback from medical staff, etc. After the experiment, statistical analysis software was used to process and analyze the data to evaluate the effectiveness of the interactive picture book. There were no significant differences in age, gender, disease type, etc. between the two groups of pediatric patients to ensure the comparability and reliability of the data. During the data collection process, we strictly followed standardized operating procedures to ensure that each child patient could accurately understand the content of the scale and truly express his or her feelings.

Acknowledgements. The authors acknowledge the funding support by the "High-Level Achievement Cultivation Project" of Shenzhen University's Phase III Construction of High-Level Universities (Project No: 24GSPCG18).

References

1. Wang, X.Y.: Research on emotional education in children's picture book reading. New Curricul. Primary School **6**(8), 109 (2014)
2. Serim-Yildiz, B., Erdur-Baker, O.: Examining fears of Turkish children and adolescents with regard to age. Gender and socioeconomic status. Procedia-Soc. Behav. Sci. **5**, 84 (2013)
3. Hart, B.E.: Self-reported fears of hospitalized school age children. J. Pediatr. Nurs. **9**(2), 83–90 (1995)
4. Broome, M.E., Hellier, A., Wilson, T.: Measuring Children's Fears of Medical Experience, pp. 201–214. Springer, New York (1988)
5. Zhou, H., Su, X.Y.: Research on influencing factors of medical fear in hospitalized school-age children. Chin. J. Nurs. **6**, 485–489 (2006)
6. Li, X.S.: The user experience design of the mobile application software for the children. Packag. Eng. **33**(10), 81–84 (2012)
7. Li, Y.Y., Zhou, L.J.: Evaluation of the effect of nursing professional experience on medical fear and treatment cooperation in children hospitalized in the ophthalmology department. Chin. J. Pract. Nurs. **31**, 2436–2439 (2017)

Case Study on the UI Design of Sports Health Management Apps for University Students Based on User Need

Ziqiang Yan[✉] [iD] and Ziyi Ma

School of Design, South China University of Technology, Guangzhou 510006, China
ziqianghello8@gmail.com

Abstract. During the epidemic of COVID-19, online working and learning patterns become the norm. After the outbreak of COVID-19, social alienation and isolation largely changed the lifestyle of university students, and this habit of staying indoors for the sake of health also reduced university students. The lack of physical exercise will undoubtedly affect the state of life and work efficiency of university students and will also worsen their health condition. Thus, this study used face-to-face individual interviews and case comparison analysis to address the above-mentioned research gap. Then in case of comparison analysis, we analyzed the App structure and GUI design of the three popular sports health management Apps. The results of this study can help more university students in need of sports health management to select suitable related Apps and also allow more researchers to study sports health management Apps. In addition, we provided the developers with university students' demand for sports health management Apps. The developers can design effective and user-friendly sports health management Apps to increase the use of the Apps among university students. As a result, the physical health of university students can be improved.

Keywords: User needs · Case studies · Health management App

1 Introduction

1.1 Background and Purpose

According to statistical surveys, the youth population aged 14–35 accounts for 25.2% of the total population of the country [1], and among them, there are many college students [2]. With the development of technology and social progress, more and more young college students feel physically and mentally exhausted from time to time. Because of the gradual increase in the pressure of school work and the decrease in after-school time [1, 3], coupled with the progress of equipment and the influence of the epidemic environment, college students exercise less and less. The data showed that 65.88% of college students would feel insufficient exercise [4]. It is also related to some bad habits and dietary habits of college students, such as staying up late and being excited, eating fried food, carbonated drinks, etc. Physical health management of college students is an issue that deserves attention because it will last forever if it is not solved. Currently, the state has adjusted the standards of physical fitness tests for college students several times but with little success. Therefore effective and comfortable physical health management has become a key consideration for designers. The design of health management Apps is constantly innovating, and the market demand for functional requirements and interface design of physical health management Apps is increasing. The purpose of analyzing the use of different physical health management Apps is to provide effective basic information for developing new user interface design for physical health self-management Apps for college students.

1.2 Background and Purpose

This paper used a literature survey, an interview survey, and a comparative case study analysis. The literature survey was used to understand the definition of physical health, what kind of physical fitness is healthy, and what behaviors and habits affect physical health, including how to manage physical health. Twenty university students were selected to participate in the interview survey for the quantitative analysis. Three university student physical health self-management Apps were chosen from the Apple App store study based on the criteria of downloads, scores, and overall functionality: KEEP, GUDONG, and Yodo Run. For users, this paper analyzed the three APPs based on comprehensibility, readability, fatigue, intuitiveness, and consistency in layout, colors, icons, text, and graphics. The functionalities and interface design of the three university student physical health self-management Apps are in use. The strengths and weaknesses of their APP interface designs were analyzed by scrutinizing the information structure of the functions used in the Apps and the five elements of GUI design in terms of layout, colors, icons, fonts and graphics, in conjunction with the findings of the in-depth interviews.

2 Investigation and Analysis of University Students

In-depth interviews were conducted with 20 university students at different levels of health, and the characteristics and needs of university students at varying levels of fitness were analyzed using the interview survey method. To conduct the survey and analysis, it is necessary to understand the behavioral status of university students and their self-assessment of their health, so the literature review method was used to investigate the overall situation of university students' physical health and its effects.

2.1 Background and Purpose

Current State of Perception of Physical Activity. College students' knowledge of physical activity will influence their practice of physical activity. University students have a certain understanding of the basic knowledge of physical exercises, such as the types of physical exercise, the content and the handling of emergencies, but they still lack the relevant cognitive system for the more in-depth parts of physical exercise, such as how to do physical exercise in a healthy way, and do not have a thorough understanding.

Current Attitudes of University Students Toward Physical Activity. The attitude of university students toward physical activity will affect their motivation towards physical activity. Most university students can correctly understand and appreciate the value of physical activity and have an optimistic attitude toward it. However, some students still do not correctly understand the significance of physical exercise to their bodies and lives, have a negative attitude towards physical exercise, are unable to correctly understand the value of physical exercise, and have a situation of "knowing but not believing".

2.2 The Impact of Physical Activity on Target Users

Physical activity has a physiological and psychological impact on the individual and creates value for society. Physical exercise exposes a person to the risks of inadequate safety supervision, forcible completion of actions and overtraining. It, therefore, requires special attention from university students to exercise in moderation [5]. A reasonable and moderate amount of physical activity can have many positive effects, mainly in the following areas.

The Impact of Physical Exercise on Individual Physiology. Physical activity strengthens one's immune system and effectively halts the development of chronic diseases. In addition, exercise is an excellent therapeutic intervention for diseases such as obesity, type 2 diabetes, neurodegeneration, osteoporosis and myasthenia gravis. In terms of efficacy, exercise can be as beneficial as the medication prescribed for many diseases (e.g., type 2 diabetes) [6]. In particular, increased physical activity can also reduce dementia. According to an experiment conducted by Eric B. Larson et al. the incidence of dementia was lower among those who exercised three or more times per week (13.0 per 1000 person-years) than among those who exercised three times per week (19.7 per 1000 person-years) [7].

In addition to enhancing one's physical function, changes in physical activity can also have a significant impact on health status and life expectancy; for example, in one study, men aged 70 or older who engaged in exercise increased their likelihood of living to age 90 from 44% (inactive men) to 54% [6].

The Impact of Physical Activity on Individual Psychology. Ccording to statistics, university students who exercise more frequently can withstand stress, a characteristic expression of their self-efficacy. The more intense the physical activity is, the higher the self-efficacy within a certain number of weekly exercise hours is. This phenomenon will be effective in reducing anxiety levels as well as having greater sensitivity to positive feedback. In addition, physical exercise regulates mood and guided rest, including the regulation of studies, the rhythm of life and harmonious emotions, and the development of emotions. It also allows university students to rest positively, thus continuously changing the way they perceive sports and improving their physical, and cognitive abilities [5].

Effects of Physical Activity on Individual Behavior and Cognition. Similarly, increased self-efficacy with physical activity increases perseverance, resilience, and subsequent performance. One becomes more motivated to reach a specific goal while using resources effectively to make decision-making judgments. Finally, self-efficacy is believed to lead individuals to perceive stressful situations as challenges rather than threats [8].

Consequences of Prolonged Physical Inactivity. A short chronology of three millennia of history can show that a lack of physical activity reduces functional capacity and health [9]. The morbidity and mortality of associated chronic diseases significantly increase if physical inactivity is prolonged. A lifestyle of cessation of physical activity leads to a rapid decrease in insulin sensitivity, triggering chronic metabolic disorders, and a rapid increase in intra-abdominal fat following a lifestyle of cessation of physical activity [10]. In particular, inflammation in certain tissues is associated with the development of many chronic diseases. Too little exercise will trigger persistent low-grade systemic inflammation, and insufficient exercise is related to the development of insulin resistance, type 2 diabetes, atherosclerosis, neurodegenerative diseases, and certain cancers [6].

2.3 Impact of Physical Activity Completion by Target Users on Social Values

Physical activity has consistently been promoted by major international schools and as such, physical activity also contributes to the achievement of performance goals desired by higher education institutions, thereby upholding academic standards [7].

2.4 Analysis of Target Users

The above analysis can help us understand the relationship between university students and physical exercise and facilitate the preparation for further interviews. We randomly selected 20 university students as respondents for an in-depth interview survey to understand their specific needs for exercise software.

Icons that Show Changes in Trends. University students are concerned about whether their efforts positively correlate with their workouts' results. Therefore, they need comprehensive data charts to help them quickly understand changes in their physical dimensions or physical skills so that they can adjust their training accordingly.

A Lively Workout Results Interface. Sharing your workout results is a prevalent way of socializing in sports and can provide outstanding achievement. University students want a workout result interface displaying workout data and beautiful, rich graphics that make people want to share.

Simplicity and Good Placement of Key Content. University students believe that the software should focus on functionality. Therefore university students need to present information simply so they can quickly find the content they want to train on. In addition, having the functions people commonly use in a prominent place will help them start a training session quickly.

Clear Training Sessions. Students want to be able to perform the exercises with the correct posture, so the screen needs clear cues, logical information, and attention to the main points of the movements and what to look for.

3   Case Investigation and Analysis

3.1   Case Investigation and Analysis

The investigation object of the case is the related health exercise management Apps. According to the download volume, scores, and comprehensive functions, three health exercise Apps were selected as research objects in the Apple App Store: Yodo Run, KEEP, and GUDONG. They are shown in Table 1.

Table 1. Survey Objects

APP	Yodo Run	KEEP	GUDONG
logo			
score	4.0points	4.9points	4.9points
Down loads	2400+	20000+	2800+
Methods	Can connect to Apple Watch	Can connect to Apple Watch	Can connect to Apple Watch
Function	It can be connected to the apple watch and is an all-in-one mobile app that combines a tool for recording exercise patterns such as walking (pedometer), running, fitness, cycling, and an interactive community. It can also accurately match personal data, customize unique fitness plans, and automatically generate weekly health reports.	It can be connected to the apple watch, according to the user worm, fitness purposes, with or without equipment to arrange a variety of training programs, and all the movements are equipped with video, can quickly start, it also has the authority of fitness experts to control the content, for each person to develop a scientific fitness program	It can be connected to apple watch, can accurately record data and analysis, easy to bind intelligent hardware, and AI fitness training system to assist training, as well as many running groups and events can participate
Features	Well laid out, easy to use, multifunctional	Reasonable layout, features strong icon guidance, easy to use and understand, multifunctional	Simple layout, easy to use and understand, multifunctional
slogan	Why fleur yourself again, the movement does not have to be tangled	There is no such thing as being born that way, we just insist on it every day.	To exercise, use Gudong

Through the investigation of the information structure of the functions used in APP and the five elements of layout, color, icon, font, and chart in GUI design, this study analyzed the advantages and disadvantages of its APP interface design [11] combined with the investigation results of deep access. The specific contents are shown in Table 1.

Information Structure Analysis
From the information structure point of view, the information structure of KEEP, GUDONG, and Yodo Run in Figs. 1, 2, and 3 are similar. They all contain three interfaces of Information, Campaigns, and Mine. The similar information structure makes it easy for first-time users to find the information they need, which provides convenience for users. The difference is that Yodo Run's shopping platform is laid in a three-level information structure, making it more difficult to find. In addition, all three Apps can be connected to the Apple Watch, which can synchronize health data from time to time and understand the state of health and life trends in more detail.

GUI Design Analysis. From the layout factors (as shown in Table 2), all three adopt a three-part distributed layout, but the layouts of the three Apps' body parts are different. Compared to GUDONG, Yodo Run and KEEP have more functional distribution in the body part, but the layout of KEEP is more straightforward, and Yodo Run looks more vivid than KEEP with pandas as embellishments in the body part. The body part of KEEP and Yodo Run is modular, and the body part of GUDONG is refreshing without

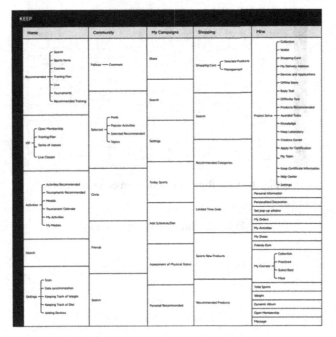

Fig. 1. KEEP information structure analysis

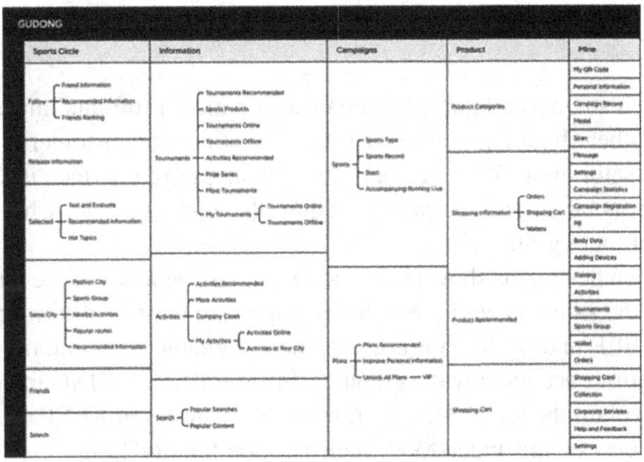

Fig. 2. GUDONG information structure analysis

cluttered elements, which are easy to operate and suitable for people who frequently use the main functions.

From the color point of view (as shown in Table 3), the colors of the three Apps are harmonious and unified, and each has its unique charm. Yodo Run's interface uses a large area of white with green icons. The overall color is rich and not monotonous. KEEP also operates a large amount of white but with blue and purple as the main accent, and most

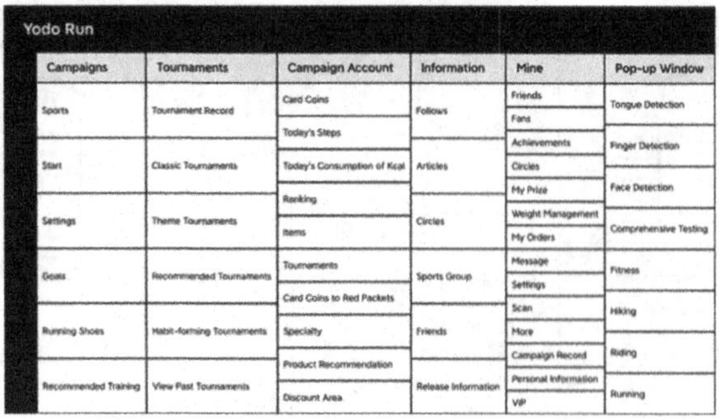

Fig. 3. Yodo Run information structure analysis

Table 2. The three Apps' layout analysis

APP	Yodo Run	KEEP	GUDONG
Layout	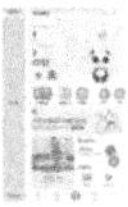	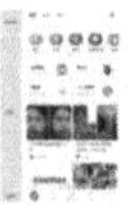	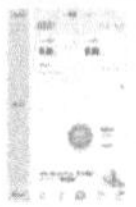
Features	The layout structure of the home page is divided into three parts, header, body and footer. There is some ambiguity in the classfication and categorization of information, which can lead to misunderstandings.	The layout structure of the home page is divided into three parts, header, body and footer. This page also has a high concentration of functions with rich visual elements but may give the impression of bloating.	The layout structure of the home page is divided into three parts, header, body and footer, compared with other two home page, this one looks more clearer is easy to understand and operate quickly.

of the icons are also blue and purple, which leaves a more profound impression. The red color used by other shopping platforms is used to stimulate customers' desire to shop. Still, the color saturation difference between the shopping interface in GUDONG and other interfaces is large, and the primary color also changes from white to red, which gives a sense of incongruity.

From the icon design (as shown in Table 4), among the icons of the three Apps, there are icons with the same meaning, but their designs are entirely different. For example, the icons of KEEP and Yodo Run use sketches of characters in motion as icons, and textual explanations accompany the graphics. In contrast, GUDONG mainly uses text to annotate and explain the icons. However, some of the icons in KEEP do not relate well to the text and may be misunderstood, such as "Community".

From the charts analysis (as shown in Table 5), there are many data involving physical health, including basic height and weight, length of each exercise, highest heart rate, average heart rate, calories consumed, etc. Take the record of a single run as an example. All three Apps use different text sizes, line graphs, and track diagrams. The line graphs of KEEP and GUDONG both analyze the height of running across and combine the line graphs to investigate the effect of height on running speed and heart rate, while Yodo Run does not examine this item. All three use the track chart to present the intuitive effect of the running path. KEEP and GUDONG's point chart records the step frequency, and

Table 3. The three Apps' color analysis

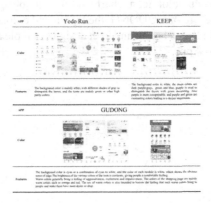

Table 4. The three Apps' icon analysis

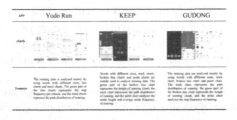

KEEP also records the total number of steps and the average stride length, so the trend of the point chart can improve the running process.

Table 5. The three Apps' charts analysis

From the font design point of view, it is found that all menus use Song font, which is easy to recognize when reading information through the text in the above chart. To show the content's priority and consistency with the layout, the font size, thickness and other changes are appropriately adjusted to increase the design sense.

A comparative analysis was made by taking the comprehension, readability, fatigue, intuition, coherence, and other information of layout, color, icon, text, chart, and other information as analysis criteria (as shown in Fig. 4). KEEP has the best GUI design. The five elements of layout, color, icon, chart, and font are designed harmoniously and uniformly. In the GUI design of GUDONG, the layout and color are slightly worse than the other two Apps. Yodo Run's layout and icon design is simple and easy to understand, superior to the other two Apps.

Fig. 4. GUI analysis results of the three Apps

3.2 Case Analysis Results

These three Apps have advantages and disadvantages regarding information structure and GUI design. After comparative analysis, KEEP's design is worth learning. Its information structure helps users solve problems through layout optimization, icon guidance and chart analysis, and mainly uses blue and purple, which is more memorable. Although KEEP has many sports, users can quickly find what they need. The information structure of GUDONG is similar to KEEP, and the layout of GUDONG is also refreshing and straightforward in style, but the colors of GUDONG are more disorganized. The color distribution of individual interfaces and the color change of jumping pages are messy. The text is mainly used in the icon part, which reduces the vividness, and The information structure of Yodo Run is slightly more chaotic than the first two Apps. The body part adopts lovely graphics, which are more vivid to use, the overall color is white, and the icons are mainly green. Border lines and shadows distinguish the hierarchy, but the data of its charts are less than the other two, which may have some influence on the user's analysis.

The five elements of information structure and GUI design are mutually optimized and promoted. The information structure improves the user's goodwill through the optimization of layout, the guidance of icons, the readability of charts, the distinction of colors and fonts, and the role of emphasis and explanation.

4   Conclusion

From a user's perspective, we investigated and analyzed three Apps: KEEP, Yodo Run, and GUDONG. Combined with the needs of college students for physical health management, we found that each App is more suitable for teenagers in terms of information structure and GUI design. All personal information must be entered manually, and users with smartwatch devices can sync their physical health data to the App. These steps are very efficient and simplify data recording for each exercise, and using the App for a long time and sticking to the exercise will achieve some results. Although using these health management Apps can help adolescents with physical data monitoring, it has aspects in motivating adolescents to exercise. Still, it cannot fully satisfy the need to mobilize teenagers' desire to exercise.

From the results of the study, the users of the health management app are not differentiated, and the content of the information structure is not consistent with the functional needs of the user groups; the primary users are self-health managers, and university students are only a small part of the main user groups; different user groups have different characteristics and functional requirements, and there is no functional classification set up specifically for university students. The difficulty of identifying and accessing information in the GUI design is also different. The interface design of the health management app should be based on the characteristics and needs of different user groups.

References

1. CSY. China Statistical Yearbook (2022)
2. The National Bureau of Statistics of China (NBSC) (2021)
3. Lin, J., Chen, Q.: Academic pressure and impact on students' development in China. McGill J. Educ. Rev. Sci. Léducation McGill. **30** (1995)
4. Kilpatrick, M., Hebert, E., Bartholomew, J.: College students' motivation for physical activity: differentiating men's and women's motives for sport participation and exercise. J. Am. Coll. Health **54**, 87–94 (2005). https://doi.org/10.3200/JACH.54.2.87-94
5. Pan, Q.: Influencing factors of college students' sports cognition based on DM technology. Secur. Commun. Netw. **2022**, e5022062 (2022). https://doi.org/10.1155/2022/5022062
6. Handschin, C., Spiegelman, B.M.: The role of exercise and PGC1α in inflammation and chronic disease. Nature **454**, 463–469 (2008). https://doi.org/10.1038/nature07206
7. Exercise Is Associated with Reduced Risk for Incident Dementia among Persons 65 Years of Age and Older | Annals of Internal Medicine. https://doi.org/10.7326/0003-4819-144-2-200 601170-00004
8. Chemers, M.M., Hu, L.-T., Garcia, B.F.: Academic self-efficacy and first year college student performance and adjustment. J. Educ. Psychol. **93**(1), 55–64 (2001). https://doi.org/10.1037/0022-0663.93.1.55
9. Booth, F.W., Roberts, C.K., Laye, M.J.: Lack of exercise is a major cause of chronic diseases. Compr. Physiol. **2**, 1143–1211 (2012). https://doi.org/10.1002/cphy.c110025
10. Booth, F.W., Laye, M.J., Lees, S.J., Rector, R.S., Thyfault, J.P.: Reduced physical activity and risk of chronic disease: the biology behind the consequences. Eur. J. Appl. Physiol. **102**, 381–390 (2008). https://doi.org/10.1007/s00421-007-0606-5
11. Case Study on the UI Design of Health Management Apps for Patients with Hypertension Based on User Need. https://doi.org/10.1007/978-3-031-06050-2_23

Author Index

Printed in the United States
by Baker & Taylor Publisher Services